Calculation and Coordi.....

Calculation and Coordination explores the founding and failure of socialism, and the attempts to reform and transform it in the twentieth century. It combines the strengths of the Austrian market-process tradition with the political economy of public choice to provide an analytical framework for theoretical and historical examination of socialist practice and post-socialist political economy.

Peter J. Boettke places particular emphasis on the difficulties of economic calculation in the absence of secure private-property rights and on the importance of establishing a credible commitment to limited government in smoothing the path from Soviet socialism to a liberal political and economic order in Post-Soviet Russia. The volume features essays on:

- The theoretical debate over socialism, and in particular the contributions of Mises and Hayek.
- The origins of socialism in Russia.
- The institutionalist maturation of socialist practice and the *de facto* organizing principles of the mature Soviet-type economy.
- The collapse of and failure to successfully reform the Soviet system.

This collection will prove to be of great interest to academics and students in the fields of economics, comparative politics, and development studies.

Peter J. Boettke is Associate Professor at George Mason University, where he also serves as the Deputy Director of the James M. Buchanan Center for Political Economy.

Foundations of the Market Economy
Edited by Mario J. Rizzo, *New York University*, and
Lawrence H. White, *University of Georgia*

A central theme in this series is the importance of understanding and assessing the market economy from a perspective broader than the static economics of perfect competition and Pareto optimality. Such a perspective sees markets as causal processes generated by the preferences, expectations and beliefs of economic agents. The creative acts of entrepreneurship that uncover new information about references, prices and technology are central to these processes with respect to their ability to promote the discovery and use of knowledge in society.

The market economy consists of a set of institutions that facilitate voluntary cooperation and exchange among indiviudals. These institutions include the legal and ethical framework as well as more narrowly 'economic' patterns of social interaction. Thus, the law, legal institutions and cultural and ethical norms, as well as ordinary business practices and phenomena, fall within the analytical domain of the economist.

The Meaning of Market Process
Essays in the development of modern Austrian economics
Israel M. Kirzner

Prices and Knowledge
A market-process perspective
Esteban F. Thomas

Keynes' General Theory of Interest
A reconsideration
Fiona C. Maclachlan

Laissez-Faire Banking
Kevin Dowd

Expectations and the Meaning of Institutions
Essays in economics by Ludwig Lachmann
Edited by Dan Lavoie

Perfect Competition and the Transformation of Economics
Frank M. Machovec

Entrepreneurship and the Market Process
An enquiry into the growth of knowledge
David Harper

Economics of Time and Ignorance
Gerald O'Driscoll and Mario J. Rizzo

Dynamics of the Mixed Economy
Towards a theory of interventionism
Sanford Ikeda

Neoclassical Microeconomic Theory
The founding of Austrian vision
A. M. Endres

The Cultural Foundations of Economic Development
Urban female entrepreneurship in Ghana
Emily Chamlee-Wright

Risk and Business Cycles
New and old Austrian perspectives
Tyler Cowen

Capital in Disequilibrium
The role of capital in a changing world
Peter Lewin

The Driving Force of the Market
Essays in Austrian economics
Israel Kirzner

An Entrepreneurial Theory of the Firm
Fréderic Sautet

Time and Money
The macroeconomics of capital structure
Roger Garrison

Microfoundations and Macroeconomics
An Austrian perspective
Steven Horwitz

Money and the Market
Essays on free banking
Kevin Dowd

Calculation and Coordination
Essays on socialism and transitional political economy
Peter Boettke

Keynes and Hayek
The money economy
Gerry Steele

Calculation and Coordination

Essays on socialism and transitional political economy

Peter J. Boettke

London and New York

First published 2001
by Routledge
2 Park Square, Milton Park, Abingdon, Oxon, OX14 4RN

Simultaneously published in the USA and Canada
by Routledge
270 Madison Ave, New York, NY 10016

Routledge is an imprint of the Taylor & Francis Group

Transferred to Digital Printing 2006

Typeset in Garamond by
Prepress Projects, Perth, Scotland

British Library Cataloguing in Publication Data
A catalogue record for this book is available
from the British Library

Library of Congress Cataloging in Publication Data

Boettke, Peter J.
    Calculation and Coordination : essays on socialism and transitional
    political economy / Peter J. Boettke.
        p. cm. – (Foundations of the market economy)
    Includes bibliographical references and index.

    ISBN10: 0-415-23813-7 (hbk)
    ISBN10: 0-415-77109-9 (pbk)

    ISBN13: 978-0-415-23813-7 (hbk)
    ISBN13: 978-0-415-77109-2 (pbk)

    1. Marxian economics. 2. Austrian school of economics. 3. Social choice.
    4. Soviet Union – Economic policy. I. Title. II. Foundations of the
    market economy series.
    HB97.5.B548 2001
    338.947–dc21   00-042218

This book has been sponsored in part by the Austrian Economics program at
New York University

To Israel M. Kirzner,
teacher, scholar, and mentor

Contents

Illustrations

Figures

Tables

Copyright acknowledgments

The authors and publishers would like to thank the following for granting permission to reproduce material in this work:

Taylor & Francis Ltd. for permission to reprint "Why Are There No Austrian Socialists? Ideology, Science and the Austrian School," *Journal of the History of Economic Thought* 17 (Spring 1995): 35–56, http://www.tandf.co.uk/journals/

Chapter 2 reprinted from *Advances in Austrian Economics*, Vol. 4, Peter Boettke, "Economic Calculation: The Austrian Contribution to Political Economy", pages 131–58, 1998, with permission from Elsevier Science.

Greg Bacher and the *Journal of Markets and Morality* for permission to reprint "Is Economics a Moral Science?" *Journal of Markets and Morality*, 1(2) (1998): 212–19.

Kenneth Koford and the *Eastern Economic Journal* for permission to reprint "Hayek's *The Road to Serfdom* Revisited: Government Failure in the Argument Against Socialism," *Eastern Economic Journal* 21(1) (Winter 1995): 7–26.

Kluwer Academic Publishers for permission to reprint "Coase, Communism, and Inside the 'Black Box' of Soviet-type Economies," in S. Medema (ed.), *On Coasean Economics*, Boston: Kluwer Academic Publishers (1998): pp. 193–207.

The Critical Review Foundation, Inc. for permission to reprint "The Soviet Experience with Pure Communism" and "The Soviet Experience with Pure Communism: Rejoinder to Nove" published in *Critical Review* (1999), 2(4): 149–82 and *Critical Review*, 5(1): 123–8 respectively.

Journal des Economistes et des Etudes Humaines for permission to reprint "The Political Economy of Utopia: Communism in Soviet Russia, 1918–1921", first published in the *Journal des Economistes et des Etudes Humaines*, 1(2) (1990): 91–138.

Kluwer Academic Publishers for permission to reprint "Soviet Venality: a Rent-seeking Model of the Communist State," written with Gary Anderson, published in *Public Choice* 93 (1997): 37–53.

"Credibility, Commitment and Soviet Economic Reform" reprinted from *Economic Transition in Eastern Europe and Russia: Realities of Reform*, edited by Edward P. Lazear, with the permission of the publisher, Hoover Institution

Press. Copyright © 1995 by the Board of Trustees of the Leland Stanford Junior University.

Kluwer Academic Publishers for permission to reprint "Perestroika and the Public Choice: the Economics of the Autocratic Succession in a Rent-seeking Society," written with Gary Anderson, published in *Public Choice* 75(2), (February 1993): 101–18.

Journal des Economistes et des Etudes Humaines for permission to reprint "The Reform Trap in Politics and Economics in the Former Communist Economies," first published in the *Journal des Economistes et des Etudes Humaines* V(2–3) (June/September 1994): 267–93.

Kluwer Academic Publishers for permission to reprint "Promises Made and Promises Broken in the Russian Transition," published in *Constitutional Political Economy* 2 (1998): 133–42.

Blackwell Publishers for permission to reprint "The Russian Crisis: Perils and Prospects for Post-Soviet Transition," published in *American Journal of Economics and Sociology* 59(3) (July 1999): 371–84.

IOS Press BV for permission to reprint "The Political Infrastructure of Economic Development," published in *Human Systems Management* 13(2) (1994): 89–100.

Professor Romano Molesti for permission to reprint "L'Economia, la Politica e il Segno della Storia" published in *Nuova Economia e Storia* 3 (1996): 189–214.

Acknowledgments

Over the years my research has been supported by various foundations, educational institutions, and individuals. For financial support I gratefully acknowledge the Earhart Foundation, the J. M. Kaplan Fund, and the Sarah Scaife Foundation. I have worked at Oakland University, New York University (NYU), the Hoover Institution on War, Revolution and Peace, Manhattan College, and George Mason University, Virginia (GMU). I have also been a visiting scholar at the Institute for the Study of Economic Culture at Boston University, the Russian Academy of Sciences in Moscow, the Central European University in Prague, and the Max Planck Institute for Research into Economic Systems in Jena. Either as a faculty or as a visiting scholar, I have benefited greatly from numerous supportive and intellectually curious colleagues.

I want to thank Mrs Kathleen Spolarich, Mrs Joan Dugan, Bob Subrick, and Christine Polek for technical and research assistance in putting this volume together, and Robert Langham of Routledge for supporting the project. I also appreciate the comments of an anonymous referee, which helped with the selection of materials to be included in the volume. I would also like to thank Mario Rizzo and Lawrence White for selecting the volume to appear in their series "Foundations of the Market Economy."

The bulk of the essays were written while I was working at New York University. I was affiliated with the Austrian Economics Program at New York University from 1990 to 1998. I continue to be affiliated with that program in my capacity as the Director of the Summer Seminar in Austrian Economics, although now that I live in Fairfax, Virginia, I can no longer benefit from the Austrian Economics Colloquium that meets weekly during the academic year. I organize a research workshop at GMU, which attempts to replicate that NYU experience, but while the intellectual level of our workshop is high it is a sad truth that Fairfax does not have the range of restaurants that one has in Greenwich Village for taking the guest speaker to lunch. For his choice of cuisine, as well as his intellectual and personal friendship, I have to thank Mario Rizzo. Mario was an amazing colleague to have as a junior faculty. He read my papers, provided constructive criticism, gave me his papers, and talked to me about ideas. His enthusiasm for ideas and the broader issues of political economy and social philosophy was contagious. From the moment I joined the faculty at NYU, he made me feel that I was a valued contributor to the research program of Austrian Economics and classical liberal political economy.

When I had the opportunity to join Israel Kirzner at NYU as a faculty member I jumped at it. The chance to work with the leading Austrian economist of his generation in the intellectual center of Austrian economics was an unbelievable opportunity offered to me. The reality of those eight years far exceeded my expectations. My time at NYU was one of great intellectual excitement and growth for me. I learned much from Kirzner, not strictly in terms of theoretical economics, but also in terms of intellectual style. Israel Kirzner is a scholar's scholar and a teacher's teacher. It was a great pleasure to work closely with him, and for the opportunities he has given me over the years I will be forever grateful. I dedicate this book to him as a small token of my appreciation.

Peter J. Boettke
George Mason University
September 2000

1 Introduction

It has become somewhat of a modern cliché to insist that the collapse of Communism is one of the defining moments of twentieth-century political economy. Next to the Great Depression, the events of the late 1980s represent *the* political economy puzzle for us to solve. If the Great Depression shook a generation's faith in the stability of the market economy, then the collapse of Communism smashed another generation's hope that a socialist political and economic system offered a solution to capitalist ills that were at one and the same time more economically rational than the capitalist order and more consistent with the democratic values that progressive liberalism demanded. The reality of socialism prior to 1989 was long lines, lousy products, corrupt politics, a history of repression, and declining social system of provision in health and human services. The environmental degradation and increasing risk of major environmental disaster in the Soviet Union, for example, were evident even prior to Chernobyl. When Tatyana Zaslavskaya's 1984 "Novosibirsk Report" was circulated among the ruling élite, nobody was really shocked by the content of her diagnosis of the existing system.[1] Rather, it was the boldness with which she put forth the need for fundamental reform of that system that was shocking to the ruling élite. The Soviet system had so eroded the "surplus fund" that even a fortuitous oil shock could not have bailed out the system this time around, as it had in the 1970s. The system crumbled from within.[2] The Soviet Union was but the most extreme form of this failed project in socialist political economy, and the rest of the Soviet Bloc followed suit. Ironically, the Soviet Union was actually the last to officially take the leap into the post-socialist era of political economy, but the reasons that this leap was necessary throughout the socialist world were strictly speaking Soviet ones.

Since 1989, the peoples of Eastern and Central Europe and, since 1992, the peoples of the former Soviet Union, have been attempting to accomplish a dual transformation in politics and economics. The euphoria of 1989 has given way to a sober reality, as this transformation has been neither easy nor obviously beneficial to the mass of citizens in terms of statistical measures of human well-being. According to official Russian statistics, 30% of the population (44 million people) was living below the poverty line (roughly $40/month) in September 1998. Life expectancy for adult males in Russia has declined from

64 in 1990 to 59 in 1998. It is estimated that 40% of Russia's children are chronically ill. Since 1992 meat and dairy production is down 75%, grain production is down 55%, milk production down 60%, and Gross National Product is down 55%. Real per capita income is down as much as 80% from 1992 according to some measures. This was not without considerable attention from the West, who provided $90.5 billion in external assistance to Russia from 1991 to 1997. Socialist political economy was horrible enough, but how do we explain post-socialist political economy?[3]

Unfortunately, the mainstream of the economics profession was ill-equipped to both explain the failure of socialist political economy and provide a workable model of post-socialist political economy. It is perfectly understandable that, at such a momentous time, leaders both at home and abroad would turn to the "best and the brightest" that the discipline of economics had to offer.[4] And the individuals called on were quite confident that they could redirect the post-socialist world in a more prosperous and peaceful direction. But the turbulent waters of post-Soviet reality have proved more difficult to navigate than was previously expected. Hindsight is, of course, 20/20, but some of these difficulties were predictable.

The biggest problem with the "transition according to Cambridge" (a phraseology introduced by Peter Murrell) was that the basic model of the Soviet period was mis-specified, and that the goal toward which the transition was to achieve has been underdefined.[5] In a sense, on the path from "here to there," the "here" wasn't specified and the "there" was not defined. Without an accurate picture of "here to there," there is no way to successfully navigate the path from socialism to capitalism.

Not everyone among the Harvard–Moscow cadre was guilty of this mis-specification, scholars such as Andrei Shleifer and Anders Åslund clearly understood more than others the "here" of the *de facto* reality of Soviet life.[6] But the standard package of reforms discussed in the "Big Bang" versus "Gradualism" debate did not reflect an understanding of this *de facto* reality. This is not to say that the issue of policy simultaneity which underlies the "Big Bang" argument doesn't hold. The "Big Bang" no doubt logically holds – tight monetary policy without fiscal restraint cannot be sustained, etc. But that doesn't mean that "Big Bang" can ignore the evolutionary type of argument associated with "Gradualism." Just as simultaneity is unassailable, so too is the argument that changes in the world largely occur in an incremental manner rather than in one shot.

There are three factors missing in this "Big Bang" versus "Gradualism" debate which cannot be overlooked if the real problems of post-socialist political economy are going to be engaged:

1   the *de facto* property rights arrangement that existed under the old system;
2   the institutional arrangements within which markets are to be embedded after reforms;
3   the historical experience and cultural legacy of the country under

examination, and specifically the question of the lived experience with market institutions as a carrier of legitimacy.

If we don't pay attention to these issues, then we risk continual frustration due to mis-specification problems and the poor design of transition policies.

The work of public choice and market process scholars which animates my work has highlighted the incentive and informational difficulties associated with alternative institutional environments.[7] However, we must also be willing to peer underneath given institutions and explore the legitimacy accorded to these institutions by different people. The basic institutions of a Western market society, for example, do not accord well with the lived experience of the Soviet peoples with markets. Formerly, the institutions of pricing and bargaining existed in both Soviet and post-Soviet periods. But during the Soviet period, the experience was one within the following situation: a black market without well-defined or enforced property rights, and a shortage of goods and lack of alternative supply networks. If we just look at the simplest depiction of this situation (see Figure 1.1), then perhaps we can begin to see the host of problems that arise under former Soviet conditions.

This very simple supply and demand configuration brings to the forefront the basic fact that in a shortage situation, the real price of obtaining the good in a shortage economy is higher than the official price. There is a gap between quantity demanded and the quantity supplied which creates a situation where there are non-monetary costs to buyers – associated with acquiring the good. Under "normal" market conditions, the costs to buyers are simultaneously benefits to sellers. But in the artificial shortage situation (caused by administered pricing), the non-monetary costs are not immediately benefits to the sellers, so the seller has a strong incentive to transform those non-monetary costs to buyers into benefits (monetary or non-monetary) for themselves. In other words, what this simple diagram reveals is the "rents" that are to be had by those who can exploit the shortage situation – rents that took the form of monetary "bribes,"

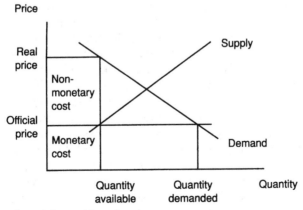

Figure 1.1 Supply and demand in a shortage economy

"black-market profits," and non-monetary "privileges" to those in special favor with the ruling élite. Markets were necessary for daily survival, but black (and other colored) markets are not the same as above-ground and legitimated markets backed by the rule of law, despite the formal similarity of prices and bargaining. The asymmetry between "markets" has to be the starting point of thinking about transition.[8]

Fixing this situation is not just a matter of freeing prices so they can adjust to the market clearing level. Of course, freeing prices is a necessary move, but it is not sufficient. "Getting the prices right" is not enough. What is required is the adoption of an intricate mix of institutions which enable individuals to realize the gains from exchange. But that intricate mix of institutions must be legitimated in the belief structures of the people. We cannot just impose whatever institutional structure we want wherever we want: the institutional structure has to be "grounded" in the everyday actions, beliefs, and ideas of the people.

The essays contained in this book, written over a decade of reflection on the founding, collapse, and transition from socialism in the former Soviet Union, were motivated by the idea that we cannot even begin to provide an answer to the political economy of the transition unless we start with an accurate description of Soviet reality. This explains the first word in the title of the book – *Calculation*. The argument, which originated in the work of Ludwig von Mises, concerning the impossibility of rational economic calculation under pure socialism, is the starting point of all my work in Soviet and post-Soviet political economy. Soviet socialism did not exist in pure form, that model was defeated by reality in the first years of the Soviet system's existence, as explained in the essays on socialism. Instead, the mature Soviet system morphed into a political patronage system which is best modeled as a rent-seeking economy. The second word in the title – *Coordination* – refers to both the problem of the Soviet system in terms of magnitude of coordination failures which were evident in the political economy of everyday life under the Soviet system, and the solution to those problems in the sense that successful reform will lead to increased coordination of plans among economic actors, such that the most willing demanders and the most willing suppliers realize the mutual gains from free exchange. The title is also meant to convey the connection between these two key concepts –advanced complex coordination requires that economic actors are able to utilize the tools of economic calculation provided by private property, market prices and profit and loss accounting.

A theme that is reiterated again and again in the essays on transitional political economy and development in general is that institutions matter. It should be understood, however, that the reason for this emphasis on institutions is the role that entrepreneurship plays in lifting people beyond subsistence and how alternative institutional arrangements direct entrepreneurial activity in either productive or unproductive directions. Entrepreneurship – as described in the work of market process economists – is a necessary ingredient in the economic process in order that individuals can realize the mutual gains from exchange. Entrepreneurship takes at least two general forms:

1   alertness to existing opportunities for mutual gain, and
2   the discovery of new opportunities for mutual gain.

The prime mover of the economic system toward progress is entrepreneurial action. It is through the entrepreneurial process that we come to detect previous errors, adjust our behavior to correct those errors, and thus move to a state of affairs less erroneous than before. Entrepreneurial action is guided by relative price signals and the lure of pure profit (which requires the calculation of profit and loss accounting). Without these important indicators of economic life, the individual would be lost amid a sea of economic possibilities. However, these indicators are a product of specific institutional configurations and cannot be derived outside of that context. Absent the intricate institutional context of a private property market society, and individuals, while still striving to achieve their goals as best as they can, will be unguided by the incentives and informational surrogates which exist only within the private property monetary price system.

In lectures I have often invoked the image of a three-legged bar-stool to make the point about the necessity of this intricate institutional context for economic progress. The legs of the bar-stool represent:

1   economics institutions,
2   political/legal institutions, and
3   social/cultural institutions.

Unless all three legs are equally strong, the bar-stool will not be able to stand when we sit on it. Russia's problems are not limited to the underdevelopment of economic institutions, but are just as much (and probably more) due to the underdevelopment (and mal-development) of political/legal and social/cultural institutions.

The essays in this volume lean toward the conclusion that while there are many different ways that people choose to live throughout our world, there are very few ways for them to live peacefully and prosperously as a society. The book begins with an essay that argues that this conclusion has as much to do with the analytical contributions of economics as it does with normative judgments. The book ends with some concluding remarks on the relationship between economic freedom, economic growth, and general measures of human well-being. I do not believe that aggregate measures of economic growth capture all there is to understand about the human condition – in fact, along with other market process economists, I am quite skeptical of aggregate economics in general and statistical analysis in particular (see Boettke 1993, pp. 21–5). But getting our best guesses on the table can be a valuable exercise, and identifying the possible proxies for human well-being does, on the margin, aid the conversation we are engaged in concerning the human condition within developing economies.

I also do not fear normative theorizing in political economy; in fact, I welcome it (see Boettke 1993, p. 146). But in my work I have tried to insist that political economy is a value-relevant discipline, precisely because economics can provide knowledge that, to the best that we are humanly capable, can be termed value-neutral. In other words, I have tried to carve out a niche where the assessment of socialism and capitalism does not solely turn on whether the analyst has individualist or collectivist values. The consequentialist arguments *for* private property, freedom of contract, open trade, free pricing, monetary stability, and fiscal restraint are not strictly speaking "value-free." To advocate a policy position requires the importation of values. But the consequentialist *critiques* of collective property or even attenuated private property rights; the abolition of commodity production or even restricted market activity; administered pricing; soft-budget constraints; and monetary instability are, in principle, "value-neutral." The logic of these arguments can be, in principle, accepted by both the advocate and the critic of the proposed policy.

The essays in this volume are not meant to close the dialog in political economy over alternative systems. I believe that there are strong arguments and evidence indicating that when ideas and institutions line up to reinforce a commitment within a society to private property, freedom of contract, open trade, monetary responsibility, and fiscal restraint economic miracles will occur and the people in that society will be able to live "better lives." I remain unpersuaded by arguments to the contrary. By stating this position as strongly as I can, I hope these essays will engage others to join the dialog, if only to expose my errors, so that our common understanding of the social–political– economic preconditions for advancing the human condition will be advanced.

References

Åslund, A. (1991) *Gorbachev's Struggle for Economic Reform*, Ithaca, NY: Cornell University Press.

Åslund, A. (1995) *How Russia Became a Market Economy*, Washington, DC: Brookings Institution.

Boettke, P. J. (1990) *The Political Economy of Soviet Socialism: The Formative Years, 1918–1928*, Boston: Kluwer Academic Publishers.

Boettke, P. J. (1993) *Why Perestroika Failed: The Politics and Economics of Socialist Transformation*, New York: Routledge.

Boettke, P. J. (ed.) (1994) *The Collapse of Development Planning*. New York: New York University Press.

Boettke, P. J. (ed.) (2000) *Socialism and the Market: The Socialist Calculation Debate Revisited*, nine volumes, New York: Routledge.

Boycko, M., Shleifer, A. and Vishny, R. (1995) *Privatizing Russia*, Cambridge, MA: MIT Press.

Buchanan, J. (1998) *Post-Socialist Political Economy*, Aldershot: Edward Elgar Publishing.

Murrell, P. (1995) "The Transition According to Cambridge, Mass.," *Journal of Economic Literature* XXXIII (March): 164–78.

Shleifer, A. and Treisman, D. (2000) *Without a Map: Political Tactics and Economic Reform in Russia*, Cambridge, MA: MIT Press.

Shleifer, A. and Vishny, R. (1998) *The Grabbing Hand: Government Pathologies and Their Cure*, Cambridge, MA: Harvard University Press.

Wedel, J. (1998) *Collision and Collusion: The Strange Case of Western Aid to Eastern Europe 1989– 1998*, New York: St Martin's Press.

Zaslavskaya, T. (1984) "The Novosibirsk Report," *Survey* 28 (Spring): 88–108.

2 Why are there no Austrian Socialists?

Ideology, science, and the Austrian school*

Introduction

The Austrian School of Economics has long been branded as a sort of radical *laissez-faire* wing within the economics profession, even much more "right wing," in fact, than Milton Friedman, the profession's most recognized "preacher" of the free market. The economics journalist Alfred Malabre, Jr., for example, in his recent critical book on modern economics, *Lost Prophets*, argues that "the monetarism that Friedman and his followers were preaching was not quite as conservative as advertised. In fact, the University of Chicago professor was treading not far from the middle of the economic road, flanked on the left by the likes of Galbraith and Leontief and on the right by Hayek, along with such other Austrian-school luminaries as Hans Sennholz, chairman of the Economics Department at Grove City College in western Pennsylvania, and Ludwig von Mises, transplanted from Austria and finishing out a distinguished academic and writing career at New York University" (Malabre 1994, p. 144).

This association of Austrian economics with a public policy position, as opposed to a set of analytical arguments, is not new. This is not surprising, given the history of the political economy conflicts in which Austrian economists have been embroiled over the 100+-year history of this school of thought. But it is somewhat surprising when you consider that such an astute *critic* of the development of modern economics as Gunnar Myrdal actually singled out the early Austrian school for being a school of thought which was not directly linked to a political or ideological agenda. Myrdal contended that "in Austria, economics has never had direct political aims in spite of the close connection of the Austrian marginal utility theory with utilitarian philosophy. The Austrians were preoccupied with value theory and never elaborated a detailed theory of welfare economics" (Myrdal 1929, p. 128). In other words, to Myrdal the Austrians (Carl Menger, Eugen von Bohm-Bawerk and Friedrich Wieser) were concerned with pure analytical questions that were not directly connected to an ideology – even though in Myrdal's framework they did reflect some visionary element, namely utilitarianism.[1]

*Originally published as Boettke, P. J. (1995) "Why are there no Austrian Socialists? Ideology, Science and the Austrian School," *Journal of the History of Economic Thought*, 17 (Spring): 35–56.

New evidence from Menger's lectures to Crown Prince Rudolf, as presented by Eric Streissler (1990), may now reveal that Menger himself was a deeply committed classical liberal.[2] Israel Kirzner (1990) has pointed out that no matter what Menger's own political policy preferences may have been, his scientific vision of a consumer-driven economy laid the groundwork for Ludwig von Mises' analytical treatment of the problems with state interventionism and socialist planning. Wieser may have been a mild Fabian in political persuasion, but his insight concerning how the decentralized decisions in the private market economy would outperform a centralized economy, precisely because of the "knowledge problem" in the latter, would become a theme repeatedly stressed by subsequent generations of Austrians in their battles with advocates of socialist and interventionist policies (see Wieser 1927, p. 396). Moreover, Bohm-Bawerk (1896) penned what many consider the most devastating polemic against Karl Marx's logical structure. So even the founding fathers of Austrian economics made fundamental contributions to the argument for economic liberalism.

The liberalism of the classical economists and the *vulgar* economics of the German Historical School were criticized, however, by Richard Strigl (1928). The Mengerian revolution changed the essential character of economics, according to Strigl, and as such the relationship between economic theory and public policy application. Classical economics (of either the French Physiocrats or the English school) *required* the economic policy of liberalism to follow from its theoretical train of thought. Austrian economics, on the other hand, "has absolutely nothing to do with the old liberalism" (Ibid., p. 14). Of course, Strigl insisted, as compared with the blind intervention of the Historical School, modern theory appeared to be liberal. But this missed a fundamental change in the content of economics since the revolution of the 1870s. Modern subjectivist economics did not concern itself with the examination of ends or goals of economic policy. Economic theory, instead, is a tool for the critical appraisement of means. "For economic policy, the setting of a goal will always stand outside the field discernible to a theory. But when a goal is set, the task is to discover means of realizing it. Economics too does not only serve the satisfaction of the baser wants; it can stand in the service of higher ends. And economic theory can teach us how to apply our means to the satisfaction of such ends" (Ibid., p. 15).

The Bolshevik leader and theoretician, Nikolai Bukharin, wrote a book largely devoted to a critique of the Austrian School because, as he states in the preface, "it is well known that the most powerful opponent of Marxism is the Austrian School" (Bukharin 1919, p. 9). Moreover, even while involved in a party dispute over the New economic policy in Russia, Bukharin singled out Mises in a polemic as "one of the most learned critics of communism" (Bukharin 1925, p. 188). It seems that even the Bolsheviks understood the ideological import as well as the scientific merit of the Austrian position.

Despite Mises' many contributions to monetary economics, comparative system analysis, methodology, and value theory, his work, especially in the reception it received in the US in the post-World War II era, was viewed as ideologically suspect. Hayek confronted the professional assessment as that of Mises. When the *American Economic Review* decided to review F. A. von Hayek's *The Road to Serfdom* (1944), for example, they arranged for two reviewers and prefaced the reviews with the following editorial: "In view of the ideological character of, and the great interest in Professor Hayek's book it was found desirable to publish two reviews written from different standpoints." Ideological dismissal substituted for serious consideration of the analytical arguments put forth by Mises and Hayek with regard to the feasibility of socialism, Keynesian macroeconomic interventionism, and microeconomic interventionism.[3]

Suffice it to say that given this historical record, most practicing economists, if asked to discuss the work of Mises or Hayek or even contemporary Austrian economists, would focus on their ideological position and not the analytical arguments. While certainly the majority of researchers working in the tradition of Mises and Hayek would not deny that their work is decidedly market-oriented compared with others in the economics profession (or other scholars working on economic questions in political science, sociology, history, etc.), they would also argue that their *critique* of government interventionism and socialism was *completely* value-free.[4] Nothing less than the scholarly integrity of a school of thought is at stake. If the Austrian method necessitates at the outset that free market conclusions be drawn, then Austrian economics does not warrant serious scholarly attention and truly is a pseudoscientific endeavor. Those within the Austrian tradition beg to differ with this inference. Austrian economics is no more or less ideologically tainted than alternative approaches to economic science, including the currently hegemonic neoclassical mainstream, and its analytical contributions to economic science demand scholarly attention if a deeper understanding of economic life is the goal of our endeavors as social scientists. But then how can the passionate commitment to *laissez-faire* (so evident in the writings of Austrian economists) be squared with an intellectual commitment to objective and dispassionate value-free analysis? Why, if Austrian economics does not imply an ideological agenda, are there no Austrian socialists?

Traditional Austrian *wertfreiheit*

Following Max Weber (1904, 1919), the Austrian School has been one of the steadfast defenders of the notion of *wertfreiheit*, or value-freedom, in economic theory.[5] Mises, for example, argued that "economics is apolitical or non-political, although it is the foundation of politics and of every kind of political action. We may furthermore say that it is perfectly neutral with regards to all judgments of value, as it refers always to means and never to the choice of ultimate ends" (Mises 1949, p. 881). The objective scientific status of bacteriology, Mises stated in an earlier work, is not doubted because the biological researcher in this field seeks to fight viruses responsible for human illness (see 1933, p. 36). Neither should the objective nature of economic knowledge be called into question when it produces a critique of "wishful thinking" with regard to proposed political action for the economy. At least that is the position which Mises was promoting.

Perhaps the most articulate statement of the doctrine of *wertfreiheit* within economics was contained in Lionel Robbins' influential essay on method. Economic science, Robbins insisted under the influence of Weber and Mises, is neutral with regard to ultimate ends. The science is not equipped to pronounce on the validity of ultimate judgments of value. Economics is "fundamentally distinct from Ethics." The value of the science of economics, however, consists in the fact that "when we are faced with a choice between ultimates, it enables us to choose with full awareness of the implications of what we are choosing ... [Economics] can make clear to us the implications of the different ends we may choose. It makes it possible for us to will with knowledge of what it is we are willing. It makes it possible for us to select a system of ends which are mutually consistent with each other" (Robbins 1933, p. 152).

Israel Kirzner (1976, 1994) has provided important surveys of the doctrine of *wertfreiheit* within Austrian economics. Kirzner's argument, in fact, is that it is precisely because of the radical subjectivist position to which Austrian economists adhere that permits value-freedom in economic science. Mises' critique of proposed government policy, for example, was never stated as a critique of the ends of the interventionist. The ends were not in dispute, but the efficacy of the proposed means for obtaining any given end was scrutinized. The critique, in other words, was always stated in terms of the purposes and plans of the agents who were proposing the policy. Rent-control was a proposed means to obtain the end of lower-cost housing. The unfortunate result of the policy, though, was to create a shortage of housing and raise the "real" price (which would include non-monetary costs) of obtaining those units that were available. The policy was self-defeating from the point of view of those who desired it in the first place. It is this self-defeating aspect of Mises' analysis of interventionism that generates the interventionist dynamic, which, under certain ideological and cultural conditions, begets additional interventions.

Mario Rizzo (1992, pp. 250–2) has recently vigorously defended the value-free nature of Austrian economics. "Austrian economics," Rizzo states, "has been called mere ideology, or even worse, an economic apologia for libertarianism. If the consequences of such accusations were not so serious, it would be easy to dismiss the whole matter as absurd because it really does arise out of a negligent misunderstanding of Austrian political economy" (Rizzo 1992, p. 251). He goes on, however, to suggest that some of the blame for misunderstanding must be shared by Austrian economists, who sometimes make reckless statements, and to suggest that we recast the political economy claims of the Austrian School in propositional form.[6] He provides a list of five positive propositions:

1   The profit and loss system possesses greater coordinative properties than alternative systems.
2   Even moderate interventionism generates unintended consequences which are unsatisfactory from the point of view of the benevolent interventionist.

3 The middle-of-the-road system is unstable.
4 Vast economic control by the government leads to resource waste and a destruction of wealth.
5 Socialism is not feasible because of the difficulties in economic calculation outside of the private property order and price system.

Rizzo argues that none of these propositions require the importation of the values of the economic theorist. The first proposition does involve the values of the agents in the economy. The second and fifth argue that the results of government policies are contrary to the values (goals) of the intervener. The third involves no value judgments, but instead examines the logic of the situation, given the second and fifth propositions. The fourth defines wealth in terms of the preferences of the agents within the economy.

These are scientific (i.e. objective) propositions, Rizzo argues, the validity of which is capable of disinterested evaluation. However, "dislike" must be distinguished from scientific disbelief, Rizzo adds. None of these propositions should be held as sacrosanct. Austrian economics is first and foremost a way of thinking, and only secondarily a system of conclusions. Those who find this way of thinking attractive but do not believe the validity of the propositions are invited by Rizzo to join the discussion and demonstrate how these propositions "do not follow from what is essential in Austrian theory, or, more simply, that they are wrong" (Rizzo 1992, p. 252). The important point to stress, for present purposes, is that it does not matter whether Rizzo or anyone else feels comfortable with these propositions, for they flow not from an ideological system of thought, but instead from a series of analytical steps that are capable of objective assessment and refutation.

Where the Austrians have historically differed from other scholars seeking to establish the objective nature of economic reasoning is in their denial that methodological monism (i.e. the adoption of the empiricist methods of the natural scent for the project in the social sciences) was the key to objective knowledge. In short, the Austrian school has traditionally held two fundamental philosophical stances. First, the social sciences in general, and economics in particular, are methodologically distinct from the natural sciences. Yet despite this fundamental difference, economics is capable of establishing general principles. Second, neither the development of these general principles (an exercise in logic), nor the application of these principles to assess the efficacy of the means chosen to satisfy stated ends, involves the importation of values. A type of non-positivistic positive economics is what the Austrians have always claimed their analytical contributions represented.

Dissension within the Austrian camp

Some Austrian economists, namely Murray Rothbard (1970, 1976, 1982), have raised some serious problems concerning the ability of neoclassical economists to engage in value-free welfare economics. Rothbard exposes the importation of non-justified philosophical arguments within most economic exercises of welfare theory and/or public policy analysis. Rothbard, however, also hits closer to home and even points out limitations to Mises' analysis (see, in particular, Rothbard 1982, pp. 205–12). To Rothbard, Misesian analysis fails on one level simply because it must assume that the stated aims of the intervener are the real goals of the policy in question. But what if the real aim of the policy is actually to produce the "undesired" consequence, say shortages caused by a price ceiling: Mises then loses his critical edge and must remain silent.

Mises believed that economic science could demonstrate how the adoption of the policies of economic liberalism would generate results deemed beneficial from the point of view of "rightly understood interests." His commitment to the assumption of public official benevolence translated into an assertion of public interest motivation behind economic policy. But, as subsequent developments in public choice theory have argued, the assumption of benevolence provides a woefully deficient foundation for understanding the logic of politics within representative democracies. That logic tends to produce a bundle of economic policies which yield short-term and easily identifiable benefits concentrated on the well-organized and well-informed mass of citizens. To Mises there simply was no conflict between good economics and good politics. Mises' exhortation for government to pursue "sound" economic policies in the face of the public choice logic was futile. Rothbard's critique of democratic government, of course, is different from that offered in the public choice literature – stressing the coercive nature of politics, in general, and the contradictory nature of democracy, in particular. Both the public choice and the Rothbardian critiques, however, challenge the effectiveness of Mises' core analytical assumptions for generating policy relevant political economy.

Rothbard concedes that Mises has an alternative position – one more consistent with the value-freedom of economics – and that is to state that economics can establish chains of cause and effect, but cannot establish the correctness of any economic policy. The economist *qua* economist can provide information, but he/she cannot advocate. Policy advocacy is the domain of the citizen. Mises did not believe that ethics was capable of generating "objective" statements and, therefore, could not be considered a science. However, as citizens, we can, and do, adopt value systems. The economist Mises may not be able to advocate *laissez-faire* liberalism, but the citizen Mises can, and certainly did (see Mises 1949, pp. 153–5). While Rothbard admits that this position saves Mises from an internal contradiction (i.e. the value-free economist vigorously advocating *laissez-faire*), the Misesian position is nevertheless seen as unsatisfactory for ethical theory reasons.[7]

Along Rothbardian lines, Hans-Herman Hoppe (1993, pp. 173–208) rejects the Humean dictum that reason is the slave of the passions, and, therefore, that the choice between ends must be arbitrary, and attempts to develop a rational ethic based on the logical priors to effective argumentation and communication. Borrowing from the German philosopher, Karl-Otto Apel, Hoppe seeks to deduce from the a priori principles of argumentation a libertarian ethic of self-ownership. The principle of self-ownership is a necessary precondition for human communication, and the consistent pursuit of this principle generates a social philosophy of non-aggression and absolute private ownership rights. To deny these propositions, Hoppe argues, entangles the party in question in a self-refuting philosophical contradiction.

Despite our judgment of the success or failure of either Rothbard's or Hoppe's attempt to develop a rational science of ethics, the important point for present purposes is to explore the implication for traditional Austrian arguments concerning *wertfreiheit*. Ironically, if we read Rothbard and Hoppe carefully, neither challenge the doctrine in economics *per se*. Instead, their argument is almost that we could have a *wertfreiheit* science of ethics! The criteria of reason (logic and evidence) controls the passions in the theoretical systems developed by Rothbard and Hoppe. Praxeology is not abandoned, but reconstructed and completed (that is especially how Hoppe sees his work).[8] "Ought" can be derived from "is" in this system. All that is really suggested in the Rothbard and Hoppe position is an explicit recognition of where economics leaves off (i.e. before policy advocacy) and the other sciences of human action take over and where ethical theory consistently fits into the interdisciplinary research program for libertarian scholarship.

Jack High (1985) has taken a slightly different twist to the Rothbardian critique of mainstream welfare economics in general, and to Austrian economics in particular. High argues that the very concepts employed in positive economics, such as exchange, are embedded in an ethical system of language. To understand voluntary exchange, for example, the concept of "voluntary" must be clearly defined, and that concept *cannot* be defined without recourse to an articulated ethical theory. The same can be said, High argues, for the concepts of "coercion," "rights," and "ownership." In fact, the "market" understood as a nexus of contracts cannot be distinguished from socialism without ethical concepts. In other words, the "is" of positive economics cannot be discussed or analyzed properly without recognizing the "ought" properties embedded in the conceptualizations of the system. High, however, is emphatic that his discussion does not challenge the *wertfreiheit* status of economic science. "The use of value judgments to define those methods of acquiring resources that fall within the scope of market activity and those methods that fall within the scope of government activity does not require the economist to agree with those value judgments.... Indeed, a socialist who defined the market this way (i.e. in terms of Lockean natural rights theory) could attack the market by attacking the moral precepts on which the market rests." Accepting "the proposition," High concludes, "that economic definitions depend upon ethical judgements does not involve the economist in taking a stand on moral issues. In this sense, the much-cherished 'value-freedom of economic science' is left untouched by our central thesis" (High 1985, pp. 14–15).

Thus, neither the Rothbardian critique nor High's demonstration of the ethical embeddness of our language challenges the doctrine of *wertfreiheit* and its central role within Austrian economics. The analytical contribution of the

Austrian school continues to be viewed as objective and value-free statements of logical chains of cause and effect.

Modern philosophy of science, however, has challenged the veracity of these claims to "objective" and "value-free" knowledge. Scholars such as Michael Polanyi and Thomas Kuhn, let alone Richard Rorty, have effectively challenged the modernist ideal of "objective" knowledge even in the natural sciences. But, as we have seen, the Austrian argument for value-freedom was couched in different terms from that offered by positivistic modernists and promised a non-positivistic positive economic analysis.[9] It was not the empirical testability of propositions that guarded against the unwarranted intrusion of values, but the givenness of ends. It was the radical subjectivism of the Austrians that provided the check against the intrusion of unwarranted value judgments into scientific analysis. Nevertheless, developments in the philosophy of science literature have led some contemporary Austrians to challenge the traditional Austrian notion of "objective" knowledge.

Don Lavoie is the one main researcher to challenge the very notion of value-freedom as a viable principle of scientific research within Austrian economics. Lavoie's position derives from a familiarity with post-positivist philosophy of science in general, and contemporary continental philosophy (hermeneutics and phenomenology) in particular (see, for example, Lavoie 1985, 1990, 1994). Among the next generation of Austrian economists, challenges to the epistemological status of *wertfreiheit* have been voiced by Boettke (1989b, 1990), D. L. Prychitko (1990), and S. Horwitz (1992, pp. 3–6).[10] The position advocated among these writers, however, is not one of abandoning scientific discourse in economics, but rather one of widening that discourse to explicitly recognize the values that accreditate the process of science, that give rise to the questions we hope to answer, that establish the standards by which we judge arguments as convincing. At the edge of this argument lurks an abyss of relativism. But is it possible to stare into the abyss and not jump? Surely we must answer in the affirmative if we hope to validate the process of the scientific search for truth. However, I contend that affirmative answer is not due to an epistemological argument for objective knowledge. Recognizing the value-ladenness of our thought does not condemn economics simply to become an ideological clash of "different perspectives."

Toward a pragmatic understanding of *wertfreiheit*

In light of modern philosophical developments, must the doctrine of *wertfreiheit* be abandoned? First, it is important to distinguish the Austrian case from the neoclassical case for the doctrine. The neoclassical case is built upon the foundation of modernist epistemology as reflected in the positivist conception of science. The Austrian case is different. The Austrians represent a non-positivistic positive social science, and, as such, they are not as completely de-legitimized in their epistemological claims to "objectivity" as the positivistic economist. Nevertheless, the critique of modernist epistemology does not leave the Austrian case intact philosophically speaking.[11] Values invade our scientific analysis at the level of the basic questions we ask, as well as at the level of what we consider to be an appropriate answer to the problems posed. We can conceptually distinguish between *vision* and *analysis*, but the interconnection between the two undermines the epistemological dichotomy assumed in the modernist enterprise. After the post-positivist revolution, *wertfreiheit* is no longer the viable epistemological project that it once was thought to be.

At least two arguments follow immediately from the epistemological challenge to *wertfreiheit*. First, economists need to be explicit about their value system. This is a variant of the Rothbardian critique of standard welfare economics. Mainstream economists did not employ rigorous philosophical arguments, Rothbard pointed out, to justify their welfare economics. But, welfare economics was grounded in moral philosophy and ethical theory – namely utilitarianism. Part of Rothbard's critique was to expose the normative underpinnings of what many thought was positive analysis, and then to demand an engagement of scholarly debate. Moral theory is capable of rational dialog, and economists ought to be knowledgeable of this dialog if they are going to employ the concepts derived within this field of study to make welfare statements and policy recommendations. For example, they ought to be informed of the critique of utilitarianism that comes out of libertarian natural rights theory, or the difficulties that moral philosophers have with social contract theories. In a recent paper surveying development in moral philosophy, Daniel Hausman and Michael McPherson (1993) make a very similar argument in making their case that economists need to take ethics seriously for both their normative and their positive work in economics. As Hausman and McPherson point out, many economists have already engaged this dialog; some, such as Amartya Sen or James Buchanan, have even fundamentally influenced developments in moral philosophy. This is a progressive sign.

As explained above, however, Rothbard would not concur with the argument that positive analysis involves moral judgments, it is just normative theorizing that is imbued with ethical considerations. Kirzner (1989) has taken a different route altogether from Rothbard's call for explicit ethical argumentation in dealing with welfare theory (although see Rothbard 1970, pp. 203–55 for a praxeological critique of anti-market ethics). Kirzner argues that standard ethical assessments of capitalism have failed not because of flaws in the ethical arguments themselves, but because they misperceive the nature of market processes; namely, the discovery function of market competition. The lure of pure profit sets in motion an entrepreneurial discovery procedure in which individuals tend to learn how to arrange resources in a more effective manner to satisfy the demands. Without the private property order, which Kirzner seeks to establish, this learning process will be absent. I would like to suggest that nothing in this Kirzner research strategy is damaged by the epistemological critique of *wertfreiheit*. In fact, it is completely consistent with the pragmatic case that I will suggest. For example, regarding the ideological import of the Cambridge–Cambridge capital theory debate and Kirzner's attempt at clarification, "the point of all this," he states, "is that we cannot, surely, close our eyes to possible ideological implications of science. Our science may well be, perhaps, ideologically untainted and value-free (or, at any rate honest efforts in this direction may be undertaken), but human beings are, as valuing citizens, vitally interested in the character of controversial phenomena." The Austrian methodological essentialism is, Kirzner points out, particularly relevant in these discussions. Science must take note of the non-scientific purposes for which it may be put to use (Kirzner 1993, pp. 190–1).

The second response to the critique of modernist ideas on objective knowledge would be to offer a pragmatic defense of *wertfreiheit*. There is no need to jettison the concept entirely just because philosophy cannot sustain its epistemological purity if it can be found that the doctrine aids rational dialog. In fact, Lionel Robbins (1933, p. 150) offered a pragmatic defense of the doctrine on the following grounds: "And, quite apart from all questions of methodology, there is a very practical justification for such a procedure. In the rough-and-tumble of political struggles, differences of opinion may arise either as a result of differences about ends or as a result of differences about the means of attaining ends. Now, as regards the first type of difference, neither economics nor any other science can provide any solvent. If we disagree about ends it is a case of thy blood or mine – or live and let live, according to the importance of the difference, or the relative strength of our opponents. But, if we disagree about means, then scientific analysis can often help us resolve our differences." While I would contest that rational dialog over ends is impossible, I would endorse Robbins' general point.

Science does not need a single Methodology[12] to insure its progress, but rather, honest practitioners willing to submit to the critical dialog of their peers and refrain from cheating and other assorted shortcuts (see McCloskey 1985, pp. 20–53). In other works, science, as Michael Polanyi often stressed, is nothing more than a set of shared values within a community which are accreditated in the process of the search for truth. The problem of ideology for the scientific enterprise is only a problem when the values of a political and ideological doctrine are exalted above the values which guide the scientific process. Ideology is ever-present, even if it is the ideology of the status quo, but it need not be an impediment to the generation of progress in thought. In fact, the reverse may be true: thought in the social sciences may crucially depend on the social philosophical visions that are held dear by many practitioners.

My proposed pragmatic employment of the doctrine of *wertfreiheit* would be similar in spirit to Bruce Caldwell's (1982) articulation of the research strategy for a critical rationalism in the post-positivist world. Within a methodologically pluralistic world – in which demarcation is not possible – the critical function of methodology can no longer be pursued under the assumption of a universalistic method. But, that does not imply silence. Methodological work can proceed along the line of immanent criticism. For the sake of argument, assume the "paradigm" of the school in question and examine the internal logic of its arguments. I do not follow Caldwell completely in this regard, because I still think that there is a large role for the clash between competing paradigms and the employment of external criteria to assess a school of thought. For example, mainstream models of market clearing may be internally consistent, given the problems that they were developed to solve, but if the paradigm masks certain important questions, features of reality that are deemed essential to a satisfying explanation, then it is legitimate to critically assess the school's contribution, despite its internal consistency. Admittedly, this inter-paradigmatic critical act moves me beyond the "objective" role of a critic, and involves my judgments about what are the good and interesting questions to be asked and what would be appropriate analytical techniques for generating persuasive answers. The fact that this results from my value judgments in no way implies that these judgments cannot be debated. As a responsible member of the community, I am responsible for providing *good reasons* for my position on the goals toward which the enterprise of economics should aspire. We can debate those reasons, using logic, evidence, scholarly authority, etc. In fact, this is why methodology remains an important field of study in economics, despite the post-modernist critique – it helps the profession define the "rules of the game" with regard to the discipline of questioning and answering.

What is true for methodological discourse, I contend, is also true for the dialog concerning the welfare properties of alternative public policies (see, for example, Boettke 1993, pp. 4–5, 108–9, 163, n. 27). For critical discourse on issues of public policy, the Misesian case for *wertfreiheit* can be employed pragmatically, if not completely justified on epistemological grounds. Recognizing that *vision* lies at the heart of our intellectual endeavors, does not mean that we cannot examine the *analytics* of an argument. In assessing a system of thought, I can first and foremost examine whether it is internally consistent (immanent criticism). If its constituent parts do not fit together, then I have demonstrated a weakness in the theoretical structure that must be repaired. On the other hand, if a theoretical structure is internally consistent, then I can ask whether it is vulnerable to external argument (interparadigmatic conflict). If it is both internally consistent and can withstand external criticism, then we will most likely be convinced of its merit and adopt it ourselves as a useful conceptual apparatus for thinking about the world.

The critical argument that Mises and Hayek presented against socialism employed this pragmatic variant of *wertfreiheit*. Given the socialist planners ends of eliminating poverty, ignorance and squalor, certain means were advocated, namely the abolition of private property in the means of production, and the substitution of a rational and unified plan for the anarchy of the market. The Mises–Hayek critique (both economic and political) was an immanent critique. The means to be employed by socialist planners were inconsistent with the ends sought. Instead, the unintended and undesirable consequence would be economic deprivation and political tyranny. In other words, theirs was an *analytical* argument concerning decentralized knowledge, the complexity of an advanced capital structure, and the functional significance of relative monetary prices and profit and loss signals, combined with a set of subsidiary *empirical* assumptions about the institutional arrangements, cultural attitudes of the population, and the magnitude of distortions that can be assessed independently of whether the individual presenting the argument is a socialist or a radical libertarian.

Rothbard's critique of Mises' position affects the epistemological status of the strategy, not its pragmatic usefulness in advancing arguments. Mises' argument is only strengthened when libertarian caste analysis or public-choice interest-group theory is incorporated. For strength of argument, the Misesian can assume benevolence, and then show that the chosen means would be ineffective to achieve the ends sought by the benevolent planner. Moreover, if the Misesian argument can be demonstrated under the heroic assumption of benevolence, then in practice the Misesian critique is even stronger as a practical guide than as theoretically stated. Of course, the assumption of benevolence does damage to epistemological reality, but it aids thought by allowing us to focus on one set of difficulties while holding another of issues constant. Thus, this is another instance where the pragmatic value of a convention out distances our epistemological capability to justify rationally.

The advocacy of classical liberalism and libertarianism, however, is another story. Now, the underlying *vision* must be explicitly admitted and defended. The vision of civil society as the by-product of self-regulation within the bounds of individual rights is radically different from a conception of society that sees civil society as the result of conscious ordering. As economists *qua* economists, we can debate the different analytical arguments that flow from these visions, but we must recognize that the visions are distinct and fundamentally important. Keynesians, for example, may be asking a different set of questions (namely, how do markets break down?) than the ones asked by Austrians (namely, how do markets coordinate?). We can choose to debate either the analytical components of each other's arguments through immanent critique and external assessment of some set of values that we define (say realism of theory), or we can examine each other's visions and debate the merit of these for understanding the world. Both exercises are rational, both may be heated and passionate, and in both situations reason and passion are what make the human search for truth interesting and progressive.

Conclusion

William Rappard, reflecting on the numerous conversations that he had with Mises during their time as colleagues at the Graduate Institute of International Studies in Geneva, stated that something puzzled him in those "always very enlightening" conversations. The two fundamental opinions on which Mises never wavered appear to be in contradiction. Mises insisted on the purely scientific character of economics, and Mises insisted on complete and uncompromising *laissez-faire* (Rappard 1957). Mises was able to square these positions because in his mind when it came to economic matters people differ not in ultimate ends but in the means recommended to achieve generally accepted ends.

More recently, Rothbard (1993) has picked up Rappard's question and provides – despite his earlier critiques of Mises mentioned above – a spirited defense of Mises as objective scientist *and* liberal social philosopher. Mises' theory of liberalism was grounded in a theory of social cooperation based on the division of labor – Ricardo's Law of Association. In other words, Mises, the social rationalist, conceived of economic liberalism as the application of the principles of economic reasoning to problems of policy. The goals of liberalism were general and non-controversial – improvements in the economic well-being of the masses. Economic science (at least in Mises' hands) taught that the unhampered market economy within a system of private property accomplished that goal more effectively than alternative systems.

Rothbard chides his fellow contemporary Austrians for not embracing Mises' concern with policy relevance for fear of the ideology charge from the profession. Historically, economists of all stripes had engaged in *political* economy. Classical British economists, Marxists, the German Historical School, American Institutionalists, the early neoclassical economists, Keynesians, etc., all eschewed the "monkish cowl" and the call for political abstinence. Rothbard makes an important point when he states that the charge of ideology is often reserved for work being done outside of the mainstream. Clearly, the policy relevance of one's work should not be a sign of illegitimacy. On the other hand, the political/ideological relevance of a set of propositions does not establish their scientific merit.

The value-free posture and the search for "objective" knowledge within the Austrian camp (or any school of economics for that matter) may be an epistemological chimera, but that does not mean that the fiction fails to serve a useful purpose. Classical liberalism and libertarianism, as an underlying *vision,* in turn provide the questions on which Austrian economists tend to focus. *Analysis* is not invariant to the underling *vision* which the analyst adopts. That does not mean that we should not make honest efforts at ideologically untainted assessments of the economic world. The analytical propositions of the Austrians can be employed as part of a critical theory framework for assessing the effectiveness of chosen means for given ends. These analytical arguments are open to critical appraisal and logical and empirical challenge.

I started this chapter with a question: Why are there no Austrian socialists? The answer has something to do with the history of modern economic thought. First, trends in philosophical and economic thought moved the economics discipline in a direction which placed the Austrians outside of the mainstream of economic teaching. Therefore, something other than puzzles in economic theory had to attract people to work in the Austrian tradition. Classical liberalism and libertarianism provided the educational impetus. Many heterodox movements in economics, I would conjecture, have a *visionary* component which serves this purpose of maintaining intellectual interest in an approach to economic questions that lies outside the normal curriculum in undergraduate and graduate courses in economics. Second, the classical liberal and libertarian visions compel a theorist to ask certain questions, or focus on aspects of empirical reality which other visions would minimize.[13] Analytical tools in modern Austrian economics were developed to address these questions. These analytical aspects of Austrian thought raised some – as yet unchallenged (as I see it) – criticisms of the socialist enterprise. Thus, the answer to my question may have as much, if not more, to do with the analytical assessment of the means of collective property for the given ends of equality and liberty than the visionary clash between individualism and collectivism.

Acknowledgments

An earlier version of this chapter was presented at the Eastern Economic Association Meetings in Boston in March 1994 (see Boettke 1994). I would like to thank Paul Davidson, Robert Solow, Donald Dewey, Roger Koppl, Sanford Ikeda, Bill Butos, Steve Sullivan, and Sean Keenan for helpful comments. In addition, I would like to thank Mario Rizzo, Israel Kirzner, David Prychitko, and Steve Horwitz for their comments on earlier drafts. I would also like to acknowledge the insightful comments of Donald Walter, editor of the *Journal of the History of Economic Thought,* and two anonymous referees. Financial assistance from the Austrian Economics Program at New York University is gratefully acknowledged. Responsibility for errors is exclusively my own.

Appendix: is economics a moral science?*

That political economy in its finest moments is a value-relevant discipline can hardly be disputed. The question is whether knowledge gleaned in the disciplines of economic and political economy can be both value-relevant and value-neutral. Adam Smith holds a claim to our intellectual attention to this day precisely because his work, as Kenneth Boulding so aptly put it, is part of our "extended present."[14] We need Smith, because Smith still speaks to us in an enabling manner about basic issues of social organization. But Smith's *analysis* of economic interdependence is something that stands independent of our judgment of his *vision* of "the system of natural liberty." Vision and analysis cannot be so neatly compartmentalized, but they can nevertheless be usefully distinguished from one another.[15]

The post-positivist critique of objective knowledge found in writers such as Michael Polanyi,[16] Thomas Kuhn,[17] and Stephen Toulmin[18] does not inevitably slide into the post-modernist critique of scientific knowledge in general. There might be strong epistemological arguments against the idea that scientific procedures can produce a "mirror of nature," but that need not imply a slip into epistemological relativism. Algorithms and methods do not necessarily make for good science; good scientists make for good science.[19] But beyond

*Originally published as Boettke, P. J. (1998) "Is Economics a Moral Science?" *Journal of Markets and Morality*, 1(2): 212–19.

admonishments to behave morally, the task of scientific discourse can be aided by certain argumentative steps.[20] Despite the critique of modernist epistemology, there are, in other words, pragmatic steps that we can take in argumentation that improve the chances for interpersonal assessment. These steps amount to accepting the ends of one's intellectual adversary and restricting analysis to an immanent critique of their system.

Ricardo Crespo does not tackle the issue of whether economics is a moral science by way of post-modernist philosophy, but instead through the lens of Aristotelian philosophy.[21] His basic claim is that economics as a practical science must of necessity address the ends toward which individuals strive. I do not have much of a problem with what is stated about the Aristotelian stance, especially with regard to expecting from a discipline only that "amount of precision which belongs to its subject matter," and I do have many problems with positivistic notions of economic science as they have developed in this century. So, why do I resist Crespo's formulation? Because I think that in his critique of economic *analysis,* Crespo undermines precisely the most important role that economics as a science can plan in developing a value-relevant political economy. Economics can provide us with as close to value-neutral knowledge as we can hope to gain, and this knowledge, in turn, provides the basis for our rational discussion of alternative *visions* of the good.

The practice of political economy as a value-relevant discipline is an interdisciplinary research program in politics, philosophy, and economics. Hyper-specialization of the disciplines has pulled these fields increasingly further apart, but, for political economy to be properly practiced, these disciplines can neither be allowed to collapse into one another through overzealous intellectual imperialism nor completely separated in the vain quest for specialization. Instead, we must respect each discipline for its unique contribution to human knowledge, yet draw on the multidisciplinary insights that reside in the section of overlap – an overlap of questions, of data, of both the object and subject of study in political economy. The unique contribution that economics has to offer to this project is a style of reasoning about means and ends, and a determination of the effectiveness of selected means to obtaining selected ends.

I will raise four separate points to argue for the role of economics as value-neutral. Before I proceed, however, I would like to make two statements. First, to say that economics can provide value-neutral knowledge does not mean that any particular economist can be value-neutral. We are human beings and in the very nature of choosing we strive for various ends by employing available means. This is as true for the scientist as it is for the stockbroker or your parish priest. Value judgments are part of our human condition and there is no way to escape them, and either we admit to them or we sneak them in through the back door. The best we can do is either openly debate and defend value-judgments, or find certain procedures in our argumentative strategy that attempt to improve interpersonal assessment of how we obtained our judgments. Second, when economists use the term *efficiency* there is no necessary judgment involved in the term. It could, in fact, be used as a term of value-judgment if we impart normative weight to ends (such as wealth-maximizing), but there is no necessary reason to take this step. All efficiency refers to is the relationship between means chosen and desired ends. Both the sinner and the saint want to be *efficient* in this sense. The criticism of economics, that it tries to substitute efficiency as the ultimate moral judgment, is, in this sense, simply misplaced. Efficiency, for example, does not mean wealth-maximization. Of course, some economists (perhaps many) may be guilty of misapplication but *economics* need not be so tarred.

I can grant many (perhaps most) of Crespo's arguments and still hold out a pragmatic defense of value-neutral economics, for it is only a value-neutral economics that enables economists and social thinkers to practice a value-relevant political economy.

Radical subjectivism

Modern economic theory stresses the subjective nature of value-judgments by choosing individuals within social processes. It is individuals that choose which ends to pursue with the means available to them. As has been stressed by Israel Kirzner (and before him by Ludwig von Mises), it is precisely the radical subjectivism of economics that assures that the discipline has any way to approximate "objective knowledge."[22] The content of ends is not the domain of economics; the logical analysis of the effectiveness of selected means to achieve given ends is the domain of economics. Economics cannot determine, for example, whether profits are deserved. But what economics can do is inform one of the consequences of various answers to that question.

Thus, *contra* Crespo, the knowledge that economics provides can be separated from ethical questions. Moreover, it is precisely because economics can provide value-neutral knowledge of the logical consequences of different ethical systems that it is an essential input to a value-relevant discipline of political economy. To put it another way, if the choice is between utility and justice, then, of course, we can agree that justice should trump. But, in the world, the choice is rarely so clear-cut. Instead, we are usually confronted with a choice between different concepts of justice, and when confronted with this choice, utility trumps justice.[23] Knowledge of the consequences of alternative social arrangements is vital to making the choice among those arrangements. If we deny that this knowledge is obtainable in any manner that allows for interpersonal assessment, then we deny from the moral science of political economy the ability to adjudicate between different conceptions of social organization. On the other hand, if we restrict our analytical attention to the relationship between means and ends, and thus treat ends as given, then we can obtain the necessary critical information that eventually makes value-relevant statements move beyond mere opinions reflecting the political and social preferences of the analyst.

Ideology and the Devil's test

The world is a rather tricky place, and utopia is not a viable option. In fact, perhaps the most important role that economics plays is in providing *negative knowledge*. By examining the logic of means–ends efficiency, economics places parameters around people's utopias. Wishing it so, in short, cannot make it so. To put it bluntly, chickens do not fly into people's mouths. Scarce resources must be allocated among competing ends in a way that minimizes waste by directing resources to their most effective use in satisfying the demands of others. Every day, however, policies are introduced that attempt to direct resources in a manner different from what would have been chosen voluntarily.[24] In some instances these policies might improve upon the situation, but in others the policy choice actually worsens the situation. How can we establish this fact? If economics is a value-laden discipline from the very beginning, does it not depend on the perspective of the analyst whether a policy is deemed good or bad? Again, the solution does not require an epistemological defense of objectivity. All that is needed is the more humble defense of an argumentative strategy that allows people to rationally discuss alternative policies.

The analyst does not debate the ends but rather restricts the analysis to the logic of means–ends. If the ends the advocate seeks are undermined by the means chosen, then even the advocate would have to admit that the chosen policy is inappropriate. That the analysis of means–ends is independent of the ideological vision of the analyst can be checked by what could be called the "Devil's test."[25] If both an angel and the Devil could agree with the means–ends analysis, then the analysis itself provides an independent or "objective" ground upon which to debate.

In economics, mistakes are often made by analysts – even assuming they employ solid economic logic – because the "holding other things constant" clause is forgotten, or the magnitude of the consequence is not dutifully noted. The minimum wage controversy, for example, highlights the problem. Blanket statements like "Minimum Wage Laws Cause Unemployment" claim too much. A proper statement must establish the context of application. A minimum wage law set above the market clearing wage rate will cause some unemployment. The extent of the unemployment effect, and the manner in which that effect will be felt depends on the extent of the deviation from the market clearing wage, and the margin of decision for employers in adjusting to the change in the legal wage rate. What can be established fairly clearly is the tendency and direction of the effect. Wage rates set above the market clearing level by law will result in disproportionately harming lower wage workers – i.e. the least well-off workers. If the end of the policy is to aid the least well-off, then the means chosen (raising the legal wage rate that must be paid to employees) will be ineffective for that task. If, on the other hand, the intended result was to harm the least well-off (the Devil's work), then establishing legal minimum wages would be an effective policy. Both the angel and the Devil can agree with the analysis, but place different weight on the normative use to which the analysis can be deployed. The analysis itself, however, is value-neutral. To deny that would, I fear, result in denying economic logic and as such would drain economics of its critical edge.

Critical appraisal and policy advocacy

There is a strict line that must be drawn between the critical appraisal of alternative public policies and advocacy of any policy. A critical appraisal can be "objective"; advocacy requires value-judgments. If we advocate free-trade, then it is appropriate for us to defend the "goodness" of free-trade and be explicit about the ends we desire. On the other hand, if we are restricting our analysis to the examination of proposed protectionist legislation, then the economist can surely critically assess the effectiveness of the proposed policy for achieving the ends (usually stated as improving the economic health of the country). Of course, this means that if someone were to argue that the majority of consumers should pay more for their products to benefit a few producers, and this is the goal toward which the proposed protectionist legislation is aimed, then the economist as economist has little to say. Most policy advocates, however, are not so brazen in their disregard for the economic interests of consumers.

Moreover, by treating the desired ends, not as a subject of debate but as given, and by restricting analysis to the relationship of the selected means in obtaining the stated ends, the economic analyst can provide "objective knowledge" or something approximating such knowledge. Many policy disputes, and especially those debates that call upon economics most urgently, are not about ends but about means to obtain rather broad ends – "provide for the least advantage"; "improve opportunities"; "social justice"; "allow people to live peaceful and fruitful lives." The examination of means to given ends can establish that policies generate consequences that are perverse with regard to the ends sought – the least well-off are disproportionately harmed; opportunities are restricted; social inequities grow worse; and social conflict and poverty ensue. In taking this critical stance with regard to the position of the advocate, the knowledge provided by economic analysis enables us to explore the limits and potential of political and social organization. Endorsing a concept of the "good life" necessarily entails value-judgments, but the tool of weighing the different concepts of the good by examining consequences need not entail any importation of values – except the value that achieving what one sets out to accomplish is worthwhile.

Pre- and post-constitutional levels of analysis

James Buchanan has made the useful distinction in his work between pre- and post-constitutional levels of analysis.[26] At the pre-constitutional level, the discussion revolves around different notions of what might constitute good rules of the game. At the post-constitutional level, the rules are treated as given and the question then becomes, which strategies players will play, given the established rules? Political economy consists of oscillating between the pre- and post-constitutional levels of analysis. The rules of the game determine the types of strategies that individuals will choose.

Choice among the rules is a normative enterprise, whereas choice of strategies is not. The choice of strategy follows a simple formula – what is the best play given the rules and the play of others. The choice among rules, however, entails determining what is considered a good game and whether a game is challenging yet fair, and so forth. The point I want to stress for present purposes is that, in deciding on the rules, it is also important to consider the consequences that this has on the choice of strategy. A game that has interesting rules in theory but is undermined by opportunistic strategies is not a very robust game, no matter how convinced we are of its righteousness. Thus, the ability to engage in a positive analysis of the consequences of alternative rules of the game on the way in which the game will be played is essential for our ability to engage in a productive normative discourse about what rules we should choose to live by.

Conclusion

Economics, as I said earlier, puts parameters on people's utopias. But it also provides insights into what might be workable utopias. Economics without history, politics, culture, and morality runs the risk of becoming a barren technical enterprise. But political economy, without a firm basis in logic and evidence, runs the risk of being mere opinion and wishful thinking. The disciplines of economics and political economy can be likened to engineering science and worldly philosophy. The great minds of political economy – independent of ideological perspective – have found a way to weave together both the technical and the philosophical aspects of these disciplines without becoming mutually exclusive of the other. Crespo's argument for economics as a moral science correctly challenges economists who believe that the "engineering aspects" of the discipline are enough to provide advice on policies. His argument also challenges those who think that economics as a discipline is best practiced in an ideological vacuum. But I sense that the argument goes too far when he suggests that economics cannot provide value-neutral knowledge. My contention is that political economy as a value-relevant discipline has a legitimate claim on our intellectual attention only to the degree that it is grounded in the value-neutral logic of economic analysis – an analysis that, while it cannot determine ultimate values, may nevertheless inform us of the consequences of alternative social and political arrangements established to serve those values.

Bibliography

Boettke, P. J. (1989a) "Evolution and Economics: Austrians as Institutionalists," *Research in the History of Economic Thought and Methodology* 6: 73–89.

—— (1989b) "Austrian Institutionalism: a Reply," *Research in the History of Economic Thought and Methodology* 6: 181–202.

—— (1990) "Interpretative Reasoning and the Study of Social Life," *Methodus* 2(2) (December): 35–45.

—— (1992) Analysis and Vision in Modern Economic Discourse," *Journal of the History of Economic Thought* 14 (Spring): 84–95.

—— (1993) *Why Perestroika Failed: The Politics and Economics of Socialist Transformation*, London: Routledge.

—— (1994) *Notes on Ideology and Austrian Economics, C. V. Starr Center for Applied Economics, New York University*, RR #94–19 (May): 37 pp.

—— (ed.) (1994) *The Elgar Companion to Austrian Economics*, Aldershot, UK: Edward Elgar Publishing.

—— (1995) "Hayek's *The Road to Serfdom* Revisited: Government Failure in the Argument Against Socialism," *Eastern Economic Journal* 20(1) (Winter): 7–26.

Bohm-Bawerk, E. (1975) (first published 1896) *Karl Marx and the Close of His System*, Clifton, NJ: Augustus M. Kelley.

Boulding, K. (1971) "After Samuelson, Who Needs Adam Smith?" *History of Political Economy* 3 (Fall): 225–37.

Buchanan, J. M. (1987) "The Constitution of Economic Policy," *American Economic Review* 77 (June): 748–50.

Buchanan, J. M. (1992) *Better Than Plowing, and Other Personal Essays*, Chicago: University of Chicago Press.

Bukharin, N. (1972) (first published 1919) *The Economic Theory of the Leisure Class*, New York: Augustus M. Kelley.

—— (1982) (first published 1925) "Concerning the New Economic Policy and Our Tasks," in M. E. Sharpe, *Selected Writings on the State and the Transition to Socialism*, Armonk, NY, pp. 183–208.

Caldwell, B. J. (1982) *Beyond Positivism*, London: George Allen & Unwin.

—— (ed.) (1990) *Carl Menger and His Legacy in Economics*, Durham, NC: Duke University Press.

—— and Boehm, S. (eds.) (1992) *Austrian Economics: Tensions and New Directions*, Boston: Kluwer Academic Publishers.

Crespo, R. (1998) "Is Economics a Moral Science?" *Journal of Markets and Morality* 1(2) (October): 201–11.

Dolan, E. G. (ed.) (1976) *The Foundations of Modern Austrian Economics*, Kansas City: Sheed and Ward.

Hausman, D. M. and McPherson, M. S. (1993) "Taking Ethics Seriously: Economics and Contemporary Moral Philosophy," *Journal of Economic Literature* 31(2) (June): 671–731.

Herbener, J. M. (ed.) (1993) *The Meaning of Ludwig von Mises: Contributions in Economics, Sociology, Epistemology and Political Philosophy*, Boston: Kluwer Academic Publishers.

High, J. (1985) "Is Economics Independent of Ethics?" *Reason Papers* 10 (Spring): 3–16.

Hoppe, H.-H. (1993) *The Economics and Ethics of Private Property*, Boston: Kluwer Academic Publishers.

Horwitz, S. (1992) *Monetary Evolution, Free Banking & Economic Order*, Boulder, CO: Westview Press.

Kirzner, I. M. (1976) "Philosophical and Ethical Implications of Austrian Economics," in E. G. Dolan (ed.) (1976) *The Foundations of Modern Austrian Economics*, Kansas City: Sheed and Ward, pp.75–88.

—— (1989) *Discovery, Capitalism and Distributive Justice*, Oxford: Basil Blackwell.

—— (1990) "Menger, Classical Liberalism, and the Austrian School of Economics," in B. J. Caldwell (ed.) *Carl Menger and His Legacy in Economics*, Durham, NC: Duke University Press, pp. 93–106.

—— (1993) "The Pure Time-Preference Theory of Interest: An Attempt at Clarification," in J. M. Herbener (ed.) *The Meaning of Ludwig von Mises: Contributions in Economics, Sociology, Epistemology and Political Philosophy*, Boston: Kluwer Academic Publishers, pp. 166–92.

—— (1994a) "Value-Freedom," in P. Boettke, *Notes on Ideology and Austrian Economics, C. V. Starr Center for Applied Economics, New York University,* RR #94–19 (May): 313–19.

—— (ed.) (1994b) *Classics in Austrian Economics,* three volumes, London: William Pickering.

Kuhn, T. (1958) *The Structure of Scientific Revolutions,* Chicago: University of Chicago Press.

Lavoie, D. (1985) "Tacit Knowledge and the Revolution in the Philosophy of Science," in D. Lavoie, *National Economic Planning: What is Left?* Washington, DC, Cato Institute, pp. 247–65.

—— (1990) "Understanding Differently," in B. J. Caldwell, *Carl Menger and His Legacy in Economics,* Durham, NC: Duke University Press, pp. 359–77.

—— (1994) "The Interpretive Turn," in P. Boettke, *Notes on Ideology and Austrian Economics, C. V. Starr Center for Applied Economics, New York University,* RR #94–19 (May): 54–62.

Malabre, A. L., Jr. (1994) *Lost Prophets: An Insider's History of the Modern Economists,* Boston: Harvard Business School Press.

McCloskey, D. (1985) *The Rhetoric of Economics,* Madison, WI, University of Wisconsin Press.

Menger, C. (1985) (first published 1883) *Investigations into the Method of the Social Sciences with Special Reference to Economics,* New York: New York University Press.

Mises, L. von (1981) (first published 1933) *Epistemological Problems of Economics,* New York: New York University Press.

—— (1949) *Human Action: A Treatise on Economics,* New Haven: Yale University Press.

Myrdal, G. (1954) (first published 1929) *The Political Element in the Development of Economic Theory,* Cambridge, MA: Harvard University Press.

Polanyi, M. (1962) *Personal Knowledge,* Chicago: University of Chicago Press.

Prychitko, D. L. (1990) "Toward an Interpretive Economics: Some Hermeneutical Issues," *Methodus* 2(2) (December): 69–72.

Raico, R. (1994) "Classical Liberalism and the Austrian School," in P. Boettke (1994) *Notes on Ideology and Austrian Economics, C. V. Starr Center for Applied Economics, New York University,* RR #94–19 (May): 320–7.

Rappard, W. E. (1957) "On Reading von Mises," in M. Sennholz (ed.) *On Freedom and Free Enterprise: Essays in Honor of Ludwig von Mises,* Irvington-on-Hudson, NY: Foundation for Economic Education, pp. 17–33.

Rizzo, M. J. (1992) "Austrian Economics for the Twenty-First Century," in B. J. Caldwell and S. Boehm (eds.) (1992) *Austrian Economics: Tensions and New Directions,* Boston: Kluwer Academic Publishers, pp. 245–55.

Robbins, L. (1933) *An Essay on the Nature and Significance of Economic Science,* London: Macmillan.

Rockwell, L. H., Jr. (ed.) (1985) *The Gold Standard: An Austrian Perspective,* Lexington, KY: Lexington Books.

Rothbard, M. N. (1970) *Power and Market,* Kansas City: Sheed Andrews and McMeel.

—— (1976) "Praxeology, Value Judgements, and Public Policy," in E. G. Dolan, (ed.) (1976) *The Foundations of Modern Austrian Economics,* Kansas City: Sheed and Ward, pp. 89–111.

—— (1982) *The Ethics of Liberty,* Atlantic Highlands, NJ: Humanities Press.

—— (1993) "Mises and the Role of the Economist in Public Policy," in J. M. Herbener (ed.) *The Meaning of Ludwig von Mises: Contributions in Economics, Sociology, Epistemology and Political Philosophy,* Boston: Kluwer Academic Publishers, pp. 193–208.

Schumpeter, J. A. (1954) *History of Economic Analysis,* New York: Oxford University Press.

Selgin, G. A. (1988) "Praxeology and Understanding: An Analysis of the Controversy in Austrian Economics," *Review of Austrian Economics* 2: 19–58.

Sennholz, H. F. (1985) "The Monetary Writings of Carl Menger," in L. H. Rockwell, Jr. (ed.) (1985) *The Gold Standard: An Austrian Perspective,* Lexington, KY: Lexington Books, pp. 19–34.

Sennholz, M. (ed.) (1957) *On Freedom and Free Enterprise: Essays in Honor of Ludwig von Mises,* Irvington-on-Hudson, NY: Foundation for Economic Education.

Streissler, E. W. (1990) "Carl Menger on Economic Policy: The Lectures to Crown Prince Rudolf," in B. G. Caldwell (ed.) *Carl Menger and His Legacy in Economics*, Durham, NC: Duke University Press, pp. 107–30.

Streissler, E. W. and Streissler, M. (eds.) (1944) *Carl Menger's Lectures to Crown Prince Rudolf of Austria,* Aldershot, UK: Edward Elgar Publishing.

Strigl, R. (1994) (first published 1928) "Economic Theory in the Service of Economic Policy," in I. M. Kirzner (ed.) *Classics in Austrian Economics*, London: William Pickering, vol. 2, pp. 3–16.

Toulmin, S. (1958) *The Uses of Argument,* Cambridge: Cambridge University Press

—— (1972) *Human Understanding,* Princeton, NJ: Princeton University Press.

Weber, M. (1947) (first published 1904) " 'Objectivity' in Social Science and Social Policy," in E. Shils and H. A. Finch (eds.) *Methodology of the Social Sciences,* Glencoe, IL: Glencoe Free Press, pp. 49–112.

—— (1946) (first published 1919) "Science as a Vocation," in M. Weber, *From Max Weber: Essays in Sociology*, Oxford University Press, New York, pp. 129–56.

Wieser, F. (1967) (first published 1927) *Social Economics*, New York: Augustus M. Kelley.

3   Economic calculation

The Austrian contribution to political economy*

If no other objection could be raised to the socialist plans than that socialism will lower the standard of living of all or at least part of the immense majority, it would be impossible for praxeology to pronounce final judgement. Men would have to decide the issue between capitalism and socialism on the ground of judgements of value and of judgements of relevance ... However, the true state of affairs is entirely different. Man is not in a position to choose between the two systems. Human cooperation under the system of the social division of labor is possible only in the market economy. Socialism is not a realizable system of society's economic organization because it lacks any method of economic calculation.

(Ludwig von Mises 1949, p. 679)

This is the decisive objection that economics raises against the possibility of a socialist society. It must forgo the intellectual division of labor that consists in the cooperation of all entrepreneurs, landowners, and workers as producers and consumers in the formation of market prices. But without it, rationality, i.e. the possibility of economic calculation, is unthinkable.

(Ludwig von Mises 1927, p. 75)

The usual theoretical abstractions used in the explanation of equilibrium in a competitive system include the assumption that a certain range of technical knowledge is 'given.' This, of course, does not mean that all the best technical knowledge is anywhere concentrated in a single head, but that people will all kinds of knowledge will be available and that among those competing in a particular job, speaking broadly, those that make the most appropriate use of the technical knowledge will succeed. In a centrally planned society this selection of the most appropriate among the known technical methods will only be possible if all this knowledge can be used in the calculations of the central authority. This means in practice that this knowledge will have to be concentrated in the heads of one or at best a very few people who actually formulate the equations to be worked out. It is hardly necessary to emphasize that this is an absurd idea, even in so far as that knowledge is concerned which can properly be said to 'exist' at any moment in time. But much of the knowledge that is actually utilized is by no means 'in existence' in this ready-made form. Most of it consists in a technique of thought which enables the individual engineer to find new solutions rapidly as soon as he is confronted with new constellations of circumstances.

(F. A. von Hayek 1935b, pp. 210–11)

*Originally published as: Boettke, P. J.(1998) "Economic Calculation: The Austrian Contribution to Political Economy," *Advances in Austrian Economics* 5: 131–58.

Introduction

The basic thesis of this chapter is that the issue of economic calculation, in both its positive and negative manifestations, is *the* contribution of twentieth-century Austrian economics to the discipline of political economy. Of course, there are other contributions worthy of mention, especially in the area of methodology. But, it is this issue of economic calculation which provides the foundation for the main contributions of the school in monetary theory, capital theory, business cycle theory, the entrepreneurial theory of the market process, and the examination of interventionism. In other words, *all* the unique contributions of the Austrian school of economics to substantive economics can be traced back to the central importance of economic calculation for human cooperation.

The scholar most responsible for highlighting the central importance of economic calculation was Ludwig von Mises. However, contrary to some recent arguments that have been put forth, Mises was joined by F. A. von Hayek in the research effort to elaborate on the implications of this insight[1]. In other words, Mises' calculation argument was in many ways the source of Hayek's knowledge argument. Demonstrating that there is no conflict between these arguments is the purpose of this chapter.

There should be no doubt that subtle and profound differences exist between Mises and Hayek, especially in the area of the philosophical justification of the sciences of man. But, while I admit that valuable research can be conducted differentiating between the research program of Mises and Hayek, it is my contention that the differences are narrow compared with the gulf that separates their shared research program from that of the rest of twentieth-century economic thought. Moreover, this is how their contemporaries saw the matter, and even more important, how they both saw it[2]. The difference in their presentation, I will contend, is a function of the intended *audience* for which they wrote. In making this argument, I will flow in and out of an examination of the history of *economic analysis*, and the *intellectual history* of economic thought.

After presenting the basic analytical issue that economic calculation addresses, I will then attempt to put the progression of the argument within the intellectual context of the socialist calculation debate, and then conclude with a short discussion of how these analytical issues represent the unique Mises–Hayek contribution to modern political economy which must now be advanced to improve our conceptualizations of the market, and to raise critical points in a renewed debate over the possibility of socialism. Since most of the literature on the dehomogenization of Mises and Hayek focuses on Mises' statements in *Human Action*, I will also concentrate on Mises' statement from his mature writings, although reference will be made to the consistency of his position from his earlier statements to the later writings. However, with regard to Hayek, I will draw from his writings across the history of the socialist calculation debate, although not much from his later writings, such as *The Fatal Conceit*. To anticipate the argument, Mises' *audience* was largely divorced from the academic economics profession, whereas Hayek's argument was always presented within the context of directly responding to an *audience* of professional academic economists who raised particular objections to Mises' challenge. Mises wrote to a wider audience and for posterity, whereas Hayek wrote for a particular time and place and to a narrow specialist audience[3]. In interpreting their respective contributions, it is vital to see how Mises' insights can be applied to resolve the particular debates which he sought to transcend, and how Hayek's insights into particular debates can transcend that context and provide lasting contributions to our pure understanding of market processes and social cooperation. And, when looked at in this manner, for all practical purposes the Mises–Hayek contribution becomes a unified (and unique) perspective on economic processes.

Economic calculation

Put simply, economic calculation refers to the decision-making ability to allocate scarce capital resources among competing uses. "Economic calculation," Mises wrote, "is either an estimate of the expected outcome of future action or the establishment of the outcome of past action. But the latter does not serve merely historical and didactic aims. Its practical meaning is to show how much one is free to consume without impairing the future capacity to produce" (1949, pp. 210–11). Acting people must mentally process the alternatives placed before them, and to do so they must have some "aid to the human mind" for comparing inputs and output. Mises' great contribution to economic science was to establish that this decision-making ability is dependent on the institutional context of private property[4]. Mises' point, while not denying the importance of incentives in executing business plans, was that the necessary informational inputs into that decision process are made available to decision-makers only through the market process. The argument went as follows:

1   Without private property in the means of production, there will be no market for the means of production.
2   Without a market for a means of production, there will be no monetary prices established for the means of production.
3   Without monetary prices, reflecting the relative scarcity of capital goods, economic decision-makers will be unable to rationally calculate the alternative use of capital goods.

In short, without private property in the means of production, rational economic calculation is not possible. Under an institutional regime which attempts to abolish private ownership in the means of production, advanced industrial production is reduced to so many steps in the dark as decision-makers are denied the necessary compass. As Mises put in *Socialism*, economic calculation "provides a guide amid the bewildering throng of economic possibilities. It enables us to extend judgements of value which apply directly only to consumption goods – or at best to production goods of the lowest order – to all goods of higher orders. Without it, all production by lengthy and roundabout processes would be so many steps in the dark ... And then we have a socialist community which must cross the whole ocean of possible and imaginable economic permutations without the compass of economic calculation" (1922, pp. 101, 105).

In the world in which we live, economic decision-makers are confronted with an array of technologically feasible production projects, what economic calculation provides is a means to select from among these projects to assure that resources are employed in an *economic* manner[5]. Waste, as a result, will be minimized as decision errors are continually detected and corrected by the aid of profit and loss accounting. Only through this process of error detection and correction within the market can it be said that entrepreneurial hunches are tied to the underlying reality of consumer tastes, resource endowment, and technological possibilities. Every entrepreneurial act is a wishful conjecture about a future which is different from today, but wishing so cannot make it so by itself[6]. Entrepreneurial wishes yield profits only when technological possibilities are arranged in a manner which best satisfies consumer preferences in the most economic fashion. Consumer preferences change, and the stock of technological knowledge changes, and the entrepreneur (perhaps a new one) is trying to bring their new wishful conjectures into life to realize profits. If their conjecture is wrong, or poorly executed, then the ensuing losses will redirect their efforts. "Every single step of entrepreneurial activities," Mises wrote, "is subject to scrutiny by monetary calculation. The premeditation of planned action becomes commercial precalculation of expected costs and expected proceeds. The retrospective establishment of the outcome of past action becomes accounting profits and losses" (Mises 1949, p. 229).

The ability to render monetary calculations is conditioned by social institutions – namely private property in the means of production. Mises' question to critics of the "anarchy" of capitalist production was what alternative to rational calculation on the basis of monetary prices do you propose?[7] If a satisfactory non-market answer is not put forth, then Mises' challenge remains unmet. And, if instead some form of "market socialism" is proposed, then it must be recognized that this is "nothing short of a full acknowledgment of the correctness and irrefutability of the economists' analysis and devastating critique of socialists' plans" (Mises 1949, p. 706).

Mises' argument was directed at a broad community of intellectuals, activists, and scientists. The intention was to demonstrate how economic science decisively challenges the claims made on behalf of the socialist project. The intellectual spirit of the age was one which accepted the superiority – both ethically and economically – of socialism. "To prove that economic calculation would be impossible in the socialist community," Mises stated, "is to prove also that Socialism is impracticable. Everything brought forward in favour of Socialism during the last hundred years, in thousands of writings and speeches, all the blood which has been spilt by the supporters of Socialism, cannot make socialism workable" (1922, p. 117). This was a conclusion that was most inconvenient to those who aspired to create a better world along "progressive" lines in the early twentieth century.

As Mises pointed out in his original essay on the subject, there were socialists who never thought of the problems of economic organization, and there were those who examined in some depth the problems in economic history, but as regards a critical examination of the economic organization of socialism there were hardly any thoughtful excursions. Economics did not seem to figure prominently in the pictures painted of the future socialist world. "They invariably explain how, in the cloud-cuckoo lands of their fancy, roast pigeons will in some way fly into the mouths of the comrades, but they omit to show how this miracle is to take place" (Mises 1920, p. 88). The investigation into the properties of a society organized along socialist lines seemed to be called for. So Mises' essay can be seen as an attempt to raise this challenge to socialist writers – to examine how the socialist commonwealth would in fact organize its economic affairs. As such, his argument was intended for a wide audience, and not a narrow subset of specialists within economics. Such a narrow subset did not yet exist to which one could aim an argument, but wide acceptance of the moral superiority and historical inevitability of socialism did exist.

In Mises' writings there are four basic warnings against socialism – the most decisive, of course, was the problem of the impossibility of rational economic calculation. Nevertheless, it is essential to recognize that Mises does present four arguments which include:

1   private property and incentives;
2   monetary prices and the economizing role they play;
3   profit and loss accounting; and
4   political environment.

In a fundamental sense, all of these arguments are derivative of an argument for private property. Without private property, there can be no advanced economic process.

To the economically illiterate, Mises had to explain how private property engenders incentives which motivate individuals to husband resources efficiently. To the more informed, but still economically uninformed, he had to explain how the exchange ratios established in a market allow individuals to compare alternatives by summarizing in a common denominator the subjective assessment of trade-offs that individuals make in the exchange and production process. To the trained economist, Mises had to explain how the static conditions of equilibrium only solved the problem of economic calculation by hypothesis, and that the real problem was one of calculation within the dynamic world of change, in which the lure of pure profit and the penalty of loss would serve a vital error detection and correction role in the economic process. And, finally, to scholars, activists, and political leaders, Mises warned that the suppression of private property leads to political control over individual decisions and thus the eventual suppression of political liberties to the concerns of the collective. *All* four arguments are criticisms of socialist proposals. On the other hand, the private-property market economy is able to solve each of the three economic issues, and constitutional democracy does seek to guarantee individual rights, and protect against the tyranny of majority. Where socialism fails, in other words, liberalism succeeds.

Mises focused most of his efforts in his critical examination of socialism on how private property was an essential precondition for the monetary exchange process which makes possible the intellectual division of labor embedded in advanced industrial production.[8] There are two motivating forces for Mises' endeavors that should be kept in mind. First, he was critically responding to the ideas of Marxist thinkers who advocated the abolition of commodity production and the substitution of a natural economy for a monetary exchange economy. Second, he was developing his thesis concerning monetary exchange within the economic process (put forth in his *Theory of Money and Credit*, 1912), and further integrating that argument with an understanding of the capital structure (made up of heterogeneous and multispecific capital goods).

It is important to keep these two factors in mind for my thesis. In response to Mises' challenge, the parameters of the debate shifted. To see how this shift affects how the economic calculation argument was presented by Hayek, it is useful to see what Hayek's argument was *before* the Lange–Lerner response was formulated. Even here it is difficult, because soon after Mises presented his challenge in 1920, there developed a German-language response and an English-language response. The English-language response included essays by F. M. Taylor and Frank Knight, as well as H. D. Dickinson, which argued that marginalist principles could be effective tools in the economic management of the socialist state.[9] In other words, even by the time Hayek had come to be involved in this analytical debate, the opponent had already shifted from the Marxist call for the abolition of commodity production to the neoclassical economists' insistence of the universal validity of marginalist principles of maximization. But we can compare Hayek's statement of the problem in his two essays from *Collectivist Economic Planning* and his critical examination of "The Competitive Solution" – all three papers were reprinted in *Individualism and Economic Order* under the title: "Socialist Calculation" – with that of the position developed by Mises that has just been presented.

Hayek's development of the economic calculation argument

Hayek's first contributions to economic science were, like his mentor Mises, in the field of monetary theory and the trade cycle. Following in the Austrian tradition, Hayek postulated a complex capital structure of heterogeneous and multispecific capital goods. Business plans required a prospective commercial calculation to direct capital allocations, and a retrospective accounting of previous decisions to judge the appropriateness of those decisions. Monetary calculation, in the theory, is essential in that it provides business decision-makers with the mental tool required to embark upon production projects, and to assess the economic viability of chosen projects. When this process of monetary calculation is impaired, economic decision-makers can *systematically* err, and a "cluster of errors" can result. The realization of the cluster of errors in unfinished projects is what is referred to as the "bust" in the "boom–bust" cycle.

This is not the time or place for an examination of the Mises–Hayek theory of the business cycle, but what is important to highlight is that Hayek's understanding of the economic process, like Mises', was grounded in a theory of the monetary exchange economy. The centrality of monetary calculation permeates both Mises' and Hayek's writing. Consider Hayek's understanding of the application of this thesis to the problems that socialism would have to confront.

First, Hayek argued that while the incentive problem "does raise some of the real difficulties, it does not really touch the heart of the problem" (1935a, p. 2). It is not that Hayek actually believes that socialist man (e.g. *Homo sovieticus*) is a realistic possibility, but Hayek believed the argument that if one limits their analysis to questions of motives, then economics as a science could not address the problem. It would be a problem of ethics and psychology. Economics, he insisted, can answer the comparative question between capitalism and socialism without regard to ethics or psychology. It was not a question of the execution of the socialist plan that was being raised. Rather, it was whether the plan – even if we assume away these motivational difficulties – would achieve the desired end. Here economics provides the essential lesson – absent the monetary price system and choice among alternatives cannot be made economically.

To get at the heart of the matter, Hayek contends, the development of the subjective theory of value was necessary – this is so because otherwise the difference between the technological and economic problems would remain hidden.[10] The economic problem, Hayek points out, arises "as soon as different purposes compete for the available resources. And the criterion of its presence is that costs have to be taken into account. Cost here, as anywhere, means nothing but that the advantages to be derived from the use of given resources in other directions" (1935a, p. 6). Economic allocation requires that decision-makers compare alternative uses of scarce resources – whether the subject of deliberation is the use of part of the workday for leisure, or the use of material resources for alternative lines of production. "Even if the director of the economic system were quite clear in his mind that the food of one person is always more important than the clothing of another, that would by no means necessarily imply that it is also more important than the clothing of two or ten others" (Hayek 1935a, p. 7). Since in the modern capitalist society, nobody is called upon to make these *system-wide* decisions, Hayek argues, most people are not conscious that they are made at all. Of course, individuals continually must assess their trade-offs and do. In order to do so, however, they require decision input – namely the exchange ratios established on the market which embody the trade-offs that other participants in the market have made.[11] The prices established on the market are vital inputs into the decision process which, when taken in *composite,* select from among the array of technologically feasible projects those which are economic. Hayek states this argument clearly in a short examination of the Russian experience. As he admitted, from a technological point of view Soviet Russia had some impressive accomplishments by the 1930s. But, as Hayek insisted: "Whether the new plant will prove to be a useful link in the industrial structure for increasing output depends not only on technological considerations, but even more on the general economic situation" (1935b, p. 204). And, once we free ourselves from the misleading impression, an uncritical observation of the Soviet colossi of industrial production, "only two legitimate tests of success remain: the goods which the system actually delivers to the consumer, and the rationality or irrationality of the decisions of the central authority" (1935b, p. 205). On these grounds, it is obvious that – except for the privileged few – consumer satisfaction was better in pre-war Russia. Moreover, the collapse of the industrial economy in 1921 demonstrated beyond doubt the "impossibility of rational calculation in a moneyless economy, which Professor Mises and Professor Brutzkus had foreseen.[12] The development since, with its repeated reversals of policy, has only shown that the rulers of Russia had to learn by experience all the obstacles which a systematic analysis of the problem reveals" (1935b, p. 206).

The key issue for Hayek, as it was for Mises, is that absent private property in the means of production rational economic calculation will be impossible.[13] Without the mental aid of monetary calculation, decision-makers will be unable to assess how to allocate scarce capital goods among alternative lines of production in an efficient manner. Before I move on to examine how Hayek restates this argument in response to different opponents, I want to clarify with a few select quotations the importance Hayek placed on Mises' contribution to *his* endeavor to respond to opponents in the socialist calculation debate. In other words, Hayek thought he was pursuing a Misesian line of argument and applying it to meet the challenge of new opponents as they moved from Marxists, such as Otto Neurath and Otto Bauer, to neoclassical socialist economists, such as Oskar Lange (1939) and Abba Lerner (1934, 1935).

Mises, according to Hayek, "went far beyond" his predecessors in his critique of socialism, and therefore Mises' work represented "the starting-point from which all the discussions of the economic problems of socialism, whether constructive or critical, which aspire to be taken seriously must necessarily proceed" (1935a, p. 33). Moreover, while it was true that both Max Weber and Boris Brutzkus presented a critique of socialism on grounds of the impossibility of economic calculation under socialism independently of Mises,[14] it was Mises who presented "the more complete and systematic exposition" of the problem (1935a, p. 36).

Hayek explains that Mises' "central thesis could not be refuted" (p. 36). But even where Mises' thesis was conceded, socialist thinkers did not abandon their aspirations. There were basically two responses to Mises[15]. The first response was to admit Mises' critique, and the implication that socialist production would entail – in the world we live in (which includes a world economy of market prices) there would be a loss of efficiency. But the loss of efficiency and decline in general wealth would be accepted on the grounds of achieving a more just distribution of income. As Hayek states, from an economic point of view, *if* this choice is made in full realization of what is implied, then there is not much left for the economist to offer to the deliberation. Analytical economics has nothing more to say. The second responses to Mises, however, left room for the analytical economist to respond. Here the argument was made that Professor Mises' criticisms were "valid only as regards the particular form of socialism against which it was mainly directed," but that hope for socialists remained in the attempt to "construct other schemes that would be immune against that criticism" (1935a, p. 38). In this regard, Hayek saw his role as "to examine in their light (i.e. Mises' critique and the developments of that critique by others) some of the more recent developments of English speculation" (1935a, p. 40).

Mises and Hayek in debate with socialist economists

In rhetoric, Mises did not have much patience with socialist intellectuals who did not attempt to meet his challenge of rational economic calculation. On the other hand, despite his fundamental disagreement, at least socialists such as Dickinson and Lange "are conversant with economic thought" (1949, p. 706, fn.4). Thus, he thought that responding to their attempts to meet his argument was worthwhile. Hayek had already taken up that challenge in his concluding essay to *Collective Economic Planning* (1935b) and his critical examination of "The Competitive 'Solution'" (1940). Hayek's knowledge problem argument emerged in this exercise, whereas Mises' theory of the entrepreneurial market process is refined in his attempt to articulate why the mathematical model of Walrasian socialism did not meet his argument (see Vaughn 1980b). The complementary nature of these two arguments is what we hope to explore in this section.

Lavoie (1985, pp. 20–1) describes the debate as going through the following stages:

1 central planning theory before 1920;
2 Mises' critique of central planning;
3 equation solving;
4 the issue of impracticability; and
5 trial and error models.

Hoff's (1949, p. 204) survey of the debate makes a similar distinction between the stages of the debate, but is more concentrated on the responses made directly to Mises' challenge:

1 solutions from the theory of the moneyless economy;
2 solutions based on the original Marxist labor theory of value;
3 mathematical solutions and models which employ the experimental method of trial and error;
4 solutions via marginal costing; and

5   those that aim to provide a solution by the introduction of competition
      into models of socialism.

As Hoff states, solutions offered in categories (1) and (2) were proven to be
futile against Mises' challenge. The interesting issue, as far as testing Mises'
proposition that meaningful economic calculation can take place only within
the private property market society, was to see how Mises' argument would
hold up against the counterarguments in (3)–(5).

   Hayek (1935b) had already begun to respond to these arguments – and, in
fact, had anticipated arguments that would only be developed in the coming
decades.[16] The debate in the English language began at "a comparatively high
level" and the first proposed solutions "were directed to show that on the
assumption of a complete knowledge of all relevant data, the values and
quantities of the different commodities to be produced might be determined
by the application of the apparatus by which theoretical economics explains
the formation of prices and the direction of production in a competitive system"
(Hayek 1935b, p. 207). There are two types of responses to make to this line of
argument. First, the easy argument would be to just point out the difficulties
such a solution would confront, even granting the assumptions. The "nature
and amount of concrete information required if a numerical solution is to be
attempted and the magnitude of the task which this numerical solution must
involve in any modern community" would represent a "statistical task" that is
"beyond human capacity" (Hayek 1935b, pp. 208, 210, 211). But this was *not*
Hayek's argument. Hayek, following Mises, offered a more fundamental second
type of argument. To argue that "a determination of prices by such a procedure"
solves the problem of economic calculation under capitalism, let alone under
socialism "only proves that the real nature of the problem has not been
perceived" (Hayek 1935b, pp. 207, 208). The formal model of general economic
equilibrium (of either a Walrasian or Casselian variant) at best represents the
rules and principles to which the actual pricing process would have to adjust
were it to achieve an optimum, and not a description of actual pricing processes.[17]
Within the actual market process, technological knowledge can become useful
to agents only via the economic calculations which the pricing process affords.
Absent this process and the data required to make the calculations "is by no
means 'in existence' " (Hayek 1935b, p. 210).

   An equilibrium model is relevant for *descriptive* purposes only if "all external
change had ceased." "The essential thing" Hayek wrote, about the market
order "is that it does react to some extent to all those small changes and
differences which would have to be deliberately disregarded" under socialism
(1953b, p. 212). The continual, and marginal, adjustment and adaptability of
the market to changes in the underlying data is the source of its relative
effectiveness in allocating scarce resources. This is particularly relevant when
assessing the "solutions" to Mises' challenge through marginal cost pricing
rules, or the so-called competitive solution. As Hayek pointed out, the "excessive
preoccupation with conditions of a hypothetical state of stationary equilibrium

has led modern economists in general, and especially those who propose this particular solution, to attribute to the notion of costs in general a much greater precision and definiteness than can be attached to any cost phenomena in real life" (Hayek 1935b, p. 226).

Readers might recognize in this concern of Hayek with economically meaningful discussions of costs simply the emphasis that Buchanan has claimed was the hallmark of the LSE approach to economics (see Buchanan 1969). Both Buchanan's and Coase's critique of Pigouvian welfare economics was grounded in the same type of criticism. Costs can only be treated as objective and measurable, assuming conditions of equilibrium, but if one were *in* equilibrium then costs cease to be a guide to *future* action, but instead are rules of action which define the situation. Pigouvian remedies, in other words, were either impracticable or redundant – in either case the Pigouvian approach was irrelevant to the real problem at hand in dealing with externalities (see Vaughn 1980a). Hayek's argument against socialist planning along marginal cost pricing lines was in part to insist that in a world of disequilibrium marginal cost pricing rules are economically meaningless in themselves. Once we:

> consider a world where most of the existing means of production are the product of particular processes that will probably never be repeated; where, in consequence of incessant change, the value of most of the more durable instruments of production has little or no connection with the costs which have been incurred in their production but depends only on the services which they are expected to render in the future, the question of what exactly are the costs of production of a given product is a question of extreme difficulty which *cannot* be answered definitely on the basis of any processes which take place inside the individual firm or industry.
>
> (Hayek 1935b, p. 227)

The constellation of market prices within the economic system, in other words, is "an indispensable guide for the determination of the appropriate volume of production." Cost cannot be determined in any manner independent of the pricing process. It is "only in this way that some of the alternative ends which are affected by the decision can be taken into account" (Hayek 1935b, p. 227).

The marginal cost rule solution in models of market socialism is proposed as if costs can be determined independently of the process within which the manager must plan. Costs during any period of production cannot be said to be dependent on prices. "Even in the very short run costs will depend on the effects which current decisions will have on future productivity. Whether it is economical to run a machine hard and to neglect maintenance, whether to make major adjustments to a given change in demand or to carry on as well as possible with the existing organization – in fact, almost every decision on how to produce – now depends at least in part on the views held about the future" (1940, p. 198).

The efficiency rule for industrial production under the direction of the

Supreme Economic Council in the market socialist scheme would be for managers to minimize average costs of production, and price equal to marginal costs (see Lange 1939, p. 77). But as Hayek points out, "What is forgotten is that the method which under given conditions is the cheapest is a thing which has to be discovered, and to be discovered anew, sometimes almost from day to day, by the entrepreneur, and that, in spite of the strong inducement, it is by no means regularly the established entrepreneur, the man in charge of the existing plant, who will discover what is the best method" (Hayek 1940, p. 196). The pressure sequence of the ability to enter at one's own risk and to attract consumers, "But, if prices are fixed by the authority, this method is excluded" (Hayek 1940, p. 196).

In other words, the benefits of competitive markets are tied to the existence of markets and *cannot* be obtained independent of that context. Hayek's argument is clear on this. The so-called "competitive solution" provides no solution to Mises' challenge, precisely because it assumes what must be demonstrated – so the third chapter in the debate must also come to a close with Mises as the victor. The *knowledge* argument is a contextual argument. Hayek's argument is not limited to the complexity issue of how various scattered bits and pieces of information held privately can be summarized in a form which is objectively useful for others, so that economic actors can coordinate their plans. This is an important problem that all economists must recognize. The price system does economize on the amount of information that we have to process, and it does allow us to coordinate decentralized decisions. But this is not the most subtle reading that can be given to Hayek.[18]

In addition to the complexity argument that most scholars read in Hayek, there is an argument – as we have seen – that the knowledge required for economic calculation is available *only* within the market process itself. Outside of that context this knowledge does not exist. And, it is precisely this contextual knowledge of the market which enables economic actors to select, from among the numerous arrays of technologically feasible production projects, those which are economically viable – in other words to engage in rational economic calculation.

The fact that Hayek's argument is made within the context of the socialist calculation debate of the 1930s and 1940s means that he was forced to stress certain arguments that would be effective against the arguments presented by his opponents. He was, to put it bluntly, part of a conversation the parameters of which were set by both parties to the conversation. Lange thought he could answer Mises by stressing that the economic problem – under whatever system – is answerable if three sets of data are available. The necessary data are:

1   individual preference scales;
2   knowledge of the terms on which alternatives are offered; and
3   knowledge of existing resource availability.

Lange asserted that knowledge of individual preference scales and resource availability is given in socialism in the same way that it is given under capitalism. The only really potential problem for socialist organization is knowledge of the terms on which alternatives are offered. On the basis of the modern marginalist theory of exchange and production, however, Lange argued that knowledge of the terms on which alternatives are offered can be derived from knowledge of the scale of preferences and resource availability. Production functions provide all that is necessary in terms of the technical possibilities of transforming inputs into outputs. But in order to assert this theoretical proposition, Lange had to assume that data on production and consumption were given, when the problem was to show how in the absence of the market process the socialist community would obtain these data. As Hoff (1949, p. 216) pointed out, none of Lange's theoretical assertions "can be considered tenable" for any other reason than that the data are "not given to the same extent in the socialist society, as they are in the capitalist one."

Precisely because Hayek was responding to Lange and others,[19] who assumed as given the very knowledge of the data which within the market process is embedded in the price system and entrepreneurial appraisement, and which serves as the basis for economic calculation, he increasingly focused on the use of knowledge in society. But if we compare Hayek's statements on this issue – once this context is remembered – with those of Mises, then a basic similarity in the argument can be seen.

Mises, in order to pinpoint the crucial failure of socialist proposals, assumed that the socialist dictator has at their disposal all the *technological* knowledge, a complete inventory of the available factors of production and the manpower available for the production period under discussion.[20] Still, with all this knowledge at their disposal, the dictator must choose among an infinite variety of projects, such that resources are employed in their highest valued use (1949, p. 696). They must decide what is the best way to execute a production plan. But in the standard equilibrium models proposed in the literature, the *economic* knowledge, which Mises and Hayek emphasized was available only within the context of the competitive market process itself, was assumed to be derivable once *technological* knowledge was assumed to be provided. The key issue to Mises and Hayek was to deny that this derivation was acceptable.

Mises, in other words, despite the assumption of given knowledge, is not assuming perfect knowledge in the usual economic meaning of that term. *If perfect knowledge was assumed, then the problem with socialism would be at best* a complexity issue which could be solved by a supercomputer. The "knowledge of the particular circumstances of time and place" and the fact that we are dealing with data which "by its nature cannot enter into statistics" does not just challenge the *practicability* of socialism (see Hayek 1945, pp. 80, 83). Rather, socialism is *impossible* precisely because the institutional configuration of socialism precludes economic calculation by eliminating the emergence of the very *economic* knowledge that is required for these calculations to be made by economic actors.

Mises' argument is subtle and must be read carefully. Not only does he contend that economic knowledge cannot be inferred directly from technological knowledge without the aid of the market process, but that knowledge of equilibrium values is irrelevant for action outside of equilibrium. In equilibrium the underlying variables of tastes and technology are perfectly reflected in the induced variables of prices and profits and loss. If this was not the case, then the conditions defined by Pareto optimality – in terms of production efficiency, exchange efficiency, and product-mix efficiency – would not hold. But this situation is irrelevant for actors in the world outside of equilibrium. "What impels a man toward change and innovation," Mises wrote, "is not the vision of equilibrium prices, but the anticipation of the height of the prices of a limited number of articles as they will prevail on the market on the date at which he plans to sell." The market economy is an entrepreneurial process which "again and again reshuffles exchange ratios and allocation of the factors of production. An enterprising man discovers a discrepancy between the prices of the complementary factors of production and the future prices of the products as he anticipates them, and tries to take advantage of this discrepancy for his own profit. The future price which he has in mind is, to be sure, not the hypothetical equilibrium price. No actor has anything to do with equilibrium and equilibrium prices; these notions are foreign to real life and action; they are auxiliary tools of praxeological reasoning for which there is no mental means to conceive the ceaseless restlessness of action other than to contrast it with the notion of perfect quiet" (1949, p. 711).

Just as in our discussion of the marginal cost solution, the optimality rule that production should be at that level which minimizes average costs, and price equals marginal cost, has no meaning to economic actors outside of the equilibrium situation. In equilibrium the rule is not a guide to action, but rather the outcome of a process set in motion outside of equilibrium. Outside of equilibrium the guide to action is the ceaseless attempt to improve one's lot by removing uneasiness and substituting the current unsatisfactory state for an anticipated better future state.[21] Equilibrium conditions, or values, have no value for the actor. Compare this reading of Mises' with Hayek's statements on the failure of the marginal cost solution, and the positions are strikingly similar and represent a *paradigmatic* alternative to the equilibrium economics of the emerging neoclassical hegemony from the mid twentieth century to this day.

"The Misesian demonstration of the logical impossibility," Salerno wrote (1994, p. 112), "is not predicated on the central planners' incapacity to perform tasks that can conceivably be carried out by individual human minds (e.g. discovery of factual and technical knowledge, mathematical computations, managerial monitoring, and prevention of labor shirking, etc.). Rather, it is concerned with the lack of a genuinely competitive and social market process in which each and every kind of scarce resource receives an objective and quantitative price appraisal in terms of a common denominator reflecting its relative importance in serving (anticipated) consumer preferences. This social appraisal process of the market transforms the substantially qualitative knowledge about economic conditions acquired individually and independently by competing entrepreneurs, including their estimates of the incommensurable subjective valuations of individual consumers for the whole array of final goods, into an integrated system of objective exchange ratios for the myriads of original and intermediate factors of production. It is the elements of this coordinated structure of monetary price appraisements for resources in conjunction with appraised future prices of consumer goods which serve as the data in the entrepreneurial profit computations that must underlie a rational allocation of resources."

If my interpretation of Hayek is correct, as I believe the above textual evidence supports, then Salerno's description also fits Hayek's rendering of the problem. Of course, neither Mises nor Hayek denied as a practical matter that socialism would confront problems of gathering vast amounts of technical knowledge; computing a set of mathematical equations for an advanced industrial economy; managerial motivation; and labor discipline. And, at different points throughout their respective careers they have both used variants of all these arguments to challenge socialist and interventionist proposals. But these difficulties were not *the* decisive objections to socialist planning. *The* decisive objection is that the social process of the market is the source itself of the knowledge required to pursue advanced industrial projects (which shuffle heterogeneous and multispecific capital goods into production combinations) and to make rational calculations about the use of scarce resources among competing projects so that resources are allocated in an *economically* efficient manner.

Hayek's "knowledge" problem is what Salerno refers to as the "data" which serve as the backdrop against which economic calculation proceeds. If these data are assumed to be given, as in the general equilibrium models of socialism, then Mises' argument becomes theoretically trivial and just practically burdensome.[22] But these data *cannot* be assumed to be given, as they are intimately tied to the institution of private property and the market process and do not come into existence in the absence of that process. It is the *context* of the market, and the complex set of institutional arrangements that the term implies, which gives rise to the market's own error-corrective character. And, it is this character of the market which is the common ground in the theory of the market economy presented by Mises and Hayek (see Kirzner 1996, p. 153).

Conclusion: the socialist calculation debate today

The collapse of state socialism in the Eastern and Central Europe, and the former Soviet Union has caused a sort of theoretical dissonance among economists. If the market socialists had demonstrated that Mises' argument was flawed and Hayek's complexity argument could be handled with the advent of modern computer technology – as was argued in the standard historiography – then why did the economies of these countries operate so inefficiently? First, the standard historiography was mistaken on several counts, as Lavoie (1985) demonstrated. Second, the relationship of the Mises–Hayek critique and the operation of former socialist economies is a subtle matter and not as easily rendered as the above statement of dissonance might suggest.[23] Nevertheless, this question has motivated economists to rethink the issue of economic organization of socialism. In particular, Bardhan and Roemer (1993) have edited a volume which attempts to establish the terms of the current debate on market socialism in the post-Communist world. It is important to contrast their understanding of the states of the debate with that presented here (following the work of Hoff and Lavoie). Bardhan and Roemer (1993, pp. 3–17) fail to recognize the *contextual* knowledge argument presented as the Austrian objection to socialism. Instead, they read Mises and Hayek through the lens of modern mechanism design theory and principal–agent models. The nature of criticism remains, in their opinion, the complexity of coordinating private information and monitoring the behavior of agents. In this rendering, a feasible model of non-private ownership can be designed which attempts to "combine democracy and a reasonably egalitarian income and wealth distribution with some of these incentive and discipline mechanisms" (Bardhan and Roemer 1993, p. 16).

Obviously, a communication failure between the Austrians and other economists persists.[24] The Austrian argument can be understood only by translating it into terms in which it is no longer the fundamental critique of the socialist project that it was intended to be. This means that the *paradigmatic* clash between the Austrians and contemporary formal theory persists. In other words, the theory of the market process in Mises and Hayek is of a different character from the theory presented in modern economics. This was true in the 1930s and 1940s, and it remains true today – and it is the divergence in meaning which continues to confuse matters with regard to the socialist calculation debate, as Lavoie (1985) contended.

The dehomogenization of Mises and Hayek will not aid in closing this communication gap. Thus, along with Kirzner, we can disagree with Salerno's "two-paradigm" thesis, yet admit that Salerno's discussion of the entrepreneurial appraisement process has drawn attention to a "significant element in Mises" (1996, p. 148). The Mises–Hayek understanding of the market as a ceaseless corrective process, which is brought to life only through the institution of private property and with the aid of monetary prices that affords monetary calculation, stands in contrast to approaches which emphasize only the incentive issues of private property, or the informational efficiency of equilibrium prices. The centrality of monetary calculation to Mises and Hayek is the *unique* contribution of the Austrian school of economics. Combined with additional Austrian assumptions and theoretical propositions – irreversibility of time, uncertainty, time structure of production, heterogeneity and multiple specificity of capital goods, non-neutrality of money, and so on – monetary calculation emerges as not just an aspect of the market process, but the crucial element which allows for the social cooperation under the division of labor. Without monetary calculation, civilization as we know it is simply not possible. As Mises put it: "Our civilization is inseparably linked with our methods of economic calculation. It would perish if we were to abandon this most precious intellectual tool of action" (1949, p. 230). And, as Hayek has said: "socialist aims and programmes are factually impossible to achieve or execute; and they also happen, into the bargain as it were, to be logically impossible ... The dispute between the market order and socialism is no less than a matter of survival. To follow socialist morality would destroy much of the present humankind and impoverish much of the rest" (1988, p. 7). Except for wording and rhetoric in argumentation, the essential argument that Mises and Hayek rose against socialist proposals – the problem of economic calculation – *and* their understanding of how the private property system enables monetary calculation are complementary contributions to economic theory, and represents one of the most important and original contributions to political economy of this (or any) century.

References

Bardhan, P. K. and Roemer, J. E. (eds.) (1993) *Market Socialism: The Current Debate*, New York: Oxford University Press.

Boettke, P. J. (1990) *The Political Economy of Soviet Socialism: The Formative Years, (1918–1928)*, Boston: Kluwer Academic Publishers.

—— (1993) *Why Perestroika Failed: The Politics and Economics of Socialist Transformation*, New York: Routledge.

Boettke, P. J. and Prychitko, D. (eds.) (1996) *Advances in Austrian Economics*, vol. 3, Greenwich, CT: JAI Press.

Buchanan, J. M. (1969) *Cost and Choice: An Inquiry in Economic Theory*, Chicago: University of Chicago Press.

Hayek, F. A. von (1935a) "The Nature and History of the Problem," in F.A. von Hayek (ed.) *Collectivist Economic Planning*, New York: Augustus M. Kelley.

—— (1935b) "The Present State of the Debate," in F. A. von Hayek (ed.) *Collectivist Economic Planning*, New York: Augustus M. Kelley.

—— (1940) "The Competitive 'Solution'," in F. A. von Hayek (ed.) *Individualism and Economic Order*, Chicago: University of Chicago Press.

—— (1945) "The Use of Knowledge in Society," in F. A. von Hayek (ed.) *Individualism and Economic Order*, Chicago: University of Chicago Press.

—— (1988) *The Fatal Conceit: The Errors of Socialism*, Chicago: University of Chicago Press.

Hoff, T. J. (1949) *Economic Calculation in the Socialist Society*, Indianapolis: Liberty Press.

Kirzner, I. (1987) "The Economic Calculation Debate: Lessons for Austrian Economics," *Review of Austrian Economics* 2: 1–18.

—— (1996) "Reflections on the Misesian Legacy in Economics," *Review of Austrian Economics* 9(2): 143–54.

Kresge, S. and Wenar, L. (1994) *Hayek on Hayek: An Autobiographical Dialog*, Chicago: University of Chicago Press.

Lange, O. (1939) "On the Economic Theory of Socialism," in B. E. Lippincott (ed.) *On the Economic Theory of Socialism*, New York: Augustus M. Kelley, pp. 57–143.

Lavoie, D. (1985) *Rivalry and Central Planning: The Socialist Calculation Debate Reconsidered*, New York: Cambridge University Press.

Lerner, A. (1934) "Economic Theory and Socialist Economy," *The Review of Economic Studies* October: 51–61.

—— (1935) "Economic Theory and Socialist Economy: A Rejoinder." *The Review of Economic Studies* February: 152–4.

Mises, L. von (1912) *The Theory of Money and Credit*, Indianapolis: Liberty Fund.

—— (1920) "Economic Calculation in the Socialist Commonwealth," in F. A. von Hayek (ed.) *Collectivist Economic Planning*, New York: Augustus M. Kelley.

—— (1922) *Socialism: An Economic and Sociological Analysis*, Indianapolis: Liberty Fund.

—— (1927) *Liberalism in the Classical Tradition*, Irvington-on-Hudson, NY: Foundation for Economic Education.

—— (1949) *Human Action: A Treatise on Economics*. Chicago: Henry Regnery.

—— (1960) "Liberty and Its Antithesis," in L. von Mises (ed.), *Planning for Freedom*, South Holland, IL: Libertarian Press.

Prychitko, D. L. (1991) *Marxism and Workers' Self-Management: The Essential Tension*, New York: Greenwood Press.

Rothbard, M. N. (1991) "The End of Socialism and the Calculation Debate Revisited," *Review of Austrian Economics* 5(2): 51–76.

Salerno, J. (1990) "Ludwig von Mises as Social Rationalist," *Review of Austrian Economics* 4: 26–54.

—— (1993) "Mises and Hayek Dehomogenized," *Review of Austrian Economics* 6(2): 113–46.

—— (1994) "Reply to Leland B. Yeager on 'Mises and Hayek on Calculation and Knowledge'," *Review of Austrian Economics* 7(2): 111–25.

—— (1996) "A Final Word: Calculation, Knowledge, and Appraisement," *Review of Austrian Economics* 9(1): 141–2.

Steele, D. R. (1992) *From Marx to Mises: Post-Capitalist Society and the Challenge of Economic Calculation*. LaSalle, IL: Open Court.

Vaughn, K. (1980a) "Does it Matter that Costs are Subjective?" *Southern Economic Journal* 46: 702–15.

—— (1980b) "Economic Calculation Under Socialism: The Austrian Contribution," *Economic Inquiry* 18: 535–54.

Yeager, L. (1994) "Mises and Hayek on Calculation and Knowledge," *Review of Austrian Economics* 7(2): 93–109.

—— (1996) "Salerno on Calculation, Knowledge and Appraisement," *Review of Austrian Economics* 9(1): 137–9.

4 Hayek's *The Road to Serfdom* revisited

Government failure in the argument against Socialism*

Introduction

In a symposium on *The Fatal Conceit*, the economic historian Robert Higgs chided Hayek for ignorance of modern developments in public choice. "From reading Hayek," Higgs argued, "one would never know that public choice had been invented. Neither Buchanan nor Tullock nor any of their followers gets a single mention. Neither does Hayek show any awareness of public choice problems" (1988–9, pp. 8–9). According to Higgs, there is no discussion of interest groups, the motivation for voting, free rider problems, constitutional rules, etc., in Hayek's work. I grant that Higgs' discussion is limited to *The Fatal Conceit* and is not meant to address the entire corpus of Hayek's work, but the impression on the reader is that this flaw in Hayek's final work is symptomatic of something that permeates his entire body of work in economics and politics. *The Fatal Conceit* is seen as simply a restatement of Hayek's earlier works and, that, in fact, is the problem, according to Higgs. Repeating familiar Hayekian themes about rational constructivism and the informational function of the price system does not suffice as an academically rigorous foundation for classical liberalism. Not only are the political issues raised by public choice scholars ignored, but so are the "market failure" arguments that have emerged from mainstream neoclassical economics. Hayek's argument is analytically weak and rhetorically vapid, and, as a result, Higgs concludes, we should not expect Hayek's argument to convince anyone who is not already deeply sympathetic to the Hayekian position.

I single Higgs out not because his discussion represents an egregious example of misreading of Hayek's work, but because he reflects a general opinion among pro-market intellectuals concerning Hayek's analytical apparatus.[1] In other words, while many individuals may nod to Hayek's valiant fight against socialism and in organizing an international resurgence of classical liberal political economy (especially with his efforts relating to the Mont Pelerin Society), the belief is that he failed to address not only the revisions of socialist

*Originally published as Boettke, P. J. (1995) "Hayek's *The Road to Serfdom* Revisited: Government Failure in the Argument Against Socialism," *Eastern Economic Journal* 21(1) (Winter): 7–26.

economic theory through the years (say post-Lange market socialist models of the kind proposed by Leonid Hurwicz or the models of workers' self-management of the type developed by Jaroslav Vanek), but also the various subtle arguments for interventionism (neo Keynesianism and market failure theory) that had developed in the post-World War II years. Even more damning is Hayek's supposed ignorance of pro-market developments in economic science, such as property-rights and transaction-cost theory, law and economics, monetarism, New Classical macroeconomics, public choice, etc. Instead, the sympathetic critic contends that Hayek was content simply to beat the intellectually dead horse of central planning.[2]

While many public choice scholars will give a nod to Joseph Schumpeter's *Capitalism, Socialism and Democracy* (1942) as an early precursor, Hayek's work in political science is barely mentioned at all with regard to the historical development of public choice theory.[3] This is quite striking since Schumpeter did not see any theoretical difficulty in the organizational logic of socialism, whereas Hayek's work explicitly dealt with the thorny economic and political logic of socialism and democratic socialism.[4] Specifically, it is curious that *The Road to Serfdom* is not seen as a volume which addressed the standard public choice problems of the operation of democracy despite its extended treatment of the limits of democracy. Sir Alan Peacock, for example, in his book, *Public Choice Analysis in Historical Perspective* (1992, pp. 59–60) uses Hayek as an example of a theorist who is decidedly *not* in the public choice tradition. According to Hayek's *The Road to Serfdom,* the bulk of humanity, Peacock argues, reacts passively to policy initiatives. Hayek is just as guilty as Keynes, Peacock states, for implicitly rejecting the wisdom of public choice analysis when he accepts the proposition that it is ideas and not vested interests which rule the world of affairs.

The Road to Serfdom, however, was not limited to a critique of comprehensive central planning, i.e. the socialism of the Bolsheviks. Neither was it limited to an examination of the ideas which fostered the rise of totalitarian Bolshevism and Nazism. Rather, the book set out to explicate how socialist ideas change the demands on democratic institutions and how these institutions are in turn transformed into instruments of totalitarian rule because of their inability to meet these changing demands in a manner consistent with democratic principles. In other words, Hayek tells a tragic story – one in which the best of intentions pave the way to a hellish political, social, and economic existence. "Is there a greater tragedy imaginable," Hayek asks, "than that, in our endeavor consciously to shape our future in accordance with high ideals, we should in fact unwittingly produce the very opposite of what we have been striving for?" (1944, p. 5).

In order to get a deeper understanding of Hayek's argument, I will attempt to reconstruct his argument in *The Road to Serfdom,* survey the reaction to his argument by his contemporaries, elaborate on why his argument was misunderstood by his contemporaries and subsequent generations, and finally explain the continuing relevance of his thesis concerning the failure of government to either control or supplant the market mechanism in a manner consistent with the principles of liberal democracy.

The central argument

The Road to Serfdom is not the usual "political" pamphlet. The argument within the text is subtle and, in fact, its central message preoccupied Hayek for the rest of his scholarly life. Hayek took time out from technical economics, as he informed his reader in the preface, "due to a peculiar and serious feature of the discussions of problems of future economic policy at the present time" (1944, p. xvii). There is no doubt that Hayek intended to return in earnest to problems of pure economic theory, and specifically to capital theory (of which his *The Pure Theory of Capital* (1940) was only the first volume of a proposed two-volume work) after completing this book in his spare time. Hayek, however, never did return to economics. Instead, he embarked upon a new career as political theorist, historian of ideas, legal philosopher, etc. In fact, it could be legitimately argued that after 1944 Hayek moved completely out of economics proper and into social theory, and arguably emerged as one of the most wide-ranging theoretical social scientists of the twentieth century. But both *The Constitution of Liberty* (1960) and *Law, Legislation and Liberty* (1973–9) are in many ways elaborations and refinements of the argument first articulated in Hayek's "political book."

The Road to Serfdom is divided into sixteen concise chapters that take us on a tour of intellectual history and abstract logical deduction interspersed with historical observation. The contribution of the book was to demonstrate the social consequence of ideas. In this regard, Peacock's reading of Hayek is correct, but misleading. While it is true that Hayek envisions ideas as the motive force in history, the tragedy of bad ideas is that they permit the rule of privileged interests over the common interest. Ideas provide the social infrastructure within which individuals pursue their own interest. If these ideas do not constrain the self-seeking behavior of individuals appropriately, then the result will be not only economically inefficient, but politically and socially obnoxious.

The theoretical core of Hayek's analysis was Mises' (1922) insight concerning the technical impossibility of economic calculation within a socialist system – socialism traditionally defined as the abolition of private property in the means of production. Hayek's twist on this Misesian argument was to elaborate the precise role that the price system played in providing the information (or knowledge) required for complex plan coordination.[5] The Mises–Hayek argument demonstrated that socialism could not replicate what the private property order and the price system provided. No one mind or group of minds could possibly possess the knowledge necessary to coordinate a complex industrial economic system. The private property order and the price system, on the other hand, through the signals of monetary prices, and profit and loss accounting engendered the appropriate incentives, economized the information that needed to be processed by economic actors, and not only provided the social context for entrepreneurial discovery that was necessary for the effective use of currently available resources but led to the innovations and technological progress that assured continued prosperity (Mises 1922, pp. 55–130; Hayek 1948, pp. 77–91, 119–209).

The Road to Serfdom proceeds under the assumption that this Misesian theoretical proposition has been established in the technical literature.[6] Hayek's task in *The Road to Serfdom* was not to establish that socialist planning could not achieve the efficiency results of capitalism, but rather to demonstrate what would structurally emerge from the failure of socialist planning to achieve its desired results. The detour into intellectual history in the first three chapters was considered necessary to show that despite the Misesian demonstration, the socialist critique of competition had effectively undermined the legitimacy of liberal institutions among the general public and especially among the intellectual élite. Hayek's assessment that one of the great advances of liberal theory was to unmask the special pleading activity of interest groups is significant when demonstrating Hayek's relevance to public choice. Liberalism, Hayek argues, had imparted a "healthy suspicion" of any argument that demanded restrictions on market competition.[7] With its critique of the competitive system, socialist theory had unfortunately swept away the liberal constraints against special pleading, and opened the door for a flood of interest groups to demand government protection from competition under the flag of socialist planning (Hayek 1944, p. 40).

Hayek even explains how the failure of *laissez-faire* liberalism against socialism was born out of its success in curbing the special interests of the mercantilist type. Hayek states:

> Against the innumerable interests which could show that particular measures would confer immediate and obvious benefits on some, while the harm they caused was much more indirect and difficult to see, nothing short of some hard-and-fast rule would have been effective ... [But since such a] strong presumption in favor of industrial liberty had undoubtedly been established [by the classical economists], the temptation to present it as a rule which knew no exception was too strong always to be resisted.
>
> (Hayek 1944, pp. 17–18)

Thus, if one of the theoretical claims of modern public choice theory is the demonstration of the logic of concentrated benefits and dispersed costs, then clearly Hayek understood this principle. Moreover, if one considers his argument for the economic importance of "the rule of law," then it becomes clear that Hayek sought to counter the logic of concentrated benefits with a fixed rule that would eliminate opportunities for special groups to capture the apparatus of the state in order to use it for their benefit.[8]

Despite the reading given by Higgs or Peacock, *The Road to Serfdom* touches upon several themes central to public choice besides concentrated benefits and dispersed costs. In his elaboration of the importance of the rule of law, for example, Hayek anticipated a theme that would be continually reiterated in the work of James Buchanan. Rules, rather than discretion, by "tying the King's hands" provide the legal certainty required for the development of commercial society. Hayek (1944, p. 73), in fact, describes formal rules as "instruments of production," a phraseology that is echoed in Buchanan's (1975) distinction between the "productive state" and the "redistributive state."

Hayek provides one of the most articulate statements of the liberal proposition that economic freedom and political freedom are linked. This argument has often been misunderstood to suggest that economic development could occur only within a liberal political order. If that were the case, empirical counter-examples could be supplied where authoritarian dictatorships produced economic growth. The liberal argument would be refuted, or at least seriously called into question.[9] Hayek's argument, of course, was more limited and not so crude as to assert such a tight social causation. He argued that economic control does not control merely "a sector of human life which can be separated from the rest; it is the control of the means for all our ends. And whoever has some control of the means must also determine which ends are to be served, which values are to be rated higher and which lower – in short, what men should believe and strive for. Central planning means that the economic problem is to be solved by the community instead of by the individual; but this involves that it must also be the community, or rather its representatives, who must decide the relative importance of the different needs" (1944, p. 92).

Perhaps Hayek's most important public choice contribution in *The Road to Serfdom* was in pointing out the organizational logic implied in the substitution of community decision-making by its representatives to form a collective plan for the private decisions of individuals within the marketplace. His discussion entails both an examination of the incentives these representatives face in the institutional context of centralized economic planning, and the evolutionary process engendered by these institutions for the selection of leaders. Remember, in my interpretation, Hayek did not seek to demonstrate the truth or falsehood of the Misesian proposition concerning the impossibility of economic calculation under socialism in *The Road to Serfdom*. This work proceeded as *if* that proposition had already been established in the technical literature of economic theory. Thus, Hayek was examining the organizational logic of central planning and what societal/institutional transformation would occur in response to the failure of planning to achieve its stated purposes.[10]

Obviously, when faced with their failure, government officials could reverse course and move toward the adoption of liberal economic policies. Crucial to Hayek's argument is the public choice wisdom that government decision-makers, within a social context where liberalism (and its institutions of governance) has been undermined by the socialist critique, do not face incentives which are likely to produce a choice of reversing course. This is how we get the "slippery slope" argument. Where Hayek differs from the extreme public choice interpretation of the incentives within politics is how ideas (by changing the social infrastructure) can change the incentives that officials face in policy decisions. In this regard, Hayek blends ideas and interests together in a more subtle manner than is available in textbook treatments of public choice theory, and he does so in a manner akin to Buchanan's important distinction between pre- and post-constitutional levels of analysis.

In examining the organizational logic of planning, Hayek warns the reader that since the economic knowledge necessary to plan the economy rationally will not be available to planners, these decision-makers will be forced to rely on the forms of information that are readily available, which in this context comes in the form of incentives to exercise political power. Hayek's argument is an application of the principle of comparative advantage to the selection of leaders within the planning system. In other words, just as we expect the division of labor within a society to reflect the opportunity costs of the various producers, so we should expect those with the requisite skills in exercising political power to advance within the political apparatus of planning. In this regard, Hayek was directly challenging the argument that experiments in real existing planning, say in the former Soviet Union, were tainted by "historical accident" and/or "bad" people, and therefore, could not be employed to illustrate the difficulties with planning. It simply was not true that if only "good" people controlled the planning bureau, then the results would be harmonious with liberal democratic values.[11] Hayek wrote:

> There are strong reasons for believing that what to us appears the worst features of the existing totalitarian systems are not accidental by-products but phenomena which totalitarianism is certain sooner or later to produce. Just as the democratic statesman who sets out to plan economic life will soon be confronted with the alternative of either assuming dictatorial powers or abandoning his plans, so the totalitarian dictator would soon have to choose between disregard of ordinary morals and failure.
>
> (Hayek 1944, p. 135)

"Success" in this arena requires a talent for unscrupulous and uninhibited moral behavior with respect to humanity. Totalitarianism is neither a consequence of "corruption" nor "historical accident," but rather a logical consequence of the institutional incentives of the attempt to centrally plan an economy.[12]

Hayek, in this context as throughout *The Road to Serfdom*, is making a subtle and tragic argument about the consequences of planning. It is not just that a band of "thugs" gets control of the coercive apparatus of the state and employs it to oppress the mass of citizens to their own benefit, the desire to organize economic life (or social life in general) in strict accordance to a scientific plan does not spring from a desire to exercise power over people. But, Hayek points out, the arbitrary employment of power is a consequence, and not a cause, of the desire to plan the economy scientifically. In order "to achieve their end, collectivists must create power – power over men wielded by other men – of a magnitude never before known, and ... their success will depend on the extent to which they achieve such power" (1944, p. 144). Even liberal socialists, as opposed to collectivists, in their desire to plan the economy, must establish institutions of discretionary planning and grant authority to the planners to exercise their political power in order to accomplish the task entrusted to them. The complexity of the task implied in rationally planning an economic system would require that planners be granted almost unlimited discretion. And, as a consequence, we should expect that only those that have a comparative advantage in exercising discretionary power will survive.

Hayek's argument was a straightforward application of economic principles to the political institutions of planning. It was an argument not unique to Hayek and should not have been a controversial proposition. Frank Knight, in fact, made quite a similar argument when he aptly stated that the planning authorities would have to:

> exercise their power ruthlessly to keep the machinery of organized production and distribution running ... They would have to do these things whether they wanted to or not; and the probability of the people in power being individuals who would dislike the possession and exercise of power is on a level with the probability than an extremely tender-hearted person would get the job of whipping-master on a slave plantation.
>
> (Knight 1938, p. 869)

If public choice theory means "The economic study of non-market decision-making or simply the application of economics to political science" (Muller 1989, p. 1), then Hayek's argument concerning the organizational logic of socialist institutions is unduly neglected within the contemporary literature in political economy. Moreover, Hayek's argument was not limited to an examination of "hot" socialism, but included an analysis of the importance of rules rather than discretion, the limits of democracy and the importance of federalism as an institutional constraint on democratic action.[13]

What I would like to suggest is that this neglect of Hayek's public choice contribution can be ascribed to the twin factors of *vision* and *analysis*.[14] The majority of his contemporaries misunderstood his insights because of visionary differences which caused them to turn a deaf ear to his argument. In addition, among those contemporaries who shared his vision, precious few followed his analytical structure.[15] Unfortunately, even as time passed and more scholars tended to share Hayek's vision concerning the failure of government planning of the economy, their mode of analysis remained antithetical to his, and thus his original analytical contribution was masked from their view.

The spirit of the age

The socialist critique of the liberal economic order had effectively changed the terms of the debate by the beginning of the twentieth century. Most participants in the intellectual and political debate agreed that *laissez-faire* liberalism had failed to provide equity and humane social conditions. Instead, progressive legislation was demanded in order to correct for the failings of free competition. The Great Depression, which by popular interpretation of the time demonstrated that not only was capitalism unjust but that it was also unstable, contributed to the critique of *laissez-faire* liberalism. The capitalist system, if it was to survive in the liberal world of the 1930s, had to be subject to democratic political forces of control to tame its operation and protect the populace from unscrupulous business and irresponsible speculation.

This general intellectual climate of opinion both altered and was reinforced by the development of neoclassical economics in the 1920s and 1930s. As academic economic theory became more technically sophisticated and rarefied in its presentation of its basic theorems, the more intuitive or appreciative understanding of rivalrous market processes that characterized the classical economists and the early development of neoclassical economics was dismissed as unscientific.[16] The flip-side of the development of the model of perfect competition and the strict conditions required was the development of the theory of market failure. Market failures were said to exist whenever capitalist reality did not meet the conditions of the textbook model of perfect competition. Externalities, public goods, monopoly, imperfect competition, and macroeconomic instability were said to characterize real-world market economies and required positive government action to curb the socially undesirable result.

These theoretical developments colored historical interpretations. The Progressive Era in the US, for example, was seen as a public interest movement to rid society of social ills through positive government action. The cynicism toward proposals by interest groups to curb the forces of free competition that Hayek rightly attributes to nineteenth-century liberalism was gone, replaced by an optimism of government officials to set right what was wrong with our world.

The Great Depression simply solidified the "victory" of the socialist critique of liberalism. The collapse of the US and UK economies shook an entire generation's faith in the capitalist system. Rational planning came to be viewed as not only a viable alternative to be debated, but the only alternative to chaos. Classical liberal economic policy reflected the beliefs of the naïve and the simple minded. The modern world had become too complex for ideas from the eighteenth and nineteenth centuries to offer anything of value.

John Maynard Keynes argued that while some may cling to the old ideas of liberal economic policy, "in no country of the world today can they be reckoned as a serious force" (1933, p. 762). The significant fact to remember is that Keynes considered himself, and was viewed by others, as a realist in the classical liberal tradition. Keynes was not a socialist radical, but rather a self-anointed savior of the bourgeois order (Keynes 1926, pp. 129–30). The Keynesian idea was for government to intervene rationally to improve the workings and outcomes of the market economy. He proposed combining the socialization of the capital market with the nineteenth-century political traditions of Great Britain. While he saw the socialization of investment as the only way of securing full employment, this change did not, in his analysis, require a general break with bourgeois society. Keynes conceived of his theory as an extension of classical liberalism, not a rejection. His advocacy of a greater role of government in planning the economy was, in his mind, a practical attempt to save individualism and to avoid the destruction of the existing economic system (Ibid. 1936, pp. 378–81).

The spirit of the age even led someone as cynical toward intellectual and political promises of human betterment through progressive legislation as Frank Knight to declare publicly the virtues of Communism (Knight, 1932). Knight argued that liberal society had failed to provide social order in the time of crisis, and, therefore, that Communism may regrettably provide the social order so desperately needed.[17] It seemed as if everyone advocated some form of government control and planning of the economy to ensure stability and equity during the 1930s and 1940s. In this intellectual climate of opinion, the challenge posed to economic planning by its critics, Mises and Hayek, was neither appreciated nor tolerated. But without understanding the theoretical difficulties with planning, the eventual disappointing experience with planning attempts in both the socialist and democratic world could not be understood. It was not just an issue of ideological apologetics; the problem was that the ideological vision produced an honest analytical blind spot in scholars and intellectuals.

The intellectual biases of the time not only failed to appreciate economic problems of planning; they also ignored political difficulties of planning. Along with the previous era's cynicism toward pleas for restrictions against competition, the victory of the socialist critique of liberal society also eliminated the justifications for constraints on democratic government that had been developed in the eighteenth and nineteenth centuries. Hayek's discussion of this delegitimation of liberal constitutionalism and the rule of law was one of the crucial arguments in *The Road to Serfdom* (1944, pp. 56–87). In order for planning to be implemented, officials cannot be constrained by formal rules, but must be entrusted with discretionary power. Moreover, planning (if it is to have any coherent meaning) requires broad agreement, and democracy is capable of only producing a certain level of agreement – usually limited to general rules within which disagreement will be tolerated. Hayek argued, "That planning creates a situation in which it is necessary for us to agree on a much larger number of topics than we have been used to, and that in a planned system we cannot confine collective action to the tasks on which we can agree but are forced to produce agreement on everything in order that any action can be taken at all, is one of the features which contributes more than most to determining the character of a planned system" (1944, p. 62). In other words, "planning leads to dictatorship because dictatorship is the most effective instrument of coercion and the enforcement of ideals and, as such, essential if central planning on a large scale is to be possible. The clash between planning and democracy arises simply from the fact that the latter is an obstacle to the suppression of freedom which the direction of economic activity requires" (1944, p. 70).

Such a warning, however, was not going to be respected during this era. Traditional limits on democracy had to be abandoned so that progressive legislation could be enacted. The classical liberal wisdom concerning constitutional constraints was lost. Instead, a naïve view of democratic governance dominated discourse. A democratic political system was envisioned as one in which individual citizens could effectively determine the rules by which they would live. The voting process unambiguously conveyed the necessary information concerning the array of public goods and services demanded and the level of taxes that must be paid. Democracy was an ideal model of self-rule. The spirit of the age demanded an expansion of democratic power, not constraint.[18] Faced with the failures of the liberal economic order, democratic government could easily set the manner straight through the judicious use of rational planning. If government action failed, it was not due to structural weaknesses in the democratic system (such as the inability of the government to calculate the alternative use of scarce resources rationally without the signals of the market). Instead, political actors would just have to gather more information and try harder next time.

Planning and the expansion of democratic procedures into areas beyond its traditional scope were not seen as a threat to political freedom. Keynes, for example, in reacting to Hayek's *The Road to Serfdom* wrote:

> I should say that what we want is not no planning, or even less planning, indeed I should say that we almost certainly want more. But planning should take place in a community in which as many people as possible, both leaders and followers, wholly share your own moral position. Moderate planning will be safe if those carrying it out are rightly oriented in their own minds and hearts to the moral issues.
>
> (Keynes 1944, p. 387)

So long as "good" people were in charge, nothing was objectionable with economic planning. In fact, planning was desirable.

Hayek's argument was not treated as kindly by most critics as it was by Keynes. Hayek had his supporters. For example, Joseph Schumpeter (1946) wrote a positive review in the *Journal of Political Economy*, as did Aaron Director (1945) in the *American Economic Review*. But most of the leading academic reviews were not favorable. Barbara Wootton (1945) wrote an even-handed and respectful critique of Hayek. In fact, Wootton's book was written in such a qualified manner that despite its general reputation as a critique of Hayek, many liberal writers who were sympathetic to Hayek viewed the book as a confirmation of Hayek's thesis.[19] Wootton was the exception as far as critics of *The Road to Serfdom* were concerned.

Herman Finer's *The Road to Reaction* (1945) set the tone. Finer accused Hayek's *The Road to Serfdom* of being "the most sinister offensive against democracy to emerge from a democratic country for many decades" (1945, p. v). The true alternative to dictatorship, Finer assured his audience, was not economic individualism and competition, but a democratic government fully responsible to the people. Hayek's world, according to Finer, would leave individuals under the control of aristocrats or the moneyed bourgeoisie. But free people can govern themselves without such masters. Economic planning was simply democracy in action, and it proved itself every time there was a successful government action. Finer accused Hayek of confused and misleading language, misunderstanding the concept of the rule of law which was out of the range of Hayek's amateur comprehension, a biased understanding of economic processes, poor scholarship, historical blindness, non-existent comprehension of the basic teachings of political science and ignorance of the science of administrative management, as well as a direct assault on the principal values of the democratic system that conveyed an attitude toward average men and women that was authoritarian.

Charles Merriam (1946), in reviewing both the Finer and Wootton volumes, spent very little time on Wootton, but instead devoted most of his energy to endorsing Finer's critique vigorously. He refers to Hayek's book as "an over-rated work of little permanent value" and states that there has not been a more effective political polemic written since Henry George's critique of Herbert Spencer in the *Perplexed Philosopher*. Finer's work, in contrast to Hayek's, we are told "breathes the democratic spirit of confidence, and contains a progressive plan based upon hope rather than upon fear" (Ibid. 1946, p. 135). In his own review of *The Road to Serfdom*, Merriam anticipated Finer's critique of Hayek as being confused, lacking in scholarship, and arrogant, and concludes by stating *contra* Hayek that:

> [O]ut of skillful planning will come human freedom in larger measure, the growth of the human personality, the expansion of the creative possibilities of mankind. Conscious creative evolution – mastery rather than drift – marks the way to higher levels and higher orders of human life. The road to serfdom is not planning but drift, unwillingness to change, incapacity for adaptation to new possibilities of human emancipation, worship of the status quo.
>
> (Merriam 1944, p. 235)[20]

Admittedly I have singled out the worst examples of critical discussion of Hayek's thesis. But Merriam's reviews were published in such prestigious journals as the *American Political Science Review* and the *American Journal of Sociology*. Joseph Mayer's (1945) review of *The Road to Serfdom*, published in *Annals of the American Academy of Political Social Science*, was lukewarm – he did not really understand Hayek's point about planning, but thought the book made some important points about the rule of law in a peace-time democracy. When the *American Economic Review* ran Director's review, the editors included an opposing review by Eric Roll and prefaced the reviews with the following note: "In view of the ideological character of, and the great interest in Professor Hayek's book it was found desirable to publish two reviews written from different standpoints." Roll's review, in fact, comes close to the standard of "scholarly" discourse established by Finer. Hayek had succumbed to the common rhetorical tactic among journalists and political pundits, Roll argues, but we should have hoped that such an experienced social scientist as Hayek would have avoided the temptation to equate socialism with Nazism. Roll states:

Hayek might have stopped to reflect upon the very different development during the last few pre-war years in Germany and in the Soviet Union, and he might have had the grace, at the least, to acknowledge the very different manner in which the war itself has been conducted by the enemy and by our ally: we have yet to be shown that Maidanek is an inevitable corollary of a collective economy. The truth is that Hayek's strong political prejudices show through the veneer of reasonableness with which he tries to impress the reader.

(Roll 1945, p. 180)[21]

The intellectual spirit of the age simply could not appreciate or incorporate the argument put forth by Mises and Hayek into the public wisdom of the time. Their vision and analysis of political and economic processes were simply inconsistent with everything that the contemporary intellectual culture in Western democracies was suggesting *c.*1930 to 1975. Even if the intellectual élite in the West expressed normative disagreements with aspects of how the Soviet Union was going about introducing a "new civilization," the attempt to bring social life under conscious and rational direction with the aid of science was to be applauded. The economic failures of the Soviet system were attributed to its historical backwardness, and the political problems were attributed to a lack of democratic traditions within Russian history. German Nazism, on the other hand, was a consequence of the German character and the failures of capitalism, and not the corruption of liberal institutions through the intrusion of socialist principles, as Hayek contended.

Subsequent historical development seems to have persuaded many that Hayek's vision was essentially correct (Heilbroner 1990).[22] Unfortunately, this does not translate into an appreciation of his analytical contribution to politics and economics, and this is no less true for those broadly sympathetic to his classical liberal vision than for those who are radically opposed to that vision.

Analytical confusions

Hayek was above all else an "Austrian" economist. The analytical propositions he worked with, the techniques of analysis utilized, his whole mode of operation was that of an Austrian economist. And, despite his departure from formal economic questions, this analytical apparatus remained intact. Hayek used Mengerian spontaneous order theory and Misesian market process theory to examine the emergence of private property rules, the development of the common law, the growth of commerce, the rules of moral conduct, etc. Obviously, Hayek was a unique scholar and read widely across disciplines – he could not be accused, for example, of being "economistic" in his research. My point is simply that he "read" this information gleaned from his wide-ranging research through his Austrian analytical lenses. This point is completely missed by those preoccupied with Hayek's liberalism. Liberalism provided Hayek with a set of problems, but the way that he went about analyzing these problems was thoroughly Austrian.

Although the visions we hold concerning "man" and "society" provide the basis of social analysis, they do not constitute it. As Schumpeter wrote, "In order to posit to ourselves any problems at all, we should first have to visualize a distinct set of coherent phenomena as a worth-while object of our analytical efforts. In other words, analytical effort is of necessity preceded by a pre-analytic cognitive act that supplies the raw material for the analytic effort" (1954, p. 41). Once we have located an "interesting" problem, we then set about analyzing it, and the outcomes of our study are not neutral with regard to our method of analysis.

Hayek's Austrian style of analysis, however, fell out of favor in the 1940s and has remained outside the mainstream of economic thinking ever since. To go back to my introductory thesis, public choice economics was the application of mainstream economic analysis to political decision-making. The mainstream tenets of economic analysis are:

1   maximizing behavior,
2   stable preferences, and
3   equilibrium.

Austrian economists, and Hayek in particular, reject at least two of these tenets, if not all three.[23] Hayek, for example, rejects the *Homo economicus* assumption as part of the rationalist tradition as opposed to the evolutionary tradition in which he places his own work (1960, p. 61). Moreover, Hayek was highly critical of the apparatus of perfect competition and the preoccupation of economists with equilibrium analysis (1948, pp. 77–106).

Thus, Hayek's contributions to public choice analysis come in the form of the application of *Austrian* economic theory to decision-making within non-market settings. I would stress even further that it is Austrian *capital theory* where the differences between Austrian and other marginalist economists are most acute.[24] In mainstream economic analysis, the strict application of the three tenets above masks the complexity of the capital structure, and thus the issue of coordination becomes relatively trivial. But in Austrian analysis the coordination of plans through time (and in an environment of uncertainty) takes center stage, and the various key *positive* propositions derived in Austrian theory (such as relative prices signals, profit and loss accounting, heterogeneity of capital, complementarity of capital goods, etc.) are employed to derive a theory of how complex plans dovetail in an industrial economy. In short, the manner in which Austrians explain the "equilibrium" outcome of market processes (if we can even use that term) is radically different from the conception within the mainstream, and as such represents a different analytical contribution to economic science. The difficulty of coordinating economic plans through time, and the vital role that a functioning capital market plays in guiding that process, focus theoretical attention on the issue of economic calculation and entrepreneurial discovery. In a standard circular flow model of the capitalist economy, on the other hand, these problems are not highlighted in the formal presentation because the underlying assumptions solve the problem of coordination by calculation by hypothesis. It is not the political–sociological vision that makes Hayek so different from other scholars; it is his analytical apparatus which forces scholars to pay attention to the dynamic capital structure of an economic system. What is most challenging to mainstream economic scholars is that if Hayek's position is proven to be more robust, then a major recasting of post-World War II developments in economic science would be in order.

Standard public choice analysis followed the path of mainstream neoclassical economics. The Virginia School, however, did not follow completely in line with the mainstream, but the Chicago School of public choice analysis certainly did – with the result that many of the institutional inefficiencies of government action are often not recognized because the equilibrium analysis does not permit their examination.[25] If, on the other hand, disequilibrium adjustment processes form the core of one's analytical structure, then inefficiencies and imperfections, and the way that individuals respond to this situation, are crucial to the analysis. Institutions, and the incentives and information they engender, drive the analysis. Economic outcomes are not invariant with respect to institutions – including forms of democratic governance.

Public choice analysis in the Austrian tradition would emphasize the *structural ignorance* that actors must confront in situations outside the context of the market economy.[26] The Arrow theorem, for example, could be reinterpreted as an application of Mises' impossibility thesis to non-market decision-making via democratic voting. In the absence of the price system, actors would confront a set of incoherent signals about how they should orient their behavior. Rather than rely on the competitive bidding of the market, the community must decide on how to allocate a scarce resource, say a vacant lot. The lot could be used for:

1 a community park,
2 an elementary school, or
3 a parking garage.

Without the price system to guide resource use, community agreement must emerge. But, as Arrow demonstrated, even in a simple example such as this one, majority-rule pairwise voting might not produce the required agreement (a highly formal result which echoes Hayek's discussion of limits of democratically derived agreement in *The Road to Serfdom*). The park may win against the school, and the school may win against the parking garage, but the parking garage would win over the park – violating the mathematical principle of transitivity. The well-known result is that given this problem the outcome can be efficient only if the political system is dictatorial, or allocations can be inefficient, but democratic. There simply is no manner in which allocations can be efficient and derived democratically.

One line of argument favored by some public choice scholars, such as Buchanan and Tullock, was to charge this result with being trivial. Why should we be surprised? Only a naïve view of democracy would have expected that individual preference rankings could be aggregated cleanly to convey unambiguously the "will of the people." This was a perfectly reasonable response by scholars working within a constitutional democratic tradition. But, the Arrow result was important precisely because it should have burst the bubble of naïve democracy of the type that informed Finer's critique of Hayek. And, moreover, to go back to my introductory remarks concerning the Higgs-type critique of Hayek – this challenge to the ability of democratic government to produce agreement beyond a certain limited range of issues informs the Hayekian examination of public goods (i.e. what are the demand revealing processes in public goods provision, and what institutions would compensate for the calculation difficulties in non-market allocations?) and externalities (i.e. what property rules and/or contract technologies would internalize external effects?). This is why, for example, in his examination of public goods problems in *Law, Legislation and Liberty*, despite his acceptance of certain aspects of the analytical arguments of standard market failure theory Hayek nevertheless derives an entirely different conclusion concerning the production and distribution of public goods. In particular, Hayek argues for a non-exclusive position for the government even when it can be technically determined that under *current circumstances* only government would in fact be able to supply the good in question. This argument is not a result of "bad economics" combined with wishful ideological thinking (e.g. assuming away free-rider problems), but rather emerges from Hayek's analytical consideration of the dynamics of technological change and his recognition that the informational requirements of matching demand and supply of *any* good are dependent upon the institutional context within which that process is to take place (Hayek 1973–9, vol. 3, pp. 41–64). Hayek is not ignorant of public choice problems: he just alters the analytical treatment of these problems in certain directions that differ from more traditional treatments in the literature.

The inability of democracy to ensure agreement means that theorists must recognize the limits of democratic decision-making and focus scholarly attention on the governance structures that permit efficient outcomes to result. The political process, just like the market process, should not be expected to generate optimal allocations. Both are imperfect. Unlike the market process, however, democratic politics does not engender the incentives and information for its own error detection and correction. The type of spontaneous adaptations that occur in the market to correct current inefficiencies cannot be expected to emerge in the political process. Instead, conscious direction and rule-making are needed. Rather than spontaneous adaptation, politics requires conscious adaptation, and there are epistemological limits to this procedure.

Conclusion

Hayek's *The Road to Serfdom* is as relevant today as when it was published fifty years ago, perhaps more so. At the time of publication it constituted a warning to the liberal democratic West that the road to totalitarianism was not paved by revolutionary bandits, but instead by high ideals. Today, we are witnessing the collapse of the state socialist system, and the attempt to transit the path to political democracy and economic prosperity. We will not find an answer to these problems by reading Hayek's great book. What we will find, however, is a set of analytical tools and insights that we can employ to address the problems of our modern world.

In this regard, Hayek leaves us:

1   a refined statement of the Misesian proposition concerning the impossibility of economic calculation in the absence of private property, and
2   an examination of the organizational logic of institutions designed to replace the private property system in allocating scarce resources.

The strength of Hayek's analysis was to show that this logic was not a function of the form of government which inspired the substitution of collective decision-making for the private choices on the market. Whether democratic or authoritarian in legitimation, the institutional incentives produced a logical pressure toward totalitarianism.

In Eastern and Central Europe and the former Soviet Union this logic is misunderstood when the intellectual élites insist that democratic politics be held up as the revolutionary values of 1989, and not economic freedom. That there can be no meaningful political freedom without a large degree of economic freedom was the core political–philosophical claim of *The Road to Serfdom*, a claim derived from an analytical argument concerning the nature of the planner's task. It will indeed be a hollow victory if the revolutions of 1989 end up by simply rejecting the totalitarian rule of the Communist Party only to embark upon a process of multi-party sanctioned dictatorship in the quest to control the process of transition. Already much of Eastern and Central Europe has failed to incorporate the constitutional lessons of liberal democracy. We are in a constitutional moment, but it still does not appear that the "democratic fetish" that Hayek warned about has subsided. Moreover, we have to convey forcefully to the people in the former Communist Bloc countries (and our own) that not all forms of democratic rule are equally effective with regard to safeguarding the market economy. Unless "enabling" institutions are established and the spontaneous adjustments of markets are permitted to guide economic decision-making, the poverty of one terrible period will only be replaced by the continued poverty and disappointment of a people who have endured so much already.

Acknowledgments

An earlier version of this chapter was presented at the Eastern Economic Association Meetings in Boston, March 1994. I would like to thank those who participated in that session for their comments and criticisms. In addition, I would like to thank Gary Becker, James Buchanan, Milton Friedman, Robert Higgs, Steve Horwitz, Israel Kirzner, Daniel Klein, Laurence Moss, Dave Prychitko, Mario Rizzo, E. C. Pasour, Hans Sennholz, Alex Tabarrock, Viktor Vanberg, Karen Vaughn and Edward Weick for critical conversation on this topic and suggestions for improvements in my argument. The comments of two anonymous referees and Harold Hochman, the editor of the *Eastern Economic Journal,* were extremely helpful. Financial assistance from the Sarah Scaife Foundation for general support of the Austrian Economics Program at New York University is gratefully acknowledged. Responsibility for remaining errors is my own.

References

Becker, G. (1985) "Public Policies, Pressure Groups, and Dead Weight Costs," *Journal of Public Economics* 28: 329–47.

—— (1991) *A Treatise on the Family*, Cambridge: Harvard University Press.

Block, W. (1994) "Hayek's *Road to Serfdom*," unpublished paper, Department of Economics, College of the Holy Cross, IN.

Boettke, P. J. (1990) *The Political Economy of Soviet Socialism: The Formative Years, 1918–1928*, Boston: Kluwer Academic Publishers.

—— (1992a) "F.A. Hayek, 1899–1992," *The Freeman* August: 300–3.

—— (1992b) "Analysis and Vision in Economic Discourse," *Journal of the History of Economic Thought* Spring: 84–95.

—— (1993) *Why Perestroika Failed: The Politics and Economics of Socialist Transformation*, London: Routledge.

Boettke, P. J. and Rizzo, M. (eds.) (1994) *Advances in Austrian Economics*, vol. 1.

Buchanan, J. (1975) *The Limits of Liberty*, Chicago: University of Chicago Press.

Director, A. (1945) "Review of F. A. Hayek, *The Road to Serfdom*," *American Economic Review* March: 173–5.

Finer, H. (1945) *The Road to Reaction*, Chicago: Quadrangle Books.

Friedman, M. (1962) *Capitalism and Freedom*, Chicago: University of Chicago Press.

Hayek, F. A. von (1940) *The Pure Theory of Capital*, Chicago: University of Chicago Press.

—— (1944) *The Road to Serfdom*, Chicago: University of Chicago Press.

—— (1948) *Individualism and Economic Order*, Chicago: University of Chicago Press.

—— (1960) *The Constitution of Liberty*, Chicago: University of Chicago Press.

—— (1973–9) *Law, Legislation and Liberty*, three volumes, Chicago: University of Chicago Press.

—— (1994) *Hayek on Hayek: An Autobiographical Dialogue*, Chicago: University of Chicago Press.

Heilbroner, R. (1990) "Analysis and Vision in the History of Modern Economic Thought," *Journal of Economic Literature* September: 1097–114.

Herring, P. (1945) "Review of Ludwig von Mises," *Bureaucracy. Annals of the American Academy of Political Social Science* March: p. 213.

Higgs, R. (1988–9) "Who'll be persuaded?" *Humane Studies Review* 8–9.

Hoppe, H. (1993) *The Economics and Ethics of Private Property*, Boston: Kluwer Academic Publishers.

—— (1994) "F. A. Hayek on Government and Social Evolution," *The Review of Austrian Economics* 7: 57–93.

Jewkes, J. (1946) "Review of Barbara Wootton," *Freedom Under Planning. The Manchester School of Economics and Social Studies* January: 89–104.

Johnson, D. (1991) *Public Choice: An Introduction to the New Political Economy*, Mountain View, CA: Mayfield Publishing.

Keynes, J. M. (1926) *Laissez Faire and Communism*, New York: New Republic.

—— (1933) "National Self-sufficiency," *The Yale Review* June: 755–69.

—— (1964) (first published 1936) *The General Theory of Employment; Interest and Money*. New York: Harcourt Brace Jovanovich.

Kirzner, I. F. A. (1991) "Hayek, 1899–1992," *Critical Review* Fall: 585–92.

Knight, F. (1991) (first published 1932) "The Case for Communism from the Standpoint of an Ex-liberal (1932)" *Research in the History of Economic Thought and Methodology: Archival Supplement* 2: 57–108.

—— (1936) "The Place of Marginal Economics in a Collectivist System," *American Economic Review* March: 255–66.

—— (1936) "Lippmann's *The Good Society*," *Journal of Political Economy* December: 864–72.

—— (1982) (first published 1940) "Socialism: the Nature of the Problem (1940)," in F. Knight, *Freedom and Reform*. Indianapolis: Liberty Classics.

—— (1941) "Professor Mises and the Theory of Capital," *Economica* November: 409–27.

—— (1946) "Freedom Under Planning," *Journal of Political Economy* October: 451–4.

Machovec, F. (1995) *Perfect Competition and the Transformation of Economics*, New York: Routledge.

Mayer, J. (1945) "Review of F. A. Hayek, *The Road to Serfdom*," *Annals of the American Academy of Political and Social Science* May: 202–3.

Merriam, C. (1944) "Review of F. A. Hayek, *The Road to Serfdom*," *American Journal of Sociology* November: 233–5.

—— (1946) "Review of Barbara Wootton, *Freedom Under Planning* and Herman Finer, *Road to Reaction*," *American Political Science Review* February: 131–6.

Mises, L. von (1981) (first published 1922) *Socialism: An Economic and Sociological Analysis*. Indianapolis: Liberty Classics.

Muller, D. (1989) *Public Choice II*, New York: Cambridge University Press.

Peacock, A. (1992) *Public Choice Analysis in Historical Perspective*, New York: Cambridge University Press.

Prychitko, D. (1991) *Marxism and Workers' Self-Management: The Essential Tension*. Westport, CT: Greenwood Press.

Przeworski, A. and Limongi, F. (1993) "Political Regimes and Economic Growth," *Journal of Economic Perspectives* Summer: 51–69.

Raico, R. (1993) "Classical Liberal Roots of the Marxist Doctrine of Classes," in Yu. N. Maltsev (ed.) *Requiem for Marx*, Auburn, AL: Ludwig von Mises Institute, pp. 189–220.

Roll, E. (1945) "Review of F. A. Hayek, *The Road to Serfdom*." *American Economic Review* March: 176–80.

Schumpeter, J. (1942) *Capitalism, Socialism and Democracy*, New York: Harper and Row.

—— (1942) "Review of F. A. Hayek, *The Road to Serfdom*," *Journal of Political Economy* June: 269–70.

—— (1954) *History of Economic Analysis*, New York: Oxford University Press.

Stevens, J.(1993) *The Economics of Collective Choice*, Boulder, CO: Westview Press.

Stigler, G. (1992) *Law or Economics? Journal of Law and Economics* April: 455–568.

Tullock, G. (1987) *The Politics of Bureaucracy*, Lanham, MD: University Press of America.

Wagner, R. (1989) *To Promote the General Welfare: Market Processes Vs. Political Transfers*. San Francisco, CA: Pacific Research Institute for Public Policy.

Weingast, B. (1993) "The Economic Role of Political Institutions," unpublished manuscript, Hoover Institution on War, Revolution and Peace, Stanford University.

Wootton, B. (1945) *Freedom Under Planning*, Chapel Hill, NC: University of North Carolina Press.

5 Coase, Communism, and the "Black Box" of Soviet-type economies*

Introduction

In his youth, like many students of his generation, Ronald Coase was favorably disposed toward socialism (Coase, 1988b, p. 5). This ideological predisposition, in fact, was one reason why he decided to study economics.[1] This attraction to socialism would eventually be dispelled by his understanding of economic processes he learned from Arnold Plant at the London School of Economics. From Plant, Coase learned to appreciate the "invisible hand" of the market economy. Though he was persuaded of the power of the market economy to coordinate the plans of diverse individuals in society, the proposition left Coase with a new question which ate away at him. If the market is so efficient and powerful in organizing our affairs, then why were there business organizations?

In fact, as Coase has stated, it was Plant's critique of rationalization schemes for British industry which motivated Coase's inquiry into business organization and management. Not that he disagreed with Plant's argument that a "normal economic system works itself," but Coase found this answer to be incomplete. He was also motivated to ask questions of economic organization due to a curiosity about Soviet Russia. As Coase puts it: "there was very little experience of economic organization in Russia to go on and economists in the West were engaged in a grand debate on the subject of planning, some maintaining that to run the economy as one big factory was an impossibility. And yet there were factories in England and America. How did one reconcile the impossibility of running Russia as one big factory with the existence of factories in the western world?" (1988b, p. 8).

Coase's answer to this question was formulated by 1932 in a letter to his friend, Ronald Fowler, and presented in a lecture at the Dundee School of Economics and Commerce. "I pointed out," Coase writes to Fowler of the lecture, "if there were atomistic competition, where every transaction involving the use of another's labour, materials or money was the subject of a market transaction,

*Originally published as Boettke, P. J. (1998) "Coase, Communism, and Inside the 'Black Box' of Soviet-Type Economies," in S. Medema (ed.) *On Coasean Economics*, Boston: Kluwer Academic Publishers, pp. 193–207.

there would be no need for an organization. In fact, this is not so. Why? I found the reason in the costs of conducting these marketing transactions. Think of the inconvenience (increased cost) if every time someone worked with someone else, there had to be a market transaction. But if the transactions are not to be governed by the price mechanism directly there *has* to be an organization ... I then asked – if by eliminating market transactions, costs were lowered, why were there market transactions at all? That is, why are there separate firms?" Coase gives two reasons relating to the organizational costs of the business enterprise. The main contribution Coase saw of his analysis was that he was able to succeed in "linking up organization with cost" (1932). He ends the letter to Fowler by stating that he plans to "work up this argument a bit more." The result was his "The Nature of the Firm" paper, which was eventually published in *Economica* in 1937, and fifty-four years later cited by the Swedish Academy as one of the two fundamental contributions Coase had made, which warranted the awarding of the 1991 Nobel Prize in Economic Science.

Coase's writings on the capitalist business enterprise have been quite influential – especially as the framework has been translated by Oliver Williamson. In other words, Coase's analysis of the nature of the firm has influenced mainly the research on the internal organization of the firm and the costs associated with pure market exchange. What I propose to do here is to look at economic organization from the opposite side, with the Soviet and post-Soviet experience as the background reality which is to be explained.

The theory of the firm as a limit "theorem"

Throughout his career Coase represented a style of economic reasoning which could be termed "economic minimalism." Simple economic concepts – some could even be termed mere tautologies – are deployed to offer insights which are of great empirical significance. They may be tautologies, but there was nothing "mere" about them. These theoretical conceptions come mainly as "limit theorems" in that they demonstrate the pure logic of a situation as the starting point of the analysis. In other words, they establish what the world is not, so that we may get on with the task of explaining the world as it is. In a world of zero transaction costs, for example, firms would not be necessary, as all economic activity could be coordinated through the market. But this is not the world we live in. By isolating the pure case, we can learn what factors in the world may lead to the emergence of practices such as the organization of production in business firms.

It is precisely because we live in a world where transactions possess costs that firms owe their existence. But if firms are so efficient at organizing economic activity in a world of positive transaction costs, then why don't we see one giant firm to coordinate all economic activity? Here Coase introduces the concept of organizational costs. So Coase was able to link the nature of economic organization to marginal cost–marginal benefit calculus. We rely on the market to coordinate affairs as long as the marginal benefits exceed the marginal costs, and similarly we rely on the firm to organize our affairs as long as the marginal benefits of organization outweigh the costs.

Such a tautology is of course limited to a large extent, but the knowledge it establishes is essential as it frames theoretical and empirical questions. Unfortunately, standard textbooks continued (and for the most part do so today) to concentrate their analytical attention on the zero transaction cost world where firms do not really exist. Firms are often treated as a "Black Box" within economic theory, as microeconomics is restricted to consumer choice theory, and production theory. Business history, of course, emphasizes the internal organization of firms and the management strategy which lead to success or failure. But a gap exists between the theory and history of market activity for the most part. This has been largely repaired by a considerable literature on the nature and evolution of the capitalist firm.[2] But the flip-side of Coase's tautology – that the costs of hierarchy preclude a pure organizational solution to economic life – has been relatively underdeveloped.

Soviet myth and Soviet reality

Standard textbooks characterized the Soviet economy as offering a radical alternative to the market economy – the centrally planned economy. This characterization belied a fundamental misunderstanding of the possible in economic life. Just as the model of perfect competition is difficult to reconcile with the lived experience of market competition and entrepreneurial activity, the material balance model of central planning was inconsistent with the intra-plan bargaining and extra-plan black-market activity. The organizing principles of Soviet economic life remain a "Black Box."

Coase's tautology – if taken to heart – could have directed research on the Soviet system in a more productive direction. Pure atomistic market competition is not a plausible framework for studying capitalist history. The very existence of business organizations implies that the transaction costs associated with market coordination are positive, and thus suppression of atomistic competition is beneficial. Theoretical and empirical research has to focus attention on the implications of positive transaction costs and the economics of hierarchical organization. But, as mentioned above, the organizational costs of hierarchy (and the suppression of markets) possesses costs that must be accounted for, and place limits of the growth of hierarchy. As organization replaces market competition, the firm must cope with problems of shirking, informational complexity, and monetary calculation.[3]

Soviet reality could not have conformed to the textbook model precisely because of these problems suggested by the flip-side of Coasean analysis of market and hierarchy. Instead of delving inside the "Black Box" of Soviet economic organization, mainstream economic analysis of the Soviet system proceeded along one of two paths. Either scholars worked out the efficiency properties of various models of central planning, or scholars attempted to rework Soviet statistics to get an accurate measure of aggregate economic performance with which to contrast with the performance of Western capitalist microeconomic and macroeconomic formal analysis was how the Soviet-type economy actually operated in practice.[4] We did get glimpses of how the system worked from historically minded scholars who provided "thicker descriptions" and journalists who traveled widely in the country. But the extremely important information provided in these accounts fell short because of the lack of an analytical framework to integrate these data into an overall analysis of Soviet economic practice. It is my contention that Coase provides that framework by forcing us to pay attention to the contractual and property rights nature of economic organization within a positive transaction cost world.

Soviet economic reality was one in which the plan served an ideological veneer. The motivating ideology of the Russian revolution was a form of Marxism which stressed that justice could only be achieved through transcendence of commodity production (see Boettke, 1990; Malia, 1994; Walicki, 1995). The project then was one of abolition of all vestiges of the market economy and the complete substitution of production for direct use through a unified plan, for a social system based on production for profit. Such a project ran aground in practice due to the difficulties associated with attempting to suppress markets completely. But the legitimating rhetoric of Soviet politics remained one of justice through transcendence. On the economic front, of course, the rhetoric–reality dichotomy set the stage for the "living the lie" that was endemic to Soviet-type societies in all walks of life (see Kuran, 1995, pp. 261–88 and Boettke, 1993, pp. 57–72). What this meant in terms of economic interaction was that the discrepancies between the *de jure* system of planning, and the *de facto* existence of internal and external markets which attempt to coordinate production plans on the one hand, and satisfy consumption demands on the other, must move to the center of our attention. "When a huge organization is this highly centralized," David Granick wrote concerning the Soviet economy, "two possibilities exist. The organization may founder in its own bureaucracy, or it may ignore its own rules ... The evidence is conclusive that formal decision-making regulations have been constantly violated. Plant managements have had to make their own decisions if they were to produce the results demanded of them. Top authorities in Moscow had to wink at violations of rules if they wished industrial production to grind ahead" (1961, pp. 132–3). The way in which the Soviet myth of Central Planning interacted with, and imprinted on, the Soviet reality of decentralized decision-making through informal channels is what must be explained if we are to understand how the system operated, and why it eventually failed.

From "here" to "there"

A Coasean perspective leads one to look for the underlying property rights arrangement within the actual organizational structure of an economy. What complex array of exchanges emerged so individuals could pursue their interests as they see fit given the incentive structure? From a property rights perspective, we can usefully distinguish between cash-flow and control rights. Soviet reality was where control rights rested to a large degree at the enterprise management level, but managers did not possess full cash-flow rights. As a consequence, the appropriability of income streams is attenuated to a large extent. But precisely because monitoring costs are positive, and thus managerial discretion is possible, potential deviations can emerge between managerial decisions and economically optimal decisions. Within developed capitalist economies, decentralized monitoring mechanisms – namely the capital market, and the internal and external managerial labor market – emerge to discipline (at least in theory, and in my judgment also in practice) the behavior of managers. One way to discipline the behavior of managers is to make sure that they have both control rights and cash-flow rights. In other words, make managers residual claimants on how well a firm performs in terms of maximizing profits. Under the socialist enterprise, however, no such decentralized monitoring mechanisms emerged, and managers certainly were not residual claimants. Monitoring remained an explicit operation of the vast state bureaucracy. The system required an expanded "span of control," not impersonal market forces to do the job of disciplining behavior.

If monitoring costs are assumed to be zero, then these questions about disciplining the discretionary behavior of managers are also assumed away. But, under both socialism and capitalism, we should expect that deviations from ideal behavior are significant and require disciplinary institutions (see Moore 1974, pp. 330–3). Since under socialism the appropriability of income streams was attenuated in terms of pecuniary rewards, one should expect that managerial discretion would lead to behavior directed toward reaping non-pecuniary benefits, or attempts to transform the non-pecuniary rewards into pecuniary benefits. The enterprise manager, in other words, was placed in the prime position for rent-seeking behavior. As Jan Winiecki (1991, pp. 1–27; 52–75) has pointed out, this rent-seeking perspective is able to explain how the inefficient property rights structure persisted in the Soviet-type economies. The economic illiteracy of economic planners, the phenomena of the shortage economy and soft-budget constraints, and the *nomenklatura* system of economic appointment are woven together under the rubric of property rights analysis and rent-seeking theory to explain the allocational pattern under Soviet socialism – which spread scarce resources – not randomly as predicted by the illiteracy model – but rather in accordance with the rent-seeking activity of the ruling élite. Anderson and Boettke (1997) offer an interpretation of the Soviet system as a rent-seeking society along lines that some historians have suggested resemble the mercantilist economies of England and France, and in so doing make an argument that economics does indeed have a useful past with regard to the transition.

Emphasizing the property rights structure of the Soviet economy does not just provide a more accurate picture of how that system operated, but also is important because that system is what is currently undergoing attempts at transformation – and not the idealized model depicted in textbooks. At the time of the introduction of radical market reforms in Russia (January 1992), there existed an array of ownership claims. The right of ownership constitutes a claim to:

1   a right to use the asset;
2   the right to appropriate the returns from the asset; and
3   the right to change the asset's form and substance (see Furubotn and Pejovich 1974, p. 4).

By institution, following the standard model in new institutionalism, I mean the formal and informal rules governing the social intercourse under discussion. In this regard, when discussing the institution of ownership we are attempting to specify those formal and informal rules which govern the use, transfer, and capitalization of an asset. In a world where formal rules are absent or defined in an incoherent manner, informal rules emerge to provide a governance structure within which economic decisions will be made. How effective or ineffective this system of governance will be is an empirical matter. Both formal and informal rules can imperfectly define rights and lead to social conflict. In pre-Yeltsin Russia, private property was not abolished, despite the formal rules which said so. As Yoram Barzel has put it: "The claim that private property has been abolished in Communist states and that all property there belongs to the state seems to me to be an attempt to divert attention from who the true owners of the property are. It seems that these owners also own the rights to terminology" (Barzel 1989, p. 104, fn. 8).

The idea of collective property is incoherent. Within the ambiguous social arrangement created by the demand for observance to an incoherent formal rule, informal rules evolve to govern social affairs and ward off collapse.[5] "The distinction between the private and public sectors," Barzel states, "is not a distinction between the presence and absence of private property rights. Such rights are necessarily present in both systems. The distinction lies instead in organization, and particularly in the incentives and rewards under which producers tend to operate" (1989, p. 107). Comparative political economy is a research program which attempts to shed light on the effect on economic performance of alternative political and economic institutional arrangements. But that requires that the analyst correctly specify the alternatives being compared.

The path from "here to there" requires then not only an idea of the "there" intended, but also the "here" from which one is starting, *before* an appropriate strategy for the path can be determined. With regard to the question under examination (i.e. the transfer of ownership) the steps required for the divesture of property from some owners, the legitimation of property held by others, and the establishment of conditions for the attainment, use, transformation, capitalization, and transfer of assets for new owners are the focus of attention. The appropriate policy path is necessarily multidimensional, and grounded in the previous historical pattern of ownership. As David Stark (1992) has argued, post-Communist developments are following a path-dependent trajectory, and therefore it is more appropriate to view post-Communism as a process of transforming existing institutions, rather than a transition to new economic order lying outside of history.

Coase and the Coaseans

Some scholars, in my opinion, have misappropriated Coase's name for transition policy, precisely because they have mis-specified the starting point of the transition. During the 1980s it was argued by some scholars that since Soviet-type economies were based on communal ownership, privatization could be accomplished roughly along the following lines.[6] First, determine the aggregate value of assets in the economy. Second, divide that aggregate value by the population. Third, provide all citizens with a certificate indicating the share value in the economy. Privatization would now be achieved. A market would immediately emerge for these share values in the economy, and, as Coase argued, the initial ownership structure would not matter as individuals would engage in mutually advantageous exchange until resources were placed in their highest valued use. Moreover, since the initial distribution of shares would be based on egalitarian principles, the Second Fundamental Welfare Theorem would have the opportunity to be operationalized in a manner not before seen in a real existing political economy. In an ironic twist of fate, efficiency and equity could be achieved through the market in the former Soviet Union through an egalitarian distribution and the unhampered operation of the market economy.

No doubt Coase's work has emphasized the robust nature of exchange behavior, but the argument offered above fails on several grounds. First, it fails to recognize the existing property rights structure in Soviet-type economies. Second, the proposal is caught in the following trap – it presupposes that we can assess the asset value of the economy, when in fact the purpose of creating the market in the first place is to find out the appropriate value of assets.[7] In other words, it presupposes what it hopes to obtain. If an accurate asset value was available to economic decision-makers prior to marketization, then in fact there would be no need for marketization. Third, the understanding of the Coase theorem is based on a zero transaction cost world. In the zero transaction cost world, the initial distribution of rights would not matter as resources would flow to their highest valued use. But, the main focus of Coase's work was to direct our attention to how institutions emerge, so that individuals can cope with a world of positive transaction costs, and how various institutional environments impact upon individuals' attempts to coordinate their behavior with one another.

Coase is certainly relevant for transition economies, and his pioneering studies on the distribution of property rights are as relevant to our discussion as his work on the theory of the firm, as emphasized above. The basic unity of this Coasean project had been demonstrated by Medema (1994) and by Coase's own autobiographical reflections (see, for example, Coase 1994, pp. 3–14 and

1997). Coase, like Buchanan, conceived of economics as a science of exchange – catallaxy. The pure logic of choice might be a necessary component, but it is certainly not sufficient.[8] Rather, the focus is on the conditions of exchange, and as I have said above, how alternative institutional configurations affect exchange behavior by changing the structure of costs and benefits. The Coase Theorem, like the theory of the firm, represents a limit theorem. By postulating a zero transaction cost world, Coase was able to establish at one and the same time the basic redundancy in the Pigouvian remedy to externalities, the limits to the pure *laissez-faire* solution, and he redirects our attention to the question of comparative institutional analysis in a world of positive transaction costs and other imperfections.[9] In the zero transaction costs world, many of the institutions that we witness in the world and associate with economic vitality are demonstrated to be unnecessary. Absent transaction costs and neither the business firm nor the law would be important components of everyday principal economic phenomena such as non-interest-bearing media of exchange, long-term contracting, and entrepreneurial discovery.

The zero transaction cost world, for Coase, was a mental tool, not an assumption about the world. Following a method of contrast style of reasoning, Coase was able to simplify the real world of everyday life in order to explain it.[10] Policy analysis based on the zero transaction cost world violates the spirit of Coase's work. Instead, the lesson from Coase that should be relevant for transition policy concerns questions of structure of the law and how that structure influences the organization of production.

Think about Coase's analysis in his project on the *political economy of broadcasting*. Starting with an analysis of the British Broadcasting Corporation (BBC), Coase was led to question the arguments which justified regulation of the airwaves in general, including the Federal Communications Commission (FCC) in the US (see Coase 1959). The paper on the FCC was where Coase first clearly states the "Coase Theorem," but for our purposes the key question is his actual argument about how property rights evolve and are transferred in emerging markets. Here Coase again calls upon the proclivity of individuals to recognize the gains from exchange and move to capture them. The chaos on the airwaves was a result not of competition, but of the failure to assign broadcast rights. "Once the legal rights of the parties are established, negotiation is possible to modify the arrangements envisaged in the legal ruling, if the likelihood of being able to do so makes it worthwhile to incur the costs involved in negotiation" (Coase 1959, pp. 26–7).

It is precisely at this juncture where Coase's emphasis on the organizational structure and the importance of establishing legal rights comes into play with regard to transition economies. As argued above, a complex array of ownership rights *already* existed prior to the reform moment. Moreover, while there was a separation between control and cash-flow rights, the system allocated resources along rent-seeking lines – explaining both its inefficiency and its persistence. This is where reform must begin. The main point to emphasize is that while we must begin with the existing *de facto* rights (and perhaps simply confer *de jure* status of them, rather than attempt to transfer them to some other owners *ex ante*), these rights are not fixed in stone. As long as conditions are so established that allow for the transfer of property rights, individuals will so exchange.[11] Of course, this exchange process is sensitive dependent so no ideal static-efficiency allocation can be claimed for the end state a priori. But, the transferring of existing resources is not what is most important with regard to the transformation of a rent-seeking economy.[12] What matters most is that the very conditions which make negotiation over existing resources possible are also those conditions which allow entry of new individuals into the system, who will discover better ways to employ existing resources or perhaps even find new resources and technologies to be employed in the production process – i.e. dynamic and adaptive efficiency. Coase's work shifts our attention in terms of both understanding how the system operated in the past and the importance of the institutional environment within which economic processes are to proceed in the future.

Conclusion

Ronald Coase does not suffer from the usual hubris of the economist, or intellectual in general. This is true, from all accounts, of Coase as a person, but it is especially true of his economics. By his own account, Coase's main contribution to economic science has been to "urge the inclusion in our analysis of features of the economic system so obvious that ... they have tended to be overlooked" (1994, p. 3). And, as he further argued, "The value of including such institutional factors in the corpus of mainstream economics is made clear by recent events in Eastern Europe. These ex-Communist countries are advised to move to a market economy, and their leaders wish to do so, but without the appropriate institutions no market economy of any significance is possible" (1994, p. 6).

Adam Smith once commented that "Little else is requisite to carry a state to the highest degree of opulence from the lowest barbarism, but peace, easy taxes, and a tolerable administration of justice; all the rest being brought about by the natural course of things" (1755, p. xliii). If we unpack this sentence, then there is probably a large degree of truth to it. But unpacking all that is packed into this program for successful development has proven more difficult. What we do know, however, is that it is not just a matter of "getting the prices right." Certainly, allowing the price system to operate is now recognized to be a vital aspect of successful economies. As Coase has argued, this price system is embedded within a set of institutions. Perhaps, then, the question is one of "getting the institutions right." Large differences in per capita income across countries, Mancur Olson (1996, pp. 3–24) has argued, cannot be explained by the variables associated with standard mainstream models of growth and development. Instead, these differences are to be explained by reference to differences in the institutional environment. "Though low-income societies obtain most of the gains from self-enforcing trades," Olson maintains, "they do not realize many of the largest gains from specialization and trade. They do not have the institutions that enforce contracts impartially, and so they lose most of the gains from those transactions (like those in the capital market) that require impartial third-party enforcement. They do not have institutions that make property rights secure over the long run, so they lose most of the gains from capital-intensive production. Production and trade in these societies is further handicapped by misguided economic policies and by private and public predation. The intricate social cooperation that emerges when there is a sophisticated array of markets requires far better institutions and economic policies than most countries have" (Olson 1996, p. 22).

Mutually beneficial bargains are not enough to ensure that the gains from specialization and trade will be realized. Realization requires a complex set of institutions. What the profession has understood as the Coase Theorem is undermined by the first sentence, but the Coase Theorem as understood by Coase focused our attention on the second sentence.

References

Alchain, A. (1977) *Economic Forces at Work,* Indianapolis: Liberty Press.

Anderson, G. and Boettke, P. J. (1997) "Soviet Venality: A Rent-seeking Model of the Communist State," *Public Choice* 93: 37–53.

Anderson, T. L. and Hill, P. J. (eds.) (1996) *The Privatization Process: A Worldwide Perspective,* Lanham, MD: Rowman and Littlefield.

Barzel, Y. (1989) *The Economics of Property Rights,* New York: Cambridge University Press.

Besançon, A. (1980) "Anatomy of a Spectre," *Survey* 25 (Autumn):.

Boettke, P. J. (1990) *The Political Economy of Soviet Socialism: The Formative Years, 1918–1928,* Boston: Kluwer Academic Publishers.

Boettke, P. J. (1993) *Why Perestroika Failed: The Politics and Economics of Socialist Transformation,* New York: Routledge.

Boettke, P. J. (1994) "The Reform Trap in Politics and Economics in the Former Communist Economies," *Journal des Economistes et des Etudes Humaines* 5: 267–93.

Boycko, M., Schleifer, A. and Vishny, R. (1995) *Privatizing Russia,* Cambridge: MIT Press.

Coase, R. (1932) "Letter dated 10 October to Ronald Fowler." As quoted in Coase 1988b, p. 4.

Coase, R. (1959) "The Federal Communications Commission," *Journal of Law and Economics* 2: 1–40.

Coase, R. (1988a) *The Firm, The Market and the Law,* Chicago: University of Chicago Press.

Coase, R. (1988b) "The Nature of the Firm: Origin," *Journal of Law, Economics, & Organization* 4: (Spring): 3–17.

Coase, R. (1994) *Essays on Economics and Economists,* Chicago: University of Chicago Press.

Coase, R. (1997) "Looking for Results: An Interview with Nobel Laureate Ronald Coase on Rights, Resources and Regulation," *Reason* January: 40–6.

Demsetz, H. (1988) *The Organization of Economic Activity* vol. 1, *Ownership, Control and the Firm,* New York: Basil Blackwell.

Demsetz, H. (1989a) *The Organization of Economic Activity* vol. 2, *Efficiency, Competition and Policy,* New York: Basil Blackwell.

Demsetz, H. (1989b) *The Economics of the Business Firm: Seven Critical Commentaries.* New York: Cambridge University Press.

Feige, E. (1990) "Perestroika and Socialist Privatization," unpublished manuscript, 31 pp.

Furubotn, E. G. and Pejovich, S. (eds.) (1974) *The Economics of Property Rights*, Cambridge: Ballinger Publishing.

Granick, D. (1961) *The Real Executive: A Study of the Organization Man in Russian Industry*, New York: Doubleday.

Klein, P. (1996) "Economic Calculation and the Limits of Organization," *Review of Austrian Economics*, 9(2): 3–28.

Kuran, T. (1995) *Private Truths, Public Lies: The Social Consequences of Preference Falsification*, Cambridge: Harvard University Press.

Langlois, R. (ed.) (1986) *Economics as a Process*, New York: Cambridge University Press.

Lazonick, W. (1991) *Business Organization and the Myth of the Market Economy*, New York: Cambridge University Press.

Malia, M. (1994) *The Soviet Tragedy: A History of Socialism in Russia (1917–1991)*, New York: Free Press.

Medema, S. G. (1994) *Ronald H. Coase*, New York: St Martin's Press.

Medema, S. G. (ed.) (1995) *The Legacy of Ronald Coase in Economic Analysis*, two volumes, Aldershot: Edward Elgar Publishing.

Milgrom, P. and Roberts, J. (1992) *Economics, Organization and Management*, Englewood Cliffs, NJ: Prentice-Hall.

Moore, J. (1974) "Managerial Behavior in the Theory of Comparative Economic Systems," in E. G. Furubotn and S. Pejovich (eds.) *The Economics of Property Rights*, Cambridge: Ballinger Publishing, pp. 327–39.

Nelson, R. and Winter, S. (1983) *An Evolutionary Theory of Economic Change*, Cambridge: Harvard University Press.

Olson, M. (1996) "Big Bills Left on the Sidewalk: Why Some Nations are Rich, and Others Poor," *Journal of Economic Perspectives* 10(2): 3–24.

Rothbard, M. N. (1962) *Man, Economy and State*, two volumes, Princeton, NJ: Van Nostrand Press.

Rubin, P H. (1996) "Growing a Post-Communist Legal System," in T. L. Anderson and P. J. Hill (eds.) *The Privatization Process: A Worldwide Perspective*, Lanham, MD: Rowman and Littlefield, pp. 57–80.

Smith, A. (1937) (first published 1775) "Notes on the Wealth of Nations," as reported in the editors' Introduction to *An Inquiry into the Nature and Causes of the Wealth of Nations*, New York: Modern Library.

Stark, D. (1992) "Path Dependence and Privatization in East Central Europe," *East European Politics and Societies* 6: 17–54.

Tollison, R, and Wagner, R. (1991) "Romance, Realism, and Economic Reform," *Kyklos* 44: 57–70.

Walicki, A. (1995) *Marxism and the Leap to the Kingdom of Freedom: The Rise and Fall of the Communist Utopia*, Stanford: Stanford University Press.

Williamson, O. E. (1975) *Markets and Hierarchies*, New York: Free Press.

Williamson, O. E. (1985) *The Economic Institutions of Capitalism*, New York: Free Press.

Winiecki, J. (1991) "Resistance to Change in the Soviet Economic System: A Property Rights Approach," New York: Routledge.

6 The Soviet experiment with Pure Communism*

Introduction

In 1957, forty years after the Russian revolution, Michael Polanyi summarized the state of Soviet studies by pointing out that despite, or because of the fact that "volume upon volume of excellent scholarship [was] rapidly accumulating on the history of the Russian Revolution ... The Revolution [was] about to be quietly enshrined under a pyramid of monographs."[1] This condition continues to persist even after seventy years of reflection upon one of the most fateful events in political–economic history. Despite heroic efforts by Paul Craig Roberts[2] and Laszlo Szamuely[3] to lift the Revolution from underneath the debris of wood pulp, confusion still permeates historical discussion of the *meaning* of the Soviet experience with Communism.[4] "We have forgotten," as Polyanyi wrote, "what the Russian Revolution was about: that it set out to establish a money-less industrial system, free from the chaotic and sordid automation of the market and directed instead scientifically by one single comprehensive plan."[5]

The grand debate over the Soviet experience from 1918 to 1921 revolves around whether the Bolsheviks followed policies that were ideological in origin or were forced upon them by the necessity of civil war. If Bolshevik economics was ideological, then Marxian socialism must confront the failure of its utopia to achieve results that are even humane, let alone superior to capitalism. If it was spawned by an emergency, then the Soviet experience from 1918 to 1921 does not provide any lesson for the economic assessment of socialism. (Some recent authors wish to argue that the policies now known as "War Communism" were produced by both ideology and emergency, and, as a result, they fundamentally misunderstand the meaning of the Soviet experience with socialism.)[6] In order to evaluate these opposing interpretations, let me first lay out points of agreement and conflict among those interpreters of the Soviet experience with socialism who have established the two poles of the grand debate.

*Originally published as Boettke, P. J. (1988) "The Soviet Experiment with Pure Communism," *Critical Review* 2(4) (Fall): 149–82.

Points of agreement

Concerning the time period from 1917 to 1921, there really is no dispute over the chronology of events or the economic conditions as they existed after three years of Bolshevik rule. (The famous disputes over Soviet economic statistics do not refer to this time period.) In particular, there exists no controversy whatsoever regarding the economic condition the Russian people found themselves in after only three years of Soviet rule. William Chamberlin, for example, stated that the Russian economy of 1921 was "one of the greatest and most overwhelming failures in history."[7] "Never in all history," H. G. Wells declared, "has there been so great a debacle before."[8] The industrial collapse can be represented in statistical terms as in Table 6.1.

By 1921, all areas of economic output had fallen far below pre-war levels.[9] Industrial life and the cities, in particular, suffered a serious setback during this time, as is evidenced in population figures. "By 1920, the number of city dwellers had fallen from 19 percent of the population in 1917 to 15 percent. Moscow lost half its population, Petrograd two-thirds."[10] In 1921 the Soviet Union, as Stephen Cohen has pointed out, lay "in ruins, its national income one-third of the 1913 level, industrial production a fifth (output in some branches being virtually zero), its transportation system shattered, and agricultural production so meager that a majority of the population barely subsisted and millions of others failed even that."[11]

There is no dispute over these facts. But what the facts mean is another story. While for Polanyi or Roberts these facts depict the failure of Soviet socialism, in the eyes of Maurice Dobb, E. H. Carr, or Cohen the same facts represent the cost of civil war. The debate over the Soviet experience with socialism from 1918 to 1921 is one of intellectual history and political economy, not economic history. It is fundamentally a debate over which theoretical framework provides the best background with which to interpret the facts.

Table 6.1 Russian industrial output

Datum	1913	1921
Gross output of all industry (index)	100.00	31.00
Large-scale industry (index)	100.00	21.00
Coal (million tons)	29.00	9.00
Oil (million tons)	9.20	3.80
Electricity (million kWh)	2,039.00	520.00
Pig iron (million tons)	4.20	0.10
Steel (million tons)	4.30	0.20
Bricks (millions)	2.10	0.01
Sugar (million tons)	1.30	0.05
Railway tonnage carried (millions)	132.40	39.40
Agricultural production (index)	100.00	60.00
Imports ("1913" roubles)	1,374.00	208.00
Exports ("1913" roubles)	1,520.00	20.00

Source: Alec Nove (1984) (first published 1969) *An Economic History of the USSR*, New York: Penguin Books, p. 68.

The standard historiography

Despite an apparent dichotomy in the ethical assessment of socialism, most scholars agree with the following rough narrative of events surrounding the origins of the Soviet system. In October of 1917 (November on the Western calendar) the Bolsheviks assumed power because the provisional government was no longer able to rule. As a result of the civil war and foreign intervention, the Bolsheviks were forced to engage in emergency policies (later referred to as "War Communism") from June 1918 to April 1921. From 1921 to 1928, after the detour necessitated by war, the Bolsheviks returned to the proper economic policies of the victorious proletariat in an economically backward country (the "New Economic Policy"). In 1928, owing to the threat of military intervention and a growing economic crisis, the Stalinist regime began its "revolution from above." Policies of collectivization and industrialization were followed as the Soviet Union established the first advanced centrally planned economy. Economic historians as diverse in their appreciation of the moral ideal of socialism as Alec Nove and the late G. Warren Nutter have endorsed this view.[12]

The standard interpretation is reiterated even by some of the most important proponents of Marxian social theory. Tom Bottomore, for example, wrote that "it is a considerable exaggeration to argue ... that the period of 'War Communism' in the USSR reflected a deliberate policy to abolish the market and the price system, rather than being in large an avoidable practical response to the conditions produced by the war, the civil war and foreign intervention."[13] Bottomore defends his position by relying upon the "more balanced view" of Alec Nove.

Economists and social theorists who stress the emergency interpretation of War Communism rely considerably upon the research of Maurice Dobb, E. H. Carr, and Alec Nove. In particular, it is Dobb and Carr who turned the scholarly literature away from the once standard view that War Communism represented an attempt to implement the Marxian project of Communism to the now prevalent emergency interpretation.

Maurice Dobb

Maurice Dobb argues that while there was some ideological justification for the policies of 1918–1921, notions of establishing an immediate socialist economic order were "no more than flights of leftist fancy."[14] We must consider the policies of War Communism within the context in which they were introduced, Dobb argues. If we remember that these centralization policies fall between the more decentralized periods of the first eight months of Bolshevik rule and the New Economic Policy (NEP), then War Communism "emerges clearly as an empirical creation, not as the a priori product of theory: as an improvisation in face of economic scarcity and military urgency in conditions of exhausting civil war."[15]

The Bolsheviks had to increase centralized direction and the use of coercive measures in order to obtain and manage the resources necessary for the war effort. Lenin's regime originally tried to obtain the necessary resources for the civil war by following inflationary policies, according to Dobb. By issuing new currency the Bolsheviks were temporarily able to procure command over the necessary resources. Inflation "acts as a forced levy or tax upon the community, forcing other people to go without, in order that the government as consumer may command a larger share of the available resources."[16] In keeping with socialist principles, however, this tax was levied upon the "moneyed class, who were extensively expropriated by the fall in the value of money, and the peasantry," not the industrial worker, who was the backbone of the revolution, since it became the practice for workers to receive an increasingly large part of their wages in kind.[17]

But these inflationary policies so devalued the currency that it was impossible for the Bolsheviks to procure enough grain from the peasants. While the issuance of new roubles only increased 119% in 1918, 1919 and 1920 saw increases of 300% and 400% respectively. By October 1920, "the purchasing power of the rouble was no more than 1 per cent of what it had been in October 1917."[18] But Dobb argues that this was all in the name of raising funds for the war effort, and had nothing to do with the Marxian desire to eliminate the monetary economy and substitute for it a comprehensive central plan.[19]

Since the Soviet government could no longer obtain resources through the normal process of market exchange, even with the aid of the printing press, it became necessary to "obtain these resources only by measures of coercion, and by centralized control and distribution of supplies." Peasants were required to forfeit any surplus beyond "essential needs of subsistence and seed corn" to the Commissariat of Supplies for allocation among the army and industrial workers. The centralization of the collection and distribution of supplies was the keystone of the system."[20]

These policies of compulsory requisitioning and centralized economic control could only have been intended as expedient measures, Dobb argues, because they threatened the alliance between the peasantry and the industrial working class which was the basis of the revolution. The Kronstadt rebellion of March 1921 brought home this point with urgency.[21] The three-year reign of War Communism had left the economy in ruins and threatened the Bolsheviks' ability to maintain political power. The decision to abandon the policies of War Communism in April 1921 is seen by Dobb, however, as a "reversion to the road which was being travelled during the early months, before the onset of the civil war." "NEP," Dobb argues, "is the normal economic policy of the proletariat after the revolution."[22]

Dobb points out that his historical interpretation of War Communism and NEP directly contrasts with the predominant Western view in the 1940s that War Communism "was a product of an attempt to realise an ideal Communism, which, coming into inevitable conflict with realities, had to be scrapped in favour of a retreat in the direction of Capitalism, as represented by the New Economic Policy."[23] In a twist of scholarly fashion, Dobb's interpretation conquered the mainstream within a matter of years.

E. H. Carr

The famous historian of the Soviet Union, E. H. Carr, reiterated Dobb's interpretation of the war emergency nature of War Communism, and is probably more responsible than anyone else for promoting the "War Communism as expedient" point of view. The Bolsheviks found themselves in a theoretical and practical paradox, Carr argues. They rose to political power smoothly because of the economic backwardness of Russia; opposition came solely from the remnants of feudalism and from elements of underdeveloped capitalism. This backwardness, however, also made the task of socialist construction that much more difficult. The Bolsheviks wished to construct a socialist economic order without the advanced political (bourgeois democratic) or economic (capitalistic) development that Marxian theory had treated as essential for social change. The situation dictated slow and cautious going. The revolutionary cadre, according to Carr, knew it was necessary in theory and in practice to complete the bourgeois revolution before moving forward to the socialist revolution.

The outbreak of civil war in the summer of 1918, however, no longer afforded the Bolsheviks the luxury of slow and cautious policies. It "removed all hesitations by driving the regime forward willy-nilly at break-neck speed along the socialist road."[24] But Carr argues that the policies of War Communism were "artificial and unstable," similar to the period known as "war socialism" in Germany.[25] "It was the product of a special emergency and lacked a sufficiently solid social and economic basis to ensure its full survival (even though some of its legacies were likely to remain) when the emergency was over."[26]

War Communism consisted of two major policy objectives:

1 centralization of economic decision-making and concentration of industry; and
2 the substitution of a "natural" economy for the market economy.

Carr argues that the objective of centralization and concentration can be clearly traced to the first period of the revolution. "Lenin had long ago insisted," Carr points out, "that socialism was the logical next step forward from state capitalism, and that forms of organization inherent in the one were equally indispensable for the other." "Here war Communism" Carr continues, "was building on a foundation of what had gone before, and many of its achievements stood the test; only in their detailed application, and in the extended scope given to them were its policies afterwards subject to criticism and reversal."[27]

Policies intended to eliminate market relations, however, are not seen as products of theory by Carr. "The second element of War Communism, the substitution of a 'natural' for a 'market' economy, had no such foundations." According to Carr, this policy objective, far from following the original path of the victorious proletariat, was the exact opposite. The attempt to substitute "production for direct use rather than for a hypothetical market ... was a direct abandonment" of the policies of the first eight months, an "unprepared plunge into the unknown."[28]

But at other places in his narrative, Carr seems to suggest that the policies of War Communism were not just emergency measures, but also seemed to be "an authentic advance into socialist order."[29] At one point he even refers to War Communism as "the attempt to implant socialism by shock tactics."[30] And in another instance, Carr states that "the real issue in the period of war communism was not the nationalization of industry ... but the attempt of the state to administer industry on socialist lines."[31] "But the civil war," he is always quick to add, "dwarfed every other issue."[32]

Forced requisitioning was introduced because the "needs of the Red Army and the urban population could not be met in a devastated, mutilated and disorganized country by anything short of the total surplus of agricultural population."[33] War emergency, in the final analysis, not adherence to any socialist principles, dictated policy objectives.

The crisis situation demonstrated the need to militarize the economy. Small-scale peasant agriculture was inconsistent with the objective of feeding the industrial workers. Large-scale, collective farming was necessary. Arguments in favor of "collective cultivation" are described by Carr as irrefutable "from the standpoint of theoretical socialism or of practical efficiency."[34] Unfortunately, collective farming was not implemented; only grain requisitioning occurred. The mistake committed during War Communism, with regard to agriculture, was treating the food shortage as a problem of "collection and distribution" and "not of production."[35]

Industry also needed to be mobilized for the war effort. All major industry had to be transformed into "a supply organization for the Red Army." Industrial policy became "an item of military strategy" where "every decision was dictated by emergency and taken without regard to long-term prospects and principles." The civil war drove home the necessity, according to Carr, for industry to come under "centralized control, direction, and planning."[36] Mobilization of labor was necessary to insure that "every man and every machine" was allocated in the "interests of military victory over the 'white' armies." Labor policy "became a matter of recruiting workers for the war effort and of sending them where they were most urgently required."[37]

Carr argues that declarations of anti-market principles and theoretical references to overcoming the "anarchy of production" by such leading theoreticians as Bukharin or Kritsman were "ex post facto justifications of something which had not been expected but which it had not been possible to prevent."[38] Carr even ascribes war expediency to passages that seem to suggest the socialist aspirations of the decision-makers. A passage from the party program at the Eighth Party Congress in March 1919, for example, states that the "maximum utilization" of the labor force for the purpose of the "planned development of the national economy" must be the "immediate task of the economic policy of the Soviet power." The program further states that the "socialist method of production" can only be made possible by such mobilization efforts.[39] But Carr argues that these passages demonstrate merely the key function of the trade unions in the civil war emergency.[40] Furthermore, he claims that "the argument for the permanent and unlimited conscription of labor by the state, like the contemporary argument for the abolition of money, reads like an attempt to provide theoretical justification for a harsh necessity which it had been impossible to avoid."[41]

So while the exigencies of War Communism, which demanded securing resources for the Red Army and the urban population, could be described by Carr at one point as "a foretaste of the future communist society" where "methods of exchange" were substituted for by "the principles of taking from each according to his capacity and giving to each according to his need," Carr opts to interpret the policy of forced requisitioning as being "rendered imperative by the civil war" and justifies it "on grounds of military necessity."[42] It is clear that War Communism was brought on by military emergency, Carr argues, because such "hand-to-mouth policies" could only be tolerated so long as the war lasted. Grain requisitioning, in particular, "whose raison d'être lay in the continuous and inexorable need to meet today's emergency," could not last beyond the emergency situation. The peasants' loyalty to the Bolshevik regime, and "reluctant submission to the requisitions" was based on the "fear of a 'white' restoration," and once that fear passed, continued adherence to "oppressive exactions" produced peasant resentment and unrest. This culminated in peasant uprising beginning in 1920 and continuing through the spring of 1921.

The financial burden of the civil war and industrialization, moreover, called for the nationalization of the banks, and the subsequent devaluing of the currency. "The printing of notes," Carr argues, "remained the sole serious available source of funds to meet current public expenditure and to make advances to industry." So although the financial policies of War Communism produced the "virtual elimination of money from the economy," it would be quite mistaken to view this result as the product of any anti-market intention. The destruction of the rouble, according to Carr, was "in no sense the produce either of doctrine or of deliberate design."[44] The collapse of the currency had originally "been treated by every responsible Soviet leader as an unmixed evil against which all possible remedies should be invoked." It was only after no remedy could be found that Soviet leaders began to make a virtue out of the elimination of money, and "the view became popular that the destruction of the currency had been a deliberate act of policy."[45]

The crisis atmosphere of March 1921 led to the substitution of the NEP for the "more extreme policies of war communism." Carr acknowledges that Lenin and the other Bolshevik leaders gave mixed accounts of the significance of the decision to change course, but claims that it was "unanimously accepted as a welcome and necessary relief."[46] This contention simply ignores the subsequent debate over NEP within the Bolshevik cadre.[47] Carr, however, finds it convenient to view NEP as an uncontroversial move away from the pragmatic, emergency-induced but problem-plagued policies of War Communism. The policies of grain requisitioning, mobilization of labor, centralization of economic decision-making, and the destruction of the currency that were followed from 1918 to 1921 are seen by Carr as predominantly the result of emergency circumstances, not adherence to Marxian principles. "NEP was a retracing of steps from a regrettable, though no doubt enforced, digression and a return to the safe path which was being followed before June 1919."[48]

While pointing out those traces of both the emergency interpretation and the ideological interpretation can be found in Lenin's writings in the post-war Communist era, Carr relies upon Lenin's description of NEP "As a resumption of the true line laid down by him in the spring of 1918 and interrupted only by the civil war emergency."[49] It was military concerns, not economic theory, that dictated the policies of War Communism. NEP was the path to the road of economic development on the way to socialism.

Stephen Cohen

The Dobb–Carr interpretation receives perhaps its strongest support from the pen of political historian Stephen Cohen. Cohen, the biographer of Nikolai Bukharin (the economic architect of both War Communism and NEP), has defended War Communism as an emergency measure in all his writings. Intimately connected to Cohen's defense of War Communism as an expedient is his commitment to NEP as a model of decentralized socialism.

The policies of War Communism, Cohen argues, "originated not in the party's ideology, but in response to the perilous military situation that suddenly confronted the Bolsheviks with the outbreak of civil war in the summer of 1918." These policies were "born and took shape in the crucible of military expediency and the Bolsheviks' desperate efforts to survive as the government of Soviet Russia."[50]

It is indeed ironic that the biographer of Bukharin would hold such a position. Bukharin himself was very explicit in his understanding of War Communism and the meaning of NEP. "We conceived War Communism" Bukharin admits, "as the universal, so to say 'normal' form of the economic policy of the victorious proletariat and not as being related to the war, that is, conforming to a definite state of the civil war."[51] Bukharin understood NEP to be an admission of, and a retreat from, the failure of War Communism. It was "not only a strategic retreat, but the solution to a large social, organizational problem." The Bolsheviks had tried to take on the organization of the entire economy, and by 1922 Bukharin readily admitted that "from the viewpoint of economic rationality this was madness."[52]

A rethinking of the principles of socialism was called for on the part of Bukharin and other Bolsheviks. As Bukharin put it, "the transition to the new economic policy represented the collapse of our illusions."[53] Socialism, in its Marxian sense, had been tried and had failed. The search began for a "feasible socialism." The search continues today. But we cannot hide from the historical lesson, and its theoretical significance: the search for "socialism with a human face" may well be inconsistent with the socialist dream of overcoming the "anarchy of production."[54] Perhaps Bukharin understood this. Perhaps he even understood the nature of the problem and its significance better than all but a few have since.

Criticisms of the standard account

The standard account is deficient for two reasons. First, economic historians and political economists have failed to take seriously the policy prescriptions of early twentieth-century European and Russian Marxism.[55] Leading economic historians, such as Alexander Gerschenkron, argue that little or nothing in the Soviet experience needs to be explained or understood in terms of Marxism. Gerschenkron summarizes his position by arguing that "the economic order (or disorder) as was developed in Soviet Russia was created not in obedience to any theoretical tenets, but as a pragmatic response to the exigencies of the practice with power mechanics of the dictatorship well in mind ... Hardly anything in the momentous story of Soviet economic policies needs, or suffers, explanation in terms of its derivation from Marx's economic theories."[56] Alec Nove, similarly, argues with regard to the early policies of the Bolsheviks that Marxian ideology was used only as an *ex post* rationalization for policies introduced as practical responses to emergency situations.[57] I contend that the standard account of historians, like Gerschenkron or Nove, misunderstands the policy prescriptions suggested by Marxian political economy and underestimates the ideological commitment of the "old" Bolshevik cadre.[58]

While Marx did not wish to write "recipes for the cookshops of the future" there is no doubt about the broad outline of Marx's project. His project entailed the rationalization of politics and economics. Rationalization of the economy required the substitution of a "settled plan," which achieved *ex ante* coordination, for the "anarchy of the market": the substitution of production for direct use for production for exchange. As Marx argued in *Capital*:

> The life-process of society, which is based on the process of material production, does not strip off its mystical veil until it is treated as production by freely associated men, and is consciously regulated by them in accordance with a settled plan.[59]

Furthermore, consider the following position taken by the young Marx in the Paris manuscripts:

> The positive transcendence of private property as the appropriation of human life, is therefore the positive transcendence of all estrangement – that is to say, the return of man from religion, family, state, etc., to his human, i.e. social, existence.[60]

The abolition of private property in the means of production and the substitution of a settled plan for the market has the consequence of rationalizing economic life and transcending man's alienated social existence. This is Marx's "economic" project.

Marx's political project, on the other hand, required the establishment of "classless" politics. Marx's political project was one of radical democracy, one which included universal suffrage and ensured full participation. Since to Marx the state was an instrument of class conflict, the disappearance of class meant the disappearance of the state and political power. But this did not mean the disappearance of social or "classless" politics.[61]

The Marxian rationalization project demanded a reconciliation of the conflict between the public and the private spheres of life. Marx's vision required the broadening of the public sphere to all areas of human existence.[62] As Don Lavoie has argued:

> Karl Marx conceived of central planning as an attempt to resolve this inherent contradiction between the private and public spheres of society. As in any genuinely radical perspective, his particular diagnosis of the problem is inextricably bound up with his utopia, his notion of the cure. Marx saw the problem as being located in the competitive private sphere, the market system, where separate, divided, or "alienated" interests contend with one another for resources. He argued that, so long as democratic institutions tried to merge themselves with this competitive sphere, they would invariably succumb to it. The solution, then, was to eradicate competitive market relations and to replace them with a broadening of the democratically based public sphere to encompass all of social life ... Social problems would henceforth be resolved not by meekly interfering with a competitive market order but by taking over the whole process of social production from beginning to end.[63]

The task of eradicating market relations and "taking over the whole process of social production from beginning to end" constitutes the economic policy followed by the Bolsheviks from 1918 to 1921. War Communism represents the conscious and deliberate attempt to realize Marx's utopia. As Alexander Rustow argued, "There can be no doubt that Lenin acted as a Marxist during this seizure of power and viewed his mission as one of carrying out the Marxist program under his regime."[64]

The second reason that standard accounts fail is that they do not account for the economic coordination problems that the Bolsheviks faced in implementing their policies. The theoretical debate over the feasibility of economic calculation under socialism (which first took place among German-speaking economists and sociologists during the 1920s and later among the technical economists in English-speaking countries during the 1930s and 1940s) seems to be irrelevant to the standard economic historian. The typical attitude appears to be that while the theoretical debate might be interesting in itself, it has nothing to add to our analysis of the practice of socialism. This kind of theory–practice split suggests an unhealthy state – either implying that theory has gone off in an esoteric direction and become irrelevant for understanding practical problems, or that economic historians are failing to use theoretical developments to aid them in interpreting reality. While both historical research on the Soviet experience and theoretical discussion about possible socialist worlds continues to accumulate, there does not appear to be a healthy cross-fertilization. As a result, both the historical interpretation of the Soviet economy and the theoretical discussion of socialist economics seem to misunderstand the significance of the historical lesson of the Soviet system.

But, as F. A. von Hayek has argued, "Even the most careful study of the Russian facts cannot lead very far if it is not guided by a clear conception of what the problem is; i.e. if it is not undertaken by a person who, before he embarks on the investigation of the special problems of Russia, has arrived at a clear idea of the fundamental task that economic planning involves."[66] Socialism, in its original intent, faces the problem of substituting for the "blind forces of the market" a conscious and deliberate plan that can maintain advanced material standards of living and promote the flourishing of human potential. The Russian experience provides important insights into the feasibility of that quest.

The alternative account

Before Dobb and Carr, most historians and political economists understood the failure of War Communism to be a direct demonstration of problems of the Marxian project. Economists such as K. Leites,[67] Arthur Shadwell,[68] Leo Pasvolsky,[69] and Boris Brutzkus[70] all understood the Russian experience as an attempt to realize Marx's utopia. This interpretation of events, however, was buried under what became the authoritative account of Dobb and Carr. The original account, though, received strong support in the hands of Michael Polanyi and Paul Craig Roberts.

Polanyi argued that the Soviet experience confirms Mises' original contention that socialism, in its original Marxian sense, is technically impossible. "The only full-scale attempt to [direct all resources of an industrial system from one center] was the one undertaken in Soviet Russia during the last six or eight months of 1920; and the results were disastrous."[71] Mises was proven right.

The program of Marxian central planning died in March 1921 with the introduction of NEP, but the ideology of socialism did not. The Soviet economy, Polanyi argues, was turned into a military state-capitalist system. "The Five-Year Plans with all their sound and fury are but the parading of a dummy dressed up in the likeness of the original purpose of socialism."[72] We have forgotten what the Revolution was all about when we view it otherwise.

Roberts, following on Polanyi, demonstrates that War Communism was not conceived as a set of emergency measures by the Bolshevik leaders at the time. Rather, it was an outright attempt to abolish market relations. He points out that in the standard account, such as that of Dobbs, Lenin is quoted only after the establishment of NEP. In addition, while several accounts allow for some ideological influence, they blend ideology and emergency in such a way such that ideology quickly falls into the background, and the conditions of the time become the motive force behind Soviet economic policy.[73]

In order to combat the emergency interpretation, Roberts turns to evidence from Marx and the "early" Lenin. He demonstrates that Lenin understood that in Marx's critique of capitalism there existed a positive vision of socialism. The Marxian theory of alienation and its relation to commodity production play a crucial role in understanding the motivation behind the attempt to abolish all market relations during War Communism. Lenin *et al.* sought to abolish the anarchy of capitalist production and substitute for it a comprehensive planning system. For in an economy where market forces were allowed to continue to operate, alienation would persist, and the Marxian dream would be unfulfilled.

The utter collapse that occurred due to the attempt to implement Marxian socialism forced Lenin to put an end to ideological aspirations, at least for the time being, in order to avoid losing control of the government. He chose to maintain political power at the expense of strict adherence to ideological principles.[74] "Lenin thought," argues Roberts, "That the reintroduction of market exchange was necessary to retain power"; he "understood the practical need to sacrifice doctrine to power rather than the other way around." Thus, "it is clear that the program of eliminating commodity production was abandoned not because it was a wartime measure unsuited to peacetime but because it had caused economic disruption and dissatisfaction that were threats to the political power of the bolsheviks."[75]

Roberts concludes by issuing a challenge to those who interpret War Communism as a set of expedient measures:

> Those who maintain that the policies of War Communism were temporary measures to cope with war and inflation rather than an effort to establish a socialist organization should explain why Lenin repeatedly described the policies as efforts to establish socialism. If they were wartime policies, why should Lenin not have said so? If in fact the measures were meant to be temporary and were a response to war and inflation, Lenin's admission that he and the R.C.P.(B.) had made mistakes in their efforts to introduce socialism was not only needless and erroneous but also a fabrication.[76]

Evidence from the old Bolsheviks

Lenin argued that the imperialist World War I had ripened the conditions for the revolution. Politically, the war had intensified the exploitation of the working class. Economically, the necessities of war planning had created a greater concentration of capital and had brought production under the conscious control of society. Lenin did not intend to abolish war planning but to transform it into a model of socialist organization. As he wrote in December 1916:

> The war has reaffirmed clearly enough and in a very practical way ... that modern capitalist society, particularly in the advanced capitalist countries, has fully matured for the transition to socialism. If, for instance, Germany can direct the economic life of 66 million people from a single, central institution ... then the same can be done, in the interests of nine-tenths of the population, but the non-properties masses if their struggle is directed

by the class-conscious workers... All propaganda for socialism must be refashioned from abstract and general to concrete and directly practical; expropriate the banks and, relying on the masses, carry out in their interests the very same thing the W.U.M.B.A. [i.e. the Weapons and Ammunition Supply Department] is carrying out in Germany.[77]

With elimination of private ownership of the means of production, and political power passing directly to the proletariat, Lenin believed that "these very conditions are a pledge of success for society's transformation that will do away with the exploitation of man by man and ensure the well-being of everyone."[78] Lenin argued that it was an utter mistake to suggest, because of some preconceived notion that conditions were not ripe, that the working class should support the bourgeois government, or that the proletariat should renounce its leading role in convincing the people of the urgency of taking practical steps toward the establishment of socialism.[79]

"We [Bolsheviks]," Lenin wrote, "put the issue of socialism not as a jump, but as a practical way out of the present debacle."[80] The steps Lenin advocated were nationalization of land, state control over banks and the establishment of a single state bank, control over the big capitalist syndicates and a progressive income tax. "Economically," Lenin argued, "these measures are timely; technically, they can be carried out immediately; politically they are likely to receive the support of the overwhelming majority of the peasants, who have everything to gain by these reforms."[81]

Only by implementing socialist policies could Russia avert catastrophe. This theme of Lenin's was reiterated in "The Impending Catastrophe and How to Combat It."[82] What was needed, according to Lenin, was for the government, a real revolutionary government, to take steps toward introducing the socialization of production; only by such steps would Russia escape disaster. The chief and principal measure for averting catastrophe was to increase control of the production and distribution of goods, i.e. to rationalize the economic process. Lenin's program of control, which he argued could be established by a workers' state "in the first weeks of its existence," consisted of:

1   nationalization of all banks and the creation of a central bank;
2   nationalization of syndicates;
3   abolition of commercial secrecy;
4   compulsory syndication; and
5   compulsory organization of the population.

The creation of a central bank, in particular, was essential to Lenin, because the principal nerve center of modern economic life was the bank. One cannot regulate economic life without taking over the banks — control over the banks allowed the unification of accountancy.[83]

"We cannot be revolutionary democrats in the twentieth century and in a capitalist country," Lenin wrote, "if we fear to advance toward socialism."[84]

There "can be no advance except towards socialism." Capitalism in Russia had become monopoly capitalism due to the imperialist war. Monopoly capitalism develops into state monopoly capitalism. Yet the state is nothing but the organization of the ruling class. If you substitute a revolutionary democratic state for a capitalist state, Lenin argued, "you will find that, given a really revolutionary-democratic state, state-monopoly capitalism inevitably and unavoidably implies a step, and more than one step, toward socialism!" "For socialism," Lenin continued, "is merely the next step forward from state-capitalist monopoly which is made to serve the interests of the whole people."[85]

These themes are perhaps best articulated in Lenin's two most important works, *Imperialism, The Highest State of Capitalism* and *The State and Revolution*.[86] *Imperialism* set out to explain how the world economic system had changed, and how the war was the inevitable outcome of this change. *State and Revolution* concerned itself with the nature of the state, its use in the revolution and subsequent dictatorship of the proletariat, and its inevitable "withering away" in the post-revolutionary world. The unifying theme in both works, from an economic perspective, is the necessity of control mechanisms for rationalizing social production.

The increasing concentration of capital in the epoch of finance capital had the advantage of bringing economic life under conscious control. The chaotic process of free competition had been overcome, Lenin argued. "Capitalism in its imperialist stage," he wrote, "leads directly to the most comprehensive socialisation of production; it, so to speak drags the capitalists, against their will and consciousness, into some sort of new social order, a transitional one from free competition to complete socialisation."[87]

The era of finance capital had laid the necessary groundwork for complete socialization. The interlocking of business and banking had transformed the world economy, shifting the social relations of production away from capitalism. As Lenin argued:

> When a big enterprise assumes gigantic proportions, and, on the basis of an exact computation of mass data, organizes according to plan the supply of primary raw materials to the extent of two-thirds, or three-fourths, of all that is necessary for tens of millions of people; when the raw materials are transported in a systematic and organized manner to the most suitable places of production, sometimes situated hundreds or thousands of miles from each other; when a single centre directs all the consecutive stages of processing the material right up to the manufacture of numerous varieties of finished articles; when these products are distributed according to a single plan among tens and hundreds of millions of consumers ... then it becomes evident that we have socialisation of production and not mere "interlocking."[88]

In *State and Revolution* Lenin repeated that the epoch of finance capital and the imperialist war had transformed capitalism into monopoly capitalism, providing the necessary prerequisites for transforming the social relations of production. "The proximity of such capitalism to socialism should serve genuine representatives of the proletariat as an argument proving the proximity, facility, feasibility and urgency of socialist revolution," Lenin wrote.[89] The "mechanism of social management" necessary for social transformation was easily at hand, and was demonstrated in such state-capitalist monopoly business organizations as the postal service. Lenin argued that once the workers overthrew the bourgeoisie then they would inherit a "splendidly-equipped mechanism" that could easily be run by the united workers. This presented the proletariat with a "concrete, practical task which [could] immediately be fulfilled." "To organize the whole economy," Lenin wrote, "on the lines of the postal service so that the technicians, foremen and accountants, as well as all officials, shall receive salaries no higher than 'a workman's wage', all under the control and leadership of the armed proletariat – that is our immediate aim. This is the state and this is the economic foundation we need."[90]

Or as Lenin put the matter later in the text:

> Given these economic preconditions, it is quite possible, after the overthrow of the capitalists and the bureaucrats to proceed immediately, overnight, to replace them in the control over production and distribution, in the work of keeping account of labour and products, by the armed workers, by the whole of the armed proletariat ... Accounting and control – that is mainly what is needed for 'smooth working', for the proper functioning, of the first phase of communist society.[91]

With the political and economic task of overthrowing the bourgeoisie and bringing social life under rational control in mind, Lenin broke off from completing *State and Revolution*. The events of the fall of 1917 had transformed Lenin's activity from theorizing about revolution to revolutionary praxis. As Lenin put it on November 30, 1917, "It is more pleasant and useful to go through the 'experience of the revolution' than to write about it."[92]

Overnight the new revolutionary government sought to implement its program by degree. Leon Trotsky, for example, described Lenin's first appearance before the Congress after taking power with the following narrative: "Lenin, gripping the edges of the reading-stand, let little winking eyes travel over the crowd as he stood there waiting, apparently oblivious to the long-rolling ovation, which lasted several minutes. When it finished, he said simply, 'We shall now proceed to construct the socialist order.' "[93] Having wrested political control from the provisional government the Bolsheviks were now "in a position to carry out the great economic revolution to which the political revolution was only a prelude, introduce socialism forthwith and transform the whole order of Society."[94]

The economic transformation of Russian society consisted of implementing five major principles of social organization:

1   Elimination of private property in land and the means of production, and the maximum extension of State ownership. This required that the working class take control of the banks, railways, shipping, mining, large-scale industry, foreign trade, etc.
2   The forced allocation and mobilization of labor. Militarization of labor was necessary in order to allocate labor resources, just like other resources, in the construction of socialism.
3   Centralized management of production and distribution of resources, deemed necessary for rationalizing the economic process.
4   The introduction of class and socialist principles of distribution.
5   The abolition of commodity and money relations and the substitution of a "natural economy" for the market economy. The elimination of the monetary economy and commodity production were deemed necessary for the "defetishization" of economic life and the transcendence of man's alienated social existence.[95]

Taken in combination, these policies constituted the economic program of War Communism, but at the time it was known simply as Communism. As Victor Serge reports in his *Memoirs of a Revolutionary, 1901–1941*, "The social system in these years was later called 'War Communism.' At the time it was called simply 'Communism,' and anyone who, like myself, went so far as to consider it purely temporary was looked upon with disdain."[96] This system attempted to substitute a unified plan of economic life, i.e. rational social relations of production, for the chaotic and exploititive relations of production that existed under capitalism.

Through a series of decrees, resolutions and party platforms, the Bolsheviks set about implementing the socialist project. By December 1917 the Supreme Economic Council was established and the banks had been nationalized. In January 1918, a declaration of the rights of working and exploited people was issued, abolishing the exploitation of man by man. The decree, however, also embodied a call for a universal labor duty. Labor conscription was introduced to ensure socialist victory in eliminating the parasitic strata of society and in rationally organizing the economy. By July 1918, the Soviet Constitution described labor as an obligation of all citizens and declared that whoever does not work shall not eat. And, throughout 1919, labor conscription, i.e. militarization, continued to extend to all categories of labor until it was declared by the State Council on Defense that leaving one's job would be considered desertion.[97]

This militarization plan was extended not only in production but in distribution. Throughout 1918 and 1919 collective exchanges were established, and the trade unions were employed to assure the central distribution of foodstuffs. Trotsky, for example, in a decree of 17 February 1918, called upon all local Soviets, railway committees and patrols to fight unorganized trading. The punishment for illegal trading of food was either confiscation of all foodstuffs or immediate death.[98]

In addition to the above-mentioned policies, the Bolsheviks issued many other decrees in order to initiate their economic program. Inheritance, for example, was abolished in May 1918, and in June 1918 large-scale industry was nationalized. The party program of the Eighth Party Congress, adopted in March 1919, called for increased centralization and for the abolition of money. And as late as November 1920 (*after* the civil war), the Supreme Economic Council nationalized all industry (even small-scale enterprises). Only the Kronstadt Rebellion of March 1921 would steer the Bolsheviks off this track of outright socialist construction.[99]

In his pamphlet, *The Immediate Tasks of the Soviet Government*, Lenin argued that the problem confronting the Bolsheviks was that of organizing social administration. The decisive means of solving this problem was implementing "the strictest and country-wide accounting and control of production and distribution of goods." The successful implementation of accounting and control alongside the amalgamation of all banks into a single state bank would transform the banks into "nodal points of public accounting under socialism" and allow the Soviets to organize "the population into a single cooperative society under proletariat management."[100] The possibility of socialism required, according to Lenin, the subordination of the desires of the many to the unity of the plan. The rhetoric of workers' control and workers' democracy meant something entirely different from the model of decentralized socialism that is promulgated today. To Lenin, as to most Marxists at that time, workers' control was a method by which central planning could be accomplished, and not a decentralized alternative to it. As Silvana Malle points out, "in Lenin's model of power, workers' control would not evolve in any decentralized form, but, on the contrary, would facilitate the flow of information to the centre and the correct implementation of central guidelines."[101]

Centralized planning and control were the essential elements of Leninist socialism. "It must be said," Lenin wrote, "that large-scale machine industry – which is precisely the material source, the productive source, the foundation of socialism – calls for absolute and strict unity of will ... The technical, economic and historical necessity of this is obvious and all those who have thought about socialism have always regarded it as one of the conditions of socialism." And how can such strict unity of will be guaranteed" Lenin asked rhetorically. "By thousands subordinating their will to the will of one."[102]

This theme of strict unity of the plan was echoed throughout various speeches and writings, and not just Lenin's. Trotsky, for example, during a speech to the Central Executive Committee on 14 February 1917, repeated the necessity of rationalizing the economic life of Russia through strict conformity to the plan. "Only a systematic organization of production," he said, "that is, one based on a universal plan – only a rational and economic distribution of all products can save the country. And that means socialism."[103] This project entailed the abolition of private ownership and the replacement of production for exchange by production for direct use. The chaotic process of market exchange and production must not merely be tampered with, but abolished. "Socialist organization of production," Trotsky declared in 1920, "begins with the liquidation of the market ... Production shall be geared to society's needs by means of a unified economic plan."[104]

The ubiquitous nature of monetary calculation under capitalist methods of production was to be replaced by the introduction of strict accounting and control. The economic transformation demanded the abolition of the "alienated ability of mankind," i.e. money, and the substitution of moneyless accounting for monetary calculation. Yu Larin, who was commissioned by Lenin to study the operation of the German war economy and ways to implement that model in Russia, argued fervently for the elimination of all market exchange and production. Larin, at the Party Congress in March 1918, argued that a moneyless system of accounting should be pursued post-haste. The nationalization of banks provided the framework to eliminate hand-to-hand currency and to transform the financial institutions of Russia into, as Lenin put it, "nodal points of public accounting." Under the new economic organization of society a circulating medium was rapidly becoming unnecessary. "Money as a circulating medium," Larin declared, "can already be got rid of to a considerable degree."[105] By May of 1918 the party declared that all state enterprises should hand over circulating media to the People's Bank, and in August 1918 the Supreme Economic Council instructed all managers of industry that settlements of deliveries and receipts of commodities should consist of book entries; in no circumstance should money be used in transactions. And Osinskii, who was the manager of the State Bank and the first chairman of the Supreme Economic Council, described the Bolshevik monetary policy in 1920 as having as "its main aim [the creation of] normal conditions of exchange without money between parts of the uniform and mostly socialized national economy."[106]

The Bolshevik program was best articulated in the Program of the Communist Party of Russia adopted at the Eighth Party Congress in March 1919, and in the popular exposition of that program, *The ABC of Communism*, by Bukharin and Preobrazhensky.[107] Bukharin gave a detailed presentation of the economic organization of Communist society in his chapter: "Communism and the Dictatorship of the Proletariat." He argued that "the basis of communist society must be the social ownership of the means of production and exchange." Under these circumstances "society will be transformed into a huge working organization for cooperative production." The anarchy of production will cease as rationality is imposed upon the economic life process. "In such a social order, production will be organized."

No longer will one enterprise compete with another, the factories, workshops, mines, and other productive institutions will all be subdivisions, as it were, of one vast people's workshop, which will embrace the entire national economy of production. It is obvious that so comprehensive an organization presupposes a general plan of production. If all the factories and workshops together with the whole of agricultural production are combined to form an immense cooperative enterprise, it is obvious that everything must be precisely calculated. We must *know in advance* how much labour to assign to the various branches of industry; what products are required and how much of each it is necessary to produce; how and where machines must be provided. These and similar details must be thought out beforehand, with approximate accuracy at least; and the work must be guided in conformity with our calculations. This is how the organization of communist production will be effected.[108]

The planning process was to be entrusted to "various kinds of bookkeeping offices and statistical bureau." Accounts would be kept (day-to-day) of production and its needs. All decisions for the allocation and distribution of resources necessary for social production would be orchestrated by the planning bureau. "Just as in an orchestra the performers watch the conductor's baton and act accordingly." Bukharin wrote, "so here all will consult the statistical reports and will direct their work accordingly."[109]

By achieving *ex ante* coordination of economic activity through the substitution of production for direct use for production for exchange, Bukharin understood that, organizationally, the need for money would disappear. "Money," he simply asserted, "would no longer be required" under these circumstances. The rationalization of economic life under Communism would eliminate the waste of capitalist production and lead to increased productivity. This burst of productivity would free individuals from the "chains imposed upon them by nature." The utopian promise of this project was that "concurrently with the disappearance of man's tyranny over man, the tyranny of nature over man will likewise vanish. Men and women will for the first time be able to lead a life worthy of thinking beings instead of a life worthy of brute beasts."[110]

Only the scientific organization of production under the direction of a unified plan constructed by the dictatorship of the proletariat could put an end to the capitalist anarchy of production and eliminate the tyranny of man over man. With the breakdown of commodity production and its replacement by the "socio-natural system of economic relations, the corresponding ideological categories also burst, and once this is so, the theory of the economic process is confronted with the need for a transition to natural economic thinking, i.e. to the consideration of both society and its parts as systems of fundamental elements in their natural form."[111] Social relations would no longer be veiled by the commodity fetishism of the monetary exchange system.

This project of rationalization and emancipation is spelled out in the party program adopted at the Eighth Congress. In the realm of economic affairs this amounted to expropriating the expropriators, increasing the productive forces of society by eliminating the contradictions of capitalism, mobilizing labor, organizing the trade unions, educating the workers, and basically, securing "the maximum solidarisation of the whole economic apparatus."[112] It was to accomplish this goal that the Bolsheviks seized the banks and merged them into a single State bank. The bank, thus, "became an instrument of the workers' power and a lever to promote economic transformation." The bank would become an apparatus of unified bookkeeping. "In proportion as the organization of a purposive social economy is achieved, this will lead to the disappearance of banks, and to their conversion into the central bookkeeping establishment of communist society." The immediate elimination of money was not yet possible, but the party was moving in that direction. "Upon the basis of the nationalisation of banking, the Russian Communist Party endeavors to promote a series of measures favouring a moneyless system of account keeping, and paving the way for the abolition of money."[113]

The Bolsheviks did not just accept this program in the heat of civil war as many historians assert. The civil war no doubt affected the way the program was implemented, but the program itself was clearly ideological in origin. It emerged out of the conscious attempt to achieve Marx's utopia. Even after the civil war had ended, the Bolsheviks embarked upon continued efforts to rationalize the economy. For example, the "Outstanding Resolutions on Economic Reconstruction" (adopted by the Ninth Congress of the Russian Communist Party in April 1920) argued that "the basic condition of economic recovery of the country is the undeviating carrying out of a *unified economic plan*."[114] And in November 1920, V. Milyutin, then Assistant President of the Supreme Economic Council, announced the decree of the Council to nationalize even small industrial enterprises and bring them under conscious control.[115] Only the insurgency of the sailors at Kronstadt convinced the Bolsheviks to reconsider their policy.

State capitalism and NEP

Those writers who support the emergency interpretation of War Communism rely upon Lenin's late description of NEP as a return to his 1918 position. But is this really the case? In his defense of the introduction of NEP, *The Tax in Kind (The Significance of the New Policy and Its Conditions)*,[116] Lenin argued that NEP was a return to his 1918 position that state capitalism was the transitional form of social organization between capitalism and socialism. But we must keep in mind Lenin's theory of the state and his theory of social relations of production under imperialism.

In *The Tax in Kind*, Lenin reprints much of the argument contained in his 1918 pamphlet, *Left-Wing Childishness and the Petty-Bourgeois Mentality*, which was a broadside against Bukharin and other left-wing Bolsheviks on the Brest Peace and the issue of "state capitalism." In the 1918 polemic, Lenin argued that history had witnessed an unusual event. The Russian people had successfully introduced the proper political basis for Communism with the dictatorship of the proletariat and the organization of the Soviets. But Russia was not fully developed economically. Germany, on the other hand, Lenin argued, was backward politically but advanced economically. The immediate task of the Russian people was to model their economy after the German war-planning machine. They were to "spare no effort in copying it and not shrink from adopting dictatorial methods to hasten the copying of it."[117]

The German model, Lenin argued, was "the last word" in modern large-scale capitalism, incorporating advanced engineering and planned organization. But the system was subordinated to a "Junker-bourgeois imperialism." If the system could be made to serve the interest of the proletariat, then socialism was not only possible, but immediate. "Cross out, the words in italics [Junker-bourgeois imperialism], and in place of the militarist, Junker, bourgeois, imperialist state put also a state, but of a different social type, of a different class content – a Soviet state, that is, a proletariat state, and you will have the sum total of the conditions necessary for socialism."[118] Thus, despite accounts that claim that Lenin did not have a model of socialist organization because Marxism was confined to a critique of capitalism, it seems that there was little doubt in Lenin's mind what socialism entailed. And it had nothing to do with the reintroduction of market methods of production, as under NEP.

The characterization of the years before the introduction of NEP as a transition period did not refer to a period of market-based "socialism," but instead to the first phase of Communism, which would last a generation or so – until the people had become so acculturated that the door would swing open for the advancement to full Communism. This was explained by both Lenin and Bukharin in their theoretical works prior to 1921. The market was to be abolished and replaced by a unified plan which would achieve *ex ante* coordination of production and distribution. War Communism was the deliberate attempt to achieve this outcome. But, as Lenin wrote in 1921, this method of economic organization proved to be a mistake. "We made the mistake," Lenin admits, "of deciding to go over directly to communist production and distribution."[119] Always the master of political double-speak, however, Lenin is able to turn this admission into an excuse for why the decision was forced upon them. It is his double-speak that caught up commentators like Dobb and Carr.

Still, Lenin understood the problems the Bolsheviks faced in trying to implement socialism. He went so far as to admit in a secret letter of 19 February 1921, written to G. M. Krzhizhanovsky, a member of the State Planning Commission, that "the greatest danger is that the work of planning the state economy may be bureaucratized. This is a great one. Milyutin does not see it ... A complete, integrated, real plan for us at present ... 'a bureaucratic utopia' ... Don't chase it."[120]

Lenin did not "deviate" from Marxist doctrine in his attempt to abolish market relations. The social ills that accompanied War Communism were consequences of precisely Lenin's faithfulness to Marx. The Marxist project of economic rationalization could not (and cannot) solve the fundamental problem of how to utilize the knowledge in society "which is not given to anyone in its totality."[121]

Lenin's deviation was NEP. The interventionist policies of NEP were an outright denial of Marx's organizational theory. Lenin not only allowed prices and profits to persist, he abandoned the cardinal goal of socialism – the substitution of a settled plan for the anarchy of the market. Even under the most extreme policies of Stalinism, monetary calculation (although highly interfered with) would serve as the basis of Soviet "planning." It was *after* the abandonment of "war" Communism that Marxism was reduced to a mere mobilizing ideology of the new ruling class.

While very few modern advocates of socialism would argue for comprehensive central planning, they hold fast to the Marxist critique of the anarchy of the market. But, as Don Lavoie has argued, "the modification from comprehensive planning, which seeks to completely replace market competition as the coordinating process of the economy, to noncomprehensive planning, which seeks to reconcile planning with market institutions, is hardly an alteration of analysis. It is the toppling of the basic pillar of Marxist analysis." Lavoie concludes that "it is by no means evident that the Marxist critique of the market order which modern planners still implicitly employ, can stand up once it is admitted that markets are necessary and that planning is to consist merely of interference in this unplannable system."[122]

Acknowledgments

I would like to acknowledge the helpful comments of Jeffrey Friedman, the editor of *Critical Review,* and two anonymous referees. Any remaining errors are exclusively my own.

Appendix: the Soviet experiment with Pure Communism: rejoinder to Nove*

Professor Nove contends that I wrongly attributed to him a myopic view of the ideological motives behind Bolshevik economic policy, when in reality it is my view that is distorted because it overemphasizes those motives. I agree with Nove that "no major action in the real world of politics can be attributed *solely* to ideology." (If I suggested that he argues in contrast for *no* ideological role, then I apologize.)

My claim is that the major role played by non-ideological factors was in influencing not the policies of "War Communism," but the manner in which they were implemented. The aspirations expressed in "War Communism" were not born in the crucible of military expediency, but originated instead in the political economy of Karl Marx and were transformed into praxis by Lenin from 1918 to 1921.[123]

Against this claim, Nove raises not only the general issue of the role of ideology in Soviet history, but also the intriguing matter of Trotsky's and Bukharin's policy positions in the period following "War Communism." Nove admits that no serious scholar of Soviet history can deny that there were ideologically inspired excesses during "War Communism," but he points out that "as soon as war communism ended Trotsky never returned to the theme of labor militarization, and Bukharin became almost overnight the principal apostle

*Originally published in Boettke, P. J. (1991) *Critical Review* 5(1) (Winter): 123–8.

of NEP." He concludes from these facts that labor militarization and opposition to economic markets must have been due primarily (although not exclusively) to "the necessities of war." But unless we are to fall into *post hoc ergo propter hoc* reasoning, more must be done to explain the reason for, and the nature of, the change in Trotsky's and Bukharin's views.

The policy pronouncements of Trotsky and Bukharin are a mixed bag in the 1920s. Although Trotsky did not continue to advocate labor militarization, he did press for planned industrialization and an anti-*kulak* campaign, and he continually referred to NEP as a temporary retreat. "Only the development of industry creates an unshakable foundation for the proletarian dictatorship," he wrote.[124]

Trotsky did not accept (at least in the 1920s) that "War Communism" had produced economic chaos because it necessarily brought too much administrative responsibility on itself. Rather, he claimed that its failure was due to lack of administrative ability. NEP, Trotsky argued, did not differ substantially from "War Communism" with regard to *the planning principle*. The difference lay in the method of planning. Under NEP, "arbitrary administration by bureaucratic agencies is replaced by economic maneuvering," but industrial development must still be guided by the State Planning Commission. The system of "one-man management must be applied in the organization of industry from top to bottom." As Trotsky saw it, the main problem in meeting this goal was "the inadequate selection of business executives."[125]

Better selection of personnel and the establishment of correct incentives for economic planners would ensure a successful extension of the planning principle. This extension would not just lead to the modification of the market, but to its eventual replacement. "In the final analysis," Trotsky said at the Twelfth Party Congress in 1923, "we will spread the planning principle to the entire market, thus swallowing and eliminating it. In other words, our successes on the basis of the New Economic Policy automatically move toward its liquidation, to its replacement by a newer economic policy, which will be a socialist policy."[126]

However, Trotsky's program of industrialization remained fundamentally incoherent throughout the 1920s. He feared concessions to foreign capital, yet he wanted to import capital resources to build up industry. He maintained a siege mentality and argued that foreign capitalists would not deal with Soviet Russia, yet he supported foreign trade. He supported NEPist reforms, yet argued that the market must be liquidated. Despite all the equivocation, however, as Nove has himself pointed out, Trotsky never fully escaped from his fear of the "market devil."[127]

Bukharin's position is even more puzzling. In fact, Bukharin's "swing to the right" is one of the great mysteries in early Soviet history. During the "War Communism" period he represented the extreme left wing of the Bolshevik party. His books: *The ABC of Communism* and *The Economics of the Transition Period* were regarded as the theoretical manifestos of "War Communism." They defended the policies of coercion and extreme centralization that the Bolsheviks had implemented from 1918 to 1921. While many readers are shocked by the conclusions that Bukharin reached in these works, it is even more amazing to witness his swing to the right under NEP. Not only was Bukharin one of the premier theorists of "War Communism," he was also the premier theorist of NEP.

The failure of "War Communism" deeply affected Bukharin's thinking, representing – along with the adoption of NEP – "a collapse of our illusions." "War communism," Bukharin argued, had been viewed "not as military, i.e. as needed at a given stage of civil war, but as a universal, general, so to speak 'normal' form of economic policy of a victorious proletariat."[128] The tentativeness of the political alliance between the workers and the peasantry and the economic annihilation of industry and agriculture in 1921 conflicted with Bukharin's original expectations of socialist construction. But, unlike the other Bolsheviks, Bukharin had a paradigm with which to interpret these failures: economic theory.

Bukharin was a serious student of bourgeois economics. During his exile from Russia, he studied economics in Vienna and attended Bohm-Bawerk's seminar on economic theory. He later embarked on a serious study of the theories of Walras and Pareto. His book *The Economic Theory of the Leisure Class* (1919) was a product of these studies.[129] Bukharin was well aware of both Bohm-Bawerk's and later Mises' criticisms of Marxian economics and socialist organization. In 1925, for example, he referred to Ludwig von Mises as "one of the most learned critics of Communism" and admitted that Mises was right about the unfeasibility of socialism, at least given the current stage of cultural development in Russia. Bukharin went on to state that, viewed in its economic essence, "War Communism" resembled the command socialism that the learned economists of the bourgeoisie predicted would lead to destruction. And NEP represented the rejection of this system and the "shift to a rational economic policy."[130]

But Bukharin's position, like Trotsky's, remained fundamentally at odds with itself. For while he admitted the necessity of the retreat to the market, but he also maintained that NEP was nevertheless a political victory of socialism. "When we crossed over to the NEP we began to overcome in practice the ... bourgeois case against socialism. Why? Because the meaning of the NEP lies in the fact that by using the economic initiative of the peasants, of the small producers, and even of the bourgeoisie, and by allowing private accumulation, we also placed these people objectively in the service of socialist state industry and the economy as a whole.[131]

Through the use of market stimuli, private interest would be mobilized for the good of social production. As long as the Bolsheviks held the "commanding heights" of the economy, the "backward strata of the proletariat (who were motivated by noncommunist ideas and private interests)" would be made to serve the interests of socialism. By means of "socialist" competition and economic struggle, the socialist sphere would eventually come to squeeze out private interests.[132]

The transition period would last a long time and would have to be managed carefully by the political leaders so that political power would remain firmly in the hands of the Bolsheviks. The creeping socialism that Bukharin advocated was a result of his recognition of the importance of balanced growth in developing the industrial base upon which the future (full) socialist society could be erected. Thus, despite the apparent drastic shift in position, Bukharin's appreciation of market forces in guiding economic development should not be exaggerated.[133]

Bukharin understood, at least to some degree, the problem of matching production plans with consumption demands that must be overcome in the process of economic development. This understanding underlies his demand for capital proportionality within his strategy for economic growth. It served as the basis for his acceptance of an essentially market-oriented model for economic development and industrialization at that stage of Soviet history. But in the ideal Marxian future, where production would be for direct use as opposed to exchange, Bukharin held the view that capital proportionality would be maintained by the planning board's calculation of the appropriate use of capital resources in advance of any economic process. Commodity exchange and production, in such a world, would be abolished – an ancient relic of a capitalist world now surpassed.

To both Trotsky and Bukharin, therefore, NEP represented a pragmatic retreat from the zealous attempt of "War Communism" to introduce socialism immediately. But the basic structural goals of "War Communism" – the liquidation of commodity production and the establishment of complete and comprehensive economic planning – remained their aims. In the future, once the appropriate industrial base was established, the full socialism of "War Communism" could be implemented again. We cannot forget these ideological aspirations if we wish to make sense of Soviet history.

My *Critical Review* paper deliberately refrained from a full treatment of Nove's interpretation of Soviet history because his views are more complex, balanced, and therefore difficult to summarize, than those of either Maurice Dobb or E. H. Carr. However, my book, *The Political Economy of Soviet Socialism*, does treat Nove's ideas at length.[134] Although the book admits that Nove's presentation is very subtle and sophisticated, it contends that his habit of introducing emergency conditions to explain away ideological aspirations produces a misreading of history.

Nove arrives at his conclusions concerning "War Communism," just as Dobb and Carr did before him, by discounting Marxian aspirations to supercede the market by eliminating money and exchange relations. Nove justifies this move by arguing that Marx's economic analysis is confined to capitalism and does not extend to the economic problems of socialism.[135] No doubt Marx did not wish to write "recipes for the cookshops of the future," but this was not in order to avoid the problem of examining socialist society. Rather, it represents a crucial aspect of Marx's particular approach to social theory. In this fashion Marx moved beyond the utopian socialists. As Don Lavoie has argued, Marx

> did not blame the [utopian socialism] so much for discussing socialist society as for the way in which they discussed it and for the contradictions within

their descriptions. Marx's scientific socialism was not merely an excuse for avoiding any examination of socialist society. It was a recommendation of a particular method for the conduct of such an excuse for avoiding any examination of socialist society. It was a recommendation of a particular method for the conduct of such an examination – that is, that socialism be described through a systematic critique of capitalism. For Marx, studying capitalism and developing a positive theory of socialism are two aspects of the same endeavor. Marx conducted a critique of capitalist society from the standpoint of socialism, intending to reveal by this study the main features of the future socialist society ... In many respects, where *Das Kapital* offers us a theoretical "photograph" of capitalism, its "negative" informs us about Marx's view of socialism.[136]

I suggest that it is Marx's implicit view of socialism that informed the Bolsheviks, inspired them, and guided them in their attempt to construct a better world order. Much of the meaning of these events is lost if this is overlooked.

References

Avrich, P. (1974) *Kronstadt 1921*, New York: W. W. Norton & Co.

Balabkins, N. (1978) "*Der Zukunftsstaat*: Carl Ballod's Vision of a Leisure-Oriented Socialism," *History of Political Economy*, 10(2): 213–32.

Berliner, J. (1964) "Marxism and the Soviet Economy," *Problems of Communism*, XII(5): 1–10.

Besancon, A. (1980) "Anatomy of a Spectre," *Survey*, 25(4).

Boettke, P. J. (1990) "The Political Economy of Utopia," *Journal des Economistes et des Etudes Humaines*, 1(2): 91–138.

——— (1990) *The Political Economy of Soviet Socialism: The Formative Years, 1918–1928*, Boston: Kluwer Academic Publishers.

Bottomore, T. (1986–87) "Is Rivalry Rational?," *Critical Review*, 1(1).

Brutzkus, B. (1935) *Economic Planning in Soviet Russia*, Westport, CT: Hyperion Press, 1981.

Bukharin, N. (1919) *The Economic Theory of the Leisure Class*, New York: Augustus M. Kelley, 1970.

——— (1920) in K. Tarbuck (ed.), *The Politics and Economics of the Transition Period*, Boston: Routledge & Kegan Paul, 1979.

——— (1924) *The Path to Socialism in Russia*, New York: Omicron Books, 1967.

——— (1925) "Concerning the New Economic Policy and Our Tasks," in N. Bukharin (ed.) *Selected Economic Writings on the Transition to Socialism*, New York: M. E. Sharpe, 1982.

Bukharin, N. and Preobrazhensky, E. (1919) *The ABC of Communism*, Ann Arbor: University of Michigan Press, 1966.

Carr, E. H. (1952) *The Bolshevik Revolution*, three volumes, New York: Norton, 1980.

Chamberlin, W. (1935) *The Russian Revolution, 1917–1921*, two volumes, Princeton: Princeton University Press, 1987.

Cohen, S. (1971) *Bukharin and the Bolshevik Revolution*, New York: Oxford University Press, 1980.

——— (1972) "In Praise of War Communism," in A. Rabinowitch and J. Rabinowitch (eds.) *Revolution and Politics in Russia*, Bloomington: Indiana University Press.

Day, R. (1973) *Leon Trotsky and the Politics of Economic Isolation*, New York: Cambridge University Press.

Djilas, M. (1957) *The New Class*, New York: Praeger.

Dobb, M. (1948) *Soviet Economic Development Since 1917*, New York: International Publishers.

Evans, A. (1987) "Rereading Lenin's *State and Revolution*," *Slavic Review*, 46(1).

Gerschenkron, A. (1969) "History of Economic Doctrines and Economic History," *American Economic Review*, LIX(2).

Habermas, J. (1986) "Ideologies and Society in the Post-War World," in P. Dews (ed.) *Habermas: Autonomy & Solidarity – Interviews with Jurgen Habermas*, London: Verso.

Hayek, F. A. (1935) "Foreword," in N. Brutzkus (ed.) *Economic Planning in Soviet Russia*, CT: Hyperion Press, 1981.

—— (1948) *Individualism and Economic Order*, Chicago: University of Chicago Press, 1980.

—— ed. (1935) *Collectivist Economic Planning*, New York: Augustus M. Kelley, 1975.

Higgs, Robert. (1987) *Crisis and Leviathan*, New York: Oxford University Press.

Hoff, T. (1949) *Economic Calculation in the Socialist Society*, Indianapolis: Liberty Press, 1981.

Keizer, W. (1987) "Two Forgotten Articles by Ludwig von Mises on the Rationality of Socialist Economic Calculation," *Review of Austrian Economics*, 1(1): 109–22.

Konrad, G. and Szelenyi, I. (1979) *The Intellectuals on the Road to Class Power*, New York: Harcourt Brace Jovanovich.

Lange, O. (1939) *On the Economic Theory of Socialism*, B. Lippincott, ed., New York: Augustus M. Kelley, 1970.

Lavoie, D. (1985) *National Economic Planning: What is Left?*, Cambridge, MA: Ballinger Books.

—— (1985) *Rivalry and Central Planning: The Socialist Calculation Debate Reconsidered*, New York: Cambridge University Press.

—— (1985) *Rivalry and Central Planning: The Socialist Calculation Debate Reconsidered*, New York: Cambridge University Press.

—— (1986–87) "Political and Economic Illusions of Socialism," *Critical Review*, 1(1).

Lawton, L. (1932) *An Economic History of Soviet Russia*, two volumes, New York: Macmillan.

Leites, K. (1922) *Recent Economic Developments in Russia*, New York: Oxford University Press.

Lenin, V. I. (1977) *Collected Works*, forty-five volumes, Moscow: Progress Publishers.

Lerner, A. (1944) *The Economics of Control*, New York: Macmillan.

Lewin, M. (1985) *The Making of the Soviet System*, New York: Pantheon Books.

Lih, L. (1986) "Bolshevik *Razverstka* and War Communism," *Slavic Review*, 45(4): 673–88.

Malle, S. (1985) *The Economic Organization of War Communism, 1918–1921*, New York: Cambridge University Press.

Marx, K. (1906) *Capital: A Critique of Political Economy*, New York: Modern Library.

—— (1969) *Selected Works*, three volumes, Moscow: Progress Publishers.

—— (1977) *Economic and Philosophical Manuscripts of 1844*, Moscow: Progress Press.

Merkle, J. (1980) *Management and Ideology*, Berkeley: University of California Press.

Mises, L. (1919) *Nation, State and Economy*, translated by Yeager, L., New York: New York University Press, 1983.

—— (1920) "Economic Calculation in the Socialist Commonwealth," in F. Hayek (ed.) (1935).

—— (1922) *Socialism: An Economic and Sociological Analysis*, Indianapolis: Liberty Press, 1981.

Moss, L. (ed.) (1976) *The Economics of Ludwig von Mises*, Kansas City: Sheed and Ward.

Murrell, P. (1983) "Did the Theory of Market Socialism Answer the Challenge of Ludwig von Mises?," *History of Political Economy*, 15(1): 92–105.

Nove, A. (1969) *An Economic History of the U.S.S.R.*, New York: Penguin Books, 1984.

—— (1979) "Bukharin and His Ideas," in A. Nove (ed.), *Political Economy and Soviet Socialism*, London: George Allen and Unwin.

—— (1979) "Bukharin and His Ideas," in A. Nove, *Political Economy and Soviet Socialism*, London: George Allen and Unwin.

—— (1981) "New Light on Trotskii's Economic Views," *Slavic Review*, 40(1): 84–97.

—— (1983) *The Economics of Feasible Socialism*, London: Allen and Unwin.

Nutter, G. W. (1962) *The Growth of Industrial Production in the Soviet Union*, Princeton: Princeton University Press.

Pasvolsky, L. (1921) *The Economics of Communism: With Special Reference to Russia's Experiment*, New York: Macmillan.

Polanyi, M. (1957) "The Foolishness of History: November 1917–November 1957," *Encounter*, IX(5).

Rathenau, W. (1921) *In Days to Come*, New York: Alfred A. Knopf.

Reed, J. (1919) *Ten Days that Shook the World*, New York: Penguin Books, 1985.

Reese, D. (1980) *Alienation, Exchange and Economic Calculation*. PhD thesis, Department of Economics, Virginia Polytechnic Institute, Blacksburg, VA.

Remmington, T. (1984) *Building Socialism in Bolshevik Russia: Ideology and Industrial Organization, 1917–1921*, Pittsburgh: University of Pittsburgh Press.

Rizzi, B. (1930) *The Bureaucratization of the World*, New York: The Free Press, 1985.

Roberts, P. C. (1971) *Alienation and the Soviet Economy*. Albuquerque: University of New Mexico Press.

—— (1988) "The Soviet Economy: A Hopeless Cause," *Reason* (July).

Roberts, P. C. and Stephenson, M. (1973) *Marx's Theory of Exchange, Alienation and Crisis*, New York: Praeger, 1983.

Rothbard, M. (1976) "Ludwig von Mises and Economic Calculation Under Socialism," in L. Moss (ed.), *The Economics of Ludwig von Mises*, Kansas City: Sheed and Ward.

Rustow, A. (1980) *Freedom and Domination: A Historical Critique of Civilization*, Princeton: Princeton University Press.

Sakwa, R. (1987) "The Commune State in Moscow in 1918," *Slavic Review* (Fall/Winter).

Salter, J. (1990) "N. I. Bukharin and the Market Question," *History of Political Economy*, 22(1): 65–79.

Selucky, R. (1979) *Marxism, Socialism, Freedom*, New York: St. Martin's Press.

Selyunin, V. (1988) "The Origins," *Novy Mir* (May): 162–89.

Serge, V. (1963) *Memoirs of a Revolutionary, 1901–1941*, New York: Oxford University Press.

Shadwell, A. (1927) *The Breakdown of Socialism*, Boston: Little Brown.

Smolinsky, L. (1967) "Planning Without Theory," *Survey*, no. 64 (July).

Szamuely, L. (1974) *First Models of the Socialist Economic System*, Budapest: Akademiai Kiado.

Treml, V. (1969) "Interaction of Economic Thought and Economic Policy in the Soviet Union," *History of Political Economy*, 1(1): 187–216.

Trotsky, L. (1923) "Theses on Industry," in R. V. Daniels (ed.), *A Documentary History of Communism*, Vol. 1, New York: Vintage, 1960.

—— (1924) *The New Course*, in L. Trotsky (ed.), *The Challenge of the Left Opposition, 1923–25*, New York: Pathfinder, 1975.

——. (1932) *The History of the Russian Revolution*, three volumes, New York: Pathfinder Books, 1987.

Vaughn, K. (1980) "Economic Calculation Under Socialism: The Austrian Contribution," *Economic Inquiry*, 18 (October): 535–54.

Weber, M. (1922) *Economy and Society*, two volumes, Berkeley: University of California Press.

Wells, H. G. (1921) *Russia in the Shadows*, New York: George H. Doran.

7 The political economy of utopia

Communism in Soviet Russia, 1918–21*

It has become a copybook maxim to assert that the policy of "War Communism" was imposed on the Bolsheviks by the Civil War and the foreign intervention. This is completely untrue, if only for the reason that the first decrees on introducing the "socialist ideal" exactly "according to Marx" in Soviet Russia were issued long before the beginning of the Civil War (the decrees of 26 January and 14 February 1918, on the nationalization of the merchant fleet and of all banks), while the last decree on the socialization of all small handicraftsman and artisans was issued on 29 November 1920, i.e. after the end of the Civil War in European Russia. Of course, the conditions of the Civil War and the intervention left an imprint. But the main thing was something else – the immediate implementation of theory in strict accordance with Marx (from "Critique of the Gotha Program") and Engels (from "Anti-During").

(Sirotkin 1989)

In the failure of War Communism and the retreat to NEP the impossibility of planning as articulated theoretically in the Mises–Hayek critique was directly demonstrated in practice.

(Lavoie 1986–7)

Introduction

The historical understanding of the Russian revolution has traveled a rather strange road. The original interpretations of this event basically agreed that Marxian socialism had been tried by the Bolsheviks and failed to such a degree that by 1921 the Bolsheviks were forced to retreat from their experiment with Marxian socialism and switch back to market institutions in the New Economic Policy (NEP).[1] During the 1940s, however, this standard interpretation was challenged by individuals such as Maurice Dobb and, later, E. H. Carr.[2] Carr's massive study of the history of the Soviet Union, perhaps more than any other source, was responsible for establishing the counterargument that the War Communism period (1918–21) was not an attempt to implement Marx's utopia, but rather was forced upon the Bolsheviks by the conditions of civil war and international intervention.

*Originally published as Boettke, P. J. (1990) "The Political Economy of Utopia: Communism in Soviet Russia, 1918–1921," *Journal des Economistes et des Etudes Humaines* 1(2): 91–138.

Recent decades, however, have seen a growing skepticism toward Carr's and other studies which disregard the ideological motivations of the Bolsheviks. The works of Paul Craig Roberts and Thomas Remington have re-emphasized the point that War Communism was a deliberate policy aimed at the elimination of all market institutions and not merely a matter of desperate emergency measures.[3] Still, the hegemony of the emergency interpretation persists and finds two of its most ardent supporters in Alec Nove and Stephen Cohen, perhaps the most influential Soviet specialists today.

The timing of the Dobb and Carr re-evaluations of Soviet history coincided with a methodological thrust in the human sciences which sought to deny the force of ideas in human history. Statistical studies would prove or disprove the effectiveness of policies, so that endless disputes over intellectual history were not necessary. Such metaphysical concepts as ideology were not important for the scientific study of society. This methodological change was responsible for the success of Dobb's and Carr's work and for the belief that central planning began not as an attempt in 1918 to eliminate the market but as the attempt to mobilize agricultural resources in 1928.

But, the decline of the positivistic model of the human sciences and the establishment of a post-positivistic philosophy of science brings in its wake a renewed appreciation of the force of ideas in human history.[4] This new philosophical thrust of the human sciences leads to a fundamental reassessment of this event and its relevance for the study of comparative political and economic systems.

Today, with full knowledge of the effects of Stalinism and the problems that continue to plague so-called socialist economies throughout the world, we can perhaps come to a better understanding of the true meaning of the War Communism period and its socioeconomic dimension. As philosopher Hans-Georg Gadamer states:[5]

> Time is no longer primarily a gulf to be bridged, because it separates, but it is actually the supportive ground of process in which the present is rooted. Hence temporal distance is not something that must be overcome. This was, rather, the naïve assumption of historicism, namely that we must set ourselves within the spirit of the age, and think with its thoughts, not with our own, and thus advance toward historical objectivity. In fact, the important thing is to recognize the distance in time as a positive and productive possibility of understanding ... It lets the true meaning of the object emerge fully ... Not only are fresh sources of error constantly excluded, so that the true meaning has filtered out of it all kinds of things that obscure it, but there emerge continually new sources of understanding, which reveal unsuspected elements of meaning ... It not only let those prejudices that are of a particular and limited nature die away, but causes those that bring genuine understanding to emerge clearly as such. It is only this temporal distance that can solve the really critical question of hermeneutics, namely of distinguishing the true prejudices, by which we understand, from the false ones by which we misunderstand.

The Soviet experience from 1918 to 1921 represents a utopian experiment with socialism. The Bolshevik revolutionaries attempted to implement a Marxian social order. Examination of the texts of Lenin, Bukharin, Trotsky, and various other party documents of the time demonstrates the intent to build socialism immediately. The Bolshevik cadre possessed a strong faith in the imminent world revolution, and, therefore, believed in the Trotskyite concept of "permanent revolutions."[6] The civil war represents not so much a distraction in the building of socialism, but rather a method by which socialism will be brought to the West.[7] "Reasoning from the premises of permanent revolution," Robert Daniels points out, "the Bolshevik left wing – Lenin now included – envisioned vast but independent possibilities of revolution in Europe as well as in Russia. Europe was ripe for revolution, and Russia would shake the tree."[8]

This faith in sparking the international revolution was demonstrated at the 6th Congress of the Russian Social-Democratic Workers' Party (Bolsheviks) held in August 1917. "History is working for us," Bukharin declared. "History is moving on the path which leads inevitably to the uprising of the proletariat and the triumph of socialism ... we will wage a holy war in the name of the interests of all the proletariat, and ... by such a revolutionary war we will light the fire of world socialist revolution."[9] And the draft resolution on the Current Movement and the War accepted at the Congress merely reiterated Bukharin's thesis.[10]

The civil war was not a surprise to the Bolsheviks, but rather an expected response from the bourgeoisie. But, while it was expected as part of the transition period, and, in fact, the *raison d'être* of the dictatorship of the proletariat, the civil war did shape the implementation of policy. As Paul Craig Roberts argues, "It was not the policy [of War Communism] but the manner in which it was applied that was determined by civil war."[11] The policies of War Communism, I hope to demonstrate, were not born "in the crucible of military expediency" as Stephen Cohen argues,[12] but originated instead from the political economy of Karl Marx and were transformed into praxis by Vladimir Illich Lenin from 1918 to 1921 in Soviet Russia.

The economic history of War Communism

There is no real dispute here over the economic facts. As Michael Polanyi wrote with regard to Maurice Dobb, "Mr. Dobb's account of the events does not materially differ from that given in my text."[13] What differs between the standard account and the one offered here is the *meaning* of these facts. It is a problem of intellectual history and not one of better fact-finding or statistical manipulation. Substantial agreement exists concerning the chronology of events following the October uprising and the implementation of certain economic policies.

The Bolsheviks rose to power with the promise of advancing Russia toward socialism. Between October 1917 and May 1918, the Bolsheviks implemented several policies intended to be steps toward the realization of socialism. "Changes of this sort," Charles Bettelheim points out, "took concrete form in certain decisive measures concerning industry and trade. Of these, the most important were the decree on workers' control, published on 19 November 1917, the decree on the formation of the Supreme Economic Council of National Economy (VSNKh), the decree on the nationalization of the banks (28 December), the decree on consumers' organizations, placing consumers' cooperatives under the control of the Soviets (16 April), and the decree on the monopoly of foreign trade (23 April)."[14]

However, the nationalization drive, which the standard account argues did not begin until after the urgency of civil war became apparent, was already in preparation in March and April of 1918; plans were being made to nationalize both the petroleum and the metal industries.[15] But the sugar industry, with the decree of 2 May 1918, became the first entire industry to be nationalized. Three hundred enterprises were nationalized on 15 May, and by the beginning of June that number exceeded five hundred, half of which represented concerns in heavy industry. This was followed by the general decree nationalizing large-scale industry issued on 28 June 1918.[16] And by 31 August the number of nationalized enterprises reached 3,000. The pace of the nationalization of industry grew throughout the War Communism period to such an extent that, by November 1920, 37,000 enterprises were nationalized: 18,000 of which did not use mechanical power and 5,000 of which employed only one person.[17]

Efforts to nationalize the economy were deemed necessary for the replacement of market methods of allocation by centralized allocation and distribution.[18] A 21 November 1918 decree, for example, forbade internal private trading and a monopoly of trade was granted to the Commissariat of Supply.[19] By March 1919 the consumer cooperatives lost their independent status and were merged with the Commissariat of Supply. And labor mobilization measures, i.e. the militarization of the labor force, were introduced in the attempt to insure the appropriate allocation of the work-force. Stern labor discipline was introduced and "deserters" were penalized accordingly.[20]

Efforts were also undertaken during this period to eliminate monetary circulation. An August 1918 decree of the Supreme Economic Council declared that all transactions had to be carried out by accounting operations without using money. The figures concerning the emission of currency during this period are shocking: 22.4 billion roubles were in circulation on 1 November 1917, 40.3 billion by 1 June 1918, and 60.8 billion by 1 January 1919. And during 1919 the quantity of money tripled, in 1920 it quadrupled, leaving the purchasing power of the rouble in October 1920 at only 1% of what it had been in October 1917.[21]

Perhaps the most ambitious effort of the Bolsheviks during the War Communism period was the attempt to organize the planning apparatus of the national economy. The Supreme Economic Council (VSNKh) was established on 2 December 1917, and three weeks later the Councils of the National Economy (the *Sovnarkozes*) were created by the Supreme Economic Council to coordinate the activities of all economic units within their provinces and districts.

As the nationalization continued to increase, the management of nationalized enterprises called for central administrations. Special departments within the Supreme Economic Council, called *Glavkis*, were formed for this task. Enterprises were integrated vertically through the *glavki* system and horizontally through the *sovarkozes*.[22]

This system of planning attempted to provide *ex ante* coordination of economic activities in place of the chaotic and *ex post* coordination provided by the market system. This planning system, while not provided in a blueprint form from Marx, was nevertheless influenced by him. As Malle writes: "Marxist ideology did not provide concrete guidance about economic organization, but it did provide a general hint about what to be kept and what had to be dropped on the path of economic development. This hint was not irrelevant in the selection of alternatives facing the leadership."[23] It is this connection and its subsequent development that I will proceed to explore.

From Marx to Lenin

While Marx did not wish to write "recipes for the cookshops of the future," there is no doubt about the broad outline of Marx's project.[24] His project entailed the rationalization of politics and the rationalization of economics. Both spheres were interdependent within the Marxian system. The interpreter of Marx cannot merely concentrate on either Marx's economics or his politics if he/she wishes to understand his project. Marx was a political economist in the broadest sense of that term.

Rationalization of the economy required the substitution of a "settled plan," which achieved *ex ante* coordination, for the "anarchy of the market"; the substitution of production for direct use for production for exchange. Consider the following statement of Marx's from *Capital*:[25]

> The life-process of society, which is based on the process of material production, does not strip off its mystical veil until it is treated as production by freely associated men, and is consciously regulated by them in accordance with a settled plan.

Furthermore, consider the following position taken by Marx in the Economic and Philosophical Manuscripts of 1844:[26]

> The positive transcendence of private property as the appropriation of human life, is therefore the positive transcendence of all estrangement – that is to say, the return of man from religion, family, state, etc. to his human, i.e. social, existence.

The abolition of private property in the means of production and the substitution of a settled plan for the market has the consequence of rationalizing economic life and transcending man's alienated social existence. This is Marx's "economic" project.

Rationalization of politics, on the other hand, required the establishment of "classless" politics. Marx's political vision was one of radical democracy; one which included universal suffrage and insured full participation.[27] Since to Marx the state was an instrument of class conflict, the disappearance of class meant the disappearance of the state and political power. But this did not mean the disappearance of social or "classless" politics. As Marx argued in *The Poverty of Philosophy*:[28]

> The condition for the emancipation of the working class is the abolition of all classes ... The working class, in the course of its development, will substitute for the old civil society *an association which will exclude classes and their antagonism, and there will be no more political power properly so-called*, since political power is precisely the official expression of antagonism in civil society ... Do not say that social movement excludes political movement. There is never a political movement which is not at the same time social. *It is only in an order of things in which there are no more classes and class antagonisms that social evolutions will cease to be political revolutions.*

Marx, it is also clear, argued that the rationalization process of both politics and economics would be conducted in the transition period by the "dictatorship of the proletariat." Moreover, it is quite clear that Marx believed the transition from capitalism to socialism would not be peaceful, but violent. "The first step in the revolution by the working class," Marx and Engels wrote, "is to raise the proletariat to the position of ruling class, to win the battle of democracy." "The proletariat," they continued, "will use its political supremacy to wrest, by degrees, all capital from the bourgeoisie, to centralise all instruments of production in the hands of the state, i.e. of the proletariat organized as the ruling class; and to increase the total of productive forces as rapidly as possible."[29]

And, though it would be violent, Marx was of the opinion that the transition would be short-lived. Capitalism would negate itself within the process of its development. But within this process of negation, capitalism would develop the material preconditions for the advancement to socialism. As he argued in *Capital*:[30]

> Hand in hand with this centralisation, or this expropriation of many capitalists by few, develop, on an ever extending scale, the cooperative form of the labour-process, the conscious technical application of science, the methodical cultivation of the soil, the transformation of the instruments of labour into instruments of labour only usable in common, the economising of all means of production by their use as the means of production of combined, socialised labour, the entanglement of all peoples in the net of the world-market, and this, the international character of the capitalist regime. Along with the constantly diminishing number of the magnates of capital, who usurp and monopolise all advantages of this process of transformation, grows the mass of misery, oppression, slavery,

degradation, exploitation; but with this too grows the revolt of the working class, a class always increasing in numbers, and disciplined, united, organised by the very mechanism of the process of capitalist production itself. The monopoly of capital becomes a fetter upon the mode of production, which has sprung up and flourished along with, and under it. Centralisation of the means of production and socialisation of labour at last reach a point where they become incompatible with their capitalist integument. This integument is burst asunder. The knell of capitalist private property sounds. The expropriators are expropriated ... Capitalist production begets, with the inexorability of a law of Nature, its own negation. It is the negation of negation ... The transformation of scattered private property, arising from individual labour, into capitalist private property is, naturally, a process, incomparably more protracted, violent, and difficult, than the transformation of capitalistic private property, already practically resting on socialised production, into socialised property. In the former case, we had the expropriation of the mass of the people by a few usurpers; in the latter, we have the expropriation of a few usurpers by the mass of the people.

There have been many recent attempts to understand Marx's project, and assess its relationship to the Soviet experience with socialism.[31] Many of these attempts, however, focus exclusively upon the relationship between Marx's political vision and Soviet authoritarianism. David Lowell, for example, concludes, after a thorough analysis and comparison of Marx's political project with that of Lenin's, that while "Lenin supplied the theoretical foundations for Soviet authoritarianism, Marx's contribution to them was not decisive. While there are many cogent reasons for rejecting Marx's project as a panacea for society's ills, the project's direct and necessary association with Soviet illiberalism is not one of them."[32]

Others, such as the critical theorists of the Frankfurt School (Horkheimer, Adorno and Marcuse), consider it one of their fundamental tasks as social theorists to explain the relationship between the Marxian promise of emancipation and the Soviet reality of illiberalism. David Held, in his informative history on the development of critical theory, points out that one of the central problems of concern to the members of the Institute of Social Research, i.e. the Frankfurt School, was to address the following questions:[33]

Given the fate of Marxism in Russia and Western Europe, was Marxism itself nothing other than a stale orthodoxy? Was there a social agent capable of progressive change? What possibilities were there for effective socialist practice?

Positive answers to these questions have not always been forthcoming from the critical theorists or Western Marxism in general. As a result, negativism and a sense of despair burdens Western Marxist discussion of the project of emancipation. Martin Jay expresses this sense of frustration when he asks, "is it too much to hope that amidst the debris there lurks, silent but still potent, the germ of a truly defensible concept of totality – and even more important, the potential for a liberating totalization that will not turn into its opposite?"[34]

Jay and Western Marxism, in general, find hope in the research program of Jurgen Habermas and the positive alternative that the Habermasian system suggests. Habermas wishes to focus on Marx's project of the rationalization of politics. In this regard, Habermas has developed his idea of "uncoerced discourse" as a model for politics.[35] Habermas, however, does not provide a cogent discussion of Marx's responsibility (if any) for Soviet authoritarianism.

Perhaps the most insightful discussion on the subject of Marx's political project and the Soviet experience, therefore, is to be found within the Praxis group philosophers of Yugoslavia. Svetozar Stojanovic, for example, argues that modern Marxists cannot escape the fact that Marx's fundamental ambiguity toward the concept of the dictatorship of the proletariat is responsible for the perversion of politics under Soviet rule. As Stojanovic argues:[36]

> No matter how we look at it, Marx's idea of the dictatorship of the proletariat was practicable only by having one group rule in the name of the proletariat as a whole. In the best of cases, it would rule in its interest and under its control. In the worst case, it would rule without any kind of supervision and against its vital interests. In conceiving a new state it is no small oversight to set out from the most optimistic assumptions, where no real thought is given to measures and guarantees against the abuse of power.

Thus, modern Marxists need to deal with the terror inflicted upon the proletariat by the dictatorship in its name that occurred during the early years of the Soviet regime.

All these interpretations, however interesting they are, have a fundamental problem; they forget the economic sphere of Marx's project and they ignore unintended consequences in social life. In this regard, the attempt by Radoslav Selucky to understand Marx's project is much more satisfying.[37] Selucky suggests that Marx's project of rationalization of the economy may be inconsistent with the rationalization of politics that Marx envisioned. The concept of a centrally planned unity in economic life is mutually exclusive from the ideal of full democratic participation within political life. This line of reasoning is also consistent with basic Marxian materialist philosophy which argued that the material base (economic life) determines the superstructure (the realm of ideas). As Selucky argues:[38]

> No Marxist may legitimately construct a social system whose political superstructure would differ structurally from its economic base ... If one accepts Marx's concept of base and superstructure, a centralized, hierarchically organized economic subsystem cannot coexist with a pluralistic, horizontally organized self-governed political subsystem.

Selucky seems to understand the institutional requirements of economic rationalization and their unintended consequences.

Those who assert that there is a line of continuity between Marx's project and Lenin's praxis need not argue that either Marx or Lenin was an authoritarian. The argument, rather, is that Marx's project of rationalization has the unintended, and undesirable, consequence of totalitarianism. Neither Marx nor Lenin needs to be viewed as a totalitarian in order to understand how the political utopia they envisioned resulted in such an order. The old Bolsheviks, Lenin, Bukharin, Trotsky, Zinoviev, etc., believed they were faithfully implementing Marx's project of social transformation.[39] In order to accomplish the process of social transformation, it would have to be directed by the dictatorship of the proletariat, i.e. the Bolsheviks, who represented the true interests of the working class. Bolshevik proposals were filled with intentions of radical democracy, both economically as well as politically, for the working man. Lenin was a faithful interpreter of Marx's project.

Don Lavoie, therefore, provides perhaps the most cogent understanding of Marx's political and economic project among recent interpretations. Lavoie presents Marx's project as an attempt to broaden the scope of democracy and public life. He states:[40]

Karl Marx conceived of central planning as an attempt to resolve this inherent contradiction between the private and public spheres of society. As in any genuinely radical perspective, his particular diagnosis of the problem is inextricably bound up with his utopia, his notion of the cure. Marx saw the problem as being located in the competitive private sphere, the market system, where separate, divided, or "alienated" interests contend with one another for resources. He argued that, so long as democratic institutions tried to merge themselves with this competitive sphere, they would invariably succumb to it. The solution, then, was to eradicate competitive market relations and to replace them with a broadening of the democratically based public sphere to encompass all of social life. No longer would politicians stoop to being tools of special and conflicting interests, since the private sector would cease to exist as a separate component of society. All social production would be carried out by the "associated producers" in conjunction with a common plan. Production would no longer be a private act of war by some market participants against others in a competitive struggle for wealth, but would instead be the main task of the self-coordinated democratic institution ... The reason for our pervasive social ills, culminating in the modern threat of total destruction in use, is perceived to be the fact that we have narrowly confined the function of democratic institutions to a tiny part of social life and have left the bulk of economic activity to the unplanned outcome of non-democratic private struggles for wealth in the market. The proposed solution is to widen democracy to the whole sphere of economics and completely abolish private ownership of the means of production, thereby eliminating the competitiveness of market relations as a basis for economic decision-making.

And, although Marx was extremely reluctant to discuss how his utopia would work in practice, Lavoie suggests that we can envision the fundamental components of Marx's political and economic project, and study their operation. So despite Marx's reluctance, Lavoie argues that:[41]

> One can still infer from his [Marx's] many indirect references to the communist society that some sort of democratic procedures would be constructed through which the goals of society could be formulated. After this is done, scientists would devise rational comprehensive planning procedures to implement these goals. Since this planning, to be meaningful and scientific, must obtain control over all the relevant variables, Marx consistently foresaw it as centralized and comprehensive. The commonly owned means of production would be deliberately and scientifically operated by the state in accordance with a single plan. Social problems would henceforth be resolved not by meekly interfering with a competitive market order but by taking over the whole process of social production from beginning to end.

This task of abolishing market relations and "taking over the whole process of social production from beginning to end" constitutes the economic policies followed by the Bolsheviks from 1918 to 1921. The policies of War Communism represent the conscious and deliberate attempt to realize Marx's utopia.

Ripeness and the rise to power

Much has been made of the issue of "ripeness" or whether Russia was sufficiently developed. Marx's model of dialectical materialism and the debate between the Mensheviks and the Bolsheviks is usually invoked to demonstrate Lenin's deviation from "real" Marxism. Russia's backward political and economic traditions, it is argued, precluded the possibility of a successful Marxist revolution. Lenin's political maneuvering was a gamble – the attempt to skip over the important historical stage of the bourgeois revolution – with the pay-off being a net loss to the Russian people.[42] Russia became stuck, as a result of Lenin's hurried attempt to achieve utopia, in the Asiatic mode of production or "oriental despotism."[43]

The tyranny of Soviet oppression under Stalin, from this perspective, is the outcome of the intentional gamble by Lenin to rush the revolution in a backward country. What is noteworthy in this analysis is that Marx's project of rationalization is understood; what is disappointing is that the economic problem this rationalization process would have to confront, no matter what stage of development the country of revolution found itself, is misunderstood. Discussion, instead, focuses upon the proper historical conditions conducive to the world revolution.

Robert Daniels, for example, argues that the key to understanding the development of Communism is to keep in mind the importance of historical conditions. The Soviet experience – a historical accident – could not possibly have succeeded in establishing socialism, because it lacked the necessary preconditions. What resulted in the Soviet Union was not the unintended outcome of attempting to implement Marx's rationalization project, but rather a different system determined by the historical stage of development. As Daniels argues in *The Conscience of the Revolution*:[44]

> The important concern from the standpoint of understanding the development of Communism is to see how the ideal proved to be unrealizable under the *particular Russian conditions* where it was attempted. The Marxian theory underlying the ideal, whenever applied objectively, actually foretold the failure: proletarian socialism required a strong proletariat and an advanced economy; Russia lacked the strong proletariat and the advanced economy. Therefore, the ideal could not be attained, and any claims to the contrary could only mask the establishment of some other kind of social order.

While Daniels sees this focus upon historical preconditions as the key to understanding this episode, I contend that it turns into the key problem to understanding, and, actually leads to misunderstanding the meaning of the Soviet experience with socialism.[45] What is disappointing about much of the analysis of the Bolshevik rise to power is the almost exclusive emphasis upon historical preconditions for successful socialist practice and the differences in *political strategy* that existed between the Mensheviks and Socialist-Revolutionaries, on the one hand, and the Bolsheviks, on the other.[46]

The Mensheviks and Socialist-Revolutionaries, after the February revolution, originally wanted to work with the Kadet government, as a critic of policy, in the belief that Russia needed to go through the bourgeois revolution before the possibility of the workers' revolution could be discussed.[47] The April days and the July demonstrations, however, brought a closer coalition between the Mensheviks, the Socialist-Revolutionaries, and the provisional government.[48] The Bolsheviks, on the other hand, wanted no part of the compromise with the government, and grew more anxious throughout 1917 to take power and bring relief (and political power) to the suffering masses. This proved to be a tactical *coup d'état*, for, as conditions worsened through the summer of 1917, the Bolsheviks were the only political group to remain untainted by association with the government. Lenin and the party took full advantage of this "higher moral ground."[49]

Lenin, for example, in his essay "Political Parties in Russia and the Task of the Proletariat," written in April 1917, set out to answer questions about the political positions of the four major political factions.[50] There existed, according to Lenin:

1   a group to the right of the Constitutional Democrats;
2   the Constitutional Democrats;

3   the Social Democrats and the Socialist Revolutionaries; and
4   the Bolsheviks.

The Constitutional Democrats, and the group to their right, represented the interests of the bourgeoisie, while the Social Democrats and the Socialist-Revolutionaries represented the interests of the petty bourgeoisie. The Bolsheviks, however, represented the interests of the proletariat and demanded all power to the Soviets, "undivided power to the Soviets from the bottom up all over the country" (1977, vol. 24, p. 99). The major difference between the political platform of the Social Democrats and the Socialist-Revolutionaries and the Bolsheviks was *pace*; the Bolsheviks demanded power to the Soviets *now*, while the Social Democrats argued that it was not time – Russia must wait until the bourgeois revolution was completed.

"The masses must be made to see," Lenin argued upon his arrival in Russia in April 1917, "that the Soviets of Workers' Deputies are the only possible form of revolutionary government, and that therefore our task is, as long as this government yields to the influence of the bourgeoisie, to present a patient, systematic, and persistent explanation of the errors of their tactics, an explanation especially adapted to the practical needs of the masses" (1977, vol. 24, p. 23). This is where he set out his famous "April Theses."[51]

As long as the Bolsheviks remained in the minority[52] their primary task was that of "criticising and exposing" the errors of the government, and to "preach the necessity of transferring the entire state power to the Soviets of Workers' Deputies" (Ibid.). It was not the task of the proletariat at that time (April 1917) to introduce socialism immediately, according to Lenin, but rather to bring social production and distribution under the control of the Soviets.[53] The Bolsheviks were urged by Lenin to take the initiative in creating the international revolution. "It must be made clear that the people can stop the war or change its character," Lenin wrote "*only* by changing the class character of the government."[54]

Lenin believed that the workers could, and should, take state power immediately. His belief was justified, he argued, because of the existence of two governments; the existence of "dual power" within Russia.[55] There existed the provisional government – which was the government of the bourgeoisie – but at the same time another government had arisen: the government of the proletariat – the Soviets of Workers' and Soldiers' Deputies. "This power is of the same type," Lenin argued, "as the Paris Commune of 1871" (1977, vol. 24, p. 38). The workers' state must assume power.

It is not a problem of ripeness, asserted Lenin.[56] The problem with the Paris Commune was not that it introduced socialism immediately (a bourgeois prejudice). "The Commune, unfortunately," Lenin asserted, "was too slow in introducing socialism. The *real* essence of the Commune is not where the bourgeois usually looks for it, but in the creation of a state of a special type. *Such a state has already arisen in Russia, it is the Soviets of Workers' and Soldiers' Deputies!*"[57]

The existence of dual power and the circumstances of the time led Lenin to declare at the 7th (April) All-Russia Conference that the whole crux of the matter can be summed up as follows: "We [Bolsheviks] put the issue of socialism not as a jump, but as a practical way out of the present debacle" (1977, vol. 24, p. 308). World War I had ripened the conditions for the revolution. Economically, the necessities of war planning had created greater concentration of capital and brought production under the conscious control of society.[58] Politically, the war had intensified the exploitation of the working class in the name of the capitalist war.[59] "But with private ownership of the means of production abolished and state power passing completely to the proletariat," Lenin argued, "these very conditions are a pledge of success for society's transformation that will do away with the exploitation of man by man and ensure the well-being of everyone" (1977, vol. 24, p. 310). Lenin argued that it was an utter mistake to suggest, because of some preconceived notion that conditions were not ripe, that the working class should support the bourgeois government, or that the proletariat should renounce its leading role in convincing the people of the urgency of taking practical steps toward the establishment of socialism. The time was ripe.

The steps Lenin advocated were nationalization of land, state control over banks and the establishment of a single state bank, control over the big capitalist syndicates and a progressive income tax. "Economically," Lenin argued, "these measures are timely; technically, they can be carried out immediately; politically they are likely to receive the support of the overwhelming majority of the peasants, who have everything to gain by these reforms" (1977, vol. 24, p. 311).

Praxis and catastrophe

Concentration upon questions of historical ripeness results in a failure to discuss, within the usual analysis of these conflicts among the different political groups, the economic content of their respective platforms, and what they hoped to accomplish by implementing their programs. As Lenin pointed out, though, in the "Impending Debacle" (1977, vol. 24, pp. 395–7), there were no substantial differences between the Narodniks and Mensheviks, on the one side, and the Bolsheviks, on the other, over the economic platform. What Lenin's complaint amounted to, therefore, was that the other groups were only socialists in word, being bourgeois when judged by their deeds. The Declaration of the "new" Provisional Government (issued on 6 May 1917 by the first coalition provisional government), for example, states that the "Provisional Government will redouble its determined efforts to combat economic disorganization by developing planned state and public control of production, transport, commerce and distribution of products, and where necessary will resort also to the organization of production."[60] Moreover, Lenin quotes at length from a resolution of the provisional government concerning economic policy (Lenin, 1977, vol. 24, p. 396):

Many branches of industry are ripe for a state trade monopoly (grain, meat, salt, leather), others are ripe for the organization of state-controlled trusts (coal, oil, metallurgy, sugar, paper); and, finally, present conditions demand in the case of nearly all branches of industry state control of the distribution of raw materials and manufactures, as well as price fixing ... Simultaneously, it is necessary to place all banking institutions under state and public control in order to combat speculation in goods subject to state control ... At the same time, the most energetic measures should be taken against the work-shy, even if labour conscription has to be introduced for that purpose ... The country is already in a state of catastrophe, and the only thing that can save it is the creative effort of the whole nation headed by a government which has consciously shouldered the stupendous task of rescuing a country ruined by war and the tsarist regime.

"We have here," Lenin commented, "state-controlled trusts, the combating of speculation, labour conscription – in what way does this differ from *terrible* Bolshevism, what more could these *terrible* Bolsheviks want?" Lenin answers his rhetorical question by simply stating that the provisional government has been "forced to accept the programme of '*terrible*' Bolshevism because no other programme offers a way out of the really calamitous debacle that is impending" (Lenin, 1977, vol. 24, p. 396). But Lenin charged the provisional government (the capitalists) with only accepting the programme "in order not to carry it out." Even though "all this can be introduced by decree which can be drafted in a single day" the new provisional government possessed no intention of taking the correct action. Disaster was imminent, Lenin warned, and action should have been immediate.[61]

Lenin summarized his argument in "Lessons of the Revolution" (1977, vol. 25, pp. 229–43). He argues that Russia was ruled as a "free" country for about four months after the overthrow of the tsarist regime on 27 February 1917. Even though the bourgeoisie were able to "capture" the government (Kadet Party), Soviets were elected in an absolutely free way – genuine organizations of the people, of the workers and peasants. Thus, there arose a situation of dual power. The Soviets should have taken state power in order to:

1   stop the war, and
2   stop the capitalists who were getting rich on the war.

But only the Bolshevik social democrats demanded that state power be transferred to the Soviets. The Menshevik social democrats and the Socialist-Revolutionaries opposed the transfer of power. "Instead of removing the bourgeois government and replacing it by a government of the Soviets," Lenin argued, "these parties insisted on supporting the bourgeois government, compromising with it and forming a coalition government with it. This policy of compromise with the bourgeoisie pursued by the Socialist-Revolutionary and the Menshevik parties, who enjoyed the confidence of the majority of the people, is the main content of the entire course of the development of the revolution during the first five months since it began" (1977, vol. 25, p. 234).

This policy of compromise represented the complete betrayal of the revolution. By April a spontaneous workers' movement was ready to assume power, but the Socialist-Revolutionaries and Mensheviks, instead, compromised with the capitalist's government, betraying the trust of the people, and allowing the capitalists to maintain state power.[62] The events of 1917, Lenin argued, merely confirmed old Marxist truths about the petty bourgeoisie and prepared the way for a true workers' revolution. The lesson was all too clear.

> The lesson of the Russian revolution is that there can be no escape for the working people from the iron grip of war, famine, and enslavement by the landowners and capitalists unless they completely break with the Socialist-Revolutionary and Menshevik parties and clearly understand the latter's treacherous role, unless they renounce all compromises with the bourgeoisie and resolutely side with the revolutionary workers. Only the revolutionary workers, if supported by peasant poor, are capable of smashing the resistance of the capitalists and leading the people in gaining land without compensation, complete liberty, victory over famine and the war, and a just and lasting peace
>
> (Lenin 1977, vol. 25, pp. 242–3).

This theme is reiterated in "The Impending Catastrophe and How to Combat It" (1977, vol. 25, pp. 327–69). There Lenin argues that six months had passed since the revolution, and, despite promises to the contrary, the catastrophe was closer than ever before. Unemployment had increased, shortages of food and other goods persisted, and yet, the "revolutionary" government did nothing to avert the catastrophe. Russia could wait no longer. The imperialist war was driving the country nearer to ruin at an ever-increasing speed. Yet the government did not implement the measures necessary to combat catastrophe and famine. The only reason, Lenin argued, that no movement was made to avert catastrophe was exclusively because their [i.e. the proper measures] realisation would affect the fabulous profits of a handful of landowners and capitalists" (1977, p. 328).

What was needed, according to Lenin, was for the government (a real revolutionary government) to take steps toward introducing the socialization of production; only such steps would avert catastrophe.[63] The chief and principal measure of combating, of averting, catastrophe and famine was to increase control of the production and distribution of goods, i.e. rationalize the economic process. "Control, supervision, accounting, regulation by the state, introduction of a proper distribution of labour-power in the production and distribution of goods, husbanding of the people's forces, the elimination of all wasteful effort, economy of effort" these are the measures necessary, Lenin argued. "Control, supervision and accounting are the prime requisites for combating catastrophe and famine." That this is so, Lenin stated, was "indisputable and universally recognized" (1977, vol. 25, p. 328).

The Mensheviks and the Socialist-Revolutionaries did nothing in the face of catastrophe. Their coalition with the government, and the government's sabotage of all attempts at control, made the Mensheviks and the Socialist-Revolutionaries "politically responsible to the Russian workers and peasants for winking at the capitalists and allowing them to frustrate all control" (1977, vol. 25, p. 330).[64] It is no wonder, given the increased suffering of the masses, that such energetic condemnations swung support from the provisional government toward the Bolsheviks.

The crux of the matter, to Lenin, was the need for a revolutionary dictatorship. "We cannot be revolutionary democrats in the twentieth century and in a capitalist country," he wrote, "if we fear to advance toward socialism" (Lenin, 1977, vol. 25, p. 360). Those who argued that Russia was not ripe for socialism, and, therefore, that the current revolution was a bourgeois revolution, had failed to "understand (as an examination of the theoretical basis of their opinion shows) what imperialism is, what capitalist monopoly is, what the state is, and what revolutionary democracy is. For anyone who understands this is bound to admit that there can be no advance except toward socialism" (Lenin, 1977, vol. 25, p. 361).

Capitalism in Russia, Lenin argued, had become monopoly capitalism due to the imperialist war. This was evidenced by the development of the syndicates, such as in sugar. Monopoly capitalism develops into state monopoly capitalism. The state, on the other hand, is nothing but the organization of the ruling class. If you substitute a revolutionary democratic state for a capitalist state "you will find that, given a really revolutionary-democratic state, state-monopoly capitalism inevitably and unavoidably implies a step, and more than one step, toward socialism!" Lenin continued by arguing:

> For socialism, is merely the next step forward from state-capitalist monopoly. Or, in other words, socialism is merely state-capitalist monopoly *which is made to serve the interests of the whole people and has to that extent ceased* to be capitalist monopoly ... The objective process of development is such that it is impossible to advance from *monopolies* (and the war has magnified their number, role and importance tenfold) without advancing toward socialism
> (Lenin, 1977, vol. 25, pp. 361–2, emphasis in original).

From imperialism to socialism

Lenin's political position can be understood more clearly if one considers his two theoretical works which basically bookend the revolutionary activity of 1917, *Imperialism, The Highest Stage of Capitalism*, and *The State and Revolution*.[65] *Imperialism* set out to explain how the world economic system had changed, and how the war was the inevitable outcome of this change. *The State and Revolution* concerned itself with the discussion of the nature of the state, its use in the revolution and subsequent dictatorship of the proletariat, and its inevitable "withering away" in the post-revolutionary world.

"Competition," Lenin argued in *Imperialism*, "becomes transformed into monopoly." "The result [of this increased monopolization of the economy]," Lenin continued, "is immense progress in the socialisation of production. In particular, the process of technical invention and improvement becomes socialised" (1977, vol. 22, p. 205). The natural operation of the capitalist mode of production leads to increased concentration of industry because of the profit advantage inherent in economies of scale.[66] The monopolization of the economy, to Lenin, is not just the result of a state-granted privilege, but inherent to the capitalist process of production.[67] The state can only affect the form the monopoly takes.

The increased concentration of industry that occurs in the highest stage of capitalism has the advantage of bringing economic life under conscious control. The chaotic process of free competition is overcome. "Capitalism in its imperialist stage," Lenin argued, "leads directly to the most comprehensive socialisation of production; it, so to speak, drags the capitalists, against their will and consciousness, into some sort of a new social order, a transitional one from complete free competition to complete socialisation" (1977, vol. 22, p. 205).

The system no longer relied upon the businessman's ability to satisfy consumer demand. The concentration of banking had made business more and more dependent upon pleasing finance capital to stay in operation.[68] Economic success was not measured by profits gathered from satisfying consumers, but by the connections one had to finance capital. Advantageous business connections and not free competition dominated economic life. "At the basis of these manipulations and swindles," Lenin observed, "lies socialised production; but the immense progress of mankind, which achieved this socialisation, goes to benefit ... the speculators" and not the people (1977, vol. 22, p. 207). The system must be made to serve the interest of the people instead.

One of the key factors in the socialization of the economic process under imperialism was the increased role of banks in economic life. "We see the rapid expansion of a close network of channels which cover the whole country," Lenin commented, "centralising all capital and all revenues, transforming thousands and thousands of scattered economic enterprises into a single national capitalist, and then into a world capitalist economy" (1977, vol. 22, p. 213). This "banking network," which under imperialism increases the power of the monopolistic giants, will provide the technical precondition for full socialization of the economy.[69]

All of industry has become interconnected (not scattered as under free competition) and dependent upon the central nerve of economic life: the bank. "As regards the close connection between banks and industry," Lenin stated, "it is precisely in this sphere that the new role of banks is, perhaps, most strikingly felt." The result of this new role "is that the industrial capitalist becomes more completely dependent on the bank" (1977, vol. 22, p. 220).

Lenin sees this, economically, as a good and natural development. It enables control over the economic life process.[70] "Finance capital," Lenin argued, "has created the epoch of monopolies, and monopolies introduce everywhere monopolist principles: the utilization of connections for profitable transactions takes the place of competition on the open market" (Lenin, 1977, vol. 22, p. 244). The era of finance capital had laid the necessary economic ground work for socialization.

On the other hand, the increased monopolization generated war as capitalists fought over economic territory and the division of the world market. "The capitalists divide the world, not out of any particular malice," Lenin stated, "but because the degree of concentration which has been reached forces them to adopt this method in order to obtain profits" (Lenin, 1977, vol. 22, p. 253). The inevitable striving of finance capital to expand its influence leads directly to colonialism and colonial conquest.[71] This increases the misery individuals suffer under capitalist rule, and brings to consciousness the antagonism of the classes. The imperialist war had laid the necessary ground work for political revolution.

Lenin argued that imperialism was capitalism in transition. As he stated (1977, vol. 22, pp. 265–6):

> Imperialism emerged as the development and direct continuation of the fundamental characteristics of capitalism in general. But capitalism only became capitalist imperialism at a definite and very high stage of its development, when certain of its fundamental characteristics began to change into, their opposites, when the features of the epoch of transition from capitalism to a higher social and economic system had taken shape and revealed themselves in all spheres. Economically, the main thing in this process is the displacement of capitalist-free competition by capitalist monopoly. Free competition is the basic feature of capitalism, and of commodity production generally; monopoly is the exact opposite of free competition, but we have seen the latter being transformed into monopoly before our eyes, creating large-scale industry and forcing out small industry; replacing large-scale by still larger scale industry, and carrying concentration of production and capital to the point where out of it has grown and is growing monopoly: cartels, syndicates and trusts, and merging with them, the capital of a dozen or so banks, which manipulate thousands of millions. At the same time the monopolies, which have grown out of free competition, do not eliminate the latter, but exist above it and alongside it, and thereby give rise to a number of very acute, intense antagonisms, factions and conflicts. Monopoly is the transition from capitalism to a higher system.

The epoch of imperialism had, according to Lenin, confirmed Marx's theory of the increased socialization of production under capitalism. Socialism was to be born in the womb of capitalism, and the transition phase would have all the pains associated with birth.[72] Imperialism signaled the advent of transition.

The interlocking of business and banking interests, and the world economy signified to Lenin the changing of social relations of production. As he wrote (Lenin, 1977, vol. 22, pp. 302–3, emphasis added):

When a big enterprise assumes gigantic proportions, and, *on the basis of an exact computation of mass data, organizes according to plan* the supply of raw materials to the extent of two thirds, or three-fourths, of all that is necessary for tens of millions of people; when the raw materials are transported in a systematic and organized manner to the *most suitable places of production*, sometimes situated hundreds or thousands of miles from each other; when a single centre directs all the consecutive stages of processing the materials right up to the manufacture of numerous varieties of finished articles; when these products are distributed *according to a single plan* among tens and hundreds of millions of consumers ... then it becomes evident that *we have socialisation of production* and not mere "interlocking."

The shell of private ownership and private enterprise no longer fits the content of the socialized mode of production; it must either decay (if its removal is artificially delayed) or be removed, but nevertheless it will inevitably fall away opening the door for people to exist in social relation with one another.

The process of removing the shell preparing for post-revolutionary social relations constitutes the subject of Lenin's *The State and Revolution*. This essay is perhaps one of the most fateful political tracts for the human condition written in the twentieth century. "The Soviet state," A. J. Polan writes, "that emerged after 1917 bore the stamp of *The State and Revolution* in all its subsequent phases, before and after the Bolsheviks secured the monopoly of power, before and after the decline of the Soviets as significant institutions, before and after the rise of Stalin."[73]

Yet there is some controversy surrounding Lenin's essay and its place within Lenin's political thinking. Robert Daniels, for example, has argued that *The State and Revolution* represents a utopian aberration in Lenin's political career – a product of revolutionary fervor – and, therefore, views it as a mistake to treat the text as representative of Lenin's political philosophy. "To consider *State and Revolution* as the basic statement of Lenin's political philosophy," Daniels states, "is a serious error." Daniels' argument amounts to pointing out that the essay's "argument for a utopian anarchism never actually became official policy after the revolution," and that the text only served as "the point of departure for the Left Opposition." It was the Leninism of 1902, the "What is to be Done" Lenin, "which prevailed as the basis for the political development of the USSR."[74]

Rodney Barfield, however, in challenging Daniels' interpretation has pointed out that Lenin's essay cannot be viewed as a product of revolutionary fervor because at the time he was researching it Lenin had no idea that revolution was looming on the horizon for Russia. "If *State and Revolution* is divorced from the revolutionary period and viewed as a theoretical work written for the future, a work intended to be Lenin's 'last will and testament,' consisting of ideas which were formulated not in the heat of revolution but in the cool detachment of the Zurich Library," Barfield argued, "then there is sufficient reason to interpret it as representing an integral part of the whole of Lenin's revolutionary thought and personal make-up. *The book may then be viewed as a serious revelation of the end to which Lenin had devoted his life.*"[75]

Alfred Evans has recently argued that *"State and Revolution* has been misinterpreted in most of the scholarly literature on Lenin's thought."[76] Lenin is simply not the utopian or quasi-anarchist, Evans argues, that people make him out to be in *State and Revolution.* Lenin did not possess a blind faith in the masses, nor did he reject authority from above. Evans contends that:[77]

> In 1917 he did not in theory or practice throw all caution to the winds and stake everything on the unskilled wisdom of the masses. Lenin's essay was vulnerable to the charge of being unrealistic, not because he failed to allow for authority from above, but because he expected centralized planning and guidance to be easily compatible with enthusiastic initiative from below.

Thus, *State and Revolution* is neither the crazy utopian tract depicted by Daniels nor the humanistic utopian tract depicted by Barfield, but a polemic in defense of the Marxian utopia of a politically and economically rationalized society. Lenin saw his "prime task" as that of re-establishing "what Marx really taught" (1977, vol. 25, p. 391). Once Lenin established, to his own satisfaction, what Marx really taught on the subject of the state, he turned his attention to clarifying the role of the state in the transition from capitalism to Communism and the tasks that the proletariat vanguard must confront in socioeconomic transformation.

Lenin defends the thesis of the withering away of the state against both the opportunists (Kautsky, etc.), who argue that the proletariat needs the state, and the anarchists, who argue that the state must be abolished without first transforming the economic system. The state – that special apparatus of coercion – is necessary during the transition, but it is a state that is withering away. Lenin asserted that (1977, vol. 25, p. 441):

> The proletariat needs the state only temporarily. We do not at all differ with the anarchists on the question of the abolition of the state as the aim. We maintain that, to achieve this aim, we must temporarily make use of instruments, resources and methods of state power against the exploiters, just as the temporary dictatorship of the oppressed class is necessary for the abolition of classes.

The proletariat state would be modeled upon the Paris Commune, Lenin argued, which could not be properly labeled a state in the sense that it no longer operated as an instrument for the suppression of the majority, but the minority (see 1977, vol. 25, pp. 441–7). The proletariat state must conduct the process of social transformation along the lines of democratic centralism.

From this point of reference, Lenin argued, following Marx, that the proletariat must win the battle of democracy in order to overcome mere bourgeois democracy. "Fully consistent democracy," Lenin wrote, "is impossible under capitalism, and under socialism all democracy will wither away."[78] But, "to develop democracy to the utmost, to find the forms for this development, to test them by practice, and so forth, all this is one of the component tasks of the struggle for the social revolution" (1977, vol. 25, p. 457). Democracy, though, is merely "a state which recognizes the subordination of the minority to the majority, i.e. an organization for the systematic use of force by one class against another, by one section of the population against another" (1977, vol. 25, p. 461). And, as Lenin pointed out, the goal of the social revolution was to transcend such a social existence (Ibid.):

> We set ourselves the ultimate aim of abolishing the state, i.e. all organized and systematic violence, all use of violence against people in general. We do not expect the advent of a system of society in which the principle of subordination of the minority to the majority will not be observed. In striving for socialism, however, we are convinced what it will develop into communism and, therefore, that the need for violence against people in general, for the subordination of one man to another, and of one section of the population to another, will vanish altogether since people will become accustomed to observing the elementary conditions of social life without violence and without subordination.

However, during the special historical stage of development, where the revolutionary dictatorship of the proletariat assumes state power, capitalist democracy (democracy for the few) will be transformed into democracy for the majority of the people. The vanguard of the oppressed ruling class must suppress the oppressors. "Simultaneously," Lenin wrote, "with an immense expansion of democracy, which for the first time becomes democracy for the poor, democracy for the people, and not democracy for the money-bags, the dictatorship of the proletariat imposes a series of restrictions on the freedom of the oppressors, the exploiters, the capitalists." "We must," Lenin emphasized, "suppress them in order to free humanity from wage slavery, their resistance must be crushed by force." And thus, Lenin concluded (1977, vol. 25, pp. 466–7)

> Democracy for the vast majority of the people, and suppression by force, i.e. exclusion from democracy, of the exploiters and oppressors of the people – this is the change democracy undergoes during the transition from capitalism to communism. Only in the communist society, when the resistance of the capitalists has been completely crushed, when the capitalists have disappeared, when there are no classes (i.e. when there is no distinction between the members of society as regards their relation to the social means of production), only then "the state ... ceases to exist," and "it becomes possible to speak of freedom." Only then will a truly complete democracy become possible and be realised, a democracy without exceptions whatever. And only then will democracy begin to wither away...

The extension of democracy under the dictatorship of the proletariat will not be without economic consequences. The political development in the transition period "will exert its influence on economic life" and "stimulate its transformation; and in its turn it will be influenced by economic development ... this is the dialectics of living history" (Lenin, 1977, vol. 25, p. 458).

The epoch of finance capital and the imperialist war had transformed capitalism into monopoly capitalism and provided the necessary prerequisites for transforming the social relations of production. "The proximity of such capitalism," Lenin wrote, "to socialism should serve genuine representatives of the proletariat as an argument proving the proximity, facility, feasibility and urgency of socialist revolution ..." (1977, vol. 25, p. 448). The "mechanism of social management" necessary for social transformation was at hand and demonstrated in such state-capitalist monopoly business organizations as the postal service. Lenin argued that once the workers overthrew the bourgeoisie they would inherit a "splendidly-equipped mechanism" that could easily be run by the united workers. This presented the proletariat with a "concrete, practical task which [could] immediately be fulfilled." "To organize the whole economy," Lenin wrote, "on the lines of the postal service so that the technicians, foremen, and accountants, as well as *all* officials, shall receive salaries no higher than "a workman's wage," all under the control and leadership of the armed proletariat – that is our immediate aim. This is the state and this is the economic foundation we need" (1977, vol. 25, pp. 431–2, emphasis in original).[79]

Or as Lenin put the matter of economic readiness later in the text (1977, vol. 25, p. 478, emphasis in original):

> Given these economic preconditions, it is quite possible, after the overthrow of the capitalists and the bureaucrats to proceed immediately, overnight, to replace them in the control over production and distribution, in the work of keeping account of labour and products, by the armed workers, by the whole of the armed population ... Accounting and control – that is mainly what is needed for the "smooth working," for the proper functioning, of the first phase of communist society.

Once all have learned to administer and control social production, then "the door will be thrown wide open for the transition from the first phase of communist society to its higher phase, and with it the complete withering away of the state" (1977, vol. 25, p. 479).

With the political and economic task of overthrowing the bourgeoisie and bringing social life under rational control in mind, Lenin broke off from completing *The State and Revolution*. The events of the fall of 1917 had transformed Lenin's activity from theorizing about revolution to revolutionary praxis. As Lenin put it on 30 November 1917: "It is more pleasant and useful to go through the experience of the revolution than to write about it" (1977, vol. 25, p. 497). Utopia had come to power.[80]

Utopia in power

The revolutionary midwife – the Party – had proceeded in assisting a successful delivery.[81] The socialist child was born and Lenin and the others were faced with the task of insuring its development and maturation. Overnight the new revolutionary government sought to implement its program by decree.[82] Referring to the Bolsheviks' economic program, K. Leites stated that: "It [was] safe to say that from the beginning of history humanity [had] never witnessed so complicated an experiment in government."[83] Having wrested political control from the provisional government the Bolsheviks were now "in a position to carry out the great economic revolution to which the political revolution was only a prelude, introduce socialism forthwith and transform the whole order of society."[84]

The economic transformation of Russian society consisted of implementing five major principles of social organization.[85] First, the elimination of private property in land and the means of production and the maximum extension of ownership. This included the working class taking control of the banks, railways, shipping, mining, large-scale industry, foreign trade, etc. Second, the forced allocation and mobilization of labor. The strictest militarization of labor was necessary to successfully construct socialism. Third, centralized management of economic production. Centralized planning of production and distribution of resources was deemed necessary for rationalizing the economic life process. Fourth, introduction of class and socialist principles of distribution. Rationing according to class was considered necessary for the achievement of an equitable distribution of resources. Fifth, the abolition of commodity and money relations and the substitution of a "natural economy" for the market economy. The elimination of the monetary economy and commodity production were deemed necessary for the "defetishization" of economic life and the transcendence of man's alienated social existence.[86]

Taken in combination, these policies constituted the economic program of the Bolsheviks from 1917 to 1921, although for purposes of exposition it is perhaps more accurate to place the beginning of this program as December 1917 or January 1918, when the Supreme Economic Council was formed and the nationalization of industry increased in pace. This period is known to economists and historians today as "War Communism," but at the time it was known simply as Communism.[87]

This system attempted to substitute a unified plan of economic life, i.e. rational social relations of production, for the chaotic and exploitative relations of production that existed under monopoly capitalism. As Leo Pasvolsky stated in 1921: "the plan, underlying the whole Soviet economic mechanism, is made up, primarily, of two elements, viz., unity and hierarchy. The first of these elements calls for an effective coordination of the various phases of the whole country's economic life and a concentration of the control over these various factors. The second makes it imperative that these various factors be classified and then subordinated one to another in an ascending order."[88] The task the Bolsheviks took upon themselves consisted not of "rebuilding the economic apparatus and organizing productive effort, but in placing both upon an entirely new basis. The Bolshevik[s] set out to purge the economic organization of Russia of its capitalist spirit and to breathe into it their version of the Socialist spirit."[89]

This program of socialist construction was presented in the Party platforms and other writings of the leading Bolsheviks during this time. Various decrees were announced and resolutions passed with the intention of building socialism in Russia (see Table 7.1). Theoretical works, socialist polemics and Party propaganda were issued to clarify and explain the Bolshevik program to the masses.

Lenin, for example, in his pamphlet *The Immediate Tasks of the Soviet Government* (1977, vol. 27, pp. 235–77), argued that "For the first time in history a socialist party has managed to complete in the main the conquest of power and the suppression of the exploiters, and has managed to *approach directly* the task of *administration*" (1977, vol. 27, p. 242, emphasis in original). Having successfully convinced the majority of the people that its program and tactics were correct, and having successfully captured political power, the Bolsheviks were faced with the immediate task of organizing social administration. The decisive aspect in accomplishing this task was organizing "the strictest and country-wide accounting and control of production and distribution of goods" (1977, vol. 27, p. 245).

The successful implementation of accounting and control, alongside the amalgamation of all banks into a single state bank, would transform the banking system into "nodal points of public accounting under socialism"[90] and allow the Soviets to organize "the population into a single cooperative society under proletariat management" (1977, vol. 27, pp. 252, 256). But because the introduction of accounting and control had lagged behind the expropriation of the expropriators, Lenin argued, socialist construction would be slower than was originally expected. "The possibility of building socialism," Lenin wrote, "depends exactly upon our success in combining the Soviet power and the Soviet organization of administration with the up-to-date achievements of capitalism."[91]

The possibility of socialism also required, according to Lenin, the subordination of the desires of the many to the unity of the plan. The rhetoric of workers' control and workers' democracy meant something entirely different from the model of decentralization that is promulgated today. To Lenin, as to most Marxists at that time, workers' control was a method by which central planning could be accomplished and not a decentralized alternative. As Silvana Malle points out: "In Lenin's model of power, workers' control would not evolve in any decentralized form, but, on the contrary, would facilitate the flow of information to the centre and the correct implementation of central guidelines."[92]

Centralized planning and control were considered the essential elements of socialist construction. "It must be said," Lenin wrote, "that large-scale machine industry – which is precisely the material source, the productive source, the foundation of socialism – calls for absolute and strict *unity of will*, which directs the joint labours of hundreds, thousands and tens of thousands of people." "The technical, economic and historical necessity of this is obvious," Lenin continued, "and all those who have thought about socialism have always

Table 7.1 Major economic decrees and resolutions passed by the Bolsheviks

Dates (Western calendar)	Decrees and resolutions
8 November 1917	The Council of People's Commissars is formed
8 November 1917	Decree on Land; abolished the landlords' right of property and called for the confiscation of landed estates
27 November 1917	Decree on Workers' Control over Production
15 December 1917	Supreme Economic Council is established
27 December 1917	Declaration of the Nationalization of Banks
15 January 1918	Dividend and interest payments and all dealings in stocks and bonds are declared illegal
16 January 1918	Declaration of the Rights of the Working and Exploited People abolished the exploitation of man by man
10 February 1918	Repudiation of all foreign debt
22 April 1918	Nationalization of foreign trade
1 May 1918	Abolition of inheritance
9 May 1918	Decree giving the Food Commissariat extraordinary powers to combat village bourgeoisie who were concealing and speculating on grain reserves
9 June 1918	Labor mobilization for the Red Army
28 June 1918	Nationalization of large-scale industry and railway transportation
2 November 1918	Decree on the Extraordinary Revolutionary Tax to support the Red Army and the International Socialist Revolution
22 March 1919	The Party Programme of the Eighth Party Congress; called for increased centralization of economic administration
29 March to 4 April 1920	The Outstanding Resolution on Economic Reconstruction is passed; called for increased centralization of economic administration to insure the unity of the plan necessary for the economic reconstruction after the civil war and foreign intervention
29 November 1920	Decree of the Supreme Economic Council on the nationalization of small industrial enterprises; all enterprises with mechanical power who employed five or more workers, and all enterprises without mechanical power who employed ten or more workers, were nationalized
March 1921	The Kronstadt Rebellion
8–16 March 1921	Resolution on Party Unity abolishing factionalism within the Party is accepted
23 March 1921	The Tax in Kind is established and the New Economic Policy is introduced

regarded it as one of the conditions of socialism." "But how can strict unity of will be ensured?" Lenin asked rhetorically. "By thousands subordinating their will to the will of one" he answered (1977, vol. 27, pp. 268–9, emphasis in original).

This theme of strict unity of the plan was echoed throughout various speeches and writings. Lenin, in fact, declared that anyone who challenged this view could not be properly considered a Marxist and was, therefore, not worth talking to. "Socialism," he wrote, "is inconceivable without large-scale capitalist engineering based on the latest discoveries of modern science. It is inconceivable without planned state organization which keeps tens of millions of people to the strictest observation of a unified standard in production and distribution. We Marxists have always spoken of this, and it is not worth while wasting two seconds talking to people who do not understand even this" (1977, vol. 27, p. 339).[93]

Such policy prescriptions were not limited to Lenin but pronounced by all the leading Bolsheviks. Trotsky, for example, during a speech to the Central Executive Committee on 14 February 1918, repeated the necessity of rationalizing the economic life of Russia through strict conformity to the plan. "Only a systematic organization of production," he said, "that is, one based on a universal plan – only a rational and economical distribution of all products can save the country. And that means socialism."[94] This project of rationalization, as we have seen, entailed the abolition of private ownership in the means of production for exchange. The chaotic process of market exchange and production must not merely be tampered with, but abolished. "Socialist organization of production," Trotsky declared in 1920, "begins with the liquidation of the market ... Production shall be geared to society's needs by means of a unified economic plan."[95]

The ubiquitous nature of monetary calculation under capitalist methods of production was to be replaced by the introduction of strict accounting and control within state enterprises. Proposals for the nationalization of the banks and the amalgamation of all banks into a single state bank was not, as Leon Smolinsky argues, a means to maintain money as the "lifeblood of the new planned economy," where "planners were to utilize the price system, making their choices on the basis of monetary values rather than physical terms." The economic transformation did not amount to utilizing "regulated markets" as a "medium through which plans would work themselves out."[96] The economic transformation demanded instead the abolition of "the alienated ability of mankind," i.e. money, and the substitution of moneyless accounting for monetary calculation.[97]

Yuri Larin, who was commissioned by Lenin to study the operation of the German economy and ways to implement that model in Russia, argued fervently for the most extreme centralization of the economy and the elimination of all market exchange and production.[98] Larin declared in the spring of 1919 that the moneyless system of accounting should be pursued post-haste. The nationalization of banks provided the framework to eliminate hand-to-hand currency and to transform the financial institutions of Soviet Russia into, as Lenin put it, "nodal points of public accounting." Under the new economic organization of society, circulating media were rapidly becoming unnecessary. "Money as a circulating media," Larin declared, "can already be got rid of to a considerable degree."[99] And at the plenary session of the Supreme Economic Council in April 1918, Larin said: "We have made up our minds to establish commodity exchange on new bases, as far as possible without paper money, preparing conditions for the time when money will only be an accounting unit."[100]

By May of 1918 the Party had declared that all state enterprises hand over all circulating media to the People's Bank, and in an August 1918 decree of the Supreme Economic Council it instructed the management of industries that, from then on, all settlements of deliveries and receipts of commodities should consist of book entries; on no account should they be used in transactions. The intent of the policy was to establish a cashless clearing system where circulating media would be replaced by bank money.[101] Osinskii, who was the manager of the State Bank and the first chairman of the Supreme Economic Council, described the monetary policy of the Bolsheviks as follows: "Our financial policy has been aimed recently at building up a financial system based on the emission of paper money, the ultimate objective of which is the natural transition to distribution of goods without using money and to transform the money tokens into accounting units ... When introducing the system of cashless clearing, our financial policy does not wish thereby to restore the disorder of monetary circulation." On the contrary, "its main aim is to create normal conditions of exchange without money between parts of the uniform and mostly socialized national economy."[102]

This program of the Bolsheviks was perhaps best articulated in the Program of the Communist Party of Russia adopted at the 8th Party Congress in March of 1919, and the popular exposition of that program by Bukharin and Preobrazhensky.[103] Bukharin gave a detailed presentation of the economic organization of Communist society in his chapter "Communism and the Dictatorship of the Proletariat." He argued that "the basis of communist society must be the social ownership of the means of production and exchange"; under these circumstances "society will be transformed into a huge working organization for cooperative production." The anarchy of production will cease as rationality is imposed upon the economic life process. "In such a social order, production will be organized."

No longer will one enterprise compete with another; the factories, workshops, mines, and other productive institutions will all be subdivisions, as it were, of one vast people's workshop, which will embrace the entire national economy of production. It is obvious that so comprehensive an organisation presupposes a general plan of production. If all the factories and workshops together with the whole of agricultural production are combined to form an immense cooperative enterprise, it is obvious that everything must be precisely calculated. We must know in advance how much labour to assign to the various branches of industry; what products are required and how much of each it is necessary to produce; how and where machines must be provided. These and similar details must be thought out beforehand, with approximate accuracy at least; and the work must be guided in conformity with our calculations. This is how the organization of communist production will be effected.[104]

The planning process was to be entrusted to "various kinds of bookkeeping offices and statistical bureau." Accounts would be kept (day-to-day) of production and its needs. All decisions for the allocation and distribution of resources necessary for social production would be orchestrated by the planning bureau. "Just as in an orchestra all the performers watch the conductor's baton and act accordingly," Bukharin wrote, "so here all will consult the statistical reports and will direct their work accordingly."[105]

By achieving *ex ante* coordination of economic activity through the substitution of production for direct use for production for exchange, Bukharin understood that, organizationally, the need for money would disappear. "Money," he simply stated, "would no longer be required" under these circumstances.[106]

The rationalization of economic life under Communism would eliminate the waste of capitalist production and lead to increased productivity. This burst of productivity would free individuals from the "chains imposed upon them by nature." The utopian promise of this project was that "concurrently with the disappearance of man's tyranny over man, the tyranny of nature over man will likewise vanish. Men and women will for the first time be able to lead a life worthy of thinking beings instead of a life of brute beasts."[107]

Only the scientific organization of production under the direction of a unified plan constructed by the dictatorship of the proletariat could put an end to the capitalist anarchy of production and eliminate the tyranny of man over man. With the breakdown of commodity production and its replacement by the "socio-natural system of economic relations, the corresponding ideological categories also burst, and once this is so, the theory of the economic process is confronted with the need for a transition to natural economic thinking, i.e. to the consideration of both society and its parts as systems of fundamental elements in their natural form."[108] Social relations would no longer be veiled by the commodity fetishism of the monetary exchange system.

This project of rationalization and emancipation is spelled out in the party program adopted at the 8th Congress. In the realm of economic affairs, this amounted to expropriating the expropriators, increasing the productive forces of society by eliminating the contradictions of capitalism, mobilizing labour, organizing the trade unions, educating the workers, and basically, securing "the maximum solidarisation of the whole economic apparatus."[109] In order to accomplish this goal the Bolsheviks seized the banks and merged them into a sole single state bank. The bank, thus, "became an instrument of the workers' power and a lever to promote economic transformation." The bank would become an apparatus of unified book-keeping. "In proportion as the organization of a purposive social economy is achieved, this will lead to the disappearance of banks, and to their conversion into the central book-keeping establishment of communist society." The immediate elimination of money was not yet possible, but the party was moving in that direction. "Upon the basis of the nationalisation of banking, the Russian Communist Party endeavours to promote a series of measures favouring a moneyless system of account keeping, and paving the way for the abolition of money."[110]

The Bolsheviks did not just accept this program in the heat of civil war as many historians assert. The civil war no doubt affected the way that the program was implemented, but the program itself was clearly ideological in origin. It emerged out of the conscious attempt to achieve Marx's utopia. Even after the civil war had ended, the Bolsheviks embarked upon continuous efforts of rationalizing the economy. For example, the "Outstanding Resolutions on Economic Reconstruction" (adopted by the 9th Congress of the Russian Communist Party in April 1920) argued that "the basic condition of economic recovery of the country is the undeviating carrying out of a unified economic plan."[111] And in November 1920, V. Milyutin, then Assistant President of the Supreme Economic Council, announced the decree of the Council to nationalize even small industrial enterprises and bring them under conscious control.[112] Only the insurgency of the sailors at Kronstadt convinced the Bolsheviks to reconsider their policy.

Utopia in disarray

The result of this policy of socialist transformation was an economic disaster.[113] "Considered purely as an economic experiment," William Chamberlin commented, "War Communism may fairly be considered one of the greatest and most overwhelming failures in history. Every branch of economic life, industry, agriculture, transportation, experienced conspicuous deterioration and fell far below the pre-War levels of output."[114] Economic life completely fell apart. "Never in all history," declared H. G. Wells, "has there been so great a debacle before."[115] As Moshe Lewin points out: "The whole modern sector of urbanized and industrialized Russia suffered a severe setback, as becomes obvious from the population figures." "By 1920," he reports, "the number of city dwellers had fallen from 19 per cent of the population in 1917 to 15 per cent. Moscow lost half its population, Petrograd two-thirds."[116] After only three years of Bolshevik rule: "The country lay in ruins, its national income one-third of the 1913 level, industrial production a fifth (output in some branches being virtually zero), its transportation system shattered, and agricultural production so meager that a majority of the population barely subsisted and millions of others failed even that."[117] This economic debacle is recorded in various memoirs and novels of the time.[118]

   The burst of productivity expected from the rationalization of economic life was not forthcoming. Instead, economic life and social relations under Communist rule merely worsened the condition of the masses of people. If "Lenin was the midwife of socialism," then the "mother's belly had been opened and ransacked, and still there was no baby."[119] The socialist project proved unrealizable; utopia became dystopia within a matter of three years.

   The Soviet socialist failure bore full witness to the Mises–Hayek critique of socialist planning. The economic disorganization of Bolshevik Russia was, as Lancelot Lawton pointed out, a result of the "disregard of economic calculation."[120] The attempt to realize a moneyless accounting system to replace the monetary calculation of capitalism proved to be an insurmountable difficulty in economic coordination.[121] "With moneyless accounting, as with all Bolshevik innovations, the simplicity of theory vanished in the unavoidable complications of practice."[122] The Bolsheviks had attempted to eliminate, by decree, the only means to achieve the economic knowledge necessary for advanced industrial production; the monetary calculation embedded within the dynamic process of exchange and production. The "attempts of the Bolsheviks to establish moneyless accounting ended with no accounting at all." In striving "to make all men wealthy, the Soviet state had made it impossible for any man to be otherwise than poor."[123] What had happened under the rule of Lenin and Trotsky was, as Mises said, "merely destruction and annihilation."[124]

Throughout 1920, Soviet power was threatened as the social order of production was destroyed. The political protests and uprisings culminated in March 1921 with the Kronstadt uprising. The "waves of uprisings of workers and peasants," the Kronstadters declared, "have testified that their patience has come to an end. The uprising of the labourers has drawn near. The time has come to overthrow the commissarocracy ... Kronstadt has raised for the first time the banner of the uprising for the Third Revolution of the toilers ... The autocracy has fallen. The Constituent Assembly has departed to the region of the damned. The commissarocracy is crumbling."[125]

The Kronstadt rebellion represented an attempt by disillusioned revolutionaries to halt what they perceived to be a perversion of the revolution at the hands of the Bolsheviks. "In its economic content," Paul Avrich points out, "the Kronstadt program was a broadside aimed at the system of War Communism. It reflected the determination of the peasantry and working class to sweep away the coercive policies to which they had been subjected for nearly three years."[126] The Bolshevik government – and the government alone – was responsible for the hardship. Little or no blame was placed upon the civil war or the Allied intervention and blockade. "All the suffering and hardship, rather, was laid at the door of the Bolshevik regime."[127]

The Bolshevik regime must be rejected, the Kronstadters argued. Only by overthrowing the Bolsheviks could the Russian worker and peasant expect to live a humane existence. "Communist rule has reduced all of Russia," they declared, "to unprecedented poverty, hunger, cold, and other privation. The factories and mills are closed, the railways on the verge of breakdown. The countryside has been fleeced to the bone. We have no bread, no cattle, no tools to work the land. We have no clothing, no shoes, no fuel. The workers are hungry and cold. The peasants and townsfolk have lost all hope for an improvement of their lives. Day by day they come closer to death. The communist betrayers have reduced you to this."[128]

The "new serfdom" associated with Bolshevik political power was condemned throughout the land. "Faced with a simultaneous revolt of both the proletariat and the peasants," Leonard Shapiro has pointed out, the Bolsheviks were "prepared for drastic measures aimed at preserving party rule."[129] And it was at this time that Lenin *et al.* decided to shift gears. The New Economic Policy (NEP) was introduced, but at the same time, it is important to remember, the Bolsheviks declared a political monopoly.

"From the standpoint of the development of the experiment in the economics of Communism," Leo Pasvolsky wrote, "these measures [i.e. NEP] are very significant. They represent the first official, generalized acknowledgement of the breaking down of the state monopoly of distribution."[130] Never again did the Soviets dare to implement such a project of economic centralization. Never again did they attempt to realize the Marxian utopia of a completely centrally planned organization superceding market modes of production and eliminating monetary calculation. Even under the most extreme policies of Stalinism, monetary calculation, though highly interfered with, served as the basis of "planning." Marxism, instead, became merely a mobilizing ideology to maintain political power for the party.

Conclusion

The Soviet experience with Communism from 1918 to 1921 bears directly upon the calculation argument advanced by Mises. The Marxian project of economic rationalization proved unrealizable in practice. Today very few advocates of socialism would argue for comprehensive central planning, but they hold fast to the Marxist critique of the anarchy of the market. "But," as Don Lavoie has argued, "the modification from comprehensive planning, which seeks to completely replace market competition as the coordinating process of the economy, to noncomprehensive planning, which seeks to reconcile planning with market institutions, is hardly an alteration of analysis. *It is the toppling of the basic pillar of Marxist analysis ... To preserve money, prices, and so on is to abandon Marx's whole system.*"[131]

Besides the point that Marx's critique is only relevant if the point of references from which he made the critique is valid, i.e. the future socialist world, there is another fundamental criticism that must be considered. As Soviet historian and philosopher A. Tsipko has recently argued in a series of essays on "The Roots of Stalinism,"[132] the question of whether a democratic socialism can be built upon a non-commodity, non-market foundation is one of importance not only to those who are thinking about the future but also fundamental to understanding the past. "Why is it," Tsipko asks, "that in all cases without exception and in all countries ... efforts to combat the market and commodity–money relations have always led to authoritarianism, to encroachments on the rights and dignity of the individual, and to an all-powerful administration and bureaucratic apparatus?" He concludes by saying that "All this bespeaks an urgent need for a serious and open 'self-audit' of Marx's teachings on the economic bases of the future society, on how the theoretical forecast relates to the real results of its implementation in real life."[133]

Acknowledgments

This chapter draws freely from material in Boettke 1988 and 1990. I would like to thank Don Lavoie, Karen Vaughn, Ronald Jensen, Viktor Vanberg, Steve

Horwitz, and David Prychitko for helpful comments and criticisms on an earlier draft. In addition, an anonymous referee provided helpful criticisms and suggestions for improving the presentation. Responsibility for remaining errors is my own.

Bibliography

Armentano, D. T. (1978) "A Critique of Neoclassical and Austrian Monopoly Theory," in L. M. Spadaro (ed.) *New Directions in Austrian Economics*, Kansas City: Sheed, Andrews and McMeel.

Avrich, P. (1970) *Kronstadt 1921*, New York: Norton.

Barfield, R. (1971) "Lenin's Utopianism: State and Revolution," *Slavic Review* 30(1).

Baron, S. (1962) "Between Marx and Lenin: George Plekhanov," in L. Labedz (ed.) *Revisionism: Essays on the History of Marxist Ideas*, New York: Praeger Publishers.

Baron, S. (1963) *Plekhanov: The Father of Russian Marxism*, Stanford, CA: Stanford University Press.

Berdyaev, N. (1972) (first published 1937) *The Origin of Russian Communism*, Ann Arbor University of Michigan Press.

Besançon, A. (1981) *The Rise of the Gulag: Intellectual Origins of Leninism*, New York: Continuum.

Bettelheim, C. (1976) *Class Struggles in the USSR, 1917–23*, New York: Monthly Review Press.

Boettke, P. J. (1988) "The Soviet Experiment with Pure Communism," *Critical Review* 2(4).

Boettke, P. J. (1990) *The Political Economy of Soviet Socialism, 1918–28*, Boston: Kluwer Academic Publishers.

Brutzkus, B. (1935/1982) *Economic Planning in Russia*, Westport, CT: Hyperion Press.

Bukharin, N. I. (1979) "The Economics of the Transition Period," in *The Politics and Economics of the Transition Period*, Boston: Routledge & Kegan Paul.

Bukharin, N. I. and Preobrazhensky, E. (1966) (first published 1919) *The A.B.C. of Communism*, Ann Arbor: University of Michigan Press.

Carr, E. H. (1980) *The Bolshevik Revolution, 1917–23*, three volumes, New York: Norton.

Chamberlin, W. H. (1987) *The Russian Revolution*, two volumes, Princeton: Princeton University Press.

Cohen, S. (1972), "In Praise of War Communism," in A. Rabinovitch and J. Rabinowitch (eds.) *Revolution and Politics in Russia*, Bloomington, IN: Indiana University Press.

Cohen, S. (1980) (first published 1971) *Bukharin and the Bolshevik Revolution*, New York: Oxford University Press.

Cowen, T. and Krozner, R. (1987) "The Development of the New Monetary Economics," *Journal of Political Economy* 95(3).

Daniels, R. V. (1960a) *The Conscience of the Revolution*, Cambridge, MA: Harvard University Press.

Daniels, R. V. (1960b) *A Documentary History of Communism*, New York: Vintage Books.

Day, R. (1973) *Leon Trotsky and the Politics of Economic Isolation*, Cambridge: Cambridge University Press.

Demsetz, H. (1982) "Barriers to Entry," *American Economic Review* 72(1).

Djilas, M. (1957) *The New Class*, New York: Praeger.

Dobb, M. (1948) *Soviet Economic Development Since 1917*, New York: International Publishers.

Evans, A. (1987) "Rereading Lenin's 'State and Revolution,' " *Slavic Review* 46(1).

Gadamer, H. G. (1960/1985) *Truth and Method*, New York: Crossroads.

Goldman, E. (1923) *My Disillusionment in Russia*, New York: Doubleday, Page & Co.

Goldman, E. (1924) *My Further Disillusionment in Russia*, New York: Doubleday, Page & Co.

Habermas, J. (1984) *The Theory of Communicative Action: Reason and the Rationalization of Society*, vol. 1, translated by Thomas McCarthy, Boston: Beacon Press.

Harding, N. (ed.) (1983) *Marxism in Russia: Key Documents 1879–1906*, New York: Cambridge University Press.

Hayek, F. A. von (1979) (first published 1952) *The Counter-Revolution of Science*, Indianapolis: Liberty Press.

Hayek, F. A. von (1980) (first published 1967) "The Theory of Complex Phenomena," in F. A. von Hayek, *Studies in Philosophy, Politics and Economics*, Chicago: University of Chicago Press.

Hayek, F. A. von (1973) *Law Legislation and Liberty*, three volumes, London and Henley: Routledge & Kegan Paul.

Held, D. (1980) *An Introduction to Critical Theory*, Berkeley, CA: University of California Press.

Heller, M. and Nekrich, A. (1986) *Utopia in Power*, New York: Summit Books.

Hilferding, R. (1985) (first published 1910) *Finance Capital: A Study of the Latest Phase of Capitalist Development*, London: Routledge & Kegan Paul.

Holman, G. P. (1973) "War Communism," or the *Besieger Besieged: A Study of Lenin's Social and Political Objectives from 1918 to 1921*, Unpublished PhD thesis, Georgetown University.

Hunt, R. N. Carew (1969) (first published 1950) *The Theory and Practice of Communism*, Baltimore: Penguin Books.

Jay, M. (1984) *Marxism and Totality: The Adventures of a Concept From Lukacs to Habermas*, Berkeley, CA: University of California.

Johnson, P. (1983) *Modern Times*, New York: Harper and Row.

Kaufman, A. (1953) "The Origin of the Political Economy of Socialism," *Soviet Studies* 4(3).

Kolakowski, L. (1985) (first published 1978) *Main Currents of Marxism*, vol. 2, New York: Oxford University Press.

Kolko, G. (1964) *The Triumph of Conservatism*, New York: Free Press.

Konrad, G. and Szelenyi, I. (1979) *The Intellectuals on the Road to Class Power*, New York: Harcourt Brace Jovanovich.

Lavoie, D. (1985a) *National Economic Planning: What is Left?* Cambridge, MA: Ballinger Press.

Lavoie, D. (1985b) *Rivalry and Central Planning*, New York: Cambridge University Press.

Lavoie, D. (1986/1987) "The Political and Economic Illusions of Socialism," *Critical Review* 1(1).

Lawton, L. (1932) *An Economic History of Soviet Russia*, two volumes, London: Macmillan.

Leites, K. (1922) *Recent Economic Developments in Russia*, New York: Oxford University Press.

Lenin, V. L (1977) *Collected Works*, 45 volumes, Moscow: Progress Publishers.

Lewin, M. (1985) *The Making of the Soviet System*, New York: Pantheon Books.

Lih, L. (1986) "Bolshevik Razverstka and War Communism," *Slavic Review* 45(4).

Lovell, D. (1984) *From Marx to Lenin: An Evaluation of Marx's Responsibility for Soviet Authoritarianism*, New York: Cambridge University Press.

McCarthy, T. (1985) *The Critical Theory of Jurgen Habermas*, Cambridge, MA: MIT Press.

McCloskey, D. (1985) *The Rhetoric of Economics*, Madison: University of Wisconsin Press.

Malle, S. (1985) *The Economic Organization of War Communism*, 1918–1921, New York: Cambridge University Press.

Marx, K. (1973) *Grundrisse*, New York: Vintage Books.

Marx, K. (1977) *Economic and Philosophical Manuscripts of 1844*, Moscow: Progress Publishers.

Marx, K. (1978) *The Poverty of Philosophy*, Moscow: Progress Publishers.

Marx, K. and Engels, F. (1969) *Selected Works*, three volumes, Moscow: Progress Publishers.

Marx, K. (1906) (first published 1867) *Capital: A Critique of Political Economy*, New York: Modern Library.

Merkle, A. (1980) *Management and Ideology*, Berkeley, CA: University of California.

Mises, L. von (1980) *Theory of Money and Credit*, Indianapolis: Liberty Press.

Mises, L. von (1957/1985) *Theory and History*, Auburn, AL: Ludwig von Mises Institute.

Mises, L. von (1975) (first published 1920) "Economic Calculation in the Socialist Commonwealth," in F. A. von Hayek (ed.) *Collectivist Economic Planning*, New York: Augustus M. Kelley.

Nove, A. (1984) (first published 1969) *An Economic History of the U.S.S.R.*, New York: Penguin Books.

Pasvolsky, L. (1921) *The Economics of Communism: With Special Reference to Russia's Experiment*, New York: Macmillan.

Polan, A. J. (1984) *Lenin and the End of Politics*, Berkeley: University of California Press.

Polanyi, M. (1980) (first published 1951) *The Logic of Liberty*, Chicago: University of Chicago Press.

Preobrazhensky, E. (1920) *Paper Money During the Proletarian Dictatorship*, University of Michigan: Ann Arbor Press.

Prychitko, D. (1988) "Marxism and Decentralized Socialism," *Critical Review* 2(4).

Prychitko, D. (1989) "The Political Economy of Worker' Self-Management: A Market Process Critique," Unpublished PhD thesis, Department of Economics, George Mason University, VA.

Rabinowitch, A. (1978) *The Bolsheviks Come to Power*, New York: Norton.

Ransome, A. (1919) *Russia in 1919*, New York: B. W. Huebsch.

Reed, J. (1985) (first published 1919) *Ten Days That Shook the World*, New York: Penguin Books.

Remington, T. (1984) *Building Socialism in Bolshevik Russia, 1917–21*, Pittsburgh: University of Pittsburgh Press.

Remnick, D. (1988) "The Victory of Bukharin's Widow," *The Washington Post* Tuesday 6 December.

Rizzi, B. (1985) (first published 1939) *The Bureaucratization of the World*, New York: Free Press.

Roberts, P. C. (1971) *Alienation and the Soviet Economy*, Albuquerque, NM: University of New Mexico Press.

Rothbard, M. N. (1970) *Man, Economy and State: A Treatise on Economic Principles*, two volumes, Los Angeles: Nash Publishing.

Rothbard, M. N. (1984) "The Federal Reserve as a Cartelization Device: The Early Years, 1913–30," in B. Siegel (ed.) *Money in Crisis*, Cambridge: Ballinger Publishing.

Rustow, A. (1980) (first published 1950–7) *Freedom and Domination: A Historical Critique of Civilization*, Princeton, NJ: Princeton University Press.

Selgin, G. (1987) "The Yield on Money Held Revisited," *Market Process* 5(1).

Selgin, G. (1988) *The Theory of Free Banking*, Totawa, NJ: Rowman and Littlefield.

Selucky, R. (1979), *Marxism, Socialism, Freedom*, New York: St Martin's Press.

Selyunin, V. (1988) "Sources," *Novy Mir* May.

Serge, V. (1963) *Memoirs of a Revolutionary, 1901–41*, New York: Oxford University Press.

Shadwell, A. (1927) *The Breakdown of Socialism*, Boston: Little, Brown & Co.

Shapiro, L. (1960/1971) *The Communist Party of the Soviet Union*, New York: Oxford University Press.

Sljapnikov, C. (1964) *The Trotsky Papers*, London: Mouton, vol. 1.

Smolinsky, L. (1967) "Planning without theory, 1917–67," *Survey* 64.

Sirotkin, V. (1989) "Lessons of N.E.P.," *Izvestiya* 9 March.

Stojanovic, S. (1987) "Marx and the Bolshevization of Marxism," *Praxis International* 6(4).

Stojanovic, S. (1988) *Perestroika: From Marxism and Bolshevism to Gorbachev*, Buffalo: Prometheus Books.

Szamuely, L. (1974) *First Models of the Socialist Economic Systems: Principles and Theories*, Budapest: Akademiai.

Trotsky, L. (1932/1987) *The History of the Russian Revolution*, three volumes, New York: Pathfinder Press.

Trotsky, L. (1947) *Permanent Revolution*, Calcutta: Atawar Rahman.

Trotsky, L. (1964) *The Trotsky Papers*, vol. 1 *(1917–19)*, London: Mouton.

Trotsky, L. (1983) "Our Revolution (1906): Extracts," in N. Harding (ed.) *Marxism in Russia: Key Documents 1879–1906*, New York: Cambridge University Press.

Tsipko (1989) "The Roots of Stalinism: Four Essays," *Current Digest of the Soviet Press*, XLI, nos. 10, 11, 12, 13 (April).

Vorhies, W. F. (1982) "Marx and Mises on Money: The Monetary Theories of Two Opposing Political Economies," Unpublished PhD thesis, University of Colorado.

Wallace, N. (1983) "A Legal Restrictions Theory of the Demand for Money and the Role of Monetary Policy," *Federal Reserve Bank of Minneapolis Quarterly Review* 4.

Weinstein, J. (1968) *The Corporate Ideal in the Liberal State*, 1900–18, Boston: Beacon Press.

Wells, H. G. (1921) *Russia in the Shadows*, New York: George H. Doran.

White, L. H. (1984) "Competitive Payment Systems and the Unit of Account," *American Economic Review* 74(4).

White, L. H. (1987) "Accounting for Non-interest-bearing Currency: A Critique of Legal Restrictions Theory of Money," *Journal of Money, Credit and Banking* 19(4).

Wilson, E. (1940) *To the Finland Station*, New York: Doubleday.

Wittfogel, K. (1964) (first published 1957) (1964) *Oriental Despotism: A Comparative Study of Total Power*, New Haven: Yale University Press.

Zaleski, E. (1971) (first published 1962) *Planning for Economic Growth in the Soviet Union, 1918–32*, Chapel Hill, NC: University of North Carolina Press.

8 Soviet venality

A rent-seeking model of the Communist state*

Introduction

We live today in what might be termed the "post-Soviet era." Soviet-style systems are an endangered species; Cuba and North Korea are really the only surviving representative examples. Around the world, the Soviet economic model has been largely overturned.

But the Soviet economic system, and the numerous copies which that system spawned, played a crucial role on the world stage until quite recently. The Soviet Union itself survived for three-quarters of a century. Therefore, the nature and functioning of this economic system remains an important problem which requires explanation.

The progress of post-Communist reform in former Soviet-style states continues to take a variety of forms, with varying degrees of success. This ongoing reform process is the object of considerable controversy among economists. However, there is a remarkably stable consensus about the Soviet past and what it represented.

According to this view, the Soviet economy was a centrally planned system, in which all productive resources were owned by the state, and all important production and distribution decisions were made by state economic planning bodies (most importantly, Gosplan). Although a small "private sector" existed in the former USSR, in which small-scale private production of various consumer goods were legally exchanged, these private exchanges were basically relatively trivial exceptions to the rule that the economy was a non-market, centrally planned system.

This view represents the core of the comparative economic systems orthodoxy. These ranks include a number of economists, who have turned their attentions to the question of how a socialist economy could actually function – in theory. Sophisticated models of "optimal" planning have been developed, which explain how a hypothetical socialist economy might operate.

*Originally published as Boettke, P. J. and Anderson, G. (1997) "Soviet Venality: A Rent-seeking Model of the Communist State," *Public Choice* 93: 37–53.

Unfortunately, the actual operation of the Soviet economy bore little resemblance to the predictions of these optimal planning models. Soviet "planning" seemed to mostly occur after-the-fact. With the breakdown, and finally the collapse, of the Soviet state, it has become increasingly apparent that central planning authorities had little real power to manage the Soviet economy. Furthermore, the theory of central planning requires us to assume that governmental authorities are selfless public servants motivated solely by their desire to maximize the social welfare. This is inconsistent with the basic assumptions about human behavior which undergird modern economics. Thus, the existing theory of the centrally planned economy has little relevance to understanding how the Soviet economy actually worked.

We propose an alternative model of the Soviet-style economy which avoids these problems. We argue that the mature Soviet system was not a hierarchical central planning system at all, but was really a market economy heavily encrusted with central government regulation and restrictions. The Soviet state employed these various interventions to extract revenue from the economy, as an alternative to collecting revenue via the use of taxation. In short, the style system can be usefully modeled as a modern example of a mercantilist economy. Like France under Louis XIV, the Soviet system was an elaborate device by which the autocrat transferred wealth to itself, and was not a radical alternative to a market economy.

This chapter is organized as follows. The first section outlines the nature of the mercantilistic model, and discusses its application to the case of seventeenth-century France, where the sale of monopoly privileges by the monarch was an important device for raising revenue. The second section applies the model to the case of the Soviet Union, and argues that this model has greater explanatory power than the orthodox alternative. The third section explains the central planning apparatus of the Soviet economy from our "neo-mercantilist" perspective. The fourth section discusses the importance of private market activity in the Soviet Union. The fifth section addresses questions concerning how the "neo-mercantilist" Soviet system monitored and controlled the flow of rents. Finally, the sixth section summarizes and concludes the chapter.

The mercantilist model: privilege for revenue

Conventional models of the Soviet economy all share a basic assumption: the Soviet Union was a novel undertaking, an economy organized around principles unique in human history. We challenge this assumption. The Soviet economy was actually a relatively minor variation on the mercantilist pattern, which had important antecedents in this history of Europe. In this section, we review the major elements in the mercantilist model.

The term "mercantilism" connotes a variety of economic tenets, including such things as the equation of specie with wealth, and the regulation of the foreign trade sector in order to generate the net inflow of specie. Certainly, many European writers of the period between approximately 1550 and 1776 did argue in favor of these tenets, but mercantilism as a system included a number of other important aspects. While regulation of external (foreign) trade was a major interest of mercantilist economic writers, "mercantilism" (as defined by Heckscher 1955, and other historians) also included an elaborate system of regulation of internal (domestic) trade. It is this latter system of internal trade which concerns us.

In seventeenth-century England and France, the government employed the sale of various monopoly rights as a means of raising revenue. That is, the monarch sold monopoly privileges for cash or another consideration (often loans on preferred terms).

Modern governments continue to provide monopoly privileges to favored groups and individuals, and the literature on interest-group models of political behavior analyze such monopolies as the marketed output of politicians and bureaucrats. Modern democratic governments, however, have instituted numerous laws against overt bribe-taking and blatant exchanges of government-supplied privileges for cash. When a modern government legislates a monopoly in some market, the political decision-makers involved typically offer some public interest argument in favor of the monopoly. In this context, an interest-group explanation for the supply of governmentally provided monopoly rights is only one plausible competing hypothesis.

The mercantilist period in England and France represents a less ambiguous problem for economic analysis (see Ekelund and Tollison 1981). Monarchs during this period were quite open in exchanging monopoly privileges for consideration from the potential monopolist. Mercantilist monarchs relied on the sale of monopoly privileges to raise revenue instead of taxation for several reasons.

Direct taxes on land had been the chief source of revenue for ancient and medieval governments, and such taxes continued to play an important role into the seventeenth century. However, the administrative costs associated with raising tax revenues were very high. Effective modern tax-collecting bureaucracies simply did not exist. Technological limitations constrained the efficiency of tax collection; before telephones, radios, and even telegraphs, not to mention typewriters and computers, the costs of administering any tax system were high and the costs of evasion low. In England, competition between the King and Parliament restricted the monarch's ability to raise money via taxation (which required Parliamentary approval), whereas venality was less restricted.[1] In any event, income taxation — the source of the bulk of modern central government revenue in developed countries — was beyond seventeenth-century administrative capabilities. From the monarch's perspective, raising revenue by means of the production and sale of monopolies made sense. For example, in the early seventeenth century in France, 30–40% of state revenue derived from this "venality" (see Webber and Wildavsky 1986, p. 267).

Operationally, the mercantilist system was at base a market economy, where most property was privately owned, but with a substantial government sector. The state intervened extensively in the private economy, in the form of detailed regulations. Many prices and wages were subject to control; movements of labor and capital were intensely restricted; numerous markets for ordinary private goods (e.g. everything from playing cards to aluminum to woolen goods) were monopolized or cartelized; and individual rights were highly vulnerable to governmental fiat, without secure protection from the Rule of Law (see Lipson 1968; Hayek 1960; and Nef 1968).

The mercantilist system did not represent itself as an effort to centrally plan the economy. Similarly, the mercantilist state did not purport to abolish private property, neither did it claim to eliminate the market price system. The ideological claims made on mercantilism's behalf were modest and diffuse.

Another characteristic of the mercantilist system was the massive expansion of standing armies. Military forces grew rapidly, and became the largest component in government expenditure. Wealth maximization by the monarch required that the King secure himself from short-run threats, internal and external, even at the expense of long-term economic development. Given this security constraint, combined with the high cost of contemporary tax collection systems, mercantilist venality was the optimal device available to the monarch to raise revenue. Thus, the sale of monopoly privileges by the monarch was efficient from the standpoint of that ruler, even if the resulting interference in markets reduced overall economic efficiency.

The Soviet economy as a neo-mercantilist state

In the 1920s through 1940s, the comparative systems literature was rocked by the "socialist calculation debate." Ludwig von Mises and (later) F. A. von Hayek argued that replacing a market economy by a centrally planned socialist state was literally impossible (see Hayek 1935/1956). Socialist theorists insisted that the socialist society could dispense with money and markets for the allocation of resources, and rely exclusively on the dictates of central planning authorities for determining efficient economic functioning. Mises and Hayek countered that in the absence of monetary prices reflecting the relative scarcities of capital goods, which could only be generated by markets, central planners would receive neither the appropriate incentives nor the information that is required to promote rational resource use. This Mises–Hayek critique, however, had minimal influence within the comparative systems literature. One reason for this neglect involved a major apparent failing of their argument: it seemed inconsistent with the actual existence of socialist economies such as the Soviet Union. Not only did the Soviet Union exist, but it appeared to achieve relatively high rates of economic growth, as well as impressive technological advances.

The counter-argument offered by the defenders of the Mises–Hayek position stressed the ability of Soviet planners to rely on world market prices to aid in the allocation of scarce resources and the empirical fact of the large-scale borrowing of technology from Western market economies (see Rothbard 1970: 933–4). In addition, pockets of private market activity existed throughout the Soviet period in agriculture and in illicit consumer markets.

There is also a more basic problem. All varieties of the socialist model presume that a monolithic state organization will expropriate productive resources and plan all future economic activity in a manner designed to maximize social welfare. Central planners are assumed to be solely dedicated to serving the public interest. The socialist model assumes that the central planners and other state decision-makers are not rational, self-interested, actors; in fact, for socialism to function efficiently it is necessary to assume that key decision-makers act solely in the public interest.[2] The socialist model is fundamentally inconsistent with the economic model of human behavior.[3]

There were major discrepancies, however, between the socialist model and "socialist" reality, obvious upon even superficial examination. Despite the presence of an intricate system of restrictions and regulations on free exchange, the Soviet-style economy possessed a large legal market sector. Moreover, even within the state sector a substantial element of underground, or non-legal, market activity was part and parcel of routine operations. Most industries were nationalized, and the state sector represented a large proportion of the overall economy. But this is also true in many Western capitalist economies.

Although the operational reality of the Soviet-style economy was empirically inconsistent with major assumptions of the socialist model of the centrally planned system, this reality was consistent with the model of the mercantilist society. The mercantilist model includes the following major elements:

1   the government is headed by an autocrat;
2   this autocratic state extensively intervenes in the private economy and sponsors a large variety of monopolies and cartel arrangements;
3   positions of monopoly status as well as various other restrictions on competitive entry are sold by the autocrat as a means of raising revenue; and
4   the autocrat employs a specialized bureaucracy whose function is to monitor the various monopolist-franchisees to ensure that they do not behave "competitively" in relation to one another, and also to enforce barriers designed to deter outside entrants.

Clearly, the mercantilist system requires a powerful government, with an extensive security apparatus. The autocrat maximizes his venal income subject to a security constraint. Providing for internal and external security against competitive entry – i.e. a *coup d'état*, violent revolution, or foreign invasion – is a cost of ruling.

A ruler will select the optimal mix of overt coercion (the secret police) and pecuniary rewards to minimize the risk of challenge from their subordinates in the state bureaucracy. The autocrat receives several advantages from assigning payments to supporters in the form of privileges instead of cash. First, supporters become residual claimants in the operation of the system of venal revenue raising, and this provides an incentive for them to actively and diligently support the mercantilist program. Residual claimants will receive benefits from their privileged positions as a function of their efficiency as exploiters of those rent opportunities. Second, the installation of supporters into strategic economic positions with commensurate responsibilities limits their ability to conspire or otherwise participate in plans aimed at deposing the autocrat; much of their time will be devoted to the extraction of rents from their privileged positions. Third, to the extent that the reward takes the form of privilege, power, and status instead of cash, the autocrat can more readily monitor and control the activities of the supporters. In contrast, if rewards take the form of liquid assets which can be readily concealed, the autocrat's ability to control supporters is limited.

Once an economy becomes encrusted with legal monopolies and cartels, and where legal institutions are directly controlled by the autocrat (a further self-protection device), a transition to a less-restricted, more productive economy becomes increasingly difficult. A rational revenue-maximizing autocrat will recognize that the optimal revenue-maximizing device is an open economy combined with an efficient tax system. But, existing monopolists, who are unable to cash-in on the capital value of their privileged positions, will oppose any such transition to an open economy. Moreover, an open market economy is a riskier internal environment to the autocrat anyway, in which domestic opposition to their rule is more likely to coalesce and lead to their overthrow. Thus it is rational for an autocrat – whether Louis XIV or Leonid Brezhnev – to favor the perpetuation of an economic system that sacrifices global economic efficiency in exchange for their enhanced security.

The central planning apparatus and restriction rents

While French mercantilism and the Soviet system bear many important similarities, there was no apparent counterpart to the Soviet central planning apparatus in mercantilist France. We propose that the Soviet-style central planning system was in actuality a mechanism which functioned to protect the value of mercantilist monopoly rights.

A mercantilist system of monopoly rights created for the purpose of raising revenue is only effective to the extent that monopolistic barriers to entry are successful. The most valuable monopoly rights tend to be those which can be defended against competing entrants at the lowest cost.

The relevant competitors may be others in possession of monopoly rights elsewhere in the economy who produce potential substitutes to the output of other monopolists. Illicit entry by one monopolist into the privileged market domain of another state-sanctioned monopolist will tend to reduce the value of the latter's monopoly right. To the extent that such illicit competition is allowed to occur, state revenues derived from the sale of (now less valuable) monopoly rights will decline. The preservation of the value of this revenue source requires the state to monitor and enforce the monopolistic economic structure.

Central planning was the mechanism to accomplish this end in the Soviet-type system. Planned output targets were not floors, but ceilings. That is, planned output targets functioned like cartel output quotas. The planned targets implicitly protected the value of monopoly rights against competition from within the "official economy." Enterprises sometimes exceeded their nominal targets, but this only suggests that the actual target was somewhat flexible. The planning system closely monitored the production and sale of enterprise output, so as to ensure that no poaching occurred. Sellers of output were assigned buyers, i.e. granted monopolies.

Some buyers were themselves privileged and allowed to purchase output from other enterprises at subsidized prices. The military, for example, received tanks, planes, and guns from various industries at subsidized, not monopoly, prices, and was allowed to shop around among enterprises.

Central planning also performed other functions for the socialist ruler. Polanyi (1951 and 1957) suggested as early as the 1950s that the plan was partly a propaganda facade that the regime created to disguise the sale of monopoly privileges. A considerable amount of internal monitoring by the CPSU and the KGB of enterprises was designed to prevent the appropriation of rents by employees from their legal recipients, and a centralized system for such monitoring was deemed to be more efficient. Of course, this implies that in the Soviet-style system one of the main functions of the police was to protect monopolists against competition.

The appropriation of rent by a ruler can take many forms. Louis XIV built the Palace of Versailles. Soviet rulers provided themselves with mechanisms designed to secure their position from internal and external competitive threats. The Soviet Union maintained a powerful military force as well as a large internal security apparatus.

Strategic positions in the economy were "sold" to those individuals willing to offer the highest bid to the central authorities, either in cash or (more typically) non-cash transfers. Thus, like in the case in the France of Louis XIV, the sale of "offices" served as an alternative device for raising government revenue. In the French case, we noted above that the inefficiency of the tax collection system encouraged the monarch to sell offices to generate funds. Though this cannot completely explain the modern Soviet-style reliance on the sale of monopoly rights to raise revenue, it should be noted that poor tax collection technology has been universally noted by Western advisors to the reforming governments of the former Soviet bloc. The reliance on mercantilist-style revenue techniques for raising revenue may be related to the origin of the ruling system of Soviet-style states. Communist regimes in the Soviet bloc were either installed by foreign military force, or else from a violent internal takeover by a revolutionary clique. Under such circumstances, pre-existing tax systems demonstrated their inability to expropriate private wealth at a sufficient rate so as to ensure secure protection for the new regime. The new autocrat required massive wealth, quickly, to shore up their political position. Large-scale nationalization and the issuance of monopoly rights to loyal supporters represented a solution to this problem.

There are, to be sure, many differences in detail between seventeenth-century mercantilism and the modern Soviet incarnation. For example, whereas the monarchs of England and France held the equivalents of open auctions at which monopoly privileges were sold to the highest bidder, the Soviet rulers appear to have instead shared in the rents with franchisees.[4] But the basic systems appear to have operated under similar principles.

The bureaucratic apparatus ostensibly tasked with "central planning," although performing many of the same functions as the differently organized mercantilist-era equivalent, seems also to have been partly designed to conceal socialist venality from consumers. This investment in concealing rent flows was an innovation of the Soviet-style system. And the Soviet Union was bureaucratically much more advanced than its seventeenth century counterparts, organizing the state-granted monopolies which dominated the economy in a more thorough-going manner. The lower cost of communications, and the greater potential for bureaucratic management, in the twentieth century surely accounts for much of this particular difference. Despite these relatively minor variations, however, the basic economic character of the state sector of the economy was similar in both the seventeenth- and the twentieth-century examples.

One further difference between sixteenth-century mercantilism and the Soviet case may be more apparent than real. The Soviet Union originated in the sudden, violent overthrow of the existing government structure by well-organized revolutionaries, but, by contrast, mercantilism in England and France accumulated gradually over time. However, while the Soviet Union as a political entity was an outcome of the Russian revolution, an extensive system of state controls over the Russian economy had developed gradually over the preceding half-century. The tsarist state had nationalized oilfields, two-thirds of the railway system and thousands of factories; regulated prices, profits, and the use of raw materials; organized much of private industry into state-managed syndicates (cartels); and placed state agents on the boards of all private joint stock enterprises (see Miller 1926, p. 299; and White 1979, p. 50). One historian concludes that in Tsarist Russia "the predominance of the state in every area of economic life was becoming the central fact of society" (Johnson, 1983, p. 14). Thus, Tsarist Russia already had developed a kind of neo-mercantilist economy before the Russian revolution. The new Soviet rulers reallocated the monopoly rents, but otherwise needed only to modify the existing mercantilist system to serve their own purposes.

The market economy in the Soviet context

The comparative systems literature has tended to emphasize the importance of the central planning apparatus in the Soviet-style economy. By all accounts, however, there was a substantial private sector in the Soviet economy.

The comparative systems literature of the 1970s and 1980s often mentioned the importance of private agriculture (on small, privately owned agricultural plots) in overall agricultural output. However, the private sector of the Soviet economy was far more extensive than this. The parallel or second economy, comprising economic activities which were illegal or quasi-legal, was very large.[5] The private sector could not be readily distinguished from the planned sector (see Feher *et al.* 1983, pp. 98–105).

Wherever there is a gap, alert economic actors will attempt to grasp the opportunity available for personal gain. In the production process, special middlemen, the *tolkachi*, were relied on to gather resources (inputs) so enterprises could meet plan targets. The *tolkachi* worked on behalf of state enterprises selling surplus commodities on the one hand and purchasing needed products on the other. There emerged an entire secondary supply system around the *tolkachi* which allowed state enterprises to appear to conform to state output targets, and thus receive the appropriate bonuses, etc., than otherwise would have been possible (see Berliner 1957, pp. 207–30). On the consumption side, unofficial market transactions attempted to correct for the long queues and the poor quality of consumer goods found in the official state stores. Private market activity enhanced consumer well-being by increasing the flow of goods and services available and by offering an additional source of income to citizens.

Unofficial economic activity was based on evasion of legal entry restrictions. Legal monopolies in the form of entry restrictions characterized the Soviet economy. The central planning system, according to Berliner (1957, p. 408), erected barriers to entry drawn along industry lines. Giant enterprise monopolies, in the strictest sense of establishing single producers of a particular good for the entire country, were created.[6] These monopolies represented opportunities to extract monopoly rents from consumers, whether in pecuniary or non-pecuniary forms.

The conventional view admits that Soviet central planning authorities used a sort of price system, but one in which all prices were supposedly set by the planners. Prices were strictly an accounting tool, and not designed to reflect the relative scarcity of resources. Described as such, the Soviet-type economy was not a monetary economy, but rather a "documentary" one, in which money serves an accounting function, but could not command resources – documents issued by the planning authorities were necessary to do so. Producers were forbidden by law from selling commodities to a purchaser who did not possess an allocation certificate issued by the supply planning agencies (see Berliner 1976, pp. 88–9).

This, of course, was only the official picture. In the Soviet-style economy, just like Western economies during periodic episodes of government price control, official prices are not equivalent to the effective prices in actual transactions. Effective prices adjusted freely despite the fixity of official prices.

"Profits" flow to those officials in the strategic position to transform these non-monetary costs to consumers into personal benefits. Enterprises, for example, often bribed (whether in money or in favors) officials in the chain of supply before necessary inputs became available to their organizations. The deputy director of the supervisory board of the Ministry for the Automobile

Industry, say, might only agree to countersign requisition notes for the supply of vehicle parts at a rate of 1,000 roubles per requisition. Regular clients might rent a flat in Moscow for Ministry officials' use for parties and orgies, and in fact this kind of non-pecuniary bribery was apparently fairly common.[7]

Positions of political authority or influence allow for the holders to extract rents from individuals throughout the economy. One crucial aspect of this market for rents, however, was the complete absence of clearly defined and enforceable property rights to rent flows. As a result, political opportunism was a serious threat at all levels. Protection from legal sanction and regulation was a lucrative source of revenue for strategically placed officials.[8]

The *nomenklatura* system ensured that appointments to strategic positions were carefully monitored and controlled by Party officials. But, as we have seen, in some instances large bribes, in addition to or as a substitute for party loyalty, were required to secure important *nomenklatura* appointments (see Willis 1985, p. 308). Bribery of state officials became commonplace, with various jobs available for established (albeit technically illegal) money prices.

Access to goods and services was frequently only available after payment of a technically illicit bribe to the appropriate official. Medical services were legally rationed according to need, but in reality were rationed by bribery. This was also true in the case of higher education, where ostensibly students were accepted or rejected on the basis of ability, but where admission was often subject to a required bribe.[8]

These examples of rent-seeking illustrate the kind of neo-mercantilist venality which motivates decision-makers in Soviet-type economies.[9] Officials in command of particular entry barriers are in a position to obtain profits resulting from the exercise of coercive restrictions on competition in the form of bribes. In the Soviet system, entry into competition with officially sanctioned suppliers was technically prohibited, but could be achieved in practice by "paying off" the enforcers of the restrictions.

The extensive and elaborate system of official prices supposedly reflected the ideological commitment to the abolition of free-market price formation under Communism, but in reality it represented a myriad of opportunities for profits on the part of those in official strategic economic positions (see Levy 1990; and Shleifer and Vishny 1992). Such rents result from actual bribery, and also from artificially increased prices creating gains in the form of legal monopoly revenue increases to favored producers.[11]

Monitoring and controlling the flow of rents

We must distinguish between two types of "second economy" activity within the Soviet-type economy. The first type involved the exploitation of monopoly positions by the officially appointed holders to extract monopoly profits or rents from consumers. The monopolist shoe producer, for example, cannot raise the official price of shoes, but he can extract surpluses from consumers by requiring "extra" unofficial payments. The second type involved attempts by outsiders to enter into competition with the established monopolists, e.g. the private shoe producer who competes with the state shoe factory. Both types of activity indicate the degree to which market exchange, without even the pretense of planning, characterized the Soviet economy.

Holders of monopoly franchises have an obvious interest in evading payments of "franchise fees" to the rulers responsible for creating the monopoly rights. In order to maximize revenue from the "sale" of monopoly franchises, the Soviet authorities needed to monitor and control opportunistic behavior of this sort on the part of "franchisees."

In order to monitor and control the flow of privilege rents within the system, the Soviet neo-mercantilist state adopted a device pioneered by earlier mercantilist regimes: the professional informer. A considerable bureaucracy arose whose principal task was protecting the monopoly rights of political patrons.

Many scholars noted that the Communist Party played a very weak active role in the Soviet economy (see, for example, Andrle 1976; Conyngham 1973; and Hough 1969). The Party maintained a large supervisory apparatus which oversaw the operation of enterprises, and was chiefly responsible for the selection of managers.

The Communist Party exercised control over managerial appointments in a number of ways. Every Communist Party member who sought to change their job could only do so with the approval of their *raikom* (Party district committee). The majority of enterprise managers were members of the Party. Every Party organization was responsible for creating a managerial reserve list of people who were potentially suitable for managerial careers, and Party organs possessed the right of veto over all appointments made to posts listed in the *nomenklatura*.[12]

In addition, Party cells existed within each enterprise. Moreover, Party industrial instructors were employed to monitor, and actually participate in, enterprise decision-making.[13] This system of Party monitoring closely resembled the practices of the *intendant* system used under French mercantilism around the time of Colbert. Any system of monopoly restrictions requires enforcement to prevent illicit competition from dissipating the monopoly rents and rendering monopoly rights worthless. In mercantilist France, the intendant system was designed to accomplish just that. Intendants were charged with monitoring markets in local areas and empowered to prevent illicit competition (see Ekelund and Tollison 1981, pp. 85–91). The Communist Party appears to have performed this function in the Soviet Union.

Thus the Party closely controlled the positions of privilege which the Soviet state awarded. This control protected the value of the "monopoly franchises" that those positions represented, a predictable concern from the perspective of a revenue-maximizing autocrat.

Managers of enterprises, officials in the Party and the central planning apparatus, as well as almost all other official positions – those which potentially provided access to a significant rent stream – were selected from approved lists, i.e. *nomenklatura*, that were drawn up by the Communist Party. In this way, the regime ensured that those in positions of economic power were loyal to the regime. The *nomenklatura* system played an important role in perpetuating the system in the face of economic inefficiency. The *nomenklatura* functioned as a large, powerful, highly organized and cohesive interest group whose members benefited from the (Soviet) status quo.[14]

A basic function of the central planning bureau in the Soviet system was that of central monitor and coordinator of the activities of the numerous monopolies and cartels in the economy. The socialist calculation debate aside, there is ample evidence that the central planning bureaucracy only planned the economy after the fact.[15] The plan was constantly revised and renegotiated throughout the planning process. Central plans reflected the expected pattern of output from state enterprises, which in turn manipulated the formation of the plan in a variety of ways.

Conclusion

Both defenders and opponents of the Soviet system have agreed on one vital point: the Soviet economy was a radical innovation, an experiment in the abolition of the market and its replacement by central planning. The present chapter challenges this assumption. The Soviet economy was a modern version of the mercantilist economies typical of sixteenth- and seventeenth-century Europe. Like those previous incarnations, the Soviet economy was a market heavily restricted by state-granted monopolies.

Ekelund and Tollison (1981) model the sixteenth- and seventeenth-century mercantilist system as devices employed by the monarch to raise revenue through the sale of monopoly privileges. While the sale of offices and other monopoly privileges hampered the efficiency of the overall economy, it nevertheless maximized the net revenue available to the monarch. The Soviet rulers confronted similar constraints on their ability to maximize revenue from an efficient tax collection system, leading to the emergence of the Soviet-style economic system that maximized the wealth available to the rulers, albeit at a substantial cost to the efficiency of the general economy.

The French mercantilist system ended when the French monarchy was violently overthrown in 1789; the English mercantilist system gradually declined (and the efficiency of the English economy increased) in consequence of a more peaceful conflict between the monarch and the Parliament for political power. The demise of the Soviet-style system in Europe fell somewhere between these two extremes, although the Soviet-style systems in parts of Eastern Europe were overthrown (e.g. Czechoslovakia, the German Democratic Republic, and Romania), the Soviet Union itself folded its tent quietly. In all of these cases the economic interests of consumers ultimately succeeded in outbidding the ruling class for the control of political institutions.

The mercantilist model of the Soviet-style economy outlined above does not imply that ideological factors played no role in the origin of the Soviet state. Revolutionary idealism may have motivated the early Bolsheviks, at least in part. But, by the time of Stalin, the economic system began to function like a mercantilist state. The Soviet Union had become a rent-seeking society by the time it entered its "mature" stage.

Acknowledgments

We received useful comments on earlier drafts from Pamela Brown, Gordon Tullock, Barry Weingast, and the participants in seminars at the Hoover Institution, Stanford University; the Department of Economics, University of California at Santa Cruz; and the Department of Economics and the Center of Economic Research and Graduate Education, Charles University, Prague, Czech Republic. The usual caveat applies.

Bibliography

Anderson, G. M. and Tollison, R. D. (1993) "Barristers and Barriers: Sir Edwin Coke and the Regulation of Trade," *Cato Journal* 13: 223–45.

Andrle, V. (1976) *Managerial Power in the Soviet Union*, London: Cambridge University Press.

Berliner, J. (1957) *Factory and Manager in the USSR*, Cambridge: Harvard University Press.

Berliner, J. (1976) *The Innovation Decision in Soviet industry*, Cambridge, MA: MIT Press.

Boettke, P. J. (1990a) *The Political Economy of Soviet Socialism: The Formative Years, 1918–28*, Boston: Kluwer Academic Publishers.

Boettke, P. J. (1990b) "Analysis and Vision in Economic Discourse," *Journal of the History of Economic Thought* 14 (Spring): 84–95.

Boettke, P. J. (1993) *Why Perestroika Failed: The Politics and Economics of Socialist Transformation*, London: Routledge.

Bolton, P. and Farrell, J. (1990) "Decentralization, Duplication and Delay," *Journal of Political Economy* 98 (December): 331–45.

Buchanan, J. M. (1980) "Reform in a Rent-seeking Society," in I. M. Buchanan, R. D. Tollison and G. Tullock (eds.) *Toward a Theory of the Rent-seeking Society*, College Station, TX: Texas A&M University Press, pp. 359–67.

Conyngham, W. J. (1973) *Industrial Management in the Soviet Union*, Stanford: Hoover Institution Press.

Ekelund, R. B. and Tollison, R. D. (1981) *Mercantilism as a Rent-seeking Society*, College Station, TX: Texas A&M University Press.

Feher, F., Heller, A. and Markus, G. (1983) *Dictatorship Over Needs*, New York: Basil Blackwell.

Fung, K. K. (1987) "Surplus Seeking and Rent Seeking Throughout Backdoor Deals in Mainland China," *American Journal of Economics and Sociology* 46 (July): 299–317.

Gregory, P. and Stuart, R. (1986) *Soviet Economic Structure and Performance*, New York: Harper and Row.

Grossman, G. (1977a) "Notes on the Illegal Private Economy and Corruption," in *Joint Congressional Economic Committee Hearings, The Soviet Economy in a New Perspective*, Washington, DC: Government Printing Office.

Grossman, G. (1977b) "The Second Economy in the USSR," *Problems of Communism* 26 (September–October): 221–9.

Harris, P. (1986) "Socialist Graft: The Soviet Union and the People's Republic of China. A Preliminary Survey," *Corruption and Reform* 1: 13–32.

Hayek, F. A. von (1956) (first published 1935) *Collectivist Economic Planning: Critical Studies on the Possibilities of Socialism*, London: Routledge & Kegan Paul.

Hayek, F. A. von (1960) *The Constitution of Liberty*, Chicago: University of Chicago Press.

Heckscher, E. (1955) *Mercantilism*, two volumes, London: George Allen & Unwin.

Hough, J. (1969) *The Soviet Prefects: The Local Party Organs in Industrial Decision-making*, Cambridge: Harvard University Press.

Johnson, P. (1983) *Modern Times: The World from the Twenties to the Eighties*, New York: Harper and Row.

Kroll, H. (1991) "Monopoly and Transition to the Market," *Soviet Economy* 7 (April–June): 143–74.

Levy, D. (1990) "The Bias in Centrally Planned Prices," *Public Choice* 67(4): 213–26.

Lipson, E. (1968) *The Economic History of England: The Age of Mercantilism*, London: Adam and Charles Black.

Miller, M. (1926), *The Economic Development of Russia, 1905–14*. London: Macmillan.

Moore, J. (1981) "Agency Costs, Technological Change, and Soviet Central Planning," *Journal of Law and Economics* 24 (October): 189–214.

Nef, J. U. (1968) *Industry and Government in France and England, 1540–1640*, Ithaca, NY: Cornell University Press.

Nove, A. (1977) *The Soviet Economic System*, New York: Harper and Row.

Ofer, G. and Vinokur, A. (1980) *Private Sources of Income in the Soviet Household*, Santa Monica, CA: Rand Corporation, Report R-2359-NA (August).

O'Hearn, D. (1980) "The Consumer Second Economy in the USSR: Size and Effects," *Soviet Studies* 32 (April): 192–205.

Pejovich, S. (1990) *The Economics of Property Rights: Towards a Theory of Comparative Systems*, Boston: Kluwer Academic Publishers.

Polanyi, M. (1940) *The Contempt of Freedom*, New York: Little, Brown & Co.

Polanyi, M. (1951) *The Logic of Liberty*, Chicago: University of Chicago Press.

Polanyi, M. (1957) "The Foolishness of History," *Encounter* 9 (November): 25–36.

Roberts, P. C. (1990) (first published 1971) *Alienation and the Soviet Economy*, New York: Holmes and Meir.

Rothbard, M. N. (1970) *Man, Economy, and State: A Treatise on Economic Principles*, Los Angeles: Nash Publishing.

Rutland, P. (1985) *The Myth of the Plan*, LaSalle, IL: Open Court.

Shleifer, A. and Vishny, R. (1992) "Pervasive Shortages Under Socialism," *Rand Journal of Economics* 9 (Summer): 213–30.

Simis, K. (1977) "The Machinery of Corruption in the Soviet Union," *Survey* 22 (Fall): 551–73.

Tullock, G. (1980) "The Welfare Costs of Tariffs, Monopolies and Theft," in J. Buchanan, R. Tollison and G. Tullock (eds.) *Toward a Theory of the Rent-seeking Society*, College Station: Texas A&M University Press, pp. 39–50.

Voslensky, M. (1994) *Nomenklatura: The Soviet Ruling Class*, New York: Doubleday.

Webber, C. and Wildavsky, A. (1986) *A History of Taxation and Expenditure in the Western World*, New York: Simon and Schuster.

White, S. (1979) *Political Culture and Soviet Politics*, London: Longman.

Willis, D. (1985) *Klass: How Russians Really Live*, New York: St Martin's Press.

Zaleski, E. (1980) *Stalinist Planning for Economic Growth, 1933–1952*, Chapel Hill, NC: University of North Carolina Press.

Zemtsov, I. (1985) *Private Life of the Soviet Elite*, New York: Crane Russak.

9   Credibility, commitment, and Soviet economic reform*

Introduction

The former Soviet Union has been in a state of economic crisis since 1917. One reform measure after another (whether inspired by socialism or liberalism) has been introduced only to be reversed within a few years. The original socialist construction project, embarked on following the November revolution in 1917, had to be abandoned in the early spring of 1921. Introduced in 1921, the New Economic Policy, which represented the first Soviet-era perestroika (but not glasnost, as all dissension within the party was outlawed by V. I. Lenin's simultaneous decree), lasted for seven years until it was drastically reversed by Joseph Stalin's revolution from above. The Stalin years (1928–53) represented a political and economic buzzsaw. Collectivization of agriculture, industrialization, political purges, mass terror, labor camps, wartime emergencies and so forth characterized Stalin's twenty-five-year reign of power. The Nikita Khrushchev years, especially the period immediately following his 1956 speech denouncing Stalin's "cult of personality," represented the second Soviet-era perestroika and a limited period of glasnost, as Stalin's crimes against humanity were partially unmasked. The "thaw generation," however, had to wait another twenty years before glasnost was to have any lasting meaning. Khrushchev's ill-conceived economic policies generated lackluster results and bolstered the political challenge to his leadership.

The ensuing Leonid Brezhnev years were a mix of half-hearted attempts to improve the economic mechanism and political corruption. From the Khrushchev years through the entire eighteen-year reign of Brezhnev, Soviet leaders embarked on a "continuous process of reforming the reforms" (Linz 1987, p. 150). The oil shock of the early 1970s gave the regime a short reprieve and hid from immediate view the deterioration of the economic situation. But by the late 1970s, it was evident to many observers that the Brezhnev era had nothing to show but economic deprivation and political cynicism. Neither Yuri

*Originally published as Boettke, P. J. (1995) "Credibility, Commitment and Soviet Economic Reform," in E. Lazear (ed.) *Economic Transition in Eastern Europe and Russia: Realities of Reform*, Stanford, CA: Hoover Institution Press, pp. 247–75.

Andropov (who may have wanted to change things) nor Konstantin Chernenko (who did not) had enough time in office to effect a change in Brezhnev's legacy. Mikhail Gorbachev, however, did have the time and the political will.

The Gorbachev period of political and economic reform, however, must be judged a failure.[1] After six years in power, the Gorbachev government left the official Soviet economy worse off, and the Soviet Union as a political entity no longer existed. Perestroika simply did not deliver the goods, and democratic political reform was much too limited. Andres Aslund, for example, even before the attempted August coup, concluded that "looking back at Soviet economic policy during the second half of the 1980s, it is difficult to avoid the impression that virtually every possible mistake has been made. Perestroika has proved to be an utter economic failure" (1991, p. 225).

The perestroika period (1985–91), along with previous attempts at economic reform such as the New Economic Policy (1921–8), Khrushchev's *sovnarkhoz* reforms (1957), and the Brezhnev–Aleksey Kosygin reforms (1965), can now be safely treated as history. These reform efforts were all heralded in their time as liberalization policies, and they all came to an end less than a decade after they were initiated. These reform packages were simply not sustainable economic policies.[2]

Understanding why these reform attempts failed is important, not only for antiquarian interests but also for what it can tell us about the general theory of social organization and public policy. An examination of previous failed reform efforts may offer invaluable insights into how to construct a workable post-perestroika constitution of economic policy in the former Soviet Union – a task that has been left to the government of Boris Yeltsin.

A basic problem in policy design

Public policy must be constructed in a manner that recognizes the obstacles presented by information and incentives. Policy must first and foremost be compatible with basic economic incentives. Policies that are based on notions of public-spiritedness and humanitarian goals but that disregard economic motivations are most likely doomed to failure. Moreover, even if public policies offer rewards to those who perform as expected, economic actors must possess the relevant information to act appropriately. If actors have the motivation to "do the right thing," they must also have access to information about what the right thing to do would be in their present context.

Unfortunately, the problem of constructing an optimal governmental policy that intervenes properly without distorting incentives and the flow of information is compounded by the passage of time. For one, the relevant economic data are contextual and not abstract. Information gathered yesterday may be irrelevant for decisions today because of changing decisions. The price system overcomes this problem by alerting individuals to these changes through the adjustment of relative prices. Political coordination, in contrast, does not have access to a similar register of changing conditions.

Even in cases where discretionary political intervention might be desired to correct for perceived market failures, the problem remains as to how to acquire the requisite knowledge to intervene properly. Ignorant or haphazard intervention will simply lead to further destabilization and exacerbate the problem it sought to correct originally.

The dynamics of change associated with the passage of time also presents a timing problem for public policy, as Milton Friedman pointed out a long time ago. A long and variable time lag exists between:

1   the need for action and the recognition of this need;
2   the recognition of a problem and the design and implementation of a policy response; and
3   the implementation of the policy and the effect of the policy (Friedman 1953, p. 145).

Because of these lags, Friedman argued that discretionary public policy will often be destabilizing. For this reason, he argued the case for rules rather than discretionary public policy.

Finally, the passage of time introduces strategic problems for policy-makers. Policies that seemed appropriate at t_1, may not be deemed appropriate at t_2. In fact, a basic presupposition of the argument for discretion is exactly that policies accepted for one period may prove to be inappropriate for another and, therefore, that policy-makers must possess the ability to shift as circumstances change. Such shifts in public policy (coupled with the impact these shifts have on the expectations of economic actors), however, may prove destabilizing to the overall economic environment.

The issues of credibility and commitment

Recognizing the temporal dimensionality of choice is fundamental in establishing viable economic policy. Our concern here is with the public choice problem that follows from the strategic interaction between rulers and citizens. A fundamental problem faces public choosers when a policy that seemed optimal when introduced appears less so as time passes. Without a binding commitment to the policy, the government will change policy to what now appears to be optimal. The problem is that economic actors who realize this will anticipate the policy change and act in a counterproductive manner from the perspective of the policy-maker.

Optimal intervention, by definition, requires that a large degree of discretionary control be entrusted to government decision-makers. The expectational problems of discretion, however, generate difficulties for government planning in general (see Kydland and Prescott 1977). One reason that discretionary control does not work as optimally as desired is that current decisions by economic actors depend on expectations concerning future policy; those expectations are not invariant of the policies chosen. For example, if, for whatever reason (either an increase in demand or reduction in supply), market conditions produced a windfall profit for the oil industry, the government could respond by proposing to tax away those profits with the argument that this will not affect the current supply of oil because it is the result of a past decision. But such a policy would lead oil companies to anticipate that similar expropriations will occur again in the future, and they will make their investment decisions so as to reduce the future supply of oil. Policy decisions and social rules create expectations, and expectations guide actions.[3] A decision tree illustrates the basic policy dilemma (see Figure 9.1).

In Figure 9.1, player 2 is the representative citizen, and player 1 is the government decision-maker. The government announces an economic reform that liberalizes trade. Player 2 must choose to enter the game or stay out. The problem is that, once player 2 enters the game, player 1 can benefit from confiscating the wealth of player 2. Knowing the sequentially rational moves of player 1, player 2 will choose the only viable equilibrium, Out, and reforms will stall unless player 1 can successfully tie his/her own hands.

This is the basic commitment game. But the actual commitment game is more complicated. In fact, the problem is one of information. The citizens do not really know who they are playing with (see Figure 9.2).

The logic and structure of the game are basically the same as in Figure 9.1, except in Figure 9.2 the informational difficulties are highlighted. The ruling regime (player 1), which can be either sincere or insincere, announces a plan to introduce an economic liberalization policy. The citizen (player 2) now must decide to enter the market or stay out. A major problem confronting the citizen, however, is that he/she does not know whether the regime is sincere or insincere. The citizen's only prior information concerning the regime is policy history, but the reform announcement was presumably intended to signal a break from

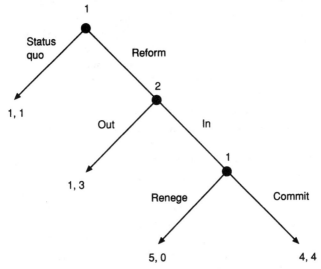

Figure 9.1 Credible commitment game

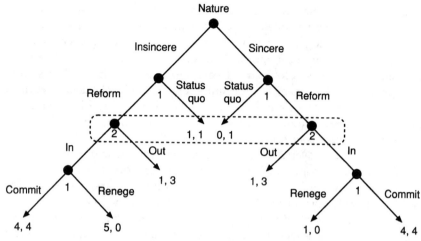

Figure 9.2 Credible commitment game with information signal

the old way of doing things. If the citizen decides to enter the official market in expectation of continued liberalization, then the regime must decide to either continue the liberalization policy that was announced or renege on the announcement and tighten political control in the second round by cracking down on individual economic activity and confiscating the wealth created in the previous period.

If the ruler is following a discretionary policy, then the citizen will foresee that the ruler may likely renege in the second period of this game and therefore will choose to stay out. But if the ruler can convey a credible commitment, he/she would announce liberalization and the citizen would choose to come into the official market. The ruler's pay-off, independent of whether the regime is sincere or insincere, will be higher with commitment conveyance than it would be without it, but the insincere ruler would be better off, once the announcement of liberalization elicited citizen market participation, to renege and crack down on private economic activity in the form of increased taxation, regulation, or confiscation. The sincere reform regime, however, will not crack down and will continue to pursue liberalization policies.

In such situations, however, because the citizens are uninformed about the sincerity of the ruling regime, and given certain probabilities that are derived from their previous experience with the regime's efforts at reform, it may be rational for them to expect that the ruler will go back on his/her announcement to pursue economic liberalization. If this is the case, citizens will choose to stay out of the economic game and thus defeat both the short-term and the long-term goals of the ruler. The only way out of this policy impasse is to establish a binding and credible commitment to economic reform.

The reform regime's problem, however, is even more difficult than solving the basic paradox of governance – establishing constraints on its activities that do not deter its positive ability to govern. To get economic reform off the ground, the regime has to simultaneously establish binding constraints on its behavior and signal a sincere commitment to reform to the citizenry. During war, for example, if the commanding officer's troops crossed over a large river to do battle with opposing forces, they may order the bridge burned – thus precommitting his troops to the battle ahead by eliminating the only possible escape. At the same time, however, opposing troops witnessing the smoke have received a signal that the other side will fight a hard battle. The reforming regime must do something similar to establish trust and bind itself to the reform policy.[4]

This simple illustration of the basic problem of policy design and the failure to solve the dilemma goes a long way, toward explaining the failures of the various reform cycles in the former Soviet Union. Marshall Goldman (1991, pp. 37–8), for example, emphasizes that all previous efforts at reform within the Soviet Union were viewed as a "big lie" by the citizens of the former Soviet Union. The suppression of the *kulaks* in the 1920s and 1930s and Khrushchev's agricultural policies in the early 1960s had not been forgotten by the population, which explains why individuals were reluctant to invest private income on economic ventures during the Gorbachev era. Hardly a family in the former Soviet Union did not have a member who was directly affected by Stalin's terror, and this served as part of a historical memory that each citizen possessed concerning the nature of the Communist Party of the Soviet Union. Obviously other issues were involved in the complex history of the design and implementation of Soviet reform, but focusing on the credibility and commitment problem allows us to highlight a key a key reason for the recurring failure of reform efforts.

Illustrations of the problem

The policy game under the New Economic Policy (NEP)

The introduction of NEP in the early spring of 1921 represented a drastic reversal from the previous policies pursued by the Bolsheviks. During War Communism the Bolshevik regime had pursued policies of extreme centralization that sought to eliminate market exchange and production completely and to establish a centrally planned economy.[5] The War Communism policies had to be reversed, for they resulted in a drastic reduction in production and threatened the political alliance between the peasant and the proletariat. NEP represented, in large part, a policy of economic liberalization that was intended to restore partial economic freedom to the peasants to appease political unrest and spur the farm production that was necessary to feed the emerging industrial strata of society.

On 24 May 1921, a decree from Sovnarkom (Council of People's Commissars) permitted not only the sale of surplus food by peasants in farmer markets but also trade by others of goods produced by small-scale private manufacturers. Whereas private trade during War Communism was basically outlawed –

although it did continue in the form of black-market bazaars – under NEP, sales could now be conducted from permanent facilities. Decrees concerning hired labor of not more than ten or twenty, leasing factories, and so forth, followed throughout 1921 and 1922. "The property rights and legalized spheres of business activity that had been granted to Soviet citizens during the first two years of NEP were collected and set down in the Civil Code of the RSFSR [Russian Soviet Federated Socialist Republic], which went into effect on 1 January 1923. Although not a dramatic extension of the rights of private businessmen, the Civil Code ... represented a clear reversal of the policies of War Communism."[6]

This policy shift to partial liberalization was meant to induce private economic initiative, and it worked to an extent. But the policy signal was not unambiguous. Nepmen, a term used to describe private businessmen in the 1920s, were subject to many taxes and fees, including business and income taxes. The most substantial of these was the fee for the use of business facilities. In fact, this fee accounted for twice as much revenue from private traders as did the business tax in 1922. In January 1923, it was announced that the fee would be increased. At this time, applications to rent facilities for private business declined 20% (see Ball 1987, p. 30).

The legal ambiguity of the nepmen was highlighted in the laws against speculation and price controls. In 1924, as a result, there was a marked decline in the economic activity of private traders. The government tried to reverse this downward trend by providing more favorable treatment – for example, easy state credit – to the nepmen. But this policy was reversed in 1926–7. State credit to private business, for example, was cut by 25% in 1926. The administrative tool that proved most devastating in the war against the nepmen was taxation. There was a 50% rate increase in the tax on profits of urban private traders from 1925 to 1927 (12.9% to 18.8%). In the Sokol'nicheski quarter of Moscow, for example, in 1929 and 1930, private traders and manufacturers represented 1.7% of the region's income taxpayers, with 8.2% of the total taxable income, but accounted for 55% of the region's income tax receipts (see Ball 1987, p. 75). The tax burden, in combination with their political status as *lishentsy* (the deprived) assured that nepmen were most vulnerable.[7] By 1928, as Aleksandr Solzhenitsyn points out, "it was time to call to a reckoning those late stragglers after the bourgeoisie – the NEPmen. The usual practice was to impose on them ever-increasing and finally totally intolerable taxes. At a certain point they could no longer pay; they were immediately arrested for bankruptcy, and their property was confiscated" (1973, vol. 1, p. 52).

The cumulative effect of these policies was to discourage individuals from investing in the official market, even though liberalization policies had been announced by the regime with the introduction of NEP. Economic actors chose to withdraw from the economic game, despite pleas from the Bolsheviks for them to invest in profitable above-ground activities (see, for example, Bukharin 1925). Ambiguity in the economic rules of the game, Bukharin argued to his fellow Bolshevik comrades, would produce nothing but contradictory expectations, which would deter economic progress. Sizing up the situation, he stated:

> Consider the fact that the well-to-do upper stratum of the peasantry, along with the middle peasant, who is also striving to join the well-to-do, are both afraid at present to accumulate. A situation has been created in which the peasant is afraid to buy an iron roof and apprehensive that he will be declared a kulak; if he buys a machine, he makes certain that the communists are not watching. Advanced technology has become a conspiracy ... The result is that the middle peasant is afraid to improve his farm and lay himself open to forceful administrative pressure; and the poor peasant complains that we are preventing him from selling his labor power to the wealthy peasants, etc. In response, Bukharin argued that 'in general and on the whole, we must say to the entire peasantry, to all its different strata: enrich yourselves, accumulate, develop your farms.'
>
> (Bukharin 1925/1982, pp. 196–7)

Price controls on grain provide another example of the contradictory expectations on the part of economic actors (alluded to by Bukharin) that were generated by discretionary Soviet policies. After the initial announcement of price liberalization in the agricultural sector, the government reversed course. In 1924, the People's Commissariat of Internal Trade attempted to fix a maximum price for grain. But over the years peasants had learned that grain was a good hedge against inflation, so they withheld grain from the market. Tax pressures to enforce sales were enacted, but peasants went to great lengths to pay the tax in anything but grain. A private illegal market developed wherein grain sold above the maximum price, creating parallel markets – with state-regulated prices, another with free prices.

In response, regional authorities attempted to issue orders declaring it obligatory to deliver 25% of all flour milled in a region to the state-purchasing authority at the fixed price, but this merely led to a cessation of above-ground milling operations. By December 1924 the state had collected less than half its projected amount of grain [118 million *pods* (Russian unit of weight equal to 36.11 pounds) out of 380 million]. Moreover, the grain stocks of the state declined, from 214 million *pods* on 1 January 1924, to 145 million *pods* on 1 January 1925. The price-fixing policy of the Soviet state had been defeated (see Carr 1958, vol. 1, pp. 208–9).

Foreign economic relations provide another example of the regime's inability to bind itself to a credible commitment undermining the reform effort, despite the announcement of liberalization. At the Genoa Conference (April–May 1922), for example, the Soviet delegation refused to conclude an agreement with Western powers on the question of Russia's debts (see Carr 1953, vol. 3, p. 377). In addition, at the end of 1922 a proposal for relaxing the foreign trade monopoly was rejected. Prospects for the expansion of foreign economic relations were, therefore, reduced considerably. Without such ties, long-term economic development was unlikely. Foreign governments simply had no reason to trust the Bolsheviks in economic deals.

The exchange-rate policy also hindered economic development and ran counter to the intentions of NEP. The hard currency reforms in the beginning of NEP – the *chervonets* reforms – were a major accomplishment. But the hard currency reforms did not even last two years. The low levels of gold reserves, the unrealistic exchange rate and the small volume of Soviet exports all undermined the monetary reform. Moreover, beginning in 1928, Gosbank refused to exchange Soviet money for foreign currency (see Khanin 1989, pp. 21, 24).

The general policy of grain procurement under NEP clearly illustrates the problem. The cornerstone of NEP was the substitution of the tax in kind for the grain requisitioning of War Communism. Peasants, however, with the War Communism period still fresh in their memories, had to be convinced that arbitrary requisitioning was not a policy option, that is, the government had to make a credible commitment to maintain NEP. As we have seen, however, the Bolsheviks did not commit to any such binding constraint. As a result, by the end of 1928, peasants no longer had an incentive to market grain surplus. From the peasants' point of view, the market was simply not a secure outlet.[8]

Thus, NEP was abandoned in 1928, and Stalin ruled over the Soviet system until his death in 1953. The reversal from the quasi-liberalization of NEP to the authoritarian measures of collectivization is one of the most drastic and fateful turn of events in the twentieth century. The abandonment of NEP, however, did possess both an economic and a political logic: NEP's failure was due neither to the inability of market institutions to provide the basis for economic development nor to the peculiarities of Stalin's personality, which thrived on political authoritarianism; rather, the internal contradictions of NEP led to an ever-increasing reliance on the substitution of political rationales for economic rationales in setting economic policy. The shifting policies produced an expectational regime that worked against the goals of policy-makers. Because the Bolsheviks were not willing to construct a binding commitment to economic liberalization, the only way out of the policy impasse was complete authoritarianism. Stalinism was the unintended consequence of the failure of the discretionary regime of the 1920s to cope with the obstacles that information and incentives present to political economies.

The policy game under Khrushchev

After Stalin's death in 1953, Soviet leaders had to face some cold facts about economic life. Collectivization, war, and political terror had taken their toll on the economic system. The post-Stalin triumvirate of Georgy Malenkov, Vyacheslav Molotov, and Lavrenty Beria could not simply continue along the path laid out by Stalin. Out of the political shakeout that followed the succession struggle, Khrushchev emerged as a major post-Stalin political figure.

Khrushchev's Central Committee speech on agriculture in 1953 detailed the results of collectivization. Productivity was down; livestock did not compare favorably with either 1928 or even 1916 figures. Peasants received low wages, and the level of investment by the collective farms was too low. Taxes levied on private plots were too high and discouraged production. All these negative policies, Khrushchev insisted, must be reversed.[9]

Malenkov, in contrast, was accused by economic planners and military leaders of over-concentrating on the consumer goods sector and thus distorting the Soviet economy by shifting priority away from heavy industry. The preoccupation with consumer material well-being associated with Malenkov did not sit well with leaders of heavy industry and the military. After Malenkov's fall, Khrushchev emerged as the dominant political figure. As the first secretary from 1955 to 1964, however, Khrushchev never achieved the dominant status that Stalin had, and political maneuvering was an omnipresent part of policy decisions. Nevertheless, Khrushchev initiated the major policies during that period.

Most of Khrushchev's reforms were directed at changing the incentives within the agricultural sector to improve the efficiency of production and improve the plight of peasants.[10] One of his most ambitious initiatives, however, was attempting to improve the economic mechanism within the Soviet system — the *sovnarkhoz* reforms of 1957.[11] In response to a political strategy on the part of his opponents to consolidate a power base in the economic planning system and establish a superministry that would coordinate the activities of all the subordinate economic ministries, Khrushchev reorganized the planning system by decentralizing power to regional economic councils (*sovnarkhozy*). This decentralization of the planning system was supposed to combat ministerial empire building and reduce the coordination problems that plagued the state-ministerial hierarchy.[12] The industrial ministries were abolished, and the regional council system (coordinated by Gosdplan) was established. Some enterprises were now subordinate to the 103 regional councils rather than to a ministry.

The danger of this policy was that localism would replace ministerial empire building as the main threat to efficient economic management. Regional councils favored their enterprises over all others, as would be expected, and economic performance suffered.[13] That Khrushchev's initiatives would substitute localism for departmentalism lends credence, Joseph Berliner argues, to the interpretation that political maneuvering rather than economic considerations provided the rationale for the 1957 reforms (Berliner 1983, p. 352). Unfortunately for Khrushchev, the reforms were correlated with a decline in the measured rates of economic growth, along with reports of the excesses of localism. As a result, even though Khrushchev reversed the 1957 reforms in March 1963, his political rivals used the failed reforms to discredit him. Khrushchev's fall in October 1964 was soon followed by a full reinstatement of the ministerial system.

The Khrushchev era, then, did nothing to convey to state enterprise managers, agricultural workers, or urban citizens that economic activity would be insulated from political manipulation. The so-called liberalization policies of decentralization were part of a larger political ploy to divest power from Khrushchev's rivals. The 1957 reforms were not only ill-conceived but reinforced the adverse reputation Soviet reform efforts possessed and thus compounded the difficulty of signaling a credible commitment to economic liberalization in the future.

The policy game under Kosygin and Brezhnev

The failure of the Khrushchev reforms did not quash debate over the problems with the Soviet economic mechanism. The *sovnarkhoz* reform did not get at the fundamental problem of incentives, but was instead limited to a question of supervision of state enterprises. Decision-making within the state enterprises was not addressed, although this was an aspect of Soviet planning that was seriously in need of reform. The gross output target of enterprise success (and the corresponding bonus system) provided incentives to the state enterprise managers (who responded rationally) that generated perverse consequences in terms of input use and output quality.

Late in the Khrushchev era, Evsei Liberman proposed a reform of the incentive system for state enterprises.[14] Liberman thought that if the state enterprise manager's reward was tied to the "profitability" of the enterprise – defined as the ratio of profit to the stock of capital – then the enterprise manager would possess the incentive to minimize costs. Under the appropriate incentive system, Liberman argued, managers would be induced to operate their enterprises at full productivity, improve the quality of goods produced, and seek out least-cost production techniques.

With Khrushchev's ousting, the debate over enterprise incentives did not wane. In September 1965, Kosygin announced the restructuring of the economic mechanism. The ministerial system was to be fully reconstituted, the basic incentive system in enterprises was to be overhauled, and a price reform was to be implemented. The ministerial system constituted a recentralization of economic decision-making away from the regional authorities and back to Moscow. As Hewett points out, this is important because many interpreters confused the incentive reform with regard to enterprises with a net decentralization of decision-making power within the economy. This was not the case in either the design or the result of the 1965 reforms.

The incentive scheme limited the number of planned targets that supervisory ministries were authorized to issue to firms. Where obligatory targets had once ranged from thirty-five to forty, they were now limited to eight: physical output, sales volume, total profit and the rate of profit on capital, total wage fund, level of payment to state budget, capital investment, introduction of new technology, and allocation of vital resources. Moreover, the sales volume target replaced the gross output target as the basis for bonuses. These new rules were supposed to give more autonomy to the enterprises, but as we will see this was not the effect, owing to the ambiguity in implementation.

As a complement to the recentralization of economic power, the 1965 reforms also entailed a centralization of price setting with the formation of Goskomtsen – which coordinated all price setting and price revision. The "price reform," however, did not intend to improve the ability of prices to convey information concerning the relative scarcities of resources in the Soviet economy. For example, prices were not to interfere with the central planning directives – they were to remain merely convenient tools for accounting purposes. As a result, prices that were set in a fashion that had little to do with the actual cost of resource use continued to distort the structure of production in the Soviet economy.

The effect of the 1965 reforms was largely limited to expanding the Soviet economic bureaucracy.[15] In terms of improving the economic mechanism, the reforms were both ill-conceived and unimplemented. In other words, they were incentive-incompatible and not credible. The policy schemes to improve incentives within the enterprises, according to Nove (1992, p. 383), were ineffective for a variety of reasons. Notably, the rules of the game were arbitrarily altered so that there was no stability in the environment even within a single planning period. Interviews with former enterprise managers concur with this interpretation of the 1965 effort to change the incentive system. "We didn't really have a reform," one former head of a planning department stated. "We were preparing for it, but it was never ratified." Another former manager summed up the enterprise reforms in the following manner: "They only poured water from one bottle to another … In practice nothing changed … One time they tried to give more rights to the enterprise … but they became afraid of private enterprise and stopped it." Another former manager had this to say: "Liberman … created a whole system in which the enterprise would have an incentive to make a profit. They introduced it almost everywhere, but then they changed it so much that it didn't even resemble itself."[16]

Again, the announcement of radical reform merely represented tinkering with the mechanism. There were no good reasons for enterprise managers or private citizens to expect a change in the situation. The only stable political economy rule in effect was that the planning bureaucracy could arbitrarily change the rules any time it desired. The expectation of arbitrary action on the part of the bureaucracy reinforced the incentives that were generated by a system of state control over the economy. Resource use was systemically wasteful, and the future was completely disregarded. The economic system generated no incentives to conserve scarce resources or employ these resources in valued uses, let alone discover better ways to allocate resources among the alternatives (i.e. to find the least-cost production techniques). As Hewett (1988, p. 240) put it: "if a 'death certificate' were issued for the 1965 reforms, it would read 'ministerial interference, aided by the lack of attention by the obstetrician (L. Brezhnev).' "

The policy game under perestroika

The key legal components of perestroika included The Law on Individual Enterprise (1986), The Law on State Enterprises (1987), and The Law on

Cooperatives (1988). Despite the rhetoric and promise of these laws, they contained contradictions and ambiguities that prevented them from achieving the objectives of economic reform. Furthermore, they failed to convey any binding commitment on the part of the Gorbachev regime to true market reform. From 1985 to 1991, Gorbachev introduced at least ten major policy packages for economic reform under the banner of perestroika, but not a single one was fully implemented.

The Law on State Enterprises, for example, was supposed to introduce self-accounting, self-financing, and self-management. But, unwilling to move too quickly with the reform of state enterprises, the government decided to stagger conformity to the law. Some enterprises would operate under the new guidelines as of 1 January 1988; others would do so in the following year, January 1989 (see Goldman 1991, p. 140).

In addition, given the commitment to full employment by the regime, there was no way to introduce self-financing in a manner consistent with a "hard budget constraint" (see Kornai 1986). Enterprise managers and employees knew that, despite whatever announcement was made concerning self-financing, as long as the regime was committed to full employment, enterprises would possess a "soft budget constraint" with all the corresponding inefficiencies.[17] Bankruptcy would not be tolerated, and state subsidies would continue as before.

Not only did the law on state enterprises fail to aid the move to the market economy, it contributed to the economic problems of the already struggling official industrial sector. Managers – in an effort to return the favor to workers to whom they owed their jobs and because they did not face hard budget constraints – approved wage increases. Average wages rose by 8% in 1988 and 13% in 1989 (see Goldman 1991, pp. 141–2). Thus, state enterprise costs increased and with them the demand for increased state subsidies from the enterprises. This, in turn, put an increased strain on the state budget and, consequently, the monetary system, as the printing press was employed to monetize the debt. The persistence of macroeconomic inefficiency bred increased macroeconomic destabilization as economic agents responded rationally to the contradictory rule changes.

The Law on Individual Enterprise was passed in November 1986 and became effective in May 1987. This law allowed individuals to engage in activities that had previously been deemed illegal. Despite several restrictions – such as the length of time that state employees could devote to individual enterprise – the intent of the law was to encourage individual economic enterprise and market experimentation. Family members of state employees or individuals such as students, housewives, and pensioners were allowed to work full time if they desired. To do so, though, individuals had to apply for a license from local authorities and pay either an annual income tax or a fee. The fee applied particularly to cases where it was difficult to monitor income, such as taxi driving. In 1987, the fee for a private taxi was 560 roubles, which meant that a worker who was moonlighting as a taxi driver had to earn the equivalent of three months' wages before driving the taxi would cover its costs (see Hewett

1988, p. 340, n. 60). The perverse consequence of this policy in terms of the persistence of a black market in taxis is described by William Taubman and Jane Taubman in their book *Moscow Spring*. The Law on Individual Enterprise, in this case, amounted to simply regulating and taxing an activity (the private market for taxi services) which had gone on "unofficially" for years. As a consequence, few if any of the Moscow *chastniki* (private taxis) that they encountered were registered and, therefore, official. "Registration," they point out, "required burdensome medical exams, payment of a fee, and of course heavy taxes ... But most burdensome was the requirement that all individual labor activity be moonlighting; the workers must have primary jobs in the State sector' " (1989, p. 46).

An even more fundamental problem with The Law on Individual Enterprise was the campaign against unearned income, which required individuals to have appropriate documentation explaining how they made their money (see Belkindas 1989). A natural market response to this was the emergence of an illicit market in documentation and a decline in economic well-being as the informal networks, which historically filled the gaps caused by the inefficient official system, were disturbed.[18] The attitude of the regime as conveyed by the campaign reinforced citizens' lack of trust concerning the government's commitment to reform. Without a credible conveyance of commitment to market reform, farmers, workers, and others had no incentive to invest in the above-ground market.

This is seen in the way in which cooperatives developed in the Soviet Union under Gorbachev.[19] The Law on Individual Enterprise (adopted November 1986) provided the legal foundation for the cooperative movement because it permitted family members who lived together to form businesses. Formal recognition of cooperatives came with the Law on Cooperation in the USSR, adopted 26 May 1988. Whereas the number of cooperatives was 8,000 employing 88,000 on 1 October 1987, by 1 July 1989, there were more than 133,000 employing 2,900,000. The output of cooperatives amounted to an estimated 350 million roubles for 1987, 6 billion roubles in 1988, and was estimated to be 12.9 billion roubles by June 1989. Despite this explosion in cooperatives, hostility from both the public and the government toward the economic success of cooperatives threatened their long-term viability.[20] Because this hostility resulted in accusations that cooperatives' financial gains were made without any real effort – just exploiting the shortage situation – the threat of the campaign to unearned income was very real. Often, state shortages got blamed on the cooperatives. A state shortage of buns and sausages translates into a cooperative-produced sandwich with a correspondingly high price – at least that is how some described the situation.

The precarious position of cooperatives was compounded because they had to rely almost exclusively on the state sector for supplies, even though they were not officially hooked up to the central supply network. Thus, cooperatives had to rely on illicit transactions, such as bribes and agreements with state enterprises, to obtain resources, which increased their vulnerability to blackmail both by officials and by criminals. In fact, cooperatives were often assumed to be fronts for criminal activity.

In addition, the legal status of cooperatives and the tax policy to which they would be subject have changed frequently. Even before the end of 1988, a resolution was passed that sought to restrict the activities of cooperatives. In February 1989, republican authorities were given the authority over taxation policy toward cooperatives and were encouraged to set differential rates based on the type of cooperative, its pricing policy, and so forth. The "speculative tendencies" of cooperatives were subject to criticism, and authorities were encouraged to take steps to bring cooperative pricing in line with state pricing. Cooperatives were subject to taxes ranging from 25–60% of their income, depending on their pricing policy. The August 1989 law on cooperative taxation, for example, established new regulations on cooperatives and tied their taxation to the relationship between state and cooperative prices.

By constraining the freedom of cooperative and private market experimentation, the Gorbachev government prevented the market from serving one of its most vital functions – inducing an increase in the supply of goods in response to excess consumer demand. The demand side of the market bid up the price of goods in short supply, but the supply side was not free to respond. When supplies failed to increase, it was inevitable that cooperative prices would rise. Consumers, therefore, could either wait in long lines at the state store and attempt to purchase goods that were becoming increasingly non-existent at the fixed state prices, or they could go to the cooperative market and purchase goods at high market prices until the shelves in those private stores were emptied. Either way, expectations of a better future were dashed, and the credibility of the reforms and perestroika was irreversibly damaged.

The undesirable effects of the policies adopted under perestroika were not limited to their incentive incompatibility with entrepreneurial activity but went much deeper, undermining the basic constitution of economic policy. The continual flux in the legal environment for the cooperatives conveyed a lack of commitment on the part of the regime to private sector experimentation. But without such a commitment, there was no way to induce the investment and hard work that were needed to develop the Soviet economy.[21] So, in addition to incentive incompatibility, there was the debilitating problem of adverse reputation that results from policy reversals and the failure to commit.

That inability to convey any kind of commitment to reform sealed perestroika's fate. The reforms could not get the economy going, and the consumer crisis grew acute (see Schroeder 1991a, 1991b; Noren 1991). The political instability of failed reforms, alongside deflated expectations on the part of the population, produced a highly troublesome situation for the Gorbachev regime. "As Gorbachev moved back and forth from one comprehensive reform to another," Marshall Goldman argues, "he became more and more uncertain about subjecting the Soviet Union to the type of shock therapy such reforms would inevitably necessitate. He also concluded that unless reined in, the reform process would ultimately shrink his powers and those of the Soviet Union over central economic control, thus reducing the Soviet Union to an ineffective economic entity" (1991, p. 222).

Gorbachev's economic zigging and zagging was not the only credibility issue at hand. The politics of discretionary power was also an issue of concern with liberal intellectuals, who were not certain that the zigs permitted today would not be superceded by repressive zags tomorrow. "Today," Andrey Sakharov warned, "it is Gorbachev, but tomorrow it could be somebody else. There are no guarantees that some Stalinist will not succeed him" (as quoted in Kaiser 1991, p. 245).

In the fall of 1990, when Gorbachev backed out of his commitment to the radical Shatalin Plan and moved to the right, he lost credibility with his liberal allies. But perestroika had already cost him his credibility with Communist conservatives, so the winter zig to the right did not gain Gorbachev much. As he tried to zag to the left in the spring of 1991, especially with the April compromise with Yeltsin, the conservative forces in the former Soviet Union prepared for one last effort to regain control.

First, they sought to regain control through "constitutional" means; when that failed, they resorted to the August 1991 coup. Even though the coup failed, the failure certainly cannot be attributed to the policies of perestroika. Rather, it was the failure of perestroika that resulted in the coup attempt. As the regime kept introducing liberalization policies only to go back on them, the official economy sank into an abyss. The bureaucracy, which was threatened by reform, knew that more and more radical measures would be necessary to get out of the abyss. Those measures, however, would be undesirable from its point of view.

The unraveling of the Soviet Union as a political entity, however, was the *unintended* by-product of Gorbachev's policy of perestroika. The regime's failure to convey the commitment to economic liberalization that was necessary to reform the Soviet system proved to be perestroika's undoing.

The policy game under Yeltsin

In January 1992, the government of Boris Yeltsin, under the orchestration of Yegor Gaidar, embarked on a liberalization program that was far more ambitious than anything introduced during Gorbachev's reign. Most consumer prices were to be liberalized overnight, mass privatization programs were to be forthcoming, a tight monetary policy was to be pursued, and a sound fiscal policy was to be instituted. This "shock therapy" program, however, was never implemented as originally announced.

Price regulations, for example, were maintained on essential consumer products, such as sugar, salt, vodka, bread, and dairy products. The authority for price regulation was delegated to local authorities. This partial liberalization produced unintended consequences that undermined the reform effort.

The price control on milk provides a perfect example of the perverse consequences of partial price reform. Milk prices were not liberalized, but sour cream prices were; in response, dairy producers shifted production out of milk and into sour cream. An abundance of sour cream and a shortage of milk resulted, as predicted by standard economic theory. Local authorities began trying to alter the perverse consequences of one set of controls with additional controls. Whereas in January 1992 only fourteen food products were under price and output controls, by the summer of 1992 that figure had risen to twenty-four. In addition to food, a wide variety of other products were under state controls, not the least being energy. The official situation was one of continued state control over the economy.

It is important to stress the word *official* because the *de facto* market escaped state controls. The continued existence of the black market during a period of economic liberalization demonstrates that liberalization has in fact not taken place. The dichotomy between the official and the *de facto* economy is a source of trouble for government leaders, especially because it represents the leakage of a source of state revenue. Victor Chernomyrdin's first decree as the new prime minister was an attempt to bring the *de facto* economy under government control by regulating prices and monitoring profits. The decree was issued on 31 December 1992, but revoked on 18 January 1993, because it was not credible.[22]

The economic situation in Russia since January 1992 has been one of continued consumer subsidies while tax revenue continued to escape into the black market. The industrial sector of the economy tells a similar story of poor policy design. Enterprise was supposed to establish hard budget constraints in the state enterprises. The consequence of enterprise reform, however, was the ballooning of debt between state firms. The inter-enterprise debt reached 3.2 trillion roubles in the summer of 1992, and many enterprises were threatened with bankruptcy.[23] The Russian parliament resisted the bankruptcy and engineered the Central Bank's issue of roubles to eliminate the debt crisis. The Central Bank remained under parliament's, not the president's, control.[24] The issuance of state credits to resolve the inter-enterprise debt crisis eliminated the impact of a hard budget constraint, and enterprise reform was stalled. Microeconomic inefficiencies at the enterprise level generated macroeconomic imbalances in the economy.

The link between macroeconomic inefficiency and macroeconomic imbalance is a holdover from the Soviet system. The Soviet system of banking involved a cash sector and a non-cash sector. The non-cash sector involved an internal accounting system that linked state enterprises. The Soviet banking system provided enterprises with the financial assets to settle accounts with one another. Unfortunately, this meant that macroeconomic inefficiencies automatically translated into macroeconomic imbalances: deficits and monetization. During the Soviet era, macroeconomic imbalances were hidden from immediate view by false accounting or repressed inflation.[25] Reform would bring these imbalances into the open; partial reform adds to them.

From July 1992 to October 1992 alone, the money supply more than doubled, from 1.4 trillion roubles to 3.4 trillion roubles. In November an additional 18.7 billion roubles, and in December another 61.5 billion roubles, were issued. This had a dramatic effect on the purchasing power of the rouble in the first year of reform under the Yeltsin government, as would be expected (see Table 9.1).

The "dollarization" of the Russian market economy reflects the unwillingness to hold roubles for market exchange and as such is perhaps a slightly better indicator of the real status of the currency than movements in the average price level. In the first months of the Yeltsin reforms, the rouble gained against the dollar in the currency market. But, beginning in June 1992, the rouble fell steadily (see Table 9.2).

Continued consumer and producer subsidies, in contrast, swelled the fiscal responsibilities of the Russian state at the same time that reliable sources of tax revenue continued to slip into the unofficial economy.[26] The central government of Russia is faced with an acute fiscal crisis.[27] Not the least of Russia's problems is the military budget. If glasnost-era data are accurate, then the Soviet Union spent around 25% of the state budget on defense. With the breakup of the Soviet Union, however, Russia has assumed that burden at the same time as its sources of revenue have been reduced. The burden of the defense sector has thus increased during the Yeltsin period.[28] Fiscal crises are usually "eliminated" through monetization. Inflationary environments, however, destroy the ability to calculate alternative investments rationally and as such deter economic development.

The Yeltsin shock therapy was ill-conceived and contradictory from the beginning.[29] Moreover, without the appropriate political changes, the economic reforms could not get implemented as the situation dictated. In combination with the economic environment, the political crisis increased the uncertainty of the situation. The "war of decrees" between parliament and the president

Table 9.1 Percentage increase in prices on average for 1992–3 as shown by monthly rates of change in the consumer price index

Month	Rate of change	
	1992	1993
January	245.0	26.5
February	38.3	25.7
March	29.8	21.4
April	21.6	24.7
May	12.0	19.3
June	18.6	19.9
July	11.0	22.0
August	9.0	26.0
September	12.0	21.0
October	23.0	21.0
November	26.0	21.0
December	25.0	19.0

Source: *PlanEcon Report*, 19 December 1993, p. 26.

Table 9.2 Rouble/dollar exchange rate at the interbank market rate

Month	Exchange rate 1992	1993
January	204	489
February	176	470
March	152	664
April	153	767
May	122	917
June	125	1,036
July	144	1,025
August	170	986
September	225	1,059
October	353	1,188
November	427	1,194
December	415	1,245

Source: *PlanEcon Report*, 19 December 1993, p. 37.

was not the only problem; many of Yeltsin's decrees were inconsistent with basic economic incentives. Tax rates and other business fees, for example, are inconsistent with the goal of attracting business investment. Foreign investment has been deterred by both economic and political uncertainty.[30]

Often the message is mixed from the government, which adds to the confusion. In addition, the vacuum and power in the central government and the fiscal crisis the center is experiencing have led regional authorities to claim more autonomy. Effective governmental power in Russia by the spring of 1993 had already shifted to the regional leaders.[31] As the events of late September and early October 1993 demonstrated, the uncertainty of the transition policy has not been overcome. And in the wake of the unexpected election results of December 1993, the Yeltsin government appears to have decided to move toward a more cautious reform program with major concessions to state enterprises and state farms.[32] For the time being, at least, it appears that the rhetoric of the Yeltsin regime has shifted from one of liberalization to conservative management.[33]

A historical perspective suggests that the troubling uncertainty in Russia is natural during a time of regime change and that there is no spontaneous mechanism that guarantees a benign outcome.[34] It took more than sixty years of turmoil in England, for example, until the political bargain of the Glorious Revolution was struck in 1688 and economic productivity increased markedly.[35]

That history offers us no easy and fixed rules for moving from an autocratic government and state-run economies to liberal political and economic arrangement does not change the basic message of the argument presented in this chapter; political rules must be established that effectively constrain discretionary behavior, and a clear and well-defined (i.e. transparent) legal system must be constructed *before* private sector economic experimentation can be expected to yield the promised welfare gains.

Conclusion

One of the most basic insights of political economy is the need for rules to govern economic activity. Modern political economy is a research program that focuses our inquiry on the working properties of rules and the processes of social interaction that take place within rules. By examining the rules of social interaction and their impact on social processes, scholars can begin to develop ideas about workable constitutions of economic policy.

In developing a workable constitution of economic policy, it must be recognized that the obstacles that incentives and information present to discretionary behavior are formidable. The Soviet experience shows that without effectively signaling and establishing a binding and credible commitment to broad liberalization, the behavior of the government simply destabilizes the situation.

The argument against government intervention in the free-market process does not amount to asserting that government intervention must necessarily lead to totalitarianism. That was a misunderstanding of the argument on the critics' part. Rather, the argument suggests that interventionism produces unintended results that will be viewed as undesirable from the government's own point of view. Thus, interventionist policy constantly forces on government officials the choice of either rejecting their previous policy or intervening even more in the attempt to correct past failings. The argument is a stability argument. Intervention is just not stable as an economic and political system. The discretionary behavior of the government results in situations that undermine its own initiatives.

Whereas the instability of the 1920s in the Soviet Union led to Stalinism, the instability of the late 1980s led to the dissolution of the Soviet Union. The efforts in the 1950s and 1960s at liberalization failed and were quickly reversed. Even under Yeltsin's post-Soviet experiment in free-market shock therapy, the new government has failed to establish the sort of binding political and legal commitments required. Each of these experiences illustrates the basic point: discretionary behavior on the part of the government fails to produce the stable environment that is necessary for economic prosperity. The insights that the Soviet and post-Soviet experience offer should become basic material in developing a workable constitution of economic policy in the post-perestroika era.

Acknowledgments

Financial assistance from the Austrian Economics Program at New York University and the Sarah Scaife Foundation, in addition to support from the Earhart Foundation and the National Fellows Program at the Hoover Institution on War, Revolution and Peace, Stanford University, is gratefully acknowledged. The usual caveat applies.

References

Aslund, A. (1991) *Struggle for Economic Reform*, 2nd edn., Ithaca, NY: Cornell University Press.

Ball, A. (1987) *Russia's Last Capitalists: The Nepmen, 1921–9*. Berkeley: University of California Press.

Belkindas, M. (1989) *Privatization of the Soviet Economy under Gorbachev*, 11 (April): Berkeley–Duke Occasional Papers on the Second Economy of the USSR, No. 14.

Berliner, J. (1983) "Planning and Management," in A. Bergson and H. Levine (eds.) *The Soviet Economy: Toward the Year 2000*, London: Allen & Unwin.

Boettke, P. J. (1990) *The Political Economy of Soviet Socialism: The Formative Years, 1918–1928*, Boston: Kluwer Academic Publishers.

—— (1993) *Why Perestroika Failed: The Politics and Economics of Socialist Transformation*, London: Routledge.

Bukharin, N. (1982) "Concerning the New Economic Policy and Our Tasks (1925)," in N. I. Bukharin, *Selected Writings on the State and the Transition to Socialism*, R. Day (ed.), New York: M. E. Sharpe.

Burke, J. (1993) "Russia's Regions Emerge as Key Power Brokers," *Christian Science Monitor* 15 March: p. 6.

Carr, E. H. (1981) (first published 1953) *The Bolshevik Revolution, 1917–23*, three volumes, New York: Norton.

—— (1958) *Socialism in One Country, 1924–1926*, three volumes, Baltimore: Penguin Books.

Conquest, R. (1986) *The Harvest of Sorrow*, New York: Oxford University Press.

Friedman, M. (1953) "A Monetary and Fiscal Framework for Economic Stability," in M. Friedman, *Essays in Positive Economics*, Chicago: University of Chicago Press.

Goldman, M. (1991) *What Went Wrong with Perestroika*, New York: Norton.

Gregory, P. (1990) *Restructuring the Soviet Economic Bureaucracy*, New York: Cambridge University Press.

Gregory, P. and Stuart, R. (1990) *Soviet Economic Structure and Performance*, 4th edn., New York: Harper and Row.

Gubsky, N. (1927) "Economic Law in Soviet Russia," *Economic Journal* 37(June).

Hewett, E. (1988) *Reforming the Soviet Economy*, Washington, DC: Brookings Institution.

Ickes, B. and Ryterman, R. (1992) "The Interenterprise Arrear Crisis in Russia," *Post-Soviet Affairs* 8.

Jones, A. and Moskoff, W. (1989) "New Cooperatives in the USSR," *Problems of Communism*, November–December: 27–39.

—— (1991) *Ko-ops: The Rebirth of Entrepreneurship in the Soviet Union*, Bloomington, IN: Indiana University Press.

Kaiser, R. (1991) *Why Gorbachev Happened?* New York: Simon and Schuster.

Khanin, G. I. (1989) "Why and When Did NEP Die?" *EKO* 10, translated in *Problems of Economics* 33 (August, 1990).

Klein, D. (1990) "The Macroeconomic Foundations of Rules versus Discretion," *Constitutional Political Economy* 1(3).

Klein, D. and O'Flaherty, B. (1993) "A Game-theoretic Rendering of Promises and Threats," *Journal of Economic Behavior and Organization* 21.

Kornai, J. (1986) "The Soft Budget Constraint." *Kyklos* 39(1).

Kydland, F. and Prescott, E. (1977) "Rules Rather than Discretion: The Inconsistency of Optimal Plans," *Journal of Political Economy* 85(3): 473–91.

The Law on Individual Enterprise (1986) *Pravda* 21 November, translated in *Current Digest of the Soviet Press* 38(46).

The Law on State Enterprises (1987) *Pravda* 1 July, translated in *Current Digest of the Soviet Press* 39(30–31).

The Law on Cooperatives (1988) in L. Black (ed.) *USSR Document Annual,* Gulf Breeze, FL: Academic International Press.

Linz, S. (1987) "The Impact of Soviet Economic Reform: Evidence from the Interview Project," *Comparative Economic Studies* 29(4) (Winter).

Litwack, J. (1991a) "Discretionary Behavior and Soviet Economic Reform," *Soviet Studies,* 43(2).

—— (1991b) "Legality and Market Reform in Soviet-Type Economies," *Journal of Economic Perspectives* 5(4) (Fall).

Noren, J. (1991) "The Economic Crisis: Another Perspective," in E. Hewett and V. Winston (eds.) *Milestones in Glasnost and Perestroika: The Economy,* Washington, DC: Brookings Institution.

North, D. (1990) *Institutions, Institutional Change and Economic Performance,* New York: Cambridge University Press.

North, D. and Weingast, B. (1989) "Constitutions and Commitment: The Evolution of Institutions Governing Public Choice in Seventeenth-Century England," *Journal of Economic History,* December.

Nove, A. (1992) *An Economic History of the USSR, 1917–1991,* New York: Penguin.

Pejovich, S. (1969) "Liberman's Reforms and Property Rights in the Soviet Union," *Journal of Law and Economics* 12 (April).

Roderik, D. (1989) "Promises, Promises: Credible Policy Reform via Signalling," *Economic Journal* 99 (September).

Rutland, P. (1993) *The Politics of Economic Stagnation in the Soviet Union,* New York: Cambridge University Press.

Schroeder, C. (1991a) "The Soviet Economy on a Treadmill of Perestroika: Gorbachev's First Five Years," in H. D. Balzer (ed.) *Five Years That Shook the World,* Boulder, CO: Westview Press.

—— (1991b) " 'Crisis' in the Consumer Sector: A Comment," in E. Hewett and V. Winston (eds.) *Milestones in Glasnost and Perestroika: The Economy,* Washington, DC: Brookings Institution.

Shelton, J. (1989) *The Coming Soviet Crash,* New York: Free Press.

Solzhenitsyn, A. (1973) *The Gulag Archipelago,* three volumes, New York: Harper and Row.

Taubman, W. and Taubman, J. (1989) *Moscow Spring,* New York: Summit Books.

10 Perestroika and public choice

The economics of autocratic succession in a rent-seeking society*

Introduction

Mikhail Gorbachev has been widely acclaimed in the West for his reform policies of perestroika and glasnost. Until quite recently, many pundits boldly declared that Gorbachev's USSR was actually embarked on an abandonment of the Communist economic system, and would eventually embrace real democracy and a free market (see, for example, Muravchik 1990, p. 25). While recent developments have rendered these forecasts obsolete, the Gorbachev round of reforms surely represents an interesting problem in public choice.

For purposes of analysis, we propose to concentrate on the period from Gorbachev's succession as Chairman of the Communist Party of the Soviet Union (CPSU) in 1985 until the end of 1989 (with occasional references to more recent events). This is the period during which both perestroika and glasnost grew to dominate the political scene in the USSR. Moreover, the first five years of Gorbachev's rule represented the period of purportedly dramatic "liberalization" within the Soviet system. Perestroika appeared to be a truly radical series of reforms, a triumph of ideals over rent-seeking.

Our purpose in the present chapter is to argue that, upon closer examination, the succession of Gorbachev in general and the perestroika/glasnost "reform" program in particular bear a close resemblance to other, earlier Soviet government policy adjustments which followed shifts in the top leadership. (Gorbachev's behavior as a "reformer" over the period 1985–9 can be explained by reference to the incentives facing the dictator of a socialist state based on the distribution of economic privilege and political patronage.) In short, during the period of perestroika, Chairman (later President) Gorbachev was an autocrat who behaved in a manner consistent with the public choice theory of autocracy, as presented by Gordon Tullock (1987). Gorbachev's period of "reform" was not an extraordinary example of the role of ideology or vision in human affairs, but a more routine episode of rent-seeking in action.

*Originally published as Boettke, P. J. and Anderson, G. (1993) "Perestroika and Public Choice: The Economics of Autocratic Succession in a Rent-Seeking Society," *Public Choice* 75(2) (February): 101–18.

Property rights to socialist rents

The "centrally planned economy" of the Soviet Union has often been portrayed as an alternative to market exchange. Supposedly, economic activity is strategically controlled from the center, which allocates quotas, provides accounting "prices" to enterprises, and generally directs the course of the economy in fine detail. Private ownership of the means of production has been abolished and replaced with "social ownership."

This "central planning model" of the USSR began to come under increasing challenge from economists in recent years. The "centrally planned economy" would appear to be "planned" only in the loosest sense, meaning that general output targets are set for the long run, but that day-to-day economic operations allow enterprise managers (in the state sector) a great deal of effective discretion.[1] In other words, managers are told what types of output to produce, but are essentially allowed to determine the quantity, quality, and distribution of that output independently of the central planners. Moreover, the "second economy," in which goods and services are exchanged at free market prices, apparently plays an important role in facilitating the operation of the "planned sector," allowing enterprises in the latter arena to function.

Furthermore, bribery (in various forms) has always been endemic to the system. The state restrictions and "central plans" constitute, in part, state-sanctioned *monopolies* which allow individuals in strategic positions to extract monopoly rents (i.e. bribes).[2]

The Soviet Union never "abolished private property" for the simple reason that such a goal is economically meaningless, hence impossible (see Hayek 1944 and 1988). In economics, ownership rights refer to the locus of effective decision-making about the use of resources (i.e. *de facto* ownership), and may or may not be consistent with legal boundaries of property (*de jure* ownership). This insight is today a standard convention among economists. While the Soviet Union has changed some aspects of the form of ownership rights, effective ownership rights remain allocated to specific individuals – as they must in *any* real-world economy.

The Soviet system, then, is not really a "non-market economy" but rather a market subject to intense governmental regulation. Market prices play an important role in allocating goods and services in the Soviet-style economy, but the "real" prices are mostly "under-the-table" (in American parlance).[3]

Understanding the property rights to rent flows in the USSR is crucial to understanding economic "reform." Among other things, perestroika has represented the redistribution of rents from their former recipients to new holders of monopoly power.

One frequently mentioned aspect of Soviet-style systems is the virtual absence of legal protection for property rights. Less frequently mentioned is the fact that this absence extends to rent flows. The individuals who have been favored by the state with positions of power (and wealth derived from that power) do not have secure property rights in those positions.

Compare this with the typical situation in Western democracies, where patterns of government redistribution of wealth tend to be based on stable long-term contracts between the legislature and particular interest groups. Landes and Posner (1975) argue that the independent judiciary plays an important role in defining and protecting such legislative contracts between the government and interest groups. The Soviet Union lacks such an independent judiciary.

In a representative democracy, the independent judiciary serves to protect wealth transfer contracts between the legislature and interest groups when the legislators retire or otherwise leave office. If, on average, the relevant decision-makers remain in office for a long period, contracts with interest groups – patterns of government taxing and spending, as well as patterns of rent-generating restrictions on markets – will tend to be stable during their tenure in office. The effective tenure in power of decision-makers (i.e. the very large number of bureaucrats and officials who regulate and oversee the economy on a day-to-day basis) in the USSR was fairly stable. In turn, the system of wealth transfer contracts with interest groups has also been fairly stable for many years.

Given the absence of an independent judiciary, formal contracts (e.g. like the judicial enforcement of "congressional intent" in the US) are not available. Instead, informal quasi-contracts form the basis for the distribution of rents. For many decades, the *nomenklatura* was a fixed group of individuals who controlled all-important positions in that country.[4] Monopoly rent rights were fairly stable, though based on verbal, personal, informal quasi-contracts.

The long period of stable rights to rent flows in the Soviet economy recently came to an end. Instead, the complex existing network of rent extraction based on political power has undergone a considerable amount of "recontracting." The period of perestroika has had important implications at the level of bureaucratic incentives and rewards. Soviet-style socialism remains alive, however, unwell, but the organizational chart of the planning apparatus has undergone a considerable amount of "restructuring."

The rhetoric and reality of perestroika

At the time of Gorbachev's rise to power, the Soviet economy had experienced a prolonged period of decline.[5] Western estimates of GNP in the Soviet Union show a marked decline from 4.7% annual growth rate during the seventh five-year planning period (1961–5) to only 2.0% during the eleventh five-year planning period that ended in 1985 (Hewett 1988, p. 52). Even more drastic figures of decline are represented in a text by two Soviet reform economists, Popov and Shmelev (1989, p. 41), who conclude that since "the late 1950s the rates of economic growth have fallen constantly and by the middle of the 1980s had dropped to almost zero." It is within this context of economic decline that Gorbachev announced his plans for the radical restructuring of the Soviet economy. The potential gains to the overall economy from "restructuring" were so obvious to outside observers that Gorbachev's "reform" efforts were largely taken at face value.

The program of perestroika, however, has been filled with ambiguities and inconsistencies from the start and continues to be plagued by them.[6] Comparative systems analysts have concluded that even assuming minimal problems of implementation, the basic "reforms" are unlikely to have much effect on overall economic performance because they fail to address the fundamental problems in the Soviet economy.[7]

For example, the Law on State Enterprises, which Gorbachev himself (1987: 86) proclaimed to be of "primary importance" to the reform of the economy, was instituted on 1 January 1988.[8] The law was ostensibly designed to grant financial autonomy to enterprises. But according to Articles 9 and 10 of the law, the enterprises were still subject to state control both in their pricing and in their output policy.[9] In other words, these "firms" remained state controlled. Thus, despite the rhetoric promising enterprise autonomy, the Law on State Enterprises – the centerpiece of perestroika – was never intended to substantially change the basis of state central planning (see Ericson, 1988, 1989). More recent "reform" decrees and laws have similarly claimed to accomplish much but in reality made little substantial difference.

Price reform has been another area rife with ambiguities. Initially, price reform was to come in 1989, then it was to start in 1991 for some products and 1993 for others.[10] For the first five years following Gorbachev's accession to power, basically nothing happened to the Soviet system of rigid price-by-government-decree. Predictably, official announcements regarding imminent price increases (ostensibly designed as a part of a "price reform" package) led to widespread hoarding by consumers, and shortages on store shelves. As of summer 1990, five years into the "Gorbachev era," there were growing shortages of virtually everything (see Gumbel 1989 and 1990). According to a state committee that monitors the availability of 1,000 products, as of October 1990, 996 of them could not be regularly found for purchase in ordinary shops.[11] Repeatedly, Gorbachev reacted by promising to bring "relief" by way of maintaining state subsidies on the prices of basic products.

Moreover, there has been a persistent gulf between the rhetoric and the reality of "price reform." The various government plans and proposals offered during the first five years of Gorbachev's purportedly "reformist" regime were not even claimed to promote freely fluctuating prices to guide exchange and production throughout the economy, but instead were all purported designs for "better" administration of prices. Prices were still assumed to be tightly controlled by central authorities. More recent plans for "price reform" continue to assume that most prices will not be decontrolled for the foreseeable future.[12]

The reforms that were actually introduced before outright political disintegration began in 1990 simply did not represent a radical restructuring of the Soviet system toward liberalization. Perestroika did represent a form of radical restructuring, but of patronage, not of the overall economic system.

The transition from a socialist to a free-market economy is fraught with political complexities to be sure, but represents a simple problem conceptually. Improving the long-term performance of the Soviet economy required implementing reforms such as permitting private ownership of productive resources, allowing free-market price formation, and eliminating prohibitions against the voluntary transfer of ownership rights. In short, simply *relaxing* controls and *reducing* the level of state intervention in the economic system could have been expected to reap substantial economic benefits. Potential political opposition (e.g. from "the bureaucracy") aside, there seems little real evidence that Gorbachev accepted the transition from socialism to a free market even as an ultimate goal of reform efforts. Yet Gorbachev is typically regarded by observers as a highly intelligent, educated man, who has rarely been accused of myopia (economic or otherwise). We suggest that this paradox is only apparent, and not real. Perestroika did not emerge as a "plan to end planning," but rather represented the "Gorbachev round" of patronage adjustment which has traditionally followed the transition to a new leader in the Soviet Union. "Reform" rhetoric constituted a quasi-ideological packaging for a rather ordinary redistribution of patronage opportunities.

Perestroika and patronage

Since its inception, the Soviet state has been an autocracy, although not necessarily a dictatorship (i.e. ultimate authority has usually been shared by a small group). However, at times, a single individual has exercised nearly absolute political power (e.g. Stalin). More often, power has been shared by members of a small clique in which one member was clearly "first among equals." For a period following the transition from one Chairman of the Communist Party to the next, the new Soviet ruler's power has usually been relatively weak as he consolidated his political position.

The Soviet state has been an exceptionally stable autocracy since its inception. Throughout history, the most common route to autocratic power has been by coup, usually involving the military. Alternatively, some autocrats have succeeded in establishing a dynasty in which their designated successor is their son or daughter, but such monastic dynasties have rarely maintained continuity for more than a few generations. The "third system" avoids many of the problems associated with these other modes of succession, and has proven very stable in the relatively few cases where it has been successfully implemented. One such case is the Soviet state.

A major characteristic of this "third system" is that the present autocrat appoints a kind of voting body which then determines the autocrat's successor after the autocrat's death. In the Soviet system, this "voting body" has been the Politburo. Tullock (1987, pp. 158–9) notes that the highly stable Soviet system of succession closely resembles another even more successful example: the Roman Catholic Church, which has used a similar system to appoint Popes for nearly a millennium. Like his predecessors before him, Gorbachev rose to the Chairmanship of the CPSU as the result of a Politburo vote.

Gorbachev's brief tenure as Chairman of the CPSU followed the routine historical pattern, up until early 1990. He never reached the position of near absolute power gained by Stalin, but neither did any of his post-Stalin predecessors.

Although there was a growing opposition movement outside of the Party, most notably Boris Yeltsin (President of the Russian Republic), Gavriil Popov (Mayor of Moscow), and Anatolii Sobchak (Mayor of Leningrad), Gorbachev emerged from the 28th Party Congress (in the Summer of 1990) in control of personnel policy within the Party and the government. In the Soviet context, this meant that Gorbachev controlled socialist patronage.

Among Sovietologists, political patronage has long been recognized as a crucial element in the succession process in the USSR (see Smith 1987, p. 343). The succession from one leader to another has typically included a substantial shift in bureaucratic appointments, mostly in the upper ranks, although this "patronage shift" has varied from the fairly minor (e.g. under Brezhnev) to the quite major (e.g. under Khrushchev).

However, much of this "patronage" appointment is only possible in the context of significant transaction costs for the new ruler. The Chairman of the CPSU does not actually have constitutional, legal authority to hire and fire very many of the individuals filling the "patronage" positions. This does not mean that the new ruler does not have the effective power to hire and fire large numbers of bureaucrats, but only that the costs of accomplishing this end may sometimes be significant.

Take, for example, the Khrushchev succession. Khrushchev instituted a wide-ranging series of changes in the planning system, including a shift in power from the Council of Ministers to the Communist Party in most spheres of policy-making, the downgrading of many ministries from All-Union to Republic status, and the regional cartelization effort (the "*sovnarkhoz* reforms"). Sovietologists generally ascribe these changes, at least in part, to political considerations – i.e. rewarding his allies, and penalizing his opponents (e.g. Hewett 1988, p. 225; and Smith 1987, p. 345).

This previous episode of "reform" illustrated a common phenomenon associated with the redistribution of patronage appointments, which has continued under Gorbachev. In some cases, the easiest way to replace the administrators of Ministry X with the new dictator's patronage choices is to first abolish Ministry X and replace it with new organization Y. This "shell game" eliminates the jobs of the previous dictator's patronage appointees and allows the distribution of the new jobs as patronage plums.[13]

As early as the fall of 1985, both of the two key central planning bodies, Gosplan and Gosnab, had new, Gorbachev-appointed leaders. The Council of Ministers also had a new chairman, and by December 1985 Gorbachev had replaced about one-third of the people heading the approximately fifty branch ministries. By early 1987 "all leading institutions in the economic hierarchy, and a good portion of the ministries, were headed by new appointees" (Hewett 1988, p. 311–12).[14]

Of course, new faces in the old jobs – or new faces in old jobs with new titles – do not in themselves imply significant "reform." On the other hand, this does not imply that the transition has no effect on the functioning of the system in the short run. It takes some time for new administrators to settle in to smoothly functioning quasi-contractual arrangements with other bureaucrats. During the period of transition from the older, stabilized regime to the new regime in a particular ministry, the bureaucracy in question will have only fairly loose quasi-contractual bonds and, consequently, will have unusually great freedom of action. This period of "experimentation" will probably be short-lived, but during its brief existence might produce impressive-looking policy shifts at the grassroots level (as the bureaucrats maneuver for better rent opportunities). While this is occurring, the appearance of "reform" is possible. But similar periods of superficial reform, which ended up never really amounting to much, have been a recurring pattern in Russian history, and have continued into the Communist era (see Starr 1989).

The recent "reforms" were essentially limited to various marginal changes in the organization of the Soviet planning bureaucracy, combined with the bumper crop of new, younger faces populating the upper reaches of that bureaucracy.[15] Both aspects of "reform" would seem to be (patronage) business as usual. Therefore, the tendency among Western observers to portray Gorbachev as locked in a mortal struggle with "the bureaucrats" over perestroika is very misleading.[16] While many bureaucrats might have expected to *lose* from perestroika, many others could expect to *gain*. Intellectuals and members of the academic bureaucracy, for example, have benefited greatly from glasnost and represented some of Gorbachev's strongest supporters in the initial phase of perestroika (1985–9).

Gorbachev's perestroika reforms were commonly portrayed as having a net decentralizing bent (cf. Hewett 1988, p. 326). Responsibilities – and resulting rents – were to be reassigned. But this "decentralization" did not represent a movement toward *laissez-faire*. The basic nature of the economy, a huge nationalized sector combined with a massive system of interlocking state monopolies, remained the same.[17] One of the apparent implications of "restructuring" in the USSR is the prospect of increased central government spending in the future. That is, the proportion of national income controlled and allocated directly by Moscow is expected by some observers to significantly increase (see Hewett 1988: 315). The changes proposed by Gorbachev in the ministerial system (including the expanded powers to "coordinate relations" to be given Gosplan) have been described as amounting "to a recentralization of economic power in a new, supra-ministerial, level of the hierarchy" (Hewett 1988, p. 338).[18]

The "anti-corruption campaign" is another interesting problem which plays an important role in the redistribution of patronage perks in Gorbachev's USSR. Such "campaigns" mask the political reallocation and redistribution of monopoly rents (pecuniary and non-pecuniary) in the Soviet system. Historically, such efforts have often come soon after the accession of a new ruler and frequently have recurred during the longer tenures of Stalin and Brezhnev. These "campaigns" might be described as "rent purges." Wealth and power are redistributed from the politically disfavored to the politically favored.

But, while these periodic "rent purges" are under way, holders of monopoly positions in the economy will tend to "lie low" for a while, waiting for the purge to end. They will then go back to business as usual. The problem is that during these periods of caution, the efficiency of the second economy of bribery is significantly reduced – and hence, so is the efficiency of the overall economy, which depends on "under the table trades" for its day-to-day functioning.[19]

One of the most dramatic changes which have taken place in the USSR has been the apparent transformation of the Communist Party itself, including changes ranging from a claimed relaxation of the rule by the Party over appointments to bureaucratic positions of responsibility (i.e. the *nomenklatura* system), to the actual abandonment of the Party's legal monopoly in Soviet politics (Parks 1990). As interesting as these developments are, they may ultimately result only in a massive reallocation of rents by way of a restructuring of the system of internal monopolies and positions of political power. These events are yet additional evidence of a massive turnover in bureaucratic personnel and patronage appointments. Simply stated, positions controlling rent flows went on the auction block in the mid-1980s.

The demographics of the purge-ocracy

In the representative democracies which have been extensively analyzed by public choice economists, government bureaucracies grow fairly slowly over time, and the current holders of positions within the bureaucracy tend to be members of a number of different age-group cohorts. The process of hiring and retiring (assuming that civil servants tend to have great security of tenure, and rarely get fired) is continuous, but gradual. Hence, "the bureaucracy" is never really the same cohort, who were all hired into their positions at about the same time, and who might be expected to remain in office as a coherent group until about the same time.

The situation in the USSR was, and until recently has been, quite different. The Communist Party of the Soviet Union was the organization that closely controlled the appointment of personnel to positions of power and responsibility. While usually one individual (and at times a tiny group) was clearly in the position of dictator, the Party organization hierarchy distributed considerable political power amongst various echelons of officials. For example, the Chairman of the CPSU may have represented the ultimate authority, exercising considerable influence over who became (and remained) the Chairman of the Communist Party of the Moldavian SSR, but the latter exercised some degree of authority over day-to-day bureaucratic appointments and affairs in Moldavia, and so on. Opportunities for patronage appointments on the part of the Chairman of the CPSU were constrained by the *nomenklatura* system, in which the Party established which individual members were "qualified" – often a strictly political judgment – for particular potential appointments. The ability of, say, Leonid Brezhnev to replace the existing manager of a large steel plant with a friend-of-a-friend of his brother-in-law was subject to many Party-determined limitations. Consequently, after changes in leadership in Moscow, the turnover in personnel in responsible positions throughout the bureaucracy tended to be fairly limited and marginal. The existing bureaucracy, and the planning apparatus, remained mostly very stable.

Stalin significantly increased stability within the Soviet bureaucracy. Brzezinski (1956) described Stalin's reign as a "permanent purge." Before, during, and after World War II, Stalin killed or imprisoned a very large proportion of the existing Soviet bureaucracy. One of the lesser-acknowledged consequences of this practice was that the average age of members of the Soviet bureaucracy fell drastically as young underlings assumed their purged seniors' former positions.[20] This "purge effect" was enhanced considerably by the war, during which an additional substantial percentage of the bureaucracy was killed off. In short, the bulk of the massive USSR state bureaucracy came to power at about the same time, and could be expected to retire (or die of natural causes) at about the same time. While the same cohort basically controlled the most important strategic positions in the bureaucracy, the system which resulted could be expected to be extremely stable in its ordinary operations until that bureaucratic cohort began to retire. Gorbachev "inherited" an imminent, massive turnover in this bureaucracy.

Numerous observers attributed the failure of Khrushchev's, Brezhnev's, and Andropov's earlier efforts at "reform" to the hostility of the "entrenched bureaucracy." But, unlike these previous autocrats, Gorbachev faced a radically different situation – the bureaucracy was about to undergo a "demographic transition." In other words, *the transaction costs associated with the realignment of rent flows and patronage opportunities were rapidly, and significantly, lowered.* Finally, by the mid-1980s the cohort which had collectively controlled the bureaucracy since Stalin's rule at last began to die, or retire. With them went the structure of informal quasi-contracts which formed the basis of the Soviet power structure.

There is abundant evidence that a massive turnover in Soviet officials occurred under Gorbachev, beside which earlier patronage appointment reallocations pale by comparison. Colton (1986, pp. 114–15) reports that by 1985–6, shortly after the Gorbachev succession, the average age of Politburo members dropped suddenly by six years, and sharp drops in age were recorded in the Party Secretariat and on the Presidium of the Council of Ministers. Further, average dates of birth were already "advancing in all segments of the élite" (Ibid.). At the middle levels of the Soviet government establishment, "functionaries have lost their positions in droves" in a series of personnel changes which "measured by the number of offices changing hands, are the most sweeping of the entire post-Stalin period" (Ibid. p. 89).[21]

Perestroika represented Gorbachev's exploitation of such an opportunity for redistribution of rent flows, which resulted from this demographic event. As the holders of major positions of power in the economy either died or retired, much of the quasi-contractual basis behind their positions of power (personal agreements, etc.) ended as well. Gorbachev seized the opportunity to reappropriate positions of power from the former holders, and reallocated them as patronage rewards to his supporters.

Glasnost as a wealth transfer

Naturally enough, the element in Gorbachev's reforms which has attracted the most attention from the Western media has been glasnost: the "new openness" and freedom of expression in the Soviet media. Although this policy has often been portrayed as the clearest expression of Gorbachev's "liberalism," an important side effect has received less attention. Glasnost has represented an effective autocratic political tactic, at least in the short run.

With the "new openness," Gorbachev has effectively "purchased" the support of (many) intellectuals by bribing them with increased freedom of expression. Landes and Posner (1975) noted that the First Amendment to the US Constitution represented, in part, a wealth transfer to publishers and writers. Similarly, by increasing freedom of expression, Gorbachev devised a wealth transfer to intellectuals which is cheap to produce: the bribe takes the form of reduced controls. The key feature of this particular "bribe" was that Gorbachev retained the reins by continuing to control the presses and TV cameras![22] Glasnost, then, represented a set of political privileges granted to intellectuals whom Gorbachev wanted to reward, not real freedoms (because the major media remain a state monopoly). Pro-Gorbachev journalists were permitted considerable leeway, while the activities of anti-Gorbachev journalists were tightly restricted.[23] In other words, with glasnost, Gorbachev offered a bid for the support of the media establishment and (many) professional intellectuals. Moreover, this wealth transfer was accomplished without any significant central government budget outlay.

The upsurge in the uncovering of corruption and inefficiency by journalists was claimed as a major piece of evidence for the significance of glasnost. However, this trend had several precedents in Soviet history. Every few years since Stalin came to power, the Soviet press has gone on an "anti-corruption" rampage – which usually occurred during the course of a Kremlin power struggle. Andropov, Brezhnev, Khrushchev, and even Stalin led campaigns against "corruption" – a term that usually referred to the ill-gotten gains of their political opponents, and overlooked the similar ill-gotten gains of their supporters.

Glasnost was consistently opposed by the KGB, and its head, Chebrikov (subsequently replaced in 1989). This was unsurprising, given that much of the "corruption" revealed in the press was KGB "corruption." These "exposés" led to major replacements of personnel at all levels.[24] Allegations of corruption among the MVD, Interior Ministry secret police, were also widespread and also preceded massive replacement of MVD personnel (Hazan 1990, p. 154). Thus, glasnost in the press functioned, partly but importantly, to facilitate the removal of officials and bureaucrats who had (for whatever reason) fallen from favor with the ruler. "Openness" in the Soviet media allowed Gorbachev and his allies to defeat and discredit at least some of their opponents in the secret police services (including the powerful KGB), organizations which many Sovietologists have long regarded as possessing "king-making" power in Soviet politics.

Of course, glasnost has produced other long-term consequences, which were probably completely unintended. "Openness" represented a low-cost wealth transfer to intellectuals and journalists, from Gorbachev's perspective, but may have contributed to the instability of the Communist regime in the longer term by depriving the CPSU of effective control over information and the media. Our point is that glasnost produced numerous short-term advantages to Gorbachev, which had nothing to do with philosophy or "liberal" values.

Free to choose, free to tax

The most dramatic evidence of "reform" in Gorbachev's USSR was the relaxation of controls on private economic activity. Until the recent law on private economic activity, put into effect in May 1987, it was illegal for individuals to engage in most private productive activities, including most services and handicrafts. Since the new law, though, many forms of private economic production are legally permitted. However, the law requires that the private economic activity does not interfere with the state employment of the individual enterpriser. Only students, housewives, members of private workers' immediate families over the age of sixteen and living with their parents, and pensioners can work full time in such businesses. Loosening the restrictions on the private sector has hitherto produced only marginal changes because the private sector in the USSR is so small relative to the overall economy.

Individuals engaged in such activities must first be licensed by local government authorities (*ispol'komy*), and must subsequently pay either an annual income tax or an up-front annual fee (patent). The income tax is progressive, and both the tax and the fees are substantial.[25] While the limited legalization of capitalist acts between consenting adults has received much press in the West, Gorbachev's motivations for promoting such "reforms" have received little scrutiny.

Given that many "illegal" private economic activities have long been tacitly permitted by the authorities, it is unclear what difference legalization will make to the average consumer.[26] Lower transaction costs would tend to improve efficiency, but some individuals will become net losers. Naturally, the well-being of those consumers with a relatively low discount rate, and/or having a comparative advantage in queuing for goods, might be temporarily reduced. Also, the former recipients of bribes from "black" or "gray" market businesses would lose income in the short run.

In contrast, from the standpoint of the central government considered as a revenue-maximizing organization, legalization does produce a tangible benefit. Legal economic activity can be made to produce tax revenue.

For purposes of comparison, recall that the Soviet Union went through a somewhat similar period of limited legalization of private trade during the 1920s (see Boettke 1990, pp. 113–46). This was termed the New Economic Policy (NEP), and has often been portrayed as a temporary reversion to full capitalism by the Bolshevik state. In reality, the NEP only permitted a fairly narrow range of private economic activities to take place in the context of a largely nationalized economy. During the period of the NEP, private enterprises were forced to pay extremely high tax and licensing fees. Although precise figures do not exist, revenues from this source appear to have been very large, and represented a significant proportion of total state revenue.[27] In addition, local administrators "frequently imposed new taxes on the Nepmen or increased old ones without permission from Moscow" (Ball 1987, p. 35) as well as overcharging for licenses.

In announcing changes in Soviet agriculture at the Twenty-seventh Party Congress, Gorbachev invoked the NEP precedent and claimed that his proposed reforms were similar (Colton 1986, p. 96). But Gorbachev's "neo-NEP" was not a freeing of markets, but the very opposite. The private sector in the USSR has long been a "gray market": technically illegal, but tacitly accepted, and essentially tax exempt. Therefore, the legalization of private domestic trade may primarily represent a large tax increase masquerading as "liberalization."[28]

Conclusion

Gorbachev "liberalized" government restrictions in some ways, although much of this "reform" activity seemed to have been primarily directed toward the reallocation of patronage opportunities, a routine activity for new autocrats throughout history. For the first five years since Gorbachev's succession, the rhetoric about market-oriented reform bore little relationship to reality. Gorbachev made no serious effort to end the domination of the economy by the central government. One of the apparent goals, and successes, of the Gorbachev era was accomplishing the transfer of resources away from the military; a goal shared by Khrushchev in the early 1960s (although with less success). More dramatically, by withdrawing the previous level of massive subsidies to the Eastern Bloc countries, Gorbachev succeeded in ending an entanglement which was a net drain on Moscow's fiscal resources. Otherwise, Gorbachev and perestroika closely resembled earlier, and equally marginal, "reform" episodes.

But even if Gorbachev's perestroika was based on the redistribution of rents disguised with "liberalization" rhetoric, it now seems obvious that a basic conflict existed between Gorbachev's short-term interests – even if they are maximizing the gains, both pecuniary and in power, from the exercise of political patronage – and the long-term stability of the Communist economic system. Some historians argue that one of the major causes of the Reformation, which limited without destroying the power of the Catholic Church, was the sudden increase in the sale of indulgences by the Papacy, which was maximizing revenue in the short run. The Gorbachev phenomenon represented a similar kind of situation. The Gorbachev perestroika/glasnost strategy for reallocating patronage, and securing his personal power, represented a kind of "capital consumption" of the infrastructure of the Communist system; the stability of Communist domination in the long run was reduced, although Gorbachev consolidated his personal power – and control over rent flows – in the short run.

Considered as a rent-seeking society, the Achilles heel of the Soviet-style economy has always been the absence of secure property rights to rent flows. The Soviet economy has grown into a complex system of market restrictions and rent opportunities for the politically favored. Those on top were given access to great wealth and tremendous power. But these advantages were inherently insecure and based on informal agreements with no strong legal protection. Positions of wealth and power were only secure until the next purge which could come any time and might well result in literal, as well as figurative, "termination." The Gorbachev succession was a kind of autonomous shock that drastically reduced the real rates of return to rent-seeking in the Soviet economy. Gorbachev may find himself presiding over the demise of Soviet state socialism as an unintended consequence of his exploitation of opportunities for the reallocation of patronage positions.

Acknowledgments

An earlier version of this chapter was presented at the Public Choice Society Meetings, Tucson, AZ, March 1990, and at the Austrian Economics Colloquium at New York University, September 1990. We would like to thank the participants at our session, and those at the Colloquium, for their comments and criticisms. In addition, Hal Hochman, Israel Kirzner, Mario Rizzo, Charles Rowley, Robert Tollison, Gordon Tullock, and an anonymous referee provided useful comments and criticisms. The usual caveat applies.

References

Abalkin L. (1987) *The Strategy of Economic Development in the USSR*, Moscow: Progress Publishers.
Abalkin, L. (1989) "The Radical Economic Reform," *Ekonomicheskaya Gazeta*, 43 (October), translated in *CDSP* 41(46) (13 December).
Aganbegyan, A. (1988) *The Economic Challenge of Perestroika*, Bloomington: Indiana University Press.
Aganbegyan, A. (1989) *Inside Perestroika*, New York: Harper and Row.
Aslund, A. (1989) *Gorbachev's Struggle for Economic Reform*, Ithaca: Cornell University Press.
Ball, A. M. (1987) *Russia's Last Capitalists: The Nepmen, 1921–1929*, Los Angeles: University of California Press.
Boettke, P. J. (1990) *The Political Economy of Soviet Socialism: The Formative Years, 1918–28*, Boston: Kluwer Academic Publishers.
Boettke, P. J. (1991) "The Austrian Critique and the Demise of Socialism: The Soviet Case," in R. Ebeling (ed.) *Austrian Economics: Perspectives on the Past and Prospects for the Future*, Hillsdale, MI: Hillsdale College Press.

Brzezinski, Z. (1956) *The Permanent Purge*, Cambridge: Harvard University Press.

Colton, T. J. (1986) *The Dilemma of Reform in the Soviet Union*, New York: Council on Foreign Relations.

D'Encausse, H. C. (1980) *Confiscated Power: How Soviet Russia Really Works*, New York: Harper and Row.

Desai, P. (1989) *Perestroika in Perspective: The Design and Dilemmas of Soviet Reform*, Princeton: Princeton University Press.

Ericson, R. (1988) "The New Enterprise Law," *The Harriman Institute Forum* 1(2) (February).

Ericson, R. (1989) "Soviet Economic Reforms: The Motivation and Content of Perestroika," *Journal of International Affairs* 42 (Spring).

Feldbrugge, F. J. M. (1988) "The Soviet Second Economy in a Political and Legal Perspective," in E. Feige (ed.) *The Underground Economies*, New York: Cambridge University Press.

Goldman, M. I. (1983) *USSR in Crisis: The Failure of an Economic System*, New York: Norton.

Goldman, M. I. (1987) *Gorbachev's Challenge: Economic Reform in the Age of High Technology*, New York: Norton.

Gorbachev, M. I. (1986) *Political Report of the CPSU to the 27th Party Congress*, Moscow: Novosti Press Agency Publishing House.

Gorbachev, M. I. (1987) *Perestroika*, New York: Harper and Row.

Gorbachev, M. I. (1989) "The Law of the Union of the Soviet Socialist Republics 'On Taxes on Cooperatives' Incomes," *Izvestiya* 8 August, translated in *Reprints from the Soviet Press*, 49(7) (15 October).

Gorlin, A. (1986) "The Soviet Economy," *Current History*, 85(513) (October).

Gumbel, P. (1989) "Soviets Have Taken Many Wrong Turns on the Road to Economic Restructuring," *Wall Street Journal* 21 November: A14.

Gumbel, P. (1990) "Out of Stock: Soviet Retail System Gets Strikingly Worse in Era of Perestroika," *Wall Street Journal* 23 July: A1.

Hayek, F. A. von (1976) (first published 1944) *The Road to Serfdom*, Chicago: University of Chicago Press.

Hayek, F. A. von (1988) *The Fatal Conceit*, Chicago: University of Chicago Press.

Hazan, B. A. (1990) "Gorbachev and His Enemies," *The Struggle for Perestroika*, Boulder, CO: Westview Press.

Hewett, E. A. (1988) *Reforming the Soviet Economy: Equality versus Efficiency*, Washington, DC: Brookings Institution.

Keller, B. (1991) "Industrial Colossus Typifies the Miseries of the Soviet Economy," *New York Times* 6 January: 8.

Lacquer, W. (1989) *The Long Road to Freedom: Russia and Glasnost*, New York: Scribner's.

Landes, W. M. and Posner, R. A. (1975) "The Independent Judiciary in an Interest-group Perspective," *Journal of Law and Economics* 18 (Fall).

Lavoie, D. (1986–7) "The Political and Economic Illusions of Socialism," *Critical Review* 1(1) (Winter).

Ledeen, M. (1990) "The Beginning of the Beginning," *The American Spectator* 23 (February).

Mises, L. von (1981) *Socialism: An Economic and Sociological Analysis*, Indianapolis, IN: Liberty Press.

Muravchik, J. (1990) "Gorbachev's Intellectual Odyssey," *The New Republic* 5 March.

Parks, M. (1990) "Soviet Party Gives Up Top Role: Historic Act Alters Entire Political, Economic System," *Los Angeles Times* 8 February: 1.

Popov, V. and Shmelev, N. (1989) *The Turning Point*, New York: Doubleday.

Roberts, P. C. (1971) *Alienation and the Soviet Economy*, Albuquerque: University of New Mexico Press.

Rutland, P. (1985) *The Myth of the Plan: Lessons of Soviet Planning Experience*, LaSalle, IL: Open Court.

Ryzhkov, N. (1989) Efficiency, Consolidation and Reform Are the Path to a Healthy Economy, *Pravda* 14 December, translated in *CDSP* 41(51) (17 January) (1990).

Ryzhkov, N. (1990) "On the Economic Situation in the Country and the Conception of a Changeover to a Regulated Market Economy," *Pravda* 25 May, translated in *CDSP* 42(21) and 42(22) (1990).

Schroeder, G. (1987) "Anatomy of Gorbachev's Economic Reforms," *Soviet Economy* 3(3) (September).

Schroeder, G. (1989) "Soviet Economic Reforms: From Resurgence to Retrenchment?" *Russian Review* 48(3) (July).

Selyunin, V. (1988) "Sources," *Novy Mir* 5 (May), translated in *CDSP* 40(40) (1988).

Shatalin, S., *et al.* (1990) "Man, Freedom and the Market," *Izvestiya* 4 September, translated in *CDSP* 42(35) (1990).

Simis, K. (1982) *USSR: The Corrupt Society: The Secret World of Soviet Capitalism*, New York: Simon and Schuster.

Smith, G. (1987) "Gorbachev and the Council of Ministers: Leadership Consolidation and Its Policy Implications," *Soviet Union/Union Sovietique* 14.

Starr, S. F. (1989) "Reform in Russia: A Peculiar Pattern," *The Wilson Quarterly* 8 (Spring).

Supreme Soviet of the USSR (1990) "Guidelines for the Stabilization of the National Economy and the Changeover to a Market Economy – as Approved by the USSR Supreme Soviet," *Izvestiya* 27 October, translated in *CDSP* 42: 43–5 (1990).

Taubman, W. and Taubman, J. (1989) *Moscow Spring*, New York, Summit Books.

Thom, F. (1989) *The Gorbachev Phenomena: A History of Perestroika*, London: Pinter Publishers.

Tullock, G. (1987) *Autocracy*, Boston: Kluwer Academic Publishers.

Voslensky, M. (1984) *Nomenklatura*, New York: Doubleday.

Willis, D. K. (1985) *Klass: How Russians Really Live*, New York: Avon Books.

Winiecki, J. (1990) "Why Economic Reforms Fail in the Soviet System – A Property rights-based Approach," *Economic Inquiry* 28(2) (April).

Zaleski, E. (1980) *Stalinist Planning for Economic Growth, 1933–1952*, Chapel Hill, NC: University of North Carolina Press.

Zaslavskaya, T. (1984) "The Novosibirsk Report," *Survey* 28(1) (Spring).

11 The reform trap in economics and politics in the former Communist economies*

Introduction

Conventional thinking with regard to economic and political reforms in Eastern and Central Europe and the former Soviet Union is "trapped" in a mindset which does not allow innovative ideas for social arrangements to be seriously considered. Sovietologists, for example, while they continue to re-examine what went wrong and why nobody was able to predict the undoing of the Soviet system, do not really address the underlying problems of the discipline.[1] What is left out of this conversation amongst Sovietologists is perhaps more important than what is included – an examination of how the economic structure of socialism generated the political system of socialism.

F. A. von Hayek, perhaps more than any other scholar, pursued the organizational logic of socialism to expose its fundamental problems as a social system. When the Berlin Wall fell in 1989, there was a brief period of adulation for Hayek (and his "teacher" Ludwig von Mises). Busts of Mises and Hayek were given to heads of former Communist governments in Eastern and Central Europe by conservative and libertarian "think-tanks" and organizations. The writings of Mises and Hayek were celebrated in universities, academic journals, and publishing houses in East and West. Hayek's *The Road to Serfdom* and *The Fatal Conceit*, for example, have been translated into Russian and can be bought at various Metro stops in Moscow. Academics, intellectuals, and politicians acknowledged the wisdom of Hayek's anti-Communism. With Hayek's death on 23 March 1992, the newspapers and magazines in the West portrayed him as the prescient one: the one who foresaw the collapse of Communism.[2] It seems that this popular pronouncement has been more of a curse than a blessing.

On the one hand, Hayek could be accused of "Chicken Littlism" by skeptics. Had not Hayek and Mises "predicted" the impossibility of socialism at least since 1920? If socialism was so bad, then how could it have lasted for so long? Even a broken clock gets the time "correct" twice a day! On the other hand, Hayek's anti-Communism was viewed as non-scientific. Prescience is not

*Originally published as Boettke, P. J. (1994) "The Reform Trap in Politics and Economics in the Former Communist Economies," *Journal des Economistes et des Etudes Humaines* V(2–3) (June/September): 267–93.

something that can be replicated or built upon. Prescience is idiosyncratic and subjective; it is visionary. Hayek is viewed as an ideological visionary and not an analytical social scientist.[3] In either case, social scientists dealing with the problems of the collapse of Communism and the transformation of these societies – whatever their ideological persuasion – do not need to examine Hayek's work for answers.

Hayek's work may not provide us with direct answers to the problems of the day, and it certainly is not all that is needed to address the pressing problems of socialist transformation.[4] However, his work does provide an analytical framework for examining the issues of the transformation of the political and economic system. Not only did Hayek provide the analytical foundation for examining the failure of Communist systems, but his work also provides the foundation for developing workable solutions.

The traps of reform

There are two traps that permeate conventional thinking in politics and economics. The basic problem with standard neoclassical economic thought on the transformation is a preoccupation with "getting the price right" and maintaining "stability."

Various privatization schemes, for example, have been introduced, ranging from vouchers to auction models. The preconditions for privatization, it has been argued, run from an egalitarian distribution to the public of shares in state enterprises to direct industrial restructuring by the World Bank. The point of the exercise is to transfer ownership as quickly as possible in a manner which is deemed sustainable on efficiency and justice grounds.[5] The problem with the conventional privatization package, however, is that one cannot value assets without a market, but a reliable market cannot exist without private property.[6] The whole point of the privatization schemes of vouchers or public auction is to create private ownership. But how is the value of assets to be determined without a market in the first place? In other words, a voucher program is predicated on the ability to value assets, even though the whole point of the exercise is to create markets that will enable participants to assess the value of assets. If valuation could take place independent of the private property context, then privatization would be redundant and unnecessary.

In addition, in order to maintain macroeconomic stability, it has been argued that the "timing" of policy and the "order" of liberalization are essential. The government must first get its fiscal home in order, then stabilize the currency, and then – and only then – open the economic system to full liberalization and domestic and foreign competition. If this gradual approach is not followed, then the ex-Communist governments will find themselves in the unenviable situation of losing their tax base (i.e. the state industrial sector) at the same time that the fiscal demands of the state have increased. Political instability and economic decline will result and liberalization will not be sustainable.[7] The squabble between the shock therapy approach of the IMF or World Bank, and the more gradual approach to liberalization is really an intramural one. Both approaches require government to manage the reform process because it is asserted that the outcome is too important to be left solely to spontaneous processes. Hayek's epistemic critique of socialism and of aggregate economics, however, is just as relevant to economic proposals for socialist transformation that rely on the use of abstract, as opposed to concrete, market knowledge for guiding resource use, and points to an alternative transformation path which avoids the economic reform trap.

Political reform is also caught in a trap laid by a preoccupation with democratic participation. Catering too much to the demands of interests is incompatible with economic reform, whereas ignoring completely the voice of the people is incompatible with notions of political liberty. Some intellectuals, such as the Polish Solidarity activist Adam Michnik, seem convinced to the contrary. Democratic forces, Michnik implies, must be unconstrained in order to constrain the inhumanity of capitalism.[8] But, Michnik's warnings of the "dogmatic faith" in the market and the need for democratic procedures to control and govern the market so that it possesses a "human face" belie a naïve faith in democracy and ignorance of economics. Rather than introducing "democracy" *per se*, the real problem to be solved for political and economic development is how to establish binding constraints on government so that rulers cannot confiscate wealth in the future for purposes of redistribution through regulation or taxation. The basic paradox of liberal governance is to first empower government with the ability to govern and then constrain government from overstepping its bounds. Hayek's political criticisms of democratic socialism and egalitarianism, and his positive contributions to constitutional political economy, are relevant in avoiding the political reform trap.

Hayek's criticisms of socialism and interventionism are intimately related to his argument for liberalism. My argument is that Hayekian economics and politics provide the most viable answer to these thought traps by offering an alternative perspective which at one and the same time respects indigenous cultural traditions and institutions, and provides a paradigm for critical reflections.

The frictionless model in politics and economics

The political economy of socialism provides an excellent foil from which to understand the workings of its antithesis – the market society and liberal government. Adam Smith's metaphor of the invisible hand, in fact, represents a quasi-foil use of direct government control to explicate the workings of a free economy. The mental experiment of a foil allows the theorist to understand the world through an exercise of contrast. The invisible hand metaphor demands a contrast with conscious design. Smith's claim was not the weak one often attributed to him – that the free economy would allocate resources in a manner which would replicate what a central planner would do. Rather, Smith's claim was that the private market economy would allocate resources in a manner superior to government direction. Moreover, this argument contained both an economic and a political dimension.

Smith's argument for free trade, for example, contained arguments concerning (1) incentives, (2) information, and (3) politics.

All three elements are essential for his argument. Consider the central passages in *The Wealth of Nations*. After stating that men pursuing their own self-interest will be led by "an invisible hand" to promote the general welfare, Smith counters with the statement that the general welfare is often not the result of government intervention. Why? Because, "What is species of domestic industry which his capital can employ, and of which the produce is likely to be of greatest value, every individual, it is evident can, in his local situation, judge much better than any statesmen, or lawgiver can do for him." The individual economic actor, in other words, possesses information and incentives which the statesman does not. But, Smith enhances his argument by adding the political dimension, and specifically the issue of the abuse of power. "The statesman," he argued, "who should attempt to direct private people in what manner they ought to employ their capitals, would not only load himself with a most unnecessary attention, but assume an authority which could safely be trusted, not only to no single person, but to no council or senate whatever, and which would nowhere be so dangerous as in the hands of a man who had folly and presumption enough to fancy himself fit to exercise it."[9]

Smith's argument has been distorted in modern times. Modem economists translated Smith's institutionally rich theory into a formal theory of general equilibrium which was conspicuous in its absence of political and economic institutions. Essential components to Smith's system of political economy were lost in the translation. The "invisible hand" postulate, for example, was not put forth by Smith as a general theoretical claim independent of property rules and political institutions. Individuals pursuing their own interests under collective property would do so in a manner radically different from individuals pursuing their own interest within an environment of private property. The welfare implications of enlightened self-interest depended on the institutional infrastructure.

The importance of institutions was lost on much of modern economics. Two examples may illuminate the problem. When Frank Knight wrote his classic *Risk, Uncertainty and Profit*, he divided the book in two parts. The first part of the book was devoted to developing a model of the world in which there was no risk or uncertainty and thus, logically no profit. It is a serious mistake, however, to examine only the first part of Knight's classic. The idealized model of perfect competition was the preliminary stage of analysis, not the end. The point of the first part was to aid the reasoning in the second part of the book dealing with the inherent imperfections of the world and how market institutions arise to cope.[10]

Ronald Coase's major contributions to economic theory – the theory of the firm and the problem of social cost – also follow a similar pattern of theorizing to that of Knight's. In the paper dealing with the theory of the firm, Coase demonstrated that, in a world of zero transaction costs, firms would not logically exist. All transactions could be conducted through atomistic markets. Similarly, the paper dealing with the problem of social cost demonstrated that, in a world of zero transaction costs, legal institutions would not be important to economic outcomes. All grievances could be negotiated away through private bargaining. It is a serious mistake, however, to confuse Coase's contribution with these logical implications of the zero transaction costs world. The zero transaction costs world was constructed as a preliminary to an examination of the real world of positive transaction costs and all that it implies for the structure of the firm, the market, and the law.[11]

Theorists must be very careful to avoid falling into error when employing idealized constructions to aid thought. This is not a criticism of abstraction; in fact, I would agree with those who argue that we cannot think in the social sciences without abstractions. It is just that we need to be quite judicious in the use of abstractions and clear in the purpose for which these abstractions are to serve. What tends to happen otherwise is that an analytical tool becomes confused with a normative ideal. Even one of the modern pioneers of the foil use of mental constructs – Frank Knight – slipped into this mistake. Knight's book *The Ethics of Competition*, for example, employs the perfectly competitive model as a normative benchmark against which market activity could be judged.[12] The benchmark use is not consistent with the general thrust of Knight's use of the analytical tool of a frictionless world in *Risk, Uncertainty and Profit* as a foil to aid thinking about the real world of uncertainty and change.

Economics was not the only discipline to slip into this problem. Whereas economics lost the wisdom of Adam Smith in the translation to modern theory, political science lost the wisdom of Liberal Constitutional Democracy found in the works of James Madison and others.[13] The ideal of democracy as the perfect model of self-rule in which the "will of the people" is unambiguously conveyed through the voting process was a view not shared by the founders of liberal democracy. This idealized model of the frictionless public conveyance of preferences was a foil, a preliminary to the real analysis of the need for institutions to allow democratic politics to operate efficiently and morally.

Socialism – as a political and economic doctrine – can be explained in terms of the confused use of the frictionless model. The critique of the market society and bourgeois democracy entailed both a moral and an economic dimension. The market economy was coordinated in a haphazard manner and was subjected to chaotic fluctuations brought on by the underlying contradictions in the system. The frictions introduced into the economy by way of monetary circulation did not allow the monetary economy to operate in the same coordinated fashion that the natural economy would. Bourgeois democracy, on the other hand, masked the dominate class interest that continued to govern state action. It was true that whereas under the previous system of autocracy and feudalism the exploitation of man was quite explicit, and now in the bourgeois market society with liberal democracy exploitation was more subtle. Nevertheless, the exploitation of man by other men continued. The clash of class interests and the corresponding exploitation was real once the underlying mechanisms of social relations were made transparent by critical theorizing. Socialism promised a better world than the one offered by the bourgeoisie.

The socialist economy would substitute production for direct use for production for exchange – social reason, in other words, for social accident. The rational use of resources would be determined *ex ante* by the planning bodies made up of the free association of men, rather than through the *ex post* coordination of the market. The socialist political system would represent classless politics. The struggle between independent private interests would disappear. The public sphere would eliminate the autonomous struggle within the private realm. A non-alienated and non-exploitative society would emerge.

In the first half of the twentieth century this political and economic project was translated into formal models of socialist political economy. Oskar Lange, for example, developed an economic theory of socialism which in essence simply substituted the Central Planning Board for the Walrasian Auctioneer of general competitive equilibrium.[14] The frictionless model of socialism could replicate the welfare results of the frictionless model of capitalism. And, given the real-world problems of monopoly and recurring business cycles, socialism would most likely outperform capitalism in practice. Similarly, frictionless democracy came to be the normative ideal in politics. If the frictionless ideal had not come to dominate democratic thinking, then the results of Kenneth Arrow's impossibility theorem simply would not have generated the surprised excitement that it did.[15] Why should anyone be surprised by Arrow's result? Individual preference ordering should not be expected to yield an aggregate preference ordering that is consistent, let alone an abstract approximate expression of the will of the people.[16]

The Arrow problem of cycling posed a challenge to the classical theory of democracy. In the face of market failure, Arrow asked, was there a democratic collective choice mechanism that was capable of allocating scarce resources efficiently. The inability to unambiguously aggregate preferences across voters led to a negative answer. Whatever collective choice mechanism we choose will be imperfect. Collective choice can be efficient but dictatorial, or it can be democratic but inefficient. Majority voting, for example, may be democratic, but the results of such voting procedures will be characterized by repetition, inconclusiveness, and waste. Social choice will therefore be without meaning in the sense that the political mechanism will be unable to provide information, for example, on whether the best use of a vacant lot would be a school, a playground, or a municipal parking garage.[17] Arrow's political failure theory is the same as his market failure theory, and just as flawed an intellectual enterprise.[18] In both cases he confused an analytical tool with a normative ideal. In his market failure theory, Arrow demonstrated that the introduction of selective realism (such as imperfections in information) resulted in market deviations from the ideal model of perfect competition and its corresponding welfare conclusions. Unfortunately, Arrow then assumed that the ideal could be obtained costlessly through substituting an unexamined alternative mechanism – namely government provision.[19]

The political failure theory is a little different. Arrow does not commit the "grass is always greener" or the "free lunch" fallacies, but his view of the political process is still representative of the "nirvana" approach to political economy. The Arrow paradox is only a paradox if the classical theory of democracy was accepted as an approximation of reality. The real paradox is why we do not see voter cycling on every issue. The empirical reality that voter cycling is not the only outcome of democratic politics suggests that political institutions and rules have emerged to channel democratic politics in certain directions which minimize the Arrow problem. Rather than examining deviations from an unobtainable ideal, the focus of scholarly attention should be on a comparison of those institutions that claim to cope with the frictions in political life.

The frictionless model is just a tool in political economy. When used correctly it allows theorists to understand the important role that institutional forms and constraints play in the functioning of social systems. But, when used incorrectly, the frictionless model truncates thought.

It must be remembered that frictions drive the social world, and are not hindrances to social order. Just as the friction between the sole of our shoes and the sidewalk enables us to walk, the frictions that exist within the political and economic system highlight the institutions that enable a political economy to sustain itself. Whereas the frictions within the economic system (such as asymmetry and other imperfections of knowledge) are the very conditions required for real world market institutions to operate in a reasonably efficient manner, the frictions within the political system highlight the required constraints and rules that the proper operation of democracy requires. Market frictions spur discovery and innovation, and political frictions reveal the necessity of rules. In both cases, it is the frictions and the institutional responses to those frictions that determine whether the social system will operate efficiently or collapse.

The Mises–Hayek critique of socialism entailed a negative assessment of the institutions of socialism to satisfy the demands of political economy. Socialist means were insufficient to obtain socialist ends, such as the abolition of ignorance, squalor, and oppression. The critique of socialism offered by Mises and Hayek also implied a positive analysis of the role of market and liberal political institutions in meeting the demands of political economy. The theory espoused by Mises and Hayek was a theory rich in institutional detail that entailed both an economic and a political dimension. The most important component of their argument was the functional significance they placed on the institution of private property and the rule of law. Property rights protected by the rule of law provide:

1   legal certainty, which encourages investment;
2   a motivation for responsible decision-making on behalf of owners;

3   the background for social experimentation, which spurs progress; and
4   the basis for economic calculation by expanding the context within which
     price, and profit and loss, signals can reasonably guide resource use.

It is precisely because the world is in a friction-ridden constant state of flux
that clearly defined property rights embedded in the rule of law are fundamental
to a sustainable political economy.[20]

Formal models of frictionless political and economic environments are not
set up to be able to deal with such institutional questions. Lange's model of
socialism, for example, explicitly denied that institutions of property mattered
for economic outcomes.[21] This problem persists today. Models of social
democracy and market socialism are still unable to come to grips with the
institutional infrastructure required for economic progress.[22]

The basic paradox of governance

Markets are like weeds. They are impossible to stamp out. Makers emerge
wherever and whenever there exist opportunities for individuals to gain through
exchange. But not all markets are equal. Market exchanges in the absence of
property rules take place, but they possess characteristics which are not desirable
for long-term economic growth. Economic activity tends to be geared toward
services rather than fixed investments. Exchange relationships are often limited
in scope. Extra-legal enforcement mechanisms are introduced. In addition, the
character of the commodities traded often changes drastically. During
prohibition in the US, for example, beer and wine basically disappeared from
the market, whereas grain alcohol emerged as the primary unit. This was because
of the nature of the market and the costs of transportation and market
distribution in the illegal environment.[23] Drug trafficking in the US is a
contemporary example which proves the general rule.

Markets do not need a *de jure* sanction to exist, but, for market activity to
serve as the basis of general economic prosperity in a given society, they must
exist within a body of law. Political institutions and the structure of law provide
the framework for economic behavior. The rules of the game are probably the
most significant determinant of economic performance.[24]

The major problem facing any regime is its ability to elicit support from the
citizenry. Economic activity must be encouraged to come above ground. Market
participation, however, requires that citizens trust that the government will
not confiscate the wealth created in future periods of the economic game. The
basic problem can be conveyed employing a simple commitment gain.[25] See
Figure 11.1.

Player 2 is the representative citizen, while player 1 is the government. The
government announces a liberal economic policy that respects property and
encourages entrepreneurial activity. Autonomy will be granted to citizens in
most economic spheres in exchange for a small share of profit income, i.e.
taxation. Player 2 must choose to enter the game or stay out of the official

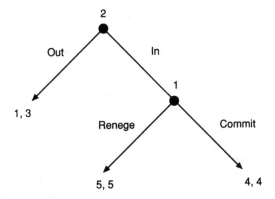

Figure 11.1 Commitment game

economy. The problem is that once player 2 enters the game, player 1 can benefit from confiscating the wealth of player 2 in the next round through increased taxation or regulation.[26] In other words, player 1 can substantially gain by engaging in post-contract opportunism. Knowing the sequentially rational moves of player 1, player 2 will choose the only viable equilibrium, OUT, and economic liberalization will stall. Unless player 1 can successfully tie his/her own hands, economic activity will not move above ground.

This is the basic commitment game. The paradox of governance is that a government strong enough to establish binding constraints is also strong enough to break those constraints. What is needed is a technology to enact a self-enforcing contract which eliminates government's discretionary ability.

Market development and preservation requires that economic activity be conducted without the threat of confiscation by authorities. If the official market does not represent a secure outlet, then economic activity will be diverted out of the official market. The key component to institutional transformation is the shackling of arbitrary behavior of rulers and the emergence of impersonal rules to govern economic activity.[27]

Democratic politics is neither a necessary nor a sufficient condition for solving the basic paradox of governance.[28] The great benefit of democratic procedures is the peaceful transition of power it engenders. But it must be remembered that democracy is merely a means, and not an end. Liberalism is a theory of what the law should be, for example, whereas democracy is simply a theoretical doctrine concerning the method by which law will be determined within a society.[29] Unless democracy is constrained, it can serve very illiberal ends.

As I argued above, the failure of unconstrained democracy to provide either an effective or moral framework was not lost on the founding fathers of the US constitution. As James Madison wrote:

> If men were angels, no government would be necessary. If angels were to govern men, neither external nor internal controls on government would

be necessary. In framing a government which is to be administered by men over men, the great difficulty lies in this: you must first enable the government to control the governed; and in the next place oblige it to control itself.[30]

In other words, a constitutional bargain must be struck which simultaneously empowers and constrains government.

It is not democracy as such that is the problem or the solution. Unconstrained democracy undermines the moral order and economic prosperity just like other forms of unconstrained government.[31] Democratic procedures tend to transform government into an engine of redistribution unless embedded within appropriate rules. Economic performance is not invariant to the form of the democratic polity established. Unfortunately, because of the deficient theoretical starting point in economics and politics, much of the technical and popular discussion of the transition problem has overlooked this problem of interdependence between the form of democratic governance and economic performance.

The public and private life

In Eastern and Central Europe and the former Soviet Union, the major issue is establishing the appropriate institutional context for economic decisions. The one thing that Western institutions and most Western advisors are silent on, however, are precisely these institutional questions. Not all democratic political systems are equal with regard to economic performance or the morality of the social order in general. In fact, one of the most serious problems in the reforming region is that the models of democratic rule chosen so far have not been the best as far as economic growth is concerned.

One of the most troublesome issues in political institution building, for example, is the role of the status quo. During reform periods, political rules should be – almost by definition – status quo breaking. However, assuming that the reforms are successful, then political rules should be status quo preserving. But, for rules to be effective they cannot change so conveniently – the reason for rules lies precisely in the problems of discretion. The status of the status quo is a function of the veto power distributed within the political system. Different forms of democratic government emerge, depending on how veto power is distributed: proportional representation, two-party systems, parliamentary systems, presidential systems, etc. The focus must be on comparative institutions and not on ideal systems of democratic procedures.

Economic and political reforms are intertwined. Many observers of contemporary reform efforts miss this point. China, for example, it is argued has successfully introduced economic reforms without changing the political system. This, however, overlooks the fundamental *de facto* change in power that has taken place in the Chinese system between central authorities and local authorities. China's successful economic reforms, in fact, could be explained on the basis of this fundamental change in the political authority structure, which has granted increased autonomy to local authorities and traditional customary practices.[32] Similarly, the economic reforms under the autocrat General Pinochet in Chile resulted in political demands for democratization. And the same is true for Spain, Taiwan, and Korea.

The argument that individuals like Hayek and Milton Friedman put forth concerning the relationship between economic and political freedom seems born out by recent experience.[33] Every move away from economic freedom entails a sacrifice of a sphere of autonomy from the political system. "Economic control," Hayek wrote, "is not merely control of a sector of human life which can be separated from the rest; it is control of the means for all our ends. And whoever has sole control of the means must also determine which ends are to be served, which values are to be rated higher and which lower – in short, what men should believe and strive for."[34]

Hayek's argument in *The Road to Serfdom* was not that economic freedom ensured political freedom, but rather that the loss of economic freedom necessarily entailed a loss of political freedom. Hong Kong, for example, is an obvious example of a relatively free economy that is not also characterized by widespread political freedom (as that term is conventionally defined). Nevertheless, the voluntary organizations of a market society do put pressure on political institutions that seek to control human interaction. Moves toward economic freedom create private spheres of autonomy. The creation of a propertied class, for example, leads to the development of an effort by those individuals to seek protection from arbitrary invasions of that property by government or others. Economic freedom does sow the seeds for the demand for political freedom.[35]

Economic growth and prosperity are political economy problems that have little or nothing to do with macroeconomic stabilization or the sequencing of industrial restructuring. And certainly foreign aid and other such programs of government to government transfers are not what is needed. What matters is the establishment of political institutions which preserve the social environment for a flood of market experiments.

The economic consequences of liberal democracy are important to understand in the wake of 1989. The collapse of Communism has thrust upon Europe a new constitutional moment, as discussed by Bruce Ackerman.[26] Ackerman, however, does not address the issue of the preservation of market institutions in the face of increased democratic appeals for a say in the distribution of wealth. The continued liberal revolution, according to Ackerman, recognizes the necessity of the market for the efficient allocation of scarce resources but allows for the distribution of the wealth created in that allocation to be subject to political decisions. Democratic freedom is incompatible with pure marketization, because the vast majority of democratic politics centers on the efforts of people to protect themselves from the market economy.

Ackerman's discussion is guilty of two related flaws common to many proposals for the democratic control of market forces. First, it is guilty of assuming that production and distribution can be separated. Production and distribution, however, are linked. Market production determines the income and functional distribution of productive factors, such as labor. There is simply no distributional process separate from the processes of exchange and production. Factors are paid according to the service they render, or are perceived to render, to others in the market. Second, since production and distribution are linked, it is a mistake to assume that one can alter distribution without adversely effecting production. Political choices are never over a desired distribution, but rather over the rules of the game which engender patterns of production and distribution.

The real problem is to create private spheres of life that are protected from public manipulation. Certainly the people in the former Communist societies must reclaim their public life. But, it is only by safeguarding the private life that a meaningful public life can emerge. This counter-intuitive notion becomes apparent when we reflect on the consequences for public life that the Communist experiment wrought.

The effect of the Communist monopoly on power was not only that experience with public administration was limited to those who served the Party loyally, but that the entire realm of public life was abdicated by the population. The use of political terror, right from the founding of the Soviet state by Lenin, subdued the population into compliance and reinforced the monopolistic situation. Soviet citizens understood, as Richard Pipes has argued, that "under a regime that felt no hesitation in executing innocents, innocence was no guarantee of survival. The best hope of surviving lay in making oneself as inconspicuous as possible, which meant abandoning any thought of independent public activity, indeed any concern with public affairs, and withdrawing into one's private world. Once society disintegrated into an agglomeration of human atoms, each fearful of being noticed and concerned exclusively with physical survival, then it ceased to matter what society thought, for the government had the entire sphere of public activity to itself."[37]

Hannah Arendt argued long ago that the defining characteristic of the totalitarian society was the elimination of the public life.[38] Public space and uncoerced discourse were the key to the free society.[39] Ironically, Communism, which sought to replace the private with the public life by subsuming everything to the public, perversely eliminated the very public spaces for participation upon which legitimacy is based. The public ideology of the revolution simply died out. But this delegitimation did not translate automatically into a challenge to the power of the regime. The delirium of earlier ideological periods simply gave way, as Vaclav Havel argued, to public passivity, opportunism, cynicism, and tacit acceptance of the way of life. Silent disagreement and conformity on the part of citizens assured that Communist power was safe. As long as the development of a civil society outside the official state sector was stifled, the Communist system could not be defeated.[40]

The economic system suffered the same fate that the political system did. The substitution of collective for private property produced a general environment in which, since everyone owned everything, no one owned anything.[41] Just as in the political sphere, individuals abdicated the official economic life. The social compact that emerged was "We pretend to work and you pretend to pay us" with deleterious consequences for both the individual and the social system. Public discourse and productive economic activity were both channeled into a *sub rosa* existence. Individuals within these societies dwelt within a dual reality in economic, political, cultural, and intellectual affairs. Jazz and rock music, for example, were for a long time an underground phenomenon in the Soviet Union. Books and articles suppressed by state censors circulated *samizdat* between scholars and intellectuals. And, the dissident political movements were formed underground to challenge the ruling regime on various fronts. The consequences of having to "live the lie," however, have not yet been fully dealt within the post-1989 era because the initial conditions of Soviet life are still little understood.

Custom as the foundation of liberal revolution

The real problem in the former Communist states is not that the private life had been completely eliminated. Market behavior, political discourse, and cultural and intellectual experimentation persisted throughout the Soviet era. This activity, however, must be transformed from its *sub rosa* existence to above-ground legitimate expressions of the meaningful life. This transformation does not require a radical change in human nature.[42] The decline of the work ethic in the official state economy was a rational response to the incentives that individuals faced, just as the hard work and ingenuity that individuals demonstrated in the black market or private plot on the collective farm were rational responses to the opportunities within that context. Undoubtedly, cultural traits and traditions matter, but the most important determinant of economic performance is the institutional rules established in any society.

Rules, however, do not spring out of nowhere. Moreover, they cannot be imposed from "the outside" and possess the legitimacy required to sustain the social system. This does not mean that rational design is eliminated from the establishment of rules, it is just that rationalism – as Hayek has argued forcefully – possesses definite limits.[43] The contrast between the American and the French revolutions demonstrates this point. The constitutional moment in America codified and refined already existing common practices and procedures. The American revolutionaries were staking a claim against the King, based on what they already had – private spheres of autonomy from public manipulation. The French revolutionaries, on the other hand, sought to establish the "rights of man," independent of context. The consequence of this difference, as Alexis de Tocqueville observed, was that the French revolution in "destroying so many institutions, ideas, and customs inimical to freedom" unfortunately "abolished so many others which were indispensable to freedom."[44]

Progress results from individual experimentation. The subordination of the individual to the whole under Communism eliminated the transparency of the law that is necessary for social harmony. The arbitrary authority of the rulers is no substitute for impersonal rules of social intercourse. The solution to social problems is not to be found in eliminating conflicting private interests, but in finding ways to adjust and ameliorate rivalries and cross-purposes through transparent political arrangements.

Establishing transparent political and legal institutions cannot be imposed, but must "bubble up" from accepted social customs. The Tocqueville warning that in moments of social change, not only institutions inimical to freedom, but also those essential to freedom, tend to get discarded, is not a trivial one. Moreover, given the complexity of the social world, it is often quite difficult to ascertain which institutions and practices are which. They must be discovered through a process of trial and error, and then must be embedded in the social wisdom of everyday customs.

The transfer of customary practice to official law is not automatic. But, it is precisely this transfer that provides the basis of the move from primitive economic accumulation and modest growth (at best) to progressive experimentation and advanced technological development.[45] Real law is built, as Hayek has argued, upon the customary practices of the people. Legislative law, on the other hand, emerges from outside the everyday life of a people, and, as such, confronts an epistemic problem not unlike the one that confronted socialist political and economic institutions. The problem of economic calculation under socialist institutions was simply one case of the more general problem confronting all complex human interaction – the discovery and use of socially useful knowledge, which is dispersed throughout society in a manner that affords individuals the ability to adjust and adapt their behavior to accommodate the constantly changing conditions of human life.[46]

Vitali Naishul has forcefully applied these Hayekian insights to understand the developments that had already taken root in the post-Stalin period in the former Soviet Union, which have laid the foundation upon which a liberal political economy could be established.[47] Naishul's main point is that as the socialist system disintegrated in the post-World War II era, organic institutions arose to accommodate daily life in law and economics. Not paying attention to these organic institutions means that reform proposals are not connected to reality.[48]

Privatization, for example, has already to a large degree occurred in the former Soviet Union. The method of privatization, however, was not officially sanctioned and therefore is not recognized by the government or many Western advisors. State enterprise managers always possessed a *de facto* ownership claim over the firm. The state enterprise manager's behavior and firm performance were rational, given the incentives that these *de facto* owners faced. Since they could not reap the capital gains from efficient resource use, these managers faced the same incentives that government and non-profit bureaucracies face. Change the context of decision-making and behavior will change accordingly.

In the late Gorbachev period, state managers asserted their claim over property more forcefully. The process of spontaneous privatization became pervasive throughout society. "State property," Naishul has argued, "is nearly non-existent. Somebody has made a common law claim to every piece of public property, and it would be impossible to take them away without force."[49] Many "democrats" argue against this claim of possession on grounds of justice. Privatization is really piratization by the *nomenklatura*.[50] But, this privatization as effected by the *nomenklatura* possesses a logic that its critics fail to recognize. Oleg Vite and Dimitry Travin, for example, point out that it is essential to distinguish between those who rose through the Communist ranks as Party functionaries and those who rose as business executives. The business executives and factory managers had not only to master the political horse-trading required of those who rose to prominence, but had also to possess an ability to bargain in the bureaucratic market over resources, plan targets, and personnel. Individuals with this experience are likely to be able to adapt quickly to the free-market environment. The managerial élite is simply seeking to retain control through privatization of what they have already laid claim to as their *de facto* property. However unappealing it may be to the romantic, the managerial élite must become an ally of economic reform. The struggle against the *nomenklatura* is not only dangerous to democracy, but economically pointless.[51]

Unless analysts begin with an understanding of the initial situation and knowledge of everyday practices, proposals for change are limited to technocratic solutions. The trap of technocracy, in fact, is the source of the reform trap in politics and economics. My contention is that reform proposals that are not grounded in the indigenous customs of the people are bound to fail. Reform must come, as it were, from the ground up and not be imposed from the outside. This contention is not based on any moral ideal of national self-sufficiency or an anti-cultural imperialism, but rather on the grounds that sustainable social change must be based in customary practices for epistemic reasons.[52] The adaptive efficiency of any social system is a function of the epistemic properties of its political, legal, economic, and customary traditions and institutions.

Technocratic policy proposals reflect the same hubris that socialist schemes were built upon. The majority of Western economists, especially those advising the governments in transition, such as Jeffrey Sachs and Stanley Fischer, are convinced that the problem with the formerly socialist economies was that the economic planning principle was pursued too comprehensively. As a result, the economic bureaucracy was overwhelmed with the task. The problem with socialism was one of incentives and complexity. The fundamental epistemological critique that Hayek offered is not yet absorbed. Without understanding this "knowledge problem," however, it is questionable as to what extent the problems of incentives and computational complexity are really appreciated.[53]

Government management of the economy is not questioned by most Western advisors. The context and implementation of planning under the old regime is challenged, not the principle of planning and government management *per se*. Mix macroeconomic stabilization with macroeconomic regulation and the conventional wisdom for economic transformation emerges rather easily.[54]

The conventional thinking translates into two trends in policy-making that undermine even the best intentions of reform. It is argued that what is needed is:

1   a careful and detailed plan for the transition, which is envisioned as a process of:
2   phasing in reforms.

Drawing up a detailed plan requires the specification of hundreds, perhaps thousands of laws concerning the regulation of markets. Phasing-in requires decisions on economic priorities before market competition is introduced. Both trends undermine structural political and economic reform.

The problems with the phasing-in strategy are twofold. First, the time lag gives opposition forces time to organize and develop their counter-strategy. In other words, phasing-in does not address the interest group question, but rather assumes that reform is taking place inside of a political vacuum. Second, if the government could decide economic priorities and enact hard budget constraints in the absence of the market process, then there would be no need for reform in the first place. Moreover, this approach to the problem neither recognizes the initial situation nor deals adequately with the institutional questions that are of importance for transforming the political economy.

Discovery, political institutions, and market preservation

Competition is one of the most important processes through which we learn to live and organize our affairs.[55] Markets are learning devices that rely on competition not only to mobilize existing information, but also to discover information that would otherwise have remained hidden from view. Political competition is also important. Competition between localities and regions (provided that citizens are free to move) sets in motion a discovery procedure that provides individuals with the incentives to reveal information through their actions concerning the level of public services and the role of the state.[56]

Social change and progress are a function of three things:

1   respect for indigenous institutions and practices;
2   competition between these practices, and
3   the establishment of political institutions which preserve (1) and (2).

Russia, for example, is experiencing a constitutional crisis unlike any other region witnessed in recent history. First, Gorbachev found that the Soviet empire was impossible to maintain, and now Yeltsin is faced with the reality that even the Russian empire may be disintegrating. Regionalism has already swept through Russia.[57]

In some sense this development of decentralization was inevitable and desirable, although of course a path fraught with danger – especially when we consider the nuclear issue. Nevertheless, the trick is to build on the existing reality and channel it in a productive direction. It will do no good to wish that the central authority was intact, and that a unified liberal policy could be imposed from the center. The disintegration of Russia is an already existing fact. As James Buchanan has repeatedly stressed in his writing, political economy reform must begin "here and now" and not in whatever ideal starting point the analyst can dream up.[58]

Regionalism, if channeled in a positive direction, sets in motion a competitive discovery procedure between local governments that is analogous to the polycentric situation that existed during the early development of capitalism.[59] Freed from central authority, local experimentation takes over – a quasi-Tiebout model of competition between governance structures is set in motion.[60] However, to realize the benefits of the competition a framework of liberal governance must be respected.

Establishing the appropriate framework is a question of constitution building. The most appropriate system to emerge that provides the proper framework is a system of federalism.[61] The richest countries of the last three centuries have been "federalist" systems by technical definitions if not by name. The Dutch Republic in the sixteenth and seventeenth centuries, England in the seventeenth and eighteenth centuries, and the US in the nineteenth and twentieth centuries can all be described as "federalist" in their essential political structure. Not only can the "take-off" of these countries be correlated with the establishment of federalist type political institutions, but the decline can be correlated with the breakdown of these institutions. Federalism entails a system of governance that possesses the following characteristics:

1   hierarchy of government;
2   delineated scope of authority;
3   guarantee of autonomy;
4   the locus of economic regulatory authority is such that (a) authority is not at the highest governmental level, and (b) lower levels of government cannot eliminate competition with trade restrictions, etc.

The benefits of federalism for economic development are considerable. It provides a unified market region. The prohibition on trade restrictions amongst local governments encourages competition and economic experimentation – both of which lead to innovation and technological development. Federalism also represents a contractual technology to minimize the threat of post-contract opportunism by the state.

Federalism, like other contracts, must be self-enforcing to be effective. It requires reactions that make it in the interest of national politicians not to respond to the inevitable political pressure that results from the interests frustrated by the restrictions of federalism. The Dutch, English, and US experience demonstrate that only fleeting self-enforcing technologies have been discovered so far. Federalism is especially vulnerable in times of crises and wars.[62] Nevertheless, so far as we can see, federalism appears to be the political system best suited to maintaining market institutions against political opportunism Strict restrictions on the federal government's responsibilities need to be established – such as defense and foreign relations. Most other governmental responsibilities should be administered at the local level. Residents should be free to move between localities or form their own localities if they so desire.

The ability of citizens to "vote with their feet" generates an incentive for the majority of residents within any locality to consider the rights of the minority, otherwise they will lose a percentage of the population which forms the tax base. Moreover, the competition between regional units "forces" the government to improve conditions so as to maintain its population, and attract additional individuals. Within the different regions, various experiments in governance can be conducted – in terms of different voting rules, different arrays of social services, and different economic regulations, etc. Successful experiments in some areas attract residents and expand the tax base, whereas unsuccessful experiments would lead to a declining population and a reduction in the tax base in others. The benign nature of this process, however, presupposes that the federalist system is self-enforcing, and does not collapse.

Federalism offers a solution to the general paradox of governance discussed above. It pre-commits the federal government to respect the economic experimentation at lower levels of government. It also pre-commits the lower levels of government to eliminating competition among themselves. The government's discretionary authority over the economy is greatly restricted.[63] In addition, this system of governance provides a framework for political tolerance of alternative experiments in living, and encourages competition among local customs and institutions in a peaceful manner. Epistemologically, federalism can potentially tap the local knowledge of its citizens in the same way that market competition relies on the local knowledge of its participants.

Conclusion

The fundamental problem with the political economy of socialism was that the epistemic demands placed on its economic institutions were not feasible. As a consequence, those economic institutions could not engender the rational assessment of alternative uses of scarce resources. Error was structurally embedded within the economic system. The error-prone nature of socialist economies possessed deleterious consequences for the political environment of socialism as the discretionary power of the government expanded to control not only economic affairs but all human affairs. The state again took on a political role far in excess of its epistemological capabilities, and error was structurally embedded into the political system. Mass terror was the only refuge from utter collapse.

Hayek spent most of his intellectual career explicating the appeal and failures of the dominant ideology of the twentieth-century socialism. His critique of socialism, however, also implied a positive image of its obverse – liberalism. Classical liberalism of the eighteenth and nineteenth centuries was far from perfect, Hayek admitted, and much of his post-*Road to Serfdom* publishing efforts were directed at refining and restating liberalism. Liberal governance, if appropriately structured, would provide the framework for the economic and social experimentation that is essential for social progress. Absent this framework, and civilization is often forced to its knees.

I have argued that the thrust of Hayek's social theory provides important insights into not only the reason why socialism collapsed, but also the preconditions for the successful transformation of the former socialist economies. If socialism distorted information and perverted incentives, then liberalization of the political economy must free information flows and provide high-powered incentives for individuals to discover and use information efficiently. Liberalization, however, cannot be imposed from above. Real transformation must be grounded in already existing practices and customs. The constitutional moment, appropriately viewed, is one of *codification*, and not the creation, of rules and rights.

Mainstream economic and political thinking fails to recognize these Hayekian insights because of the predominance of non-contextual thinking as reflected in classic models of frictionless political and economic worlds. The epistemic problem of socialism, according to Hayek, emerged because of the context of choice within which decision-makers were thrust. In the absence of private property and the freely established exchange ratios of the market economy, decision-makers were left adrift in a sea of economic possibilities. Property and monetary prices provide the necessary anchor and, thus, the social context within which rational economic decisions are made. Economic performance is a function of the social system within which the individual dwells.

That the social system cannot be imposed upon a society without negatively distorting its operation is not fully understood by scholars attempting to examine the transformations in Eastern and Central Europe and the former Soviet Union. Certainly ideas can be imported. Liberal political economy, for example, is not a native Russian system of thought, and yet I am of the firm conviction that radical liberalism possesses many of the answers to Russia's (and the other reforming countries') problems, from industrial and monetary policy to foreign relations. What the Hayekian critique of hubris implies is a position of critical rationalism, not blind conservativism. All traditions and practices are up for examination, although not at the same time.

Critical rationalism, however, does respect the importance of organic institutions and traditions and seeks to rely on the *de facto* patterns of behavior to organize affairs. Probably its most important lesson to get across is the acceptance of already existing practices as the initial situation. Pierce through the veneer of official rhetoric or idealized formal explanations and examine the *de facto* relations – economic, political, legal, and cultural. Growth and progress will follow from channeling these practices in certain directions rather than from creating a social world anew.

Acknowledgments

An earlier draft of this chapter was presented at the Friedrich A. von Hayek Memorial Symposium (sponsored by the Walter Eucken Institut and the International Institute at George Mason University, Virginia), held in Bleibach, Germany, June 9–12, 1993, and at the Department of Economics Research Seminar at California State University in Hayward. I would like to thank the participants at the symposium and the seminar for their comments and criticisms. I also want to thank Barry Weingast, Hilton Root, Tom Metzger, Ramon Myers, Robert Conquest, and Annelise Anderson of the Hoover Institution for many beneficial conversations on the issues of transition and their helpful comments on an earlier draft. In addition, financial assistance from the National Fellows Program at the Hoover Institution on War, Revolution and Peace, Stanford University, the Earhart Foundation, and the Austrian Economics Program at New York University is gratefully acknowledged. Responsibility for errors is exclusively my own.

References

Anon. (1993) "Two Cheers for Demokratiya," *US News and World Report* 5 April.

Ackerman, B. (1992) *The Future of Liberal Revolution*, New Haven: Yale University Press.

Aranson, P. (1992) "The Common Law as Central Economic Planning," *Constitutional Political Economy* 3(3) (Fall).

Arendt, H. (1958) *The Origins of Totalitarianism*, New York: World Publishing.

Arrow, K. (1951) *Social Choice and Individual Values*, New York: John Wiley.

Baechler, J. (1975) *The Origin of Capitalism*, Oxford: Basil Blackwell.

Benson, B. (1990) *The Enterprise of Law*, San Francisco: Pacific Research Institute for Public Policy.

Berman, H. (1983) *Law and Revolution*, Cambridge: Harvard University Press

Bish, R. (1988) "Federalism: A Market-Economics Perspective," in J. Gwartney and R. Wagner (eds.) *Public Choice and Constitutional Economics*, Greenwich, CT: JAI Press.

Boettke, P. J. (1990) *The Political Economy of Soviet Socialism, The Formative Years, 1918–1928*, Boston: Kluwer.

Boettke, P. J. (1992a) "Friedrich A. Hayek (1899–1992)," *The Freeman* 42(8) (August).

Boettke, P. J. (1992b) "Analysis and Vision in Economic Discourse," *Journal of the History of Economic Thought* 14 (Spring).

Boettke, P. J. (1993) *Why Perestroika Failed: The Politics and Economics of Socialist Transformation*, London: Routledge.

Buchanan, J. M. (1975) *The Limits of Liberty*, Chicago: University of Chicago Press.

Buchanan, J. M. (1993) "Asymmetrical Reciprocity in Market Exchange: Implications for Economies in Transition," *Social Philosophy and Policy* 10 (Summer).

Coase, R. (1988) *The Firm, The Market and The Law*, Chicago: University of Chicago Press.

Dallin, A. (1992) "Causes of the Collapse of the USSR," *Post-Soviet Affairs* 18(4).

de Soto, H. (1993) "The Missing Ingredient," *The Economist*, 11–17 September.

Demsetz, H. (1989) (first published 1969) "Information and Efficiency, Another Viewpoint," in H. Demsetz, *Efficiency, Competition, and Policy*, New York: Basil Blackwell.

Fischer, S. and Gelb, A. (1991) "The Process of Socialist Economic Transformation," *Journal of Economic Perspectives* 5(4) (Fall).

Friedman, M. (1982) (first published 1962) *Capitalism and Freedom*, Chicago: University of Chicago Press.

Gligorov, V. (1992) "Justice and Privatization," *Communist Economies and Economic Transformation* 4(1).

Havel, V. *et al.* (1985) *The Power of the Powerless*, New York: M. E. Sharpe.

Hayek, F. A. von (1960) *The Constitution of Liberty*, Chicago: University of Chicago Press.

Hayek, F. A. von (1973) *Law Legislation and Liberty*, vol. 1, Chicago: University of Chicago Press.

Hayek, F. A. von (1976) (first published 1944) *The Road to Serfdom*, Chicago: University of Chicago Press.

Hayek, F. A. von (1978a) "Competition as a Discovery Procedure," in F. A. von Hayek (ed.) *New Studies in Philosophy, Politics, Economics, and the History of Ideas*, London: Routledge & Kegan Paul.

Hayek, F. A. von (1978b) "Whither Democracy?" in F. A. von Hayek (ed.) *New Studies in Philosophy, Politics, Economics, and the History of Ideas*, London: Routledge & Kegan Paul.

Hayek, F. A. von (1979) *Law, Legislation and Liberty*, vol. 3, Chicago: University of Chicago Press.

Hayek, F. A. von (1980) (first published 1948) "The Economic Conditions of Interstate Federalism [1939]," in F. A. von Hayek (ed.) *Individualism and Economic Order*, Chicago: University of Chicago Press.

Heilbroner, R. (1990) "Analysis and Vision in the History of Modern Economic Thought," *Journal of Economic Literature* 28(3) (September).

Higgs, R. (1987) *Crisis and Leviathan*, New York: Oxford University Press.

Higgs, R. (1988) "Can the Constitution Protect Private Rights During National Emergencies?" in J. Gwartney and R. Wagner (eds.) *Public Choice and Constitutional Economics*, Greenwich, CT: JAI Press.

Kiser, E. and Barzel, Y. (1991) "The Origins of Democracy in England," *Rationality and Society* 3(4) (October).

Klein, D. (1990) "The Microfoundations of Rules versus Discretion," *Constitutional Political Economy* Fall.

Klein, D. and O'Flaherty, D. (1993) "A Game-theoretic Rendering of Promises and Threats," *Journal of Economic Behavior and Organization*, 21.

Knight, F. (1935) *The Ethics of Competition and Other Essays*, New York: Harper and Brothers.

Knight, F. (1971) (first published 1921) *Risk, Uncertainty and Profit*, Chicago: University of Chicago Press.

Kristof, N. (1993) "Riddle of China, Repression and Prosperity Can Coexist," *New York Times* 7 September.

Lange, O. (1970) (first published 1939) *On the Economic Theory of Socialism*, New York: Augustus M. Kelley.

Lavoie, D. (1985) *Rivalry and Central Planning*, New York: Cambridge University Press.

Lavoie, D. (1992) "Glasnost and the Knowledge Problem," *The Cato Journal* 11 (Winter).

Lavoie, D. (1993) "Democracy, Markets, and the Legal Order," *Social Philosophy and Public Policy* 10 (Summer).

Leitzel, J. (1993) "Russian Market Activity," *Sanford Institute of Public Policy, Mimeo, Duke University* January.

Leoni, B. (1972) *Freedom and the Law*, Los Angeles, CA: Nash Publishing.

212 Calculation and Coordination

McKinnon, R. (1991) *The Order of Economic Liberalization*, Baltimore: Johns Hopkins University Press.

Metzger, T. and Myers, R. (1991) "Two Diverging Societies," in R. Myers (ed.) *The Republic of China and the People's Republic of China*, Stanford, CA: Hoover Institution Press.

Michnik, A. (1990) "The Two Faces of Eastern Europe," *The New Republic* 12(November).

Mises, L. von (1980) *The Theory of Money and Credit*, Indianapolis: Liberty Classics.

Naishul, V. (1991a) *The Supreme and Last Stage of Socialism*, London: Centre for Research into Communist Economies.

Naishul, V. (1991b) "Byurokraticheskiy rynok: Skrytyye prava i ekonomicheskaya reforma," *Nezavisimaya Gazeta* 26 September (5), translated by Clifford Gaddy.

Naishul, V. (1992a) "Institutional Developments in the USSR," *The Cato Journal* 11(3) (Winter).

Naishul, V. (1992b) "The Limits of Market Economics Under Soviet Conditions," in B. Roberts and N. Belyaeva (eds.) *After Perestroika: Democracy in the Soviet Union*, Washington, DC: Center for Strategic and International Studies.

Naishul, V. (1993) "Liberalism, Customary Rights and Economic Reforms," *Communist Economies and Economic Transformation* 5.

North, D. (1990) *Institutions, Institutional Change and Economic Performance*, New York: Cambridge University Press.

Nutter, W. (1983) "Markets Without Property: a Grand Illusion," in W Nutter (ed.) *Political Economy and Freedom*, Indianapolis: Liberty Press.

Oi, J. (1992) "Fiscal Reform and the Economic Foundations of Local State Corporatism in China," *World Politics* 45 (October).

Olson, M. (1983) *The Rise and Decline of Nations*, New Haven: Yale University Press.

Pipes, R. (1990) *The Russian Revolution*, New York: Alfred Knopf.

Przeworski, A. (1991) *Democracy and the Market*, New York: Cambridge University Press.

Rizzo, M. (1980) "Law Amid Flux," *Journal of Legal Studies* 9(2) (March).

Schumpeter, J. (1942) *Capitalism, Socialism, and Democracy*, New York: Harper and Brothers.

Selgin, G. (1994) "On Ensuring the Acceptability of a New Fiat Money," *Journal of Money, Credit and Banking* 26(4) (November): 808–26.

Smith, A. (1937) (first published 1776) *The Wealth of Nations*, New York: Modern Library.

Spencer, H. (1897) *The Principle of Ethics*, New York: Appleton, p. 2.

Stevens, J. (1993) *The Economics of Collective Choice*, Boulder, CO: Westview Press.

The Economist (1992) "Behind Democracy's Facade," *The Economist* 18 April.

The Economist (1993) 12 June: 41–2.

The Federalist Papers (1961) New York: New American Library.

The National Interest (1993) 31 (Spring).

Thomsen, E. (1992) *Prices and Knowledge*, London: Routledge.

Thornton, M. (1992) *The Economics of Prohibition*, Salt Lake City: University of Utah Press.

Tocqueville, A. (1955) (first published 1856) *The Old Regime and the French Revolution*, New York: Doubleday.

Tollison, R. and Wagner, R. (1991) "Romance, realism, and economic reform," *Kyklos*, 44.

Vanberg, V. (1993) "Cultural Evolution, Collective Learning and Constitutional Design," *Working Paper, Center for Study of Public Choice* August.

Vihanto, M. (1992) "Competition between Local Governments as a Discovery Procedure," *Journal of Institutional and Theoretical Economics* 48.

Vite, O. and Travin, D. (1991) "Privatization as Effected by the Nomenklatura," *Moscow News* 1–8 December.

Weingast, B. (1992) "The Economic Role of Political Institutions," *Mimeo Stanford University* September.

12 Promises made and promises broken in the Russian transition*

Introduction[1]

For the better part of a decade now the Russian people have been attempting to make a clear break from their past system of economic and political organization and make the decisive step toward a more open and prosperous society. The path has not been easy. In fact, the picture rendered by official economic statistics reveals an economic system which has continually contracted since 1989, so that, at the end of 1996, the economy was basically half the size it was in 1989 – a steeper fall than the United States experienced during the Great Depression of the 1930s. There are good reasons to doubt the official statistics, namely that the 1989 figure overstated economic growth, and that the 1996 data understate economic growth by failing to account for the expansion of the black market. Nevertheless, there can be little doubt that the Russian people have had to endure great economic hardship all through the 1990s, with an estimated 22% of the population living below the official poverty line in 1998.

When asked to comment on Russia's problems, it is my common refrain to insist that Russia has *no* economic problems *per se*, only political and legal. My argument is basically that economic life, for the most part, takes care of itself when permitted. This does not mean that certain economic institutions are non-essential for development, they most certainly are, but these institutions are generally by-products of a process of social interaction which takes place against the backdrop of a specified institutional environment. The trick is specifying precisely that institutional environment which stimulates economic life to move in a direction that exploits the gains from mutual exchange rather than impeding that process. Contrary to an emerging consensus among some scholars and public intellectuals, the market system itself is not the source of Russian despair and global confusion in general.[2] Markets are neither "good" nor "bad," they are mere instruments through which individuals pursue their projects. The manner in which people will pursue those projects depends on

*Originally published as Boettke, P. J. (1998) "Promises Made and Promises Broken in the Russian Transition," *Constitutional Political Economy* 2: 133–42.

factors outside the market, as the market mechanism is simply a means by which people coordinate their affairs with others to pursue their own ends.

Even if we discount the Gorbachev reform experiment with the Soviet system, Russia has been attempting to change the political and legal system and introduce above-ground and operational markets since 1992.[3] From all reports, walking through the streets of Moscow nowadays, it seems that everything is for sale. But, from these same reports we rarely hear that this is a sign of social progress. Of course, there is a common revulsion to the "ugliness" of the rough and tumble of market activity, and even in advanced market economies it is rare for market activity to be singled out for esthetic praise. What one reads about Russian developments, however, goes beyond the mere disenchantment with crass materialism. Instead, what is being reported on is the very breakdown of society. A rise in murder, prostitution, drugs, and criminal behavior in general, namely the dominance of mafia-type organizations in all of economic life, combined with reports of increased social inequity and declining life-expectancy, the deterioration of social services (including health care), paints a very unpleasant picture.[4] Soviet life expectancy declined from 67 to 62 for men, and from 76 to 73 for women during the period from 1964 to the 1980s. The common explanation of this was the environmental damage wrought by Soviet economic industrialization, the harsh economic realities of the system, and the personal despair associated with underemployment and political repression reflected in the rate of alcoholism among Russian males. But that was under the Soviet system that has supposedly been overturned. Since 1992, life expectancy has dropped even further, to 58 for men and 72 for women.

It is my hypothesis that this sad predicament has little or nothing to do with the transition to a market economy in general, and instead reflects the complexity of the legal and political changes required for successful economic experimentation in the market to emerge as a vehicle for social betterment. It is a problem of the institutional infrastructure, and not something inherent to the pursuit of self-interest and wealth through market exchange. And, it is precisely in spelling out this hypothesis that Richard Epstein's *Simple Rules for a Complex World* (1995) provides the crucial framework for analysis.

How economies grow

Adam Smith once commented that:

> Little else is requisite to carry a state to the highest degree of opulence from the lowest barbarism, but peace, easy taxes, and a tolerable administration of justice; all the rest being brought about by the natural course of things.
>
> [Smith 1937 (first published 1776), p. xiii]

If we unpack this sentence, then no doubt there is a large degree of truth. But unpacking all that is packed into this Smithian program for successful development has proven more difficult. What we do know, however, is that it is not just a matter of "getting the prices right." Certainly, allowing the price system to operate is now generally recognized to be a vital aspect of successful economic development (see, for example, Krueger 1997). But the market price system is always embedded within a set of institutions. Perhaps then, the question is one of "getting the institutions right." Large differences in per capita income across countries, Mancur Olson (1996) has argued, cannot be explained by the variables associated with standard mainstream models of growth and development. Instead, these differences are to be explained by reference to differences in the institutional environment. He maintains (Olson 1996, p. 22)

> Though low-income societies obtain most of the gains from self-enforcing trades, they do not realize many of the largest gains from specialization and trade. They do not have the institutions that enforce contracts impartially, and so they lose most of the gains from those transactions (like those in the capital market) that require impartial third-party enforcement. They do not have institutions that make property rights secure over the long run, so they lose most of the gains from capital intensive production. Production and trade in these societies is further handicapped by misguided economic policies and by private and public predation. The intricate social cooperation that emerges when there is a sophisticated array of markets requires far better institutions and economic policies than most countries have.

The opportunity for mutually beneficial bargains is not enough to insure that the gains from specialization and trade will be realized. Realization of those gains from trade requires a complex set of institutions which engenders a process which provides an incentive for individuals to both discover better ways to arrange existing affairs, and to imagine alternative ways by which affairs might be arranged. For example, the economic developments in Holland in the sixteenth century that led to an "embarrassment of riches" has been the subject of serious inquiry, at least since Max Weber. Markets alone have existed in some form or another since antiquity, and even specific forms of economic institutions like basic money and banking and double-entry book-keeping existed in China and Southern Europe; yet the "economic miracle" took place in north-western Europe. Explanations as to why capitalism developed there, and at that time, center on specific economic institutions, such as the relatively advanced development of institutions of financial intermediation, the emergence of insurance contracts, and various additional institutions of risk assessment and management which enabled the expansion of markets beyond what they had previously developed. But, it is important in the analysis to point out that even within that explanation of the development of the institutions of capitalism there is another layer of institutions which provide the given backdrop against which this birth of modernity took place. In the example that we are discussing, north-western Europe was divided into small city-states and there was a lack of a unified empire during the time period. In China or Russia, by contrast, the situation was one of a centralized empire. North-west Europe was able to tap into the competition among the city-states to provide incentives to the rulers to adopt rules that would expand economic output – the rulers of a unified empire do not face the same incentives (see Rosenberg and Birdzell 1986, pp. 136–9).

These days there really should be little doubt that economic development is a function of allowing individuals within a society to realize the gains from trade, and, in order to realize those gains, various exchange-promoting institutions must be adopted.[5] In addition, these institutions must be embedded in a broader historical circumstance, including the legitimating ideology (the most common, historically, being the religious beliefs of a people). History and culture feed into political and legal institutions, which in turn provide the conditions for cultivating economic life. Markets exist everywhere and always, but they do not exist in a vacuum. Instead, they are always embedded, and that embeddedness determines how effectively they will operate with regard to serving as mechanisms of social progress. In short, economies "take-off" because of the adoption of certain institutions that structure incentives and engender a flow of information that motivates and enables economic actors to realize the gains from specialization and trade. Absent those institutions, and generalized economic prosperity will also be absent.

Rules to live by

Institutions can be defined as the formal and informal rules which govern human behavior. The interconnection between the formal and informal rules is a major research subject for classical liberal political economists, such as F. A. von Hayek (see, for example, Hayek 1973 and Benson 1990). For our present purposes, however, the focus will be on the formal rules, and in particular the relationship between the legal system and economic performance. The main characteristic of the formal rules which correlate with the economic development period mentioned in the section above is "a legal system designed to give predictable, rather than discretionary, decision" (Rosenberg and Birdzell 1986, p. 113). The development of such a legal system is closely linked to the formal recognition of private property rights. As Richard Epstein puts it, "permanence and stability are the cardinal virtues of the legal rules that make private innovation and public progress possible," and there can be little doubt that "a legal regime that embraces private property and freedom of contract is the only one that in practice can offer that permanence and stability" (1995, p. xii).

Max Weber's analysis of the development of capitalism (and modernity in general) centered on the predictability of the law. Capitalism requires law "which can be counted upon, like a machine; ritualistic-religious and magical considerations must be excluded" (Weber 1961, p. 252). The Western system of law lent itself to calculability among participants, as it enabled individuals to predict the behavior of others in various economic and social contexts.[6] Increasing the predictability of the behavior of others reduces the risk of trading and investing with individuals that you do not know intimately, and thus expands the domain of market activity. Without this predictability, trading would often remain too risky to engage in, and opportunities for economic growth through the division of labor would have to be forgone.

The key to the expansion of markets, as Adam Smith wrote, was to enable economic participants to interact with the anonymous other, rather than just the familiar faces of family and friends. The division of labor in civilized society enlists the specialized skills and efforts of individuals in a number of exchanges that "exceeds all computation." Furthermore, the individual finds him/herself in modern society "at all times in need of the cooperation and assistance of great multitudes, while his whole life is scarce sufficient to gain the friendship of a few persons" (1776/1937, pp. 11, 14). The two great principles that enable this cooperation in anonymity to occur are:

1   individual self-love, and
2   abstract rules which establish the boundaries of human behavior so that self-love will be enlisted to improve the human predicament.

The argument for simplicity in the law, Epstein argues, amounts to an argument in favor of private property fights and limited government. Formal rules are necessary to define property and contract, but only up to a point. In the absence of such rules, economic production will be very limited to only interaction with familiar parties, and trust between actors in dealing will only be possible with known kin and friends. Too many rules and too much of the administration necessary to enforce those rules prove to be counterproductive to economic life. Thus, there exists a relationship between rules (and the administration of those rules) and economic productivity that can be summed up as follows:

1   An increase in administrative costs will lead to the creation of superior incentive structures.
2   An increase in administrative costs will lead to the creation of inferior incentive structures.
3   A decrease in administrative costs will lead to the creation of superior incentive structures.
4   A decrease in administrative costs will lead to the creation of inferior incentive structures (Epstein 1995, p. 34f.).

The trade-offs evident in these four cases can be represented in Figure 12.1.[7] The argument for simplicity and predictability in the law in negotiating this trade-off can take the form of at least three arguments:

1   a cost–benefit efficiency argument, which weighs the cost of administration against the benefits of expanded economic activity;

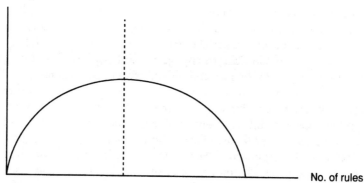

Productivity

No. of rules

1. An increase in laws increases productivity.

2. An increase in laws decreases productivity.

4. A decrease in laws decreases productivity.

3. A decrease in laws increases productivity.

Figure 12.1 Productivity of rules

2   the time consistency problem and the importance of commitment devices for economic activity over time; and

3   the necessity of stability in the points of orientation in a world of dynamic change.[8]

One way to characterize the Russian situation is that there must be a simultaneous move with regard to the law which decreases the administrative costs of the old legal system to create superior incentives, and an increase in the administrative costs of the new legal system to create superior incentives, without confusing the situation for economic actors so that inferior incentives and mistaken signals are produced and acted upon. This task requires those in charge to signal and commit to the new system so as to avoid confusion and distrust among economic participants. Soviet and now Russian reform efforts have largely failed in this task, and that is the major reason for the failure of the old system to reform and the negative picture that is drawn of the current reform situation.[9] The problem remains one of the rulers making a sincere promise to the people that the law (and with that tax and regulation of commerce) will not be arbitrary, and that there are in place institutions which will secure that the promise made by the rulers will be kept.

Promises, promises

Soviet and Russian leaders over the years have failed to keep their promises, and as a result the citizens as players in the economic game do not possess an incentive to play the game in the above-ground and legal economy. This explains the paradoxical situation of the declaration of economic liberalization and the continuation, even expansion, of black-market economic activity since 1992.

Official economic statistics continue to be highly dubious indicators of the economic situation. Russian privatization, for example, is simultaneously over- and underestimated. Privatization is overestimated because of the ambiguous definition of what constitutes privatized – so that firms which are of mixed-ownership are counted as now being private. In other words, the main empirical question which must be answered is where effective decision-making power resides – with truly private firms unconnected to the state, or with mixed or hybrid ownership firms. Privatization is underestimated because much of the private economic activity that does take place in Russia goes unreported to avoid the threat of confiscation of wealth through tax and regulation by authorities. Just consider the following two statements taken from within a few pages of each other in one of the most recent works reporting on Russian privatization:

> Russian privatization was rapid, extensive, and unprecedented in world history. The enterprises at the heart of an entire economic and political system were fundamentally changed. Almost 90 per cent of industrial output and 80 per cent of industrial enterprises passed mainly into private hands ... State ownership in 60 per cent of the firms covered by the 1996 Russian National Survey was zero.
>
> (Blasi *et al.* 1997, p. 167).

But then they report that:

> The market is risky, it is unpleasant, it is not egalitarian; and it tempts the Russian state – whoever possesses the state power at the end of each election – to try to tame and control it in the interests of politicians. The fact is that the Russian state still owns more than 10 per cent of about a third of all the already privatized corporations in the country and more than 20 per cent of a quarter of them. On average, according to recent estimates, the state owns over a third interest in the top fifty corporations in the country and may own a modest interest in the next 250 large corporations, which may help determine who ultimately controls those companies. The state and existing owners or aspiring owners will struggle over what happens to this residual state interest – which does not include several thousand firms that were never privatized in areas as diverse as coal, precious metals, health and communication services. The partial or full state role in these firms suggests a continuation of subsidies, a drain on the state budget, and ongoing attempts to combine economic and political activity
>
> (Ibid. 168 f.).

So what is actually the situation? From the reports we appear to have "unprecedented" privatization, combined with continued state control even of a large share of these supposedly privatized firms. In addition, the Yeltsin years have witnessed what was already prevalent under Gorbachev, the continuation – in fact, the expansion – of the black-market activity (or at least unrecorded economic activity) at a time when the policy regime is supposedly favorable toward the development and expansion of markets. This is because registration fees, economic regulations, and taxation remain impediments to the development of new enterprise and the discovery of better ways to satisfy consumers. Moreover, ambiguity and poor enforcement of property and contract by the official government have led to the rise of alternative enforcement mechanisms – some desirable, some not.

In other words, the Yeltsin reform team has failed to negotiate the trade-off between the administrative costs of law and economic performance in any way that credibly commits the regime to keep their promise of protection of private property, freedom of contract, and market expansion in general. Moreover, a major point to emphasize is that each time that a regime fails to live up to its promise, it reinforces the expectation that it will never keep its promises, and this means that in the future a more drastic signal and commitment device will be needed than otherwise would have been necessary to accomplish the task. In other words, the regime must overshoot in the policy game if they are going to persuade others of the sincerity of their promise to protect private property and freedom of contract. An unwillingness to make such a binding commitment will simply signal to citizens that it is best not to believe the promise made, because previous similar promises have simply been broken as easily as they were made.

The dilemma of making a credible promise highlights the general paradox of governance that has been repeatedly emphasized by Barry Weingast. "The fundamental political dilemma of an economic system," Weingast states, "is this: A government strong enough to protect property rights and enforce contracts is also strong enough to confiscate the wealth of its citizens."[10] The solution to this dilemma has to be found in the ability of the political legal system to credibly commit to limit its own power with respect to the economy. The key to establishing limited government is that the limits be self-enforcing, so that future opportunities for political–legal discretion which would benefit particular political–legal officials are *not* pursued. The governance structure of the political–legal game must be so structured that the pay-offs are such that respecting the limits on government action is the dominant strategy. Weingast finds the solution in what he terms "market-preserving federalism," a political–legal system which provides self-enforcing restrictions that make it in the interest of national leaders to respect the autonomy of the lower levels of government, and thus not to intervene in the economy.

There is no doubt that aligning the incentives within the system of governance is vital, but establishing a credible commitment during a time of transition also requires an unambiguous signal to be sent which builds trust, among economic actors, in the promise to limit power. Consider the problem that we are confronted with, as laid out above. The Russian leaders must negotiate a trade-off between the establishment and administration of law which defines and enforces property rights, and economic productivity (in terms of realizing the gains from exchange in above-ground and transparent markets). Economic productivity requires a state strong enough to establish and enforce property rights, but limited enough so that it will not confiscate wealth. Under the Soviet system, the economy operated in the region where increasing the costs of administration engendered an inferior incentive system. Russian reformers have had to simultaneously decrease the administration of the old system of law (perhaps to zero) and yet increase the administrative costs of the new system to define and enforce new property rights (perhaps by codifying the pre-existing *de facto* rights). But how is an economic actor to know which act the state is engaged in, especially when many of the same faces are populating the political–legal system, and the signal being sent is far from unambiguous? In this setting, a strong state and a weak state are interpreted identically by the relevant economic actors, and both are to be either avoided by those unconnected, or exploited by those connected.

As a consequence of this setting, economic actors are unsure of the viability of their investment in wealth creation. Economic activity will flourish in the form of short-term investment and exchange behavior, but few will "bet" on longer-term investment projects. Moreover, the economic activity that does occur will tend to go unreported so as to avoid taxation and regulation. The political–legal vacuum will be filled by alternative enforcement mechanisms, namely mafia-type organizations. It is estimated that 20% of business profits in Russia are currently paid out in the form of protection money. In Russia, the key point to remember with regard to the mafia is that organized crime has historically been (and remains) largely connected to the state apparatus in various ways, and thus efforts to deal with the situation by the state are interpreted by most as just so many words.[11] A continuation of the cycle of promises made and promises broken provides not only incentive problems, but also affects the quality of the information that is signaled by political–legal steps.

Conclusion

The difficulty of the task, combined with the confusion in the signals, suggests a stronger endorsement of simplicity than might otherwise be the case in contemporary Russia. Only a firm establishment of, and commitment to, simple and clear rules to govern economic interaction can accomplish what is needed – namely the move from the discretionary rule of the Party to the rule of law, which will protect the ability of individuals to solve most of their daily problems through private negotiation and voluntary exchange. Epstein (1995, p. 53) suggests that "the simple rules are self-ownership, or autonomy; first possession; voluntary exchange; protection against aggression; limited privilege for cases of necessity; and takings of property for public use on payment of just compensation." As the Russian political–legal system is currently structured, no such simple rules are either defined or enforced in the legal code.

Arbitrariness, not permanence and stability, continues to define the system. The incentive, therefore, is for individuals to engage in anti-social acts, and thus violates Epstein's first ambition of the law – avoid harm (Epstein 1995, p. 31).

The legal challenge that the Russian people confront joins the political challenge of finding the appropriate system of governance in general. The two major political puzzles relate to:

1 the trade-off between too much voice, and too little voice – where too much voice is inconsistent with notions of economic reform, and too little voice is inconsistent with notions of political reform, and
2 the relative position of the status quo – where by definition the time of transition requires a status-breaking set of political institutions, whereas after a successful transition (again by definition) it would seem to be required to have a status quo-preserving set of political institutions. Not only must these puzzles be solved, but they must be solved in a manner which negotiates the conflict between them – to break the existing status quo requires that we ignore the voice of those who most benefit from the existing status quo, and to preserve the status quo requires that we resist the voice of those least advantaged under the new status quo.

This is a complicated intellectual and historical task. Commitment devices have historically been stumbled upon – and often result from a by-product of other activities, such as competition between cities or nation-states. Moreover, the commitment devices that have provided a viable contract technology for governance appear to be largely fleeting, as they are vulnerable to opportunistic deviation, especially in times of crisis and war. Nevertheless, the complexity does not belie the notion that the solution to the dilemma is to be found in a political–legal system which restricts its own power.

Precisely because the task is so complex and difficult, simplicity in the rules provides the best answer. Just as the complexities and dynamism of economic life require stable and permanent simple rules as points of orientation, the complexities and dynamism of social change demand that these stable and permanent simple rules find their place. The Russian people are involved in a triple transition: they are redefining their political–legal system; they are redefining their economic system; and they are redefining their national identity. The least difficult of these tasks is the economic transition as considered in isolation, but that task will continue to appear insoluble unless the political–legal transition is accomplished in a way so that promise-making by political and economic actors can be easily understood as promise-keeping. Until that happens, promises made will simply be promises broken and the market will be constrained as a vehicle for social progress.

References

Amsden, A., Kochanowicz, J. and Taylor, L. (1994) *The Market Meets Its Match: Restructuring the Economies of Eastern Europe*, Cambridge MA, Harvard University Press.

Anderson, A. (1995) "The Red Mafia: A Legacy of Communism," in E. P. Lazear (ed.) *Economic Transition in Eastern Europe and Russia: Realities of Reform*, Stanford: Hoover Institution Press, pp. 340–66.

Anderson, G. and Boettke, P. J. (1997) "Soviet Venality: A Rent-Seeking Model of the Communist State." *Public Choice* 93 (October): 37–53.

Bauer, P. (1979) *Dissent on Development*, Cambridge, MA: Harvard University Press.

Benson, B. (1990) *The Enterprise of Law*, San Francisco: Pacific Research Institute for Public Policy.

Blasi, J., Kroumova, M. and Kruse, D. (1997) *Kremlin Capitalism*, Ithaca, NY: Cornell University Press.

Boettke, P. J. (1993) *Why Perestroika Failed: The Politics and Economics of Socialist Transformation*, London: Routledge.

Boettke, P. J. (ed.) (1994) *The Collapse of Development Planning*, New York: New York University Press.

Boettke, P. J. (1995) "Credibility, Commitment, and Soviet Economic Reform," in E. P. Lazear (ed.) *Economic Transition in Eastern Europe and Russia: Realities of Reform*, pp. 247–75.

Brennan, G. and Buchanan, J. M. (1985) *The Reason of Rules: Constitutional Political Economy*, New York: Cambridge University Press.

Buchanan, J. M. (1975) *The Limits of Liberty: Between Anarchy and Leviathan*, Chicago: University of Chicago Press.

Epstein, R. (1995) *Simple Rules for a Complex World*, Cambridge: Harvard University Press.

Hall, R. and Rabushka, A. (1995) *The Flat Tax*, Stanford: Hoover Institution Press.

Hayek, F. A. von (1973) *Law, Legislation and Liberty*, vol. 1, Chicago: University of Chicago Press.

Krueger, A. (1997) "Trade Policy and Economic Development: How We Learn," *American Economic Review* 87 (March): 1–22.

Mises, L. V. (first published 1922) (1981) *Socialism: An Economic and Sociological Analysis*, Indianapolis: Liberty Classics.

Olson, M. (1996) "Big Bills Left on the Sidewalk: Why Some Nations Are Rich, and Others Poor," *Journal of Economic Perspectives* 10(2): 3–24.

Remnick, D. (1997) *Resurrection: The Struggle for a New Russia*, New York: Random House.

Rizzo, M. (1980) "Law Amid Flux: The Economics of Negligence and Strict Liability in Tort," *Journal of Legal Studies* IX(2): 291–318.

Roberts, P. C. (1971) *Alienation and the Soviet Economy*, Albuquerque, NM.: University of New Mexico Press.

Rosenberg, N. and Birdzell, L. E. (1986) *How the West Grew Rich: The Economic Transformation of the Industrial World*, New York: Basic Books.

Smith, A. (1937) (first published 1776) *The Wealth of Nations*, New York: Modern Library.

Soros, G. (1997) "The Capitalist Threat," *Atlantic Monthly* February: 45–58.

Weber, M. (1961) *General Economic History*, New York: Collier Books.

Weimer, D. (ed.) (1997) *The Political Economy of Property Rights: Institutional Change and Credibility in the Reform of Centrally Planned Economies*, New York: Cambridge University Press.

Weingast, B. (1995) "The Economic Role of Political Institutions: Market-Preserving Federalism and Economic Development," *Journal of Law, Economics and Organization* II(1): 1–31.

13 The Russian crisis

Perils and prospects for post-Soviet transition*

Introduction

Russia is a country of unpaid taxes, unpaid wages, of poorly produced products and poor service; of credit expansion, but little long-term investments; of announced liberalization, but a growing black market; of great opportunity, but intense capital flight. In short, today's Russia, like its Soviet predecessor, remains "an enigma wrapped in a contradiction."

Since 1991, the international community has provided $90.5 billion of external assistance to aid the Russian transition. Thirty-five per cent of that has been directed toward investment, 25% for export credit, 7% for technical assistance, 4% for humanitarian and food aid, and 29% for balance of payments and budget support. Sixty per cent of this foreign aid has come from bilateral programs from G7 countries (Canada, France, Germany, Italy, Japan, United Kingdom, and the United States) and the non-G7 countries (Denmark, Finland, Netherlands, Norway, Sweden, and Switzerland). Assistance from the International Financial Institutions (the IMF, IBRD, IFC, and EBRD) accounts for 37% of the $90.5 billion committed to the Russian Federation.

This is not a trivial effort to aid Russia.[1] But there is also little to show for this effort in foreign aid. What has emerged in Russia over the past six years has not been a move toward the market, but a new variation on the older economic system known as the Soviet-type economy.[2] This is an economic system in which the main function of enterprises is not to compete in the open marketplace for goods and services, but is instead to protect oneself from the marketplace (see Gaddy and Ickes 1998). It is an economic system of innovative strategies to insulate itself from the rigors of market competition. The money sent to "prepare" for marketization, in other words, was money spent on insulating strategies to protect enterprises from the promised marketization. Hindsight is 20/20, but the logic of the situation is straightforward. Announcements of new economic measures will lead to fairly predictable responses by those who expect to be adversely affected by the proposed changes in the existing rules of the game, i.e. they will use whatever existing means are

*Originally published as Boettke, P. J. (1999) "The Russian Crisis: Perils and Prospects for Post-Soviet Transition," *American Journal of Economics and Sociology* 59(3) (July): 371–84.

available to mitigate the adverse affects. Russia remains perhaps the prime exemplar of a "rent-seeking" economy in the modern world.[3] And, until that basic structural issue in the polity and the economy is addressed, efforts at transformation of the economic system in a direction that will enable the Russian people to live peaceful and prosperous lives will continue to fall short.

Background to the current situation

Beginning in 1992, the rhetoric of the Russian government has been one of full-speed ahead into a democratic capitalist society. The reality of Russian economic and political life, however, has fallen far short of that rhetoric. This is not unlike the foundational Gorbachev years, from which the Yeltsin government emerged. Gorbachev's reign from 1985 to 1991 set the stage for both the perils and the prospects of the post-Soviet transitions.[4]

Yeltsin did not start from scratch. He started in an already-existing political economy reality, and that reality was one of negative value-added production; no alternative supply network other than the state; black markets both internal and external to the official state planning system; interlocking interest-group relationships in politics and economics; a high level of distrust between private and public individuals; and little incentive for economic actors to behave in a transparently entrepreneurial manner. Entrepreneurship existed throughout the history of the Soviet Union, but it was limited to a range of arbitrage activities within the structure of the plan, or to the black market for consumer goods. In other words, individuals recognized opportunities for mutual gain in the gaps caused by the failure of the official system, but there was no effective way for that "alertness to opportunities" to be transformed from arbitrage reshuffling to creative innovation. Gorbachev did not change that. In fact, Gorbachev's failed reforms simply exacerbated the basic problem, i.e. that any reform government must confront the quality of the signal concerning the credibility of the reforms proposed. The constant back and forth on reform measures that characterized Gorbachev's years reinforced the distrust that actors possessed in both the private and the public sector.[5] Yeltsin's reform strategy requires that a credible commitment to reform be conveyed effectively to the populace, and yet that remains *the* major shortcoming of Russian transition policy since 1992.

Without a strong signal of binding reforms in the political, legal, and economic structure promises made are not trusted and thus the hoped-for results do not materialize. If every promise made is understood to be nothing but another promise broken, then economic actors will not engage in the sort of long-term investment and productive activity that is correlated with material progress.[6] Economic activity will focus on short-term and easily transferable assets, and money made will find a more secure home outside Russia's borders.

The "enigma wrapped in a contradiction" which represents current Russia unravels once we separate rhetoric from reality. The logic of the situation actually requires only a rudimentary knowledge of economics to both understand and propose viable solutions. When walking through Washington Square Park in New York's Greenwich Village, as I did daily through most of the 1990s, it was a common occurrence for me to be propositioned to purchase some illicit substance or another. If tonight it was announced that the "War on Drugs" was over and all substances previously illegal could now be traded above ground, then my Washington Square Park "entrepreneur" would disappear. If I walked through the park in six months and he was still there, then it would seem obvious that something wasn't so clear in that earlier legal announcement. That is Russia. Liberalization has been announced for close to a decade, yet underground markets dominate economic life. The enforcement of contracts in this underground market creates opportunities for extralegal mechanisms, what we term "mafia."[7]

In addition to the broad topic of economic liberalization, there are also very specific reform measures where the rhetoric and the reality diverge so significantly that it is worth pointing out. One of the major problems with the Soviet system of economic management was that firm-level inefficiencies were converted into macroeconomic imbalances through the mechanism of "soft-budget" constraints. Subsidies to firms were paid for by budgetary imbalances, which in turn were financed through money creation. Since prices were administered during the Soviet era, this led to what was then referred to as the "rouble overhang" problem. Since the liberalization of many prices, the continuation of inflation finance has led to rising prices and a move out of the rouble and into harder currency (such as the US dollar). The point that I want to stress, however, is that inflation finance has continued throughout the Yeltsin years.[8] Despite claims of monetary and fiscal restraint, the reality of policy has been one of continued subsidies to inefficient state and quasi-state firms.[9]

To this monetary and fiscal policy environment add the regulation and tax policies that have been adopted, and the sorry state of post-Soviet affairs is not surprising. Registration, regulation, and tax policies have become major impediments to the development of new enterprises in an above-ground market economy. The ambiguity and poor enforcement of property and contract by the official government has led to the rise of alternative enforcement mechanisms – some desirable, some not.[10] Compare the situation in Moscow and Warsaw for setting up a private shop. In a study reported in *Russian Economics Trends* (April 1997), it is reported that the average time for registration (in months) is 2.7 in Moscow, but only 0.7 in Warsaw. The average number of inspections in 1996 per private shop was nineteen in Moscow and nine in Warsaw. In Moscow, 83% of those inspections resulted in fines, whereas the corresponding number in Warsaw was 46%. Finally, 39% of private shops in Moscow reported being contacted by the "mafia" within the last six months, while only 8% report similar contacts in Warsaw.

The Russian people have had to endure a collapse of the economic system – as depicted by official economic statistics – that surpasses the decline experienced in the US during the "Great Depression." During the last decade, the Russian economy has contracted by roughly half, although there are problems with this official view which should be mentioned, namely that:

1   economic statistics overstate the health of the Soviet economy in 1989;
2   official statistics understate economic activity today because of the inability
    to accurately account for black-market dealings; and
3   it is difficult to "read" production figures in a world of negative value-
    added firms.

The last point is important because, in such a world, curtailing production
(which is measured as a decline in output) is actually a step toward increasing
production and exchange efficiency. Unfortunately, in the former Soviet economy
the welfare state was tied to state firms – in some cases the entire range of
health and human services – and, if the firms are forced to shut down, then the
social safety net (however ineffective it was) is also shut down. It is now estimated
that 30% of the population is now living below the official poverty line.[11] Basic
human indicators of well-being – life expectancy, infant mortality rates, etc. –
are heading in a direction opposite to what might be hoped. From the 1960s to
the 1980s, life expectancy declined from sixty-seven to sixty-two years for men,
and since 1992 the decline has continued so that the life expectancy for a
Russian male is now in the mid- to upper-50s.

Russia's problems are enormous. Quick remedies are not possible, as the
problems are deep seated within the system and the history and culture of the
people. It is not that entrepreneurship or freedom of expression is alien to
Russians – the Soviet period saw a great entrepreneurial spirit in the black
market and a brave *samizdat* political culture. Moreover, Russian immigrants
as a group do not have difficulty adjusting to the capitalist and democratic
environments of Western Europe and the United States.[12] Nevertheless, the
experience of ordinary Russians with markets and political decision-making is
different from that experienced by those individuals who have been born in
societies firmly rooted in Western values (see Buchanan 1997a, 1997b and
1997c). Cultural constraints are felt at the level of the "legitimacy" accorded
to the basic institutions of a market-order, civil society, and political freedom.
One of the important lessons of the faded experiments with development
planning throughout the world is that, despite noble intentions, the most
sustainable path to progress is an indigenous one. In other words, history and
culture do indeed constrain our reformist zeal and, as such, must be taken into
account in the analysis of any social transformation. While history and culture
matter, they need not represent such a binding constraint that we must
necessarily adopt a fatalistic conservatism. Cultural values can mutate, and
history changes so as to direct people along a path different to that previously
traveled. We can use the background problem situation to highlight the issues
which must be addressed and to suggest institutional remedies.

Shock therapy as a path to a cure, not as a cure in itself

The difficulties experienced in Russia have led many to criticize the
transformation strategy for:

1   the uncritical adoption of a Western model, which is claimed to represent neither the only model of development, nor one particularly applicable to Russia, and

2   going too fast, where a more gradual strategy of transformation would have been more successful. The Chinese model is often invoked as the counterweight to arguments for rapid transformation in former socialist economies.

In my assessment, both of these arguments miss their target for a variety of reasons. I will state those reasons in as bold a manner as I can, in order to invite discussion. First, the conclusion to be drawn from world history of development patterns is that, while there are many ways for people to live their lives, there are very few ways for those lives to be lived prosperously, as we currently define that term (see Landes 1998; Diamond 1997; and Sowell 1998). The Western model works for advanced material production; alternatives do not. This does not mean that the Western model can be imposed wherever and whenever we desire, but it does mean that without the adoption of the broad outline of that model, an "economic miracle" is not to be expected. Second, the comparison with China misses the crucial point that while the Chinese have made very little *de jure* reforms of their political system, the *de facto* changes have been enormous since 1985.[13] In fact, an interesting proposition to explore would be that while China has had less *de jure* reform, the *de facto* changes are far greater than in Russia, while in Russia there has been much *de jure* reform, but the *de facto* changes have been quite small. The follow-up proposition could then be that what fundamentally matters for economic interaction is the *de facto* organizing principles of everyday life. Obviously, official rules are vital, but only to the extent that these statements on paper are interpreted to be binding rules in the everyday life of people.

Now is not the time to explore those propositions. I raise them only to suggest that the speed and timing debate could be argued to be misplaced. It is not really an issue of gradualism therapy, but an issue of no reform versus movement to a path of reform (however treacherous that path may be). In fact, the analogy to "shock therapy" should have suggested this formulation of the debate. Whatever the merits or demerits of the treatment with patients deemed mentally ill, shock therapy was not proposed as a cure in and of itself. The therapy was prescribed because in the judgment of the attending doctor the patient had so lost sight of reality that a drastic measure was required to get the patient back on a path toward recovery. Recovery, however, was a different matter altogether and could take quite a long time. To restate the analogy, the Soviet economy was structured in a manner so far from the reality of market competition that only an immediate step into the market context could initiate a process of social transformation. There are major problems with the shock therapy argument – namely, that history does not move in leaps, but in marginal adjustments from an existing context, and that no context (no matter how bizarre) exists outside the history and culture of a people. Peter Murrell was right to challenge the model of the "Transition according to Cambridge," but not because of speed-related issues. The criticism, instead, should be grounded in a critique of the cultural *naïveté* and the economistic arrogance that the history and deep-seated beliefs of a people can safely be ignored, a belief that characterizes so much of orthodox economic policy advice (Murrell 1995; see also Boettke 1994).

But this criticism must be weighted against arguments for the "shock." It is my contention that a concern with history and custom need not be viewed in opposition to a demand for a shock. The demand for the shock, in this regard, follows from a set of arguments concerning the necessary simultaneity of monetary, fiscal, privatization, and domestic and foreign trade policy, and the question of pre-commitment in a world of rational distrust (see Boettke 1993, pp. 106–31) As we have seen with regard to monetary policy, without appropriate fiscal changes a restrictive monetary policy cannot be sustained. Unless privatization takes place and the subsidization of inefficient economic organizations stops, fiscal restraint cannot be established. And, unless there is freedom of entry, price liberalization will neither serve as an effective guide in resource allocation nor serve as an inducement for the development of new entrants who will try to meet market demand. In addition, unless these policies are introduced against a backdrop of a political–legal structure which secures property and contract, the reform measures will possess incoherent incentives and signal a weak commitment to the reforms. The phrase "once bitten, twice shy" is particularly apt for economic actors in Russia.

Reform in real time must:

1 start from the existing status quo;
2 unearth the *de facto* organizing principles of that status quo;
3 design a set of reforms which address the incentive and informational problems associated with that *de facto* system; and
4 send a clear, high-quality signal that the proposed reforms are credible and commit the governance structure to the new system, and, in doing so, close the gap for the *de jure* and *de facto* organizing system in the new regime.

While these various steps must be made together, the consequences of making them should be expected only to be a movement on to the path of reform. Reforms in real time might require quick introduction, but results are a long time in coming. History does indeed only move in small steps, and not in giant leaps. Reform measures, however, should not be viewed as a historical leap, but part of history in the making.

The real difficulty with the post-Soviet era in Russia has been that most of the reform packages have been inconsistent and have provided incentives which are incompatible with the necessary restructuring. Even worse, many of the proposed reforms have not even been implemented. Shock therapy has not failed as much as it has not been tried (Sachs 1998).

The signal sent to economic actors continues to be one which suggests that private and public predation of wealth creation are to be expected, and thus, economic actors do what is predictable – escape to the black market, hide assets or move them abroad, and engage only in short-term investment. In short, the markets are evident for all to see in a way that they were not during the Soviet period, but the view of markets is one of kiosks and bazaar-style street trading, combined with crony-capitalist-style small-scale production, and crony-socialist-style large-scale production.

Conclusion

It seems appropriate at this point to mention Henry George. George turned his attentions to political economy because of the contradictions evident in the persistence of poverty amid advancing wealth. He sought to explore the discipline and examine the logic of social relations which would explain the discrepancy and offer effective remedies to the social ill of poverty. George was concerned that political economy had been unable to unmask the source of inequity. I do not intend to comment on George's own proposed reconstruction of political economy, but I do wish to draw some parallels between his task and the task confronting us today as it relates to the post-Soviet transformation. His *Progress and Poverty* is not just an analytical tract, it is also a "transition" blueprint, and what he said about the state of political economy in 1879 still rings true today. That "after a century of cultivation," George wrote, "during which it has engrossed the attention of some of the most subtle and powerful intellects, [political economy] should be spurned by the statesman, scouted by the masses, and relegated in the opinion of many educated and thinking men to the rank of a pseudo-science in which nothing is fixed or can be fixed – must, it seems to me, be due not to any inability of the science when properly pursued, but to some false step in its premises, or overlooked factors in its estimates" (George 1879/1942).

The political economy of the transition that emerged in the 1990s to a large extent focused on the wrong questions, approached the subject "with some false step in its premises, or overlooked factors in its estimates." This was mainly manifested in the failure to account for questions of history, culture, legitimacy, and so on. Russia's problems are not of a "technical nature." It is not a question of figuring out correct accounting practices, or voting procedures – no matter how important these issues are for Russia's future. In developing a political economy of transition, we should, following George, "beg no question, shrink from no conclusion, but to follow truth wherever it may lead."

I believe that such a pursuit will lead us back to certain concerns which occupied the classical political economists. If Adam Smith were to go to Moscow, then I imagine he would highlight fiscal restraint, monetary stability, freedom of pricing and contract, and free and open international trade. But Smith would also counsel that "history matters," and that the pursuit of self-interest can only be the source of social betterment within the confines of a very specific institutional configuration. Therefore, while the promise of progress is universal, it will not be realized by all because of a variety of human foibles and mishaps. Russia does not have an "economic" problem; it has a political, legal, and cultural problem and this results in an extremely difficult political economy problem that must be solved if Russia is to overcome its problem with poverty by economic progress.

Smithian political economy sought to discover that set of institutional constraints which would enable men to peacefully coexist and prosper. Smith did not seek to create the best of all possible worlds, but instead to find a set of robust institutions of governance. F. A. von Hayek sums up the research program as follows:

> [T]he main point about which there can be little doubt is that [Adam] Smith's chief concern was not so much with what man might occasionally achieve when he was at his best but that he should have as little opportunity as possible to do harm when he was at his worst. It would scarcely be too much to claim that the main merit of the individualism which he and his contemporaries advocated is that it is a system under which bad men can do least harm. It is a social system which does not depend for its functioning on our finding good men for running it, or on all men becoming better than they now are, but which makes use of men in all their given variety and complexity, sometimes good and sometimes bad, sometimes intelligent and more often stupid
>
> (Hayek 1948, pp. 11–12).

This is both a positive and normative enterprise. It is a positive enterprise in the sense that we can examine alternative governance structures and how they impact economic performance by structuring incentives and determining the flow and quality of information that economic actors can utilize in orienting their behavior. It is a normative exercise in the sense that on the basis of the positive knowledge gained in the comparative analysis of governance structures, we can strive to introduce a robust set of political, legal, and economic institutions.[14] The further development of the Russian economy requires that both these positive and normative exercises are pursued. That development will rest with the ability of the Russians themselves to establish institutions of governance which reduce political uncertainty by restricting the opportunities for public and private predation, and enhance the willingness of individual actors to "bet on their ideas" in the marketplace for goods and services. Unless this step is taken, the Russian people will not confront Henry George's puzzle – how could there be poverty amidst progress? – because without material progress in the first place there will be no way to even make a step in the direction of addressing the problem of poverty that the Russians have had to endure during the Soviet and post-Soviet eras.

Acknowledgments

This chapter was originally given as the Henry George Lecture at St John's University on 27 October 1998. I would like to thank the Robert Schalkenback Foundation for support of this program, and Professor Joseph Giacalone for the invitation. I gratefully acknowledge the financial support of the J. M. Kaplan Foundation. I have benefited from the research assistance of Daniel Lin and Andrew Farrant and technical assistance from Mrs. Kathleen Spolarich. I also gratefully acknowledge the insightful comments from Laurence Moss, the editor of the *American Journal of Economics and Sociology*. The usual caveat applies.

References

Anderson, A. (1995) "Red Mafia," in E. Lazear, (ed.) *Economic Transition in Eastern Europe and Russia: Realities of Reform*, Stanford: Hoover Institution Press, pp. 340–66.

Anderson, G. and Boettke, P. J. (1997) "Socialist Venality: A Rent-seeking Model of the Communist State," *Public Choice* 93 (October): 37–53.

Bethell, T. (1998) *The Noblest Triumph: Property and Prosperity Through the Ages*, New York: St Martin's Press.

Blasi, J., Kroumova, M. and Kruse, D. (1997) *Kremlin Capitalism*, Ithaca: Cornell University Press, p. 168.

Boettke, P. J. (1990) *The Political Economy of Soviet Socialism: The Formative Years, 1918–1928*, Boston: Kluwer Academic Publishers.

—— (1993) *Why Perestroika Failed: The Politics and Economics of Socialist Transformation*, London: Routledge.

—— (1994) "The Reform Trap in Economics and Politics in the Former Communist Economies," *Journal des Economistes et des Etudes Humaines* 5 (June/September): 267–93.

—— (1995) "Credibility, Commitment, and Soviet Economic Reform," in E. Lazear (ed.) *Economic Transition in Eastern Europe and Russia: Realities of Reform*. Stanford: Hoover Institution Press, pp. 247–75.

—— (1998) "Promises Made and Promises Broken in the Russian Transition," *Constitutional Political Economy* 9: 133–42.

Buchanan, J (1997a) "Tacit Presuppositions of Political Economy," in *Post-Socialist Political Economy*, Aldershot: Edward Elgar Publishing, pp. 93–107.

Buchanan, J (1997b) "Asymmetrical Reciprocity in Market Exchange," in *Post-Socialist Political Economy*, Aldershot: Edward Elgar Publishing, pp. 108–21.

Buchanan, J (1997c) "Why the Soviets Cannot Understand the Market (and Why We Cannot Understand Why They Cannot Understand)," *Journal of Private Enterprise* (Special Issue): 40–9.

Diamond, J (1998) *Guns, Germs and Steel: The Fate of Human Societies*, New York: Norton.

Gaddy, C and Ickes, B. (1998) "Russia's Virtual Economy," *Foreign Affairs* (September/October).

George, H. (1942) (first published 1879) *Progress and Poverty*, New York: Schalkenbach Foundation, pp. 12–13.

Goldman, M. (1996) *Lost Opportunity: What Has Made Economic Reform in Russia So Difficult?* New York: Norton.

Goldman, M. (1991) *What Went Wrong with Perestroika*, New York: Norton.

Hayek, F. A. von (1948) "Individualism: True and False," *Individualism and Economic Order*, Chicago: University of Chicago Press.

Hiatt, F. (1998) "Lots of Bright Ideas for Russia," *Washington Post* 26 October: A17.

Krugman, P. (1998) "The Other Bear Market: The Run on Russia," *Slate* 10 September.

Landes, D. (1998) *The Wealth and Poverty of Nations*, New York: Norton.

Mises, L. von (1966) *Human Action: A Treatise on Economics*, Chicago: Henry Regnery.

Montinola, G., Yingyi Qian and Weingast, B. (1995) "Federalism, Chinese Style: The Political Basis for Economic Success in China," *World Politics* October: 50–81.

Murrell, P. (1995) "The Transition According to Cambridge, Mass.," *Journal of Economic Literature* 33 (March): 164–78.

Sachs, J. (1998) "The Dismal Decade," *Los Angeles Times* 22 November.

Sowell, T. (1998) *Cultures and Conquest*, New York: Basic Books.

14 The political infrastructure of economic development*

Introduction

The revolutions of 1989 tore asunder many a conventional wisdom. Cherished beliefs on both the right and the left had to be discarded. That totalitarian systems could indeed be overturned without mass bloodshed took some conservative intellectuals by surprise, just as the extent of the economic degradation in Eastern and Central Europe surprised many liberal intellectuals. One implication of the collapse of Communism that I want to focus on is the rethinking of economic development that must follow. The Soviet model of planned industrialized development no longer represents a promising path to the non-capitalist world. Government planning of economic development, not only in Eastern and Central Europe, but also in China, Africa, and India, has proven to be a chimera.[1] Moreover, the interpretation of the experience of industrialization in Japan, Taiwan, and Korea must be rethought, given the general theoretical and practical difficulties that government management of economic development confronts.[2]

The empirical record demands a reconsideration of not only the various formal models of development, but also the basic orientation of research on economic development. Thirty years ago the mainstream consensus among economists was that the Soviet model did achieve what was promised in terms of industrial growth, despite whatever trade-off was made in terms of human freedom. When an economist such as Warren Nutter provided evidence to the contrary he was often dismissed as an ideological naysayer (Nutter 1962). That basic attitude about the capability of the Soviet system was maintained by most scholars until quite recently. Nowadays the empirical record on Soviet performance presented by Russian economists themselves, such as Grigory Khanin and Vasily Selyunin, demonstrates that even Nutter was too optimistic in his claims about the Soviet model (Khanin and Selyunin 1987).

The point that I wish to stress, however, is not that Soviet economic performance was poor throughout its history. Rather, I would like to focus

*Originally published as Boettke, P. J. (1994) "The Political Infrastructure of Economic Development," *Human Systems Management* 13(2): 89–100.

attention on why economists, and other social scientists, could not see that the system was not working. There must have been something in our techniques which masked the Soviet reality from the scientific community. The questions that development economists asked, and the tools that they employed to answer those questions, hid from view the structural problems with the Soviet model of planned industrialization. These problems with the research orientation of development economics not only hindered the understanding of the Soviet system, but they also hinder our ability to understand contemporary problems in both the capitalist and the non-capitalist world.

The basic thesis of this chapter is that twentieth-century economic thought turned away from the fundamental institutional and cross-cultural questions which had been raised by social scientists from Adam Smith to Herbert Spencer in the vain search of more exact measurements of industrial development and welfare. As the aggregate techniques developed to measure growth came to dominate development research, the kind of comparative historical analysis conducted by an earlier generation of scholars was crowded out, to the detriment of scientific thought. What scholars need to do today, I contend, is to take one step backward in terms of technique in order to take two steps forward in terms of understanding.

A short course on modern development economics

Adam Smith's *An Inquiry into the Nature and Causes of the Wealth of Nations* (1776/1976) set the general tone for economic debate on the determinants of prosperity for about 100 years. Smith argued that economic development was the result of expanding the division of labor within society. This expansion was due to the adoption of certain political, legal, and economic institutions and practices. Private property rights, monetization, the elimination of trade restrictions, etc., sustained specialized production and exchange, and as such led to the increased substitution of market forces for centralized decision-making within the economic affairs of society. The division of labor, Smith pointed out, was limited by the extent of the market. Expanding the market allowed individuals to capture the gains from specialized production and exchange. In short, the source of economic development and prosperity was the adoption of institutions and policies that approximated the system of "natural liberty" – i.e. the limited government, night-watchman state of classical liberalism.

As the fate of classical liberalism as a political and economic doctrine waned in the twentieth century, the focus of attention with regard to economic development shifted. Questions of the institutional infrastructure were replaced with those dealing with the appropriate policy mix to be implemented by the state to achieve economic development. Discretionary government planning replaced the concern with government rules, economic institutions, and indigenous cultural practices.[3]

Three developments in thought and history worked to undermine the emphasis on institutional infrastructure:

1   the formalist and positivist revolution in economics;
2   the Bolshevik Revolution and the rise of socialism; and
3   the Keynesian Revolution in macroeconomics.

Each of these three shifted attention away from the appropriate institutional structure of governance to the necessary activities that government must undertake – a move from designing rules to direct action.

The marginalist revolution in the 1870s was a great advance in economic understanding. Unfortunately, the formal properties of the logic of choice tended to distract theoretical attention from the institutional context of choice. The great advance of marginalism was the development of a universal theory of human action to aid our understanding of economic behaviour. But, despite the formal similarity of the choice problem across time and place, the fact remains that the institutional context of choice changes the margins on which economic decisions are based. Unfortunately, the preoccupation with equilibrium states that soon came to dominate economics after the 1930s completely eliminated institutions from mainstream economics. What emerged was a theory of choice within a vacuum.

Oskar Lange, for example, argued that economics was a universal science, applying to socialist as well as capitalist economies. One might not disagree with Lange on this point, but within Lange's comparative analysis of capitalism and socialism the formal similarity of the choice problem was transformed into a study of the static allocation problem. In fact, Lange explicitly assumed away the importance of institutions in economic interaction, and, thus, in the comparison between socialism and capitalism (1939, pp. 61–2).

Lange was not alone in this assessment. As brilliant as they were, and as much as their own work remained rich in institutional analysis, Joseph Schumpeter (1942) and Frank Knight (1936) concurred with Lange. Leading thinkers were led into this error, as Hayek pointed out, because of the preoccupation with equilibrium states that the formalist revolution engendered (1948, p. 91).

Positivism also contributed to the shift of focus away from institutional infrastructure by de-legitimizing the study of ideology as an important component in social theory. Political, legal, and economic institutions are sustained on the basis of ideological systems of thought. Out of fear of ideological campaigns, positivism sought to eliminate all non-testable empirical propositions from science.

Combine the formalist preoccupation with equilibrium with the positivist disregard for ideas, and the kinds of questions that Adam Smith raised about the nature and causes of economic development and lasting prosperity are eliminated from the field. The natural tendency of neoclassical development economics was to ignore political, legal, and economic institutions and instead to search for measures of development. The question of the institutional infrastructure of sustainable development was considered to be unscientific. Measurement alone equaled science.

The Bolshevik revolution and the rise of socialism also transformed the way that scholars approached economic development. After the initial failure of the policies of War Communism (1918–21), the Bolsheviks introduced a partial liberalization known as the New Economic Policy (1921–8). This partial liberalization led to a relative recovery of the Russian economy from the disaster of War Communism. The New Economic Policy, however, did not produce the desired results in terms of industrialization and agricultural development, as it suffered from internal contradictions which made official market exchange an insecure outlet due to arbitrary intervention (see Boettke 1990, pp. 113–46; Boettke 1993, pp. 25–30, 96–9). Net official marketings of grain, for example, in 1926–7 were only 50% and 57% of their pre-World War I level, although grain output for that period was almost equivalent to pre-World War I levels of output.

Lenin's death in 1924, along with these uncomfortable results of the New Economic Policy, led to a protracted debate among Soviet economists concerning the path to be followed in industrial development. The debates and controversies of the 1920s contain much that is of importance to economic and intellectual historians (see Erlich 1960 and Boettke 1990, pp. 147–9 for a summary of the terms of the Soviet debate). As Alec Nove has pointed out, modern "Development economics could be said to have been born here" (Nove 1969, p. 129).

The Stalinist model of industrialization emerged out the 1920s controversy, and the Five-Year Planning System was born. Forced industrialization and collectivization, it was argued, were necessary to transform a backward economy into an advanced industrial power which could simultaneously defend itself against hostile capitalist encirclement and serve as a beacon to the modern world. The early reports of success from the Soviet government (at the same time that the Great Depression had destroyed faith in the market system in the West) were reinforced by the outcome of World War II. That the Stalinist model had prepared the Soviet Union to defeat Nazism became the standard justificatory explanation for forced industrialization and collectivization of agriculture. Whatever cost the Soviet policies of the 1930s imposed on the people, it was argued, the avoidance of an economic crisis such as the Great Depression and the victory over Nazism justified the expense. A new path to economic development had been discovered, a new industrialized world had been created. No longer was the world divided into developed capitalist countries and underdeveloped non-capitalist countries, now the classification included the First World (capitalist developed economies), the Second World (socialist developed economies), and the Third World (underdeveloped economies).[4] Development was no longer synonymous with capitalism.

The Keynesian revolution also contributed significantly to the shift of focus in development economics. First, the Keynesian theory re-enforced the socialist viewpoint that capitalism was inherently unstable. The Great Depression, for example, was a consequence of aggregate demand failure which periodically results from chaotic and irrational investment decisions. Free-market competition could not be relied upon to self-correct for the systemic consequences of errors committed by private economic actors, let alone promote stability and security. John Maynard Keynes argued persuasively that *laissez-faire* was dead as a legitimating ideology.

Second, the aggregate techniques developed in the Keynesian revolution provided economists with a way to measure economic development. Economic development became synonymous, as Arndt (1981) has pointed out, with measured growth in per capita income. This equating of economic development with neoclassical growth theory had severe consequences for the theoretical foundations of development economics. The preoccupation with "growth" and "long-range" economic planning were reminiscent of the debates of the Soviet economists of the 1920s. This was not a coincidence. The development of the Harrod–Domar model of economic growth was directly influenced by the Soviet debates.

Evsey Domar remarked that the 1920s Soviet journal, *The Planned Economy*, was "a valuable source of ideas" for the development of his own approach. Soviet society represented a sort of economic laboratory where the social scientist could examine "his whole intellectual apparatus in light of a social and economic system sufficiently different from ours to make the experiment rewarding, and yet not so different to make it impossible" (1957, p. 10). Domar's model was an elaboration of the theory of growth worked out by the Soviet economist Fel'dman. In extending Fel'dman's model, however, Domar replaced the Marxist concern with capital proportionality with Keynesian aggregation. As a result, modern growth theory was completely separated from the traditional concerns of capital theory. But capital theory, properly understood, provides the basis for the microeconomic foundations for macroeconomic analysis. Without these foundations the theorist is left with a world in which there are either no market problems (the Walrasian world of general equilibrium) or no market solutions (the Keynesian world of aggregate demand failure). Neither theoretical world does much to advance our understanding of real existing economies and the preconditions for their economic development (see Garrison 1984).

Modern development economics incorporated all three trends, each tending to reinforce the others. The formalist and positivist revolution demanded measurement; Keynesian techniques of aggregation supplied the needed tools for measurement. The socialist idea of the chaos of capitalism received additional support from Keynesian theory. Moreover, the Soviet experience seemed to lend credence to the notion of comprehensive economic planning, while the Keynesian theory of demand management provided a policy technique for noncomprehensive planning of the economy.

Economic thought in both East and West accepted the idea that government management of the economy was the way not only to run a modern economy, but to transform a backward economy into a modern one. Alternative models of government management of economic development were exported from the First and Second Worlds to the Third World.

The hegemony of this paradigm for economic development has been seriously challenged by intellectual developments and political events in the past 1980s and 1990s. The Keynesian model fell out of vogue in the 1970s; then, in the mid- to late 1980s, the Communist model of political economy collapsed. The traditional Keynesian model was proven to be logically flawed and empirically weak. The protracted stagnation of the British and United States economies, combined with high inflation, represented a serious anomaly in the Keynesian system. The rejection of the Communist Party throughout Eastern and Central Europe in 1989 and the abolition of the Soviet Union in 1991 called into question the desirability of the Leninist political system. The terrible economic conditions in every one of the Communist countries were witness to the folly of economic planning.

Redefining development

The revelations from inside the former Soviet Union during the Gorbachev and continuing into the Yeltsin period are particularly relevant since they radically question all previous estimates of Soviet economic performance throughout its history (see Boettke 1993, pp. 12–45). Given the implicit centrality of the Soviet model in the economic development literature, its complete discrediting must be understood. These glasnost revelations did not simply demonstrate the systematic falsification of statistics by the Soviet government, but challenged the accuracy of even the CIA statistics for measuring Soviet economic performance. Living standards in the former USSR had been falling for decades, but this decline was not grasped by the CIA. In 1986, for example, the CIA estimated that Soviet per capita GNP was about 49% of the US. The revised estimates now put that figure at about 25%. Had the CIA figures been accurate, the Soviet economy would have been a maturing industrialized economy. The revised estimates, however, revealed that the Soviet economy provided a standard of living to its citizens equivalent to that of a well-developed Third World economy.

Even these revised statistics fail to capture the true picture of Soviet economic life. Neither the low quality of Soviet products, nor the persistent shortages of goods and the corresponding queuing for goods are reflected in the statistics. Moreover, the low percentage of Soviet GNP (never more than fifty per cent) that went to household consumption is not captured by these aggregate measures. Obviously, even these revised figures cannot be relied upon to get a clear understanding of Soviet economic performance. Nevertheless, if anything the revised statistics again overestimate the economic performance of the former Soviet Union.

Not only were the growth rates challenged, but all the claims for success of the Soviet model were brought into question by Soviet scholars and intellectuals. The full extent, for example, of the planned loss of human lives from collectivization and political persecution in the 1930s under Stalin's direct orders began to be unearthed from under the debris of state propaganda and censorship. Even the Great Patriotic War (World War II) did not escape scrutiny. The

1939 Stalin–Hitler Pact was officially acknowledged. The murder of Polish officers at Katyn was debated and finally confessed. Soviet officials admitted that Stalin's purge of the Red Army's Generals just before the outbreak of war cost the Soviet army dearly. Without the assistance of its Western allies, the Soviet Union might very well have fallen to Hitler. It was not the Stalinist model that provided the resources or unity of will to defeat Nazism, but rather the ultimate resolve of the Soviet people and the assistance of the Western allies. The Stalinist model, in fact, had made the Soviet Union highly vulnerable to Hitler's attack by crippling the Soviet economy and breaking the spirit of millions of Soviet subjects.

The sacrifices of the Soviet people were real, but what success story could this model claim in terms of enhanced consumer well-being or an improved way of living? All of this demands a re-evaluation of the economic development literature. The Soviet model no longer represents an alternative to the capitalist model of the West. A new agenda for studying development economics must be forged.

To understand economic development, what is needed is not more elaborate formal models of growth or better techniques for measurement, but more detailed historical studies of the pattern of development across countries and periods. These studies, however, must be informed by a theory of economic and political processes which is rich in institutional analysis. In other words, what is required to forge a new agenda in development economics is a return to Adam Smith's concern with social institutions and their impact on economic behaviour. Economic development can be seen as part of a general theory of economic processes and social evolution.

Prerequisites for progress

Max Weber, whether we agree with his answer or not, asked the right kind of question with regard to economic development. Why did industrial capitalism appear in the West, and specifically north-western Europe, and not in China, even though, only a few centuries earlier, China was by far richer and more technologically advanced than Europe? Weber did not provide a mono-causal answer to that question, although that is what he is mostly remembered for. Protestantism is only one of the differentiating characteristics. Protestantism provided the needed ethical or moral justification for practices conducive to economic development; it was not the source of development. In his General Economic History, for example, Weber contrasts the legal structure of the Chinese, which was non-conducive to the development of capitalism, with the Western legal structure, which was conducive to capitalist development. The Chinese law in Weber's analysis was based on certain spiritual and magical practices, but Western legal tradition was inherited from the formal legal rules of Judaism and Roman law. The Western tradition relied on a logical mode of juristic reasoning, instead of the discretionary, ritualistic, religious, or magical considerations often found in alternative legal traditions.[5]

Comparative historical political economy provides a suggestive framework for research because it forces scholars to pay attention to the institutional infrastructure of society, the impact of alternative institutional environments on human action, and the consequences in terms of social and economic progress. In other words, it encourages the kind of macroeconomic analysis of legal, political and cultural institutions that neither the "old" nor "new" growth theories can provide.

It is often only remembered in passing that Weber was one of the few social scientists in the early part of this century to foresee the fundamental problems that socialism would confront as an economic and social system. In *Economy and Society*, Weber details the problem of economic calculation that socialism would not be able to solve (1922, vol. 1, pp. 86–107). In this line of argument, Weber was repeating the argument made by Ludwig von Mises (1920 and 1922). Mises' argument was then further elaborated on by Hayek during the socialist calculation debate of the 1930s and 1940s (Hayek 1948).

The most important component of the Mises–Hayek argument was the functional significance that they placed on the institution of private property and the rule of law. Property rights protected by the rule of law provide

1   legal certainty, which encourages investment;
2   a motivation for responsible decision-making on behalf of owners;
3   the background for social experimentation, which spurs progress; and
4   the basis for economic calculation by expanding the context within which price – and profit-and-loss – signals can reasonably guide resource use.

Moreover, it was precisely because economic life is dynamic and in a constant state of flux that the clearly defined property rights embedded in the rule of law are fundamental to a sustainable political economy.

Far from the armchair theorizing that this critique of socialism was accused of, the Mises–Hayek argument was grounded in an appreciation of economic, political and social history. Their argument was consistent with the one found in the historical literature on the rise of the West.[6] The flip-side of the critique was a positive vision of how European liberalism developed and provided the institutional framework for economic development.

Capitalism developed in some regions and not in others precisely because certain institutionalized practices which were conducive to economic experimentation were adopted and reinforced. Market exchange, for example, existed throughout world history. Monetary circulation and even certain elementary banking operations existed for centuries. However, the development of capitalism went beyond the mere existence of market activity.

What we find in common to the historical examples of economic "take-off" in the West is the development of a respect for private property embodied in a rule of law. It seems sensible to reassert the hypothesis that economic take-off is associated with the extension of property ownership to capital goods. As property ownership is respected in goods further remote from consumption,

242 Calculation and Coordination

then practices emerge which lead to development. The banking system, for example, is transformed so as to provide an additional role as a financial intermediary – private savings are channeled into investment funds. The transformed banking system facilitates the growth of the capital market. Longer-term investments in productive activity (which promise greater returns in consumer goods) are undertaken and prove to be the vehicle through which sustainable growth is achieved.[7]

The extension of property ownership to capital resources is fundamental for several reasons. First, recognized property ownership establishes the legal certainty necessary for individuals to commit resources.[8] The threat of confiscation, by either other market participants or political actors, undermines confidence in market activity and limits investment possibilities. Individuals tend to get around the lack of *de jure* property rights through:

1   the tacit acceptance of *de facto rights*, which is self-enforced because of the discipline of repeated dealings;
2   the use of extensive family networks (kinship); and
3   the employment of extra-legal contract enforcement.

This activity allows markets to develop without clear property ownership, and these markets may even provide the base for the legal order that may later appear. Nevertheless, markets without clearly defined rules tend to be limited and constrained as vehicles for economic development.[9]

Second, recognized property generates incentives for the use of scarce resources that markets without recognized property do not possess. If we absent property rights, for example, the time discount on resource use will tend to be higher, and resource conservation will be discouraged. With clear property ownership, however, economic actors possess an incentive to pay close attention to resource use and the discounted value of the future employment of scarce resources.

Third, recognized property is a precondition for the emergence of stable capital markets. The market for capital goods establishes the exchange ratios for scarce resources (reflected in the relative money price of capital goods) which guide investment activity. In other words, recognized property rights in the means of production, combined with a sound monetary system, allow the process of economic calculation to work. Economic calculation provides economic actors with vital knowledge, which enables the social system of production to separate out from among the numerous array of technologically feasible projects those projects which are economically feasible. Without this process of economic calculation, as Mises often stated, industrial production would be reduced to so many steps in the dark.

Finally, secure property rights provide the foundation for the establishment of the fiscal nation state. The elimination of arbitrary confiscation and the establishment of regular taxation at announced rates enabled merchants to calculate the present value of investment decisions and pass judgment on alternative allocations of capital. This leads to economic progress, as I have argued above, but, more to the present point, even the ruler found this substitution in his/her interest. The ruler learned, as David Landes put it, "that it was easier and in the long run more profitable to expropriate with indemnification rather than confiscate, to take by law or judicial proceedings rather than by seizure. Above all, he came to rely on regular taxes at stipulated rates rather than on emergency exactions of indefinite amount" (1969, pp. 16–17). The older, arbitrary method of raising revenue was in some sense less burdensome on the ruler's subjects, since it extracted a smaller sum of their wealth, but the uncertainty associated with the older method diverted investment into activities which were easily concealed from the ruler. The diverting of investment in this manner, however, severely constrained the wealth-creating activity of individuals. The older method of raising revenue (precisely because of the incentive effect it engendered), according to Landes' interpretation of history, proved to be a hindrance to economic development and, as evidence, he points to the experience of the great Asian empires and the Muslim states of the Middle East (which maintained the old system) in comparison with that of Europe (which substituted the new system). In addition, without the substitution of fixed rates for discretionary levies, public resistance and the cumulative disruptive effect on economic activity would threaten the monarch's ability to provide for its own defense.

The rise of the nation-state and its correlation with the development of capitalism necessitates clarification of the particular historical conditions present in the West at this time. Europe was fragmented into a multitude of states and principalities. This polycentricism was essential for providing the competition between the various monarchies and city-states. Competition among the political leaders constrained their behaviour. It is highly doubtful that if Europe was instead unified as one empire that capitalist progress would have occurred there.

Competition is one of the most important processes through which we learn to live and organize our affairs.[10] Markets are learning devices that rely on competition not only to mobilize existing information, but also to discover information that would otherwise have remained hidden from view. Political competition is also important. Competition among localities and regions sets in motion a discovery procedure that provides individuals with the incentives to reveal information through their actions concerning the level of public services and the role of the state.

In providing for political competition, federalist political institutions seem to be the most effective devised so far.[11] In fact, the economic take-off of Holland, Great Britain, and the United States (the three richest countries in the last few centuries respectively) can be dated to their adoption of federalist-type institutions, and the relative decline of these countries can also be correlated with the breakdown of those very institutions. Federalism, thus, provides a time-tested model of political institutions that are conducive to economic development.[12]

Conclusion

Discrediting the Soviet model not only questions the viability of central planning models of development, but the entire array of command and control approaches to economic policy in general. Economic and social progress lie beyond the direct control of government officials. The positive role that state officials can play in economic development is limited.

Rather than command and control, the agenda for studying economic development that I have alluded to appears to suggest that state action be limited to the establishment of rules which cultivate economic experimentation and competition. Property rights need to be clearly defined and strictly enforced. Economic progress is a function of the "rules of the game." Legal, political, and cultural institutions combine to provide the effective rules within any society, and as such determine whether that society will progress or stagnate.

The uninhibited state of development planning models simply does not provide the appropriate institutional environment for economic progress.[13] Arbitrary behavior on the part of the government deters investment and retards experimentation. On the other hand, the implicit constraints on state action provided by cultural and religious traditions (the inhibited state) can be relied on only up to a point. Economic development demands that anonymous economic transactions can be imbued with trust. Kinship as an economic organization overcomes credible commitment problems, but only in small-scale instances. Economic progress requires that the implicit constraints of custom be codified in an explicit body of law. The establishment of a rule of law transforms the inhibited state into a subordinated one. It is in the subordinated state that the foundation for economic progress and development is laid. Transparency of the law, sound monetary policy, and restricted fiscal policy are the key political elements.

There remains, however, an open question with regard to development that is particularly relevant for our time. Can one move directly from an uninhibited state to a subordinated state? My own predilection would be to suggest that the subordinated state cannot emerge unless it is grounded first in an inhibited state. In other words, cultural practices and spontaneous social arrangements must already exist which encourage and sustain production and exchange before explicit rules can be codified in the law and be binding on individual behaviour. Thus, social progress and development are a function of indigenous institutions, and cannot be imposed from above. But, given the fact that not all cultural practices, belief systems, or folk traditions are favorable to economic development, some societies seem destined to poverty and squalor unless the institutional infrastructure is allowed to gradually change. To see whether this conjecture is warranted, scholars will have to give priority to historical background and view economic development as an ongoing process.

Appendix: The argument applied to post-perestroika Russia

In the spring of 1993, while watching the *McNeil–Lehrer News Hour*, I was struck by how the question of Russia highlights the difficulties of cross-disciplinary discourse. Harvard economist and Yeltsin advisor Jeffrey Sachs was a guest on the news show, along with Princeton political historian and Sovietologist Stephen Cohen. Cohen, who was (is) an unreconstructed Gorbachev supporter, was attacking the Yeltsin program of "shock therapy." Russian history, Cohen stated bluntly, dictates an alternative path of development. Sachs, on the other hand, pointed out that economic theory predicts that when the money supply is doubled the general price level will double, and that this prediction is borne out across time and place. Price liberalization, tight monetary policy, fiscal balance, and mass privatization were the path to Russian prosperity, Sachs argued forcefully. "You may have economic theory," Cohen retorted, "but we are talking about 1,000 years of Russian history."

The problem was not just that they were talking past one another. The problem was that they were both right and wrong. Sachs was certainly right that economic theory provides important insights about the effect of incentives on human behavior, and Cohen was right to stress that Russian history and culture matter. Both are wrong, however, to the extent that they believe these arguments to be mutually exclusive. Russian history and culture matter precisely because of the institutional imprint and the effect of that imprint on the incentive structure individuals face. The argument of this chapter, in fact, emphasizes the theoretical import of history and culture for development economics. Sachs is guilty of disregarding history and culture, and Cohen is guilty of disregarding economics, and it is this gap between the disciplines (and the corresponding suspicion of the other that it engenders) that undermines the kind of interdisciplinary research on developmental questions that I allude to in the main body of this chapter.

In order to understand economic development we must respect the history and culture of a people, especially how this manifests itself in the indigenous institutions of the society under study. Political and economic reforms, however correct in their abstract design, will not produce the intended results unless they are able to tap into the customary practices and indigenous institutions of a society. Custom provides the foundation for sustainable liberal revolution.[14]

The problem with the Yeltsin political and economic reforms, however, is not just limited to the issue of Russian history and culture. Yeltsin's transformation program, like the Gorbachev reform program before, has not been implemented as announced.[15] The Yeltsin "shock therapy" was ill-conceived and contradictory from the beginning.[16]

Moreover, without the appropriate political changes, the economic reforms could not be implemented as the situation dictated. In combination with the economic environment, the political crisis increased the uncertainty of the situation. The "War of Decrees" between the Parliament and the President was not the only problem. Many of Yeltsin's decrees that did emerge were simply inconsistent with basic economic incentives. Tax rates and other business fees, for example, are inconsistent with the goal of attracting business investment. Foreign investment was deterred by both economic and political uncertainty.[17]

The vacuum of power in the central government and the fiscal crisis the center has experienced led regional authorities to claim more autonomy. Effective governmental power in Russia shifted to the regional leaders. As the events of late September and early October 1993 demonstrate, the uncertainty of the transition policy has not been overcome, and the relationship between the center and the regions still needs to be settled. Historical perspective would suggest that this troubling uncertainty is natural during a time of regime change, and that there is no spontaneous mechanism that guarantees a benign outcome.[18] It took over sixty years of turmoil in England, for example, until the constitutional bargain of the Glorious Revolution was struck in 1688, and economic productivity then increased markedly.[19]

That history offers us no easy and fixed rules for moving from an autocratic government and state-run economy to liberal political and economic arrangements, does not change the basic message that I tried to convey in this chapter – political rules must be established which effectively constrain the discretionary behaviour of the government, and a clear and well-defined (i.e. transparent) legal system must be constructed before private-sector economic experimentation can be expected to yield the welfare gains promised.

Acknowledgments

I have benefited greatly from various conversations concerning economic development and social evolution with Hilton Root, Thomas Metzger, Ramon Myers, Robert Conquest, and Ralph Raico. I would also like to thank E. S. Djimopoulos for helpful suggestions on an earlier draft. Financial assistance from the National Fellows program at the Hoover Institution and the Earhart Foundation is gratefully acknowledged. Responsibility for remaining errors is exclusively my own.

References

Arrant, H. A. W. (1981) "Economic Development: A Semantic History," *Economic Development and Cultural Change* April: 457–66.

Boettke, P. J. (1990) *The Political Economy of Soviet Socialism: The Formative Years, 1918–1928*, Boston: Kluwer Academic Publishers.

Boettke, P. J. (1993) *Why Perestroika Failed: The Politics and Economics of Socialist Transformation*, London: Routledge.

Boettke, P. J. (ed.) (1994) *The Collapse of Development Planning*, New York: New York University Press.

Domar, E. (1957) *Essays in the Theory of Economic Growth*, New York: Oxford University Press.

Erlich, A. (1960) *The Soviet Industrialization Debate, 1924–1928*, Cambridge, MA: Harvard University Press.

Garrison, R. (1984) "Time and Money: the Universals in Macroeconomic Theorizing," *Journal of Macroeconomics* 6(2): 197–213.

Hayek, F. A. von (1948) *Individualism and Economic Order*, Chicago: University of Chicago Press, Chicago.

Hayek, F. A. von (1978) "Competition as a Discovery Procedure," in *New Studies in Politics, Philosophy, Economics and the History of Ideas*, Chicago: University of Chicago Press.

Khanin, G. and Selyunin, V. (1987) "The Elusive Figure," *The Current Digest of the Soviet Press* 39(25): 10–12.

Kirzner, I. (1994) "The Limits of the Market: The Real and The Imagined," in W. Möschel, M. Streit and U. Witt (eds.) *Marktwirischaft und Rechtsordnung*, Baden-Baden: Verlagsgesellschaft, pp. 101–10.

Knight, F. (1936) "The Place of Marginal Economics in a Collectivist System," *American Economic Review* 26(1): 255–66.

Landes, D. (1969) *The Unbound Prometheus*, Cambridge, UK: Cambridge University Press.

Lange, O. (1970) (first published 1939) *On the Economic Theory of Socialism*, New York: Augustus M. Kelley.

Mises, L. von (1935) (first published 1920) "Economic Calculation in the Socialist Commonwealth," translated and reprinted in F. A. von Hayek (ed.) *Collectivist Economic Planning*, London: Routledge.

Mises, L. von (1981) (first published 1922) *Socialism: An Economic and Sociological Analysis*, Indianapolis, IN: Liberty Classics.

North, D. and Weingast, B. (1989) "Constitutions and Commitment: The Evolution of Institutions Governing Public Choice in Seventeenth-century England," *Journal of Economic History* December: 803–32.

Nove, A. (1984) (first published 1969) *An Economic History of the U.S.S.R.*, New York: Penguin Books.

Nutter, G. W. (1962) *The Growth of Industrial Production in the Soviet Union*, Princeton, NJ: Princeton University Press.

Rosenberg, N. and Birdzell, L. E. (1986) *How the West Grew Rich*, New York: Basic Books.

Schumpeter, J. (1942) *Capitalism, Socialism and Democracy*, New York: Harper & Row.

Smith, A. (1776/1976) *An Inquiry into the Nature and Causes of the Wealth of Nations*, Chicago: University of Chicago Press, 1976.

Weber, M. (1961) *General Economic History*, New York: Collier Books.

Weber, M. (1978) (first published 1922) *Economy and Society*, two volumes, Berkeley, CA: University of California Press.

15 Why culture matters

Economics, politics, and the imprint of history*

Is there some action a government of India could take that would lead the Indian economy to grow like Indonesia's or Egypt's? If so, *what*, exactly? If not, what is it about the "nature of India" that makes it so? The consequences for human welfare involved in questions like these are simply staggering: Once one starts to think about them, it is hard to think about anything else.

(Lucas 1988, p. 5)

Social theory has here much to learn from the two young sciences of ethology and cultural anthropology which in many respects have built on the foundations of social theory initially laid in the eighteenth century by the Scottish moral philosophers. ... The chief points on which the comparative study of behavior has thrown such important light on the evolution of law are, first, that it has made clear that individuals had to learn to observe (and enforce) rules of conduct long before such rules could be expressed in words; and second, that these rules had evolved because they led to the formation of an order of the activities of the group as a whole which, although they are the results of the regularities of the actions of individuals, must be clearly distinguished from them, since it is the efficiency of the resulting order of actions which will determine whether groups whose members observe certain rules of conduct will prevail.

(Hayek 1973, pp. 73–4)

Introduction

In this age of a shrinking globe, where world news travels almost instantaneously and computers link individuals from one continent to another, and financial markets follow developments from the most mature industrial democracies to the newly emerging market economies, why don't all economies converge to a single economic growth path? As Gregory Mankiw has recently stated: "It is apparent to anyone who travels the world that these large differences in income (i.e. the fact that average incomes in the richest countries are more than ten times as high as in the poorest) lead to large differences in the quality of life. Less apparent are the reasons for these differences. What is it about the United

*Originally published as Boettke, P. J. (1996) "L'economia, la Politica e il Segno della Storia," *Nuova Economia e Storia* 3: 189–214.

States, Japan and Germany that makes these countries so much richer than India, Indonesia, and Nigeria? How can the rich countries be sure to maintain their high standard of living? What can the poor countries do to join the club?" (Mankiw 1995, p. 275).

Why can't economics – a discipline that has at least for two hundred years attempted to do so – explain the nature and causes of the wealth of nations in an unambiguous manner? Or are these questions just intellectual puzzles that we have invented for ourselves? Mankiw (1995, pp. 303–7), for example, highlights three problems that exist in the econometrics literature on growth (simultaneity, multicollinearity, and degrees of freedom). These problems question the ability of the "data" to adjudicate between different hypotheses on the causes of growth and development. But, as Mankiw states: "It is not that we have to stop asking so many questions about economic growth. We just have to stop expecting the international data to give us all the answers" (1995, p. 307). That conclusion, of course, depends on what the analyst means by "data" and "empirical" analysis. Aggregate macroeconomic data are not the only data available from which we can learn about the nature and causes of the wealth of nations – we can approach the question in a *multidisciplinary* manner and incorporate arguments and empirical information developed in other areas of the social sciences, such as the results of case studies and the evidence gleaned from ethnography. In fact, a plausible argument can be made that the techniques and data we economists have come to rely on are too "thin" for our own good, and that perhaps it is high time that we sought the "thicker" description provided by an ethnographic turn (see Mischel 1996). In making this turn, individual decision-making is not to be overlooked, but the context of decision moves to the center of analysis as opposed to the behavioral assumptions, and economic actions are recognized as embedded within an environment, rather than disembedded and abstract. In other words, there is no necessary reason to jettison the methodological individualism – the hallmark of rational-choice social science – but the methodological individualism practiced would not be the atomistic individualism of mainstream price theory. A more institutional individualism – which steers between both atomistic individualism and holistic institutionalism – emerges as the basic methodological starting point of analysis for political economy and social theory (see Boettke 1989a, 1989b, 1990b).

Context matters for economic outcomes. The question does not turn on whether actors are more or less rational due to cultural background. The question turns on how alternative institutional contexts affect economic performance. We now have significant empirical evidence that the socialist model of planned industrialization doesn't hold the answer to economic development (see, for example, Boettke 1990a, 1993, 1994). There are even significant theoretical arguments and factual evidence that what we once thought of (however begrudgingly) as Soviet industrial development was manufactured mismeasurement (see Boettke 1993, pp. 21–32). On the other hand, we *do know* that market economies within a rule of law which protect private property rights and freedom of contract do demonstrate robust growth and lift the masses of such societies from subsistence and the struggle for daily survival.[1] In a recent work by James Gwartney, Robert Lawson, and Walter Block (1996), which explored the relationship between public policy and economic development world-wide, the findings presented were unambiguous. Countries which adopted policies which fit with the Gwartney *et al.* definition of economic freedom – namely personal choice, protection of private property, and freedom of exchange – outperformed countries which failed to adopt such policies. The components of their index included measures on how well the policy regime:

1   protected money as a store of value and medium of exchange;
2   ensured the freedom to decide what is produced and consumed;
3   limited discretionary taxation and regulatory/legal takings so that individuals could keep what they earned; and
4   maintained open borders for trade so that individuals were free to exchange with foreign parties.

Each country was graded according to this index, and then the Economic Freedom grade was correlated with the Summers and Heston, Penn World Tables data on economic growth. As measured in 1985 US dollars, the average per capita GDP by 1995 Economic Freedom generated the results depicted in Figure 15.1.

This is not just the ideological wishful thinking on the part of classical liberal economists, it is an empirical proposition (also see Berger 1986). Where is the example to the contrary? Where has an economic system which can be characterized as respecting private property, maintaining sound money, free pricing, and freedom of contract (including trade liberalization) collapsed into

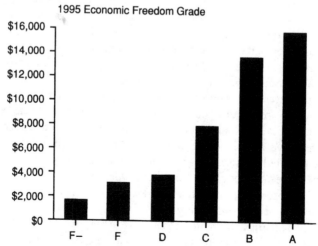

Figure 15.1 Economic freedom and per capita GDP

economic depravation? Certainly the experience in the former Soviet-type economies and in so-called Third World experiments with development planning reflects poorly on the model of collective property, restrictions on trade, and governmental planning of economic life.

If this empirical proposition is right, then part of the puzzle mentioned above is solved. Economies don't converge because they fail to adopt "correct" public polices.[2] However, this only pushes the question back to another puzzle. If we *know what* is necessary to make a miracle, then why don't we *know how* to make one? If the benefits from expanding the market are so overwhelmingly obvious upon reflection, then why don't all economic policy-makers converge to the "correct" set of policies? Robert Lucas (1993) in a paper entitled "Making a Miracle" put the matter simply – if we know what it takes to make an economic miracle, we should be able to make one. Who could doubt such straightforward reasoning?

But policies counter to economic logic are introduced every day throughout the world, and economic theory is hard pressed to provide an adequate answer (Rodrik 1996). Hard public choice logic can only get us so far in offering an explanation.[3] It is true that the logic of concentrated benefits and dispersed costs is a formidable enemy to a democratically stable minimal state. There doesn't appear to be a sustainable winning coalition for the minimal state that can emerge out of normal democratic politics for more than fleeting moments, and such a fleeting coalition is certainly vulnerable in times of political crisis, especially war (see Higgs 1987). The trend line of government involvement in the economic system is always upward sloping, but the great growth of government appears to result from the ratcheting up of government in times of crisis and the inability of democratic system to ratchet down after the crisis is over.

But autocratic governments don't suffer from this sort of "democratic sclerosis" so why don't they adopt the more encompassing perspective and simply establish an optimal tax? The autocratic government – under the assumption of a secure time horizon – will secure the greatest amount of revenue by ensuring the highest possible growth of Q (output) and simply establishing an appropriate extraction rate t (see Olson 1993, and McGuire and Olson 1996). Why don't we see this outcome more often?

To start to grope for an answer to that question, what must be done is to square two seemingly contradictory propositions in a non-*ad hoc* manner. Namely, the propositions:

1   that we *know* more of *what* it takes to create an "economic miracle" than we often admit as economic scientists;
2   that we *know* less about *how* to make an "economic miracle" than we want to admit as economic policy-makers.

In demonstrating how both of these propositions can be correct, we must maintain the contrast between *know what* (or *know that*) versus *know how*.[4] This distinction in the types of knowledge that we possess both as scientists and as actors within the model must be incorporated into our thinking about the social world if we hope to avoid the "constructivist" errors about which Hayek so often warned us. In doing so, perhaps we can offer an economic and epistemological argument for the lack of convergence between countries that is not only consistent with both propositions, but actually unifies these propositions within an analytical framework.

Culture as the core concept and the economist's critique

Could it be that the answer as to why economies diverge rather than converge in terms of economic growth lies outside of economic logic and rests instead in the fuzzy area of culture and history? The institutionalist critique of economics is that culture is a core concept that has been eliminated in the striving for a universal explanation (see Mayhew 1987). Mayhew's argument is more subtle than I will present here, but the basic argument does boil down to the claim that "the core idea of culture comes under subtle attack when insistence upon the universality of instrumental reasoning becomes insistence upon the universality and centrality of a rational strategy of human behavior and when the study of rational strategy comes to be seen as *the* important task of social science" (Ibid. p. 587, emphasis in original). Thus, the diversity of mankind defeats the striving for a universal explanation, and what standard economists assume as characteristics of human nature are instead behavioral regularities that are specific to time and place and persist because of enculturation. Outside of the particular time and place and the enculturation processes of the specific historical period, the assumptions of economic theory (as standard theory understands them) do not hold. In other words, outside of Western capitalism, principles of economic theory do not hold. Of course, the institutionalist argument would be even stronger than that – challenging even the idea that standard theory describes Western capitalism – but this would be a minimum implication of the argument. Beyond developed capitalism, economic theory doesn't hold. One cannot look to economic theory to solve the problems of poverty and deprivation in non-Western cultures. Solutions there must be found in the historical and cultural practices of the time and place under consideration. Culture and historicity are the core concepts of social analysis.

The problems with this reliance on culture as the core concept is that it ignores what we do know from cross-sectional and time series analysis of economic development. Consider, for example, the classic economist rebuttal to cultural critics – the case of the three China's: mainland China, Taiwan, and Hong Kong (see Rabushka 1987). Under the reasonable assumption that the populations of these three regions are more or less homogeneous, sharing a similar cultural heritage, an examination of the development pattern of these regions shows radical differences based on the economic institutions adopted. Rising above poverty is a consequence of adopting economic institutions approximating the private property, free pricing, sound money, open trade program mentioned above. Economic backwardness is a consequence of deviation from that institutional recipe.

The gulf between Mayhew and Rabushka simply reflects the classic social science dichotomy between "thick" and "thin" description.[5] Economists possess a penchant for "thin" description (and the scientific value of parsimony), while area studies scholars and historians value "thick" description (and the scholarly value of thoroughness). The social scientific methodological question for over a century has been whether meaningful "thick" description is possible without the guidance of "thin" description (see Geertz 1973, pp. 3–30, and Hirschman 1986, pp. 142–60). On the one hand, "thin" description unconcerned with the underlying reality conveyed in "thick" descriptions describes little of relevance to our daily lives.[6] On the other hand, "thick" description unaided by an articulated theory cannot help but bring on-board theoretical baggage that defies critical scrutiny. The social world is far too complex to access directly; our understanding must of necessity be theory-impregnated.

We need, in other words, both "thin" and "thick" description for our social theory to possess both meaning and relevance – coherence and correspondence so to speak. To put it bluntly, if there was nothing universal in the human experience (the basis for "thin" description) then even our "thick" description of different people would remain beyond our ability to understand. Alien cultural practices would forever remain *alien* and inaccessible to others. At the same time, if all there was to the human condition was the universal, then culture and history and area studies in general would disappear. We could learn as much about a people by sitting at our computer as we could by studying their history. Both extremes of exclusivity in social explanation are obviously to be avoided. We need universal theory to understand, but we need uniqueness to whet our desire to understand *the other*. We are enough alike to learn from one another, but we are also different enough so as to have something to learn.

Thus, contrary to my non-subtle reading of the institutionalist critique of economics, economic theory must not be contrasted against the diversity of humanity and the particularities of time and place.[7] Instead, economic theory is a necessary (though not sufficient) component of a social analysis which hopes to make sense of that human diversity and the particularities of the human experience. Institutions are constraints as well as shapers of human behavior, and social analysis must be prepared to deal with this complex interaction. The justification of the "thin description" of economic theory is that it affords us more compelling "thick descriptions" of the social experience of particular times and places. Rather than denying, for example, that principles of economics apply because cultural commitments preclude the buying and selling of cattle in Africa, we must open our eyes to the lived experience of Africans who trade their cattle in unlicenced markets. Fieldwork and ethnographic study, in this case, lead to an appreciation of the applicability of economic theory (see Bates 1990). The *de facto* everyday life of a people is what we want to understand, not the official life as dictated by government. In the former Soviet Union, for example, private property and markets were *de jure* non-existent, yet *de facto* attenuated private property and black markets were the primary organizing principles of social order (see Boettke 1993, pp. 57–72). The experience in both Africa and the former Soviet Union (and elsewhere throughout the world, from local trading in primitive bazaars to the high finance of the international currency exchanges) suggests that markets exist everywhere and always, but not all markets are equal with regard to the properties of providing for overall progress and prosperity. Economic principles hold, but the welfare properties that we associate with economic arrangements are a function of the institutional arrangement within which economic life is played out.[8] Moreover, the legitimacy of particular institutional arrangements within a people is a function of the "culture" of a people.

Rules and the epistemology of custom

The argument presented so far can be summed up in the following basic statement:

Economic performance is a function of the rules of the game.

Rules influence the strategies that players will employ, and the strategies that the players employ reflect back on the desirability of the rules. We can study the evolution of basketball rules, for example, as a concern with the fairness and interest in the game under one set of rules when players (and coaches) discovered ways to exploit the existing rules to their advantage. Changes in the rules do not transform the nature of the players, but they do affect what strategies the players perceive as productive. Another way of stating the proposition above is simply to insist on the basic economic insight that *people respond rationally to incentives as they perceive them.*

"Rationally" in this formulation is nothing more than a basic notion of instrumental rationality, and must be understood as entirely individually subjective and forward-looking. Only individuals act, and in acting they weigh the costs and benefits of alternative ways to arrange their means to obtain the ends they seek. Their perception of the costs and benefits depends on the institutional context of their choices. The institutional context of choice is defined by the rules (both explicit and implicit) of the social game that the individual is playing.

Economics is quite good at examining the consequences of alternative rules. But can economics help us understand why some rules can "stick" in one particularity, yet possess no meaning in another? What is required is a theory of institutional change and *acceptability*. Institutions, following the New Institutionalist literature, are defined as those formal and informal rules which govern human behavior. Culture, as I am discussing the term, refers to those beliefs and ritual practices which legitimate institutions. In order to develop a theory of institutional change and acceptability, institutions must be linked to culture. This is where the work of Menger, Mises, and Hayek may provide insights which could improve our account of social evolution. The example most often used in the Austrian literature of spontaneous-grown institutions is money, although Hayek has extended the argument to law and markets in general. In Menger's theory of money, a common medium of exchange emerges out of a barter economy as individuals strive to overcome the double-coincidence of wants. By holding more and more marketable commodities, individuals find that this expands their range of choices in the market and fuels the expansion of the division of labor in society. Individuals who hold more marketable goods as vehicles for *indirect* exchange do "better," and through a process of imitation the participants in the social process will settle on a common medium of exchange, *even though no one person sought to invent money.* Menger's theory demonstrated that money could indeed evolve spontaneously within the economic interaction of people – a central authority need not design and create money.

Mises interpreted the implication of Menger's theory in even stronger terms. Mises offered as an additional aspect of Menger's theory the "regression theorem". Technically, Mises' "regression theorem" employed marginal utility theory to monetary analysis in order to offer an explanation out of the circularity problem associated with the value of money. The value of money is determined by the purchasing power of money yesterday, but that is determined by the value of money. As Rothbard stated: "But how, then, can value scales and utilities be used to explain the formation of money prices, when these value scales and utilities themselves depend upon the existence of money prices?" (Rothbard 1993, p. 231). The circularity problem – that X depends on Y, while Y depends on X – permeates all exchanges in a monetary economy. Mises was able to offer a solution to the problem by introducing the time component into the analysis of the formation of monetary prices. The reason why the introduction of time into the analysis doesn't just push the explanation back further is that the regression is not infinite. The value of money is rooted in both its exchange value and its historical value as a commodity under the conditions of a barter economy. The implication of which Mises argued was that "Business usage alone can transform a commodity into a common medium of exchange. It is not the state, but the common practices of all those who have dealings in the market that creates money" (1912/1980, p. 93). Not only did Mises' theorem confirm Menger's theory of the evolution of money, it also refuted alternative theories which argued that the state could consciously create a monetary system through a general agreement independent of commercial activity. In other words, whereas Menger's theory argued that commercial activity *could* generate a monetary unit, Mises' theory argued that the state *could not* create a monetary unit outside the context of the accepted practice of commercial life. *It was epistemologically impossible for the State to create a common medium of exchange outside the context of exchange practice.*

Mises' further development of Menger's theory of money was not limited to monetary theory, but permeated his formulation of the theory of monetary calculation within the market process. The evolution of money made possible the expanding of the division of labor and more roundabout processes of production which led to economic development. Monetary calculation, in Mises' formulation of the market process, is the key "aid to the human mind" which afforded advanced production and rational calculation of alternative investment opportunities by economic actors (see Mises 1922/1981, part II). In fact, Mises did not simply extol the virtues of the division of labor as the engine of economic growth, he exalted the division of labor to the central position in the general theory of social cooperation (see Mises 1949, pp. 143–76). The foundations of the liberal order were the recognized benefits of specialization and exchange and the institutional preconditions necessary to realize those benefits, i.e. the respect for private property that emerged through the discipline of repeated dealings in the market.[9]

Thus, in Mises' rendering, commercial life and modern civilization were the outcome of a process rooted in the trading behavior of individuals and the expansion of that trading circle made possible by the emergence of a common medium of exchange. Outside the development of commercial norms of behavior (and the evolution of institutions which afford and re-enforce these norms), trading life would be severely restricted and economic development beyond simple production would not be sustainable. Monetary calculation, in Mises' theory of economic interaction, is "the intellectual basis of the market economy" (1949, p. 259). This, of course, is the foundational proposition which underlies Mises' famous critique of socialism. Socialism would have to forgo the "intellectual division of labor" of the liberal order that was made possible by monetary calculation. Aspects of this argument, however, permeate Mises' theory of interventionism and his theory of the unhampered market economy.[10]

Hayek also used Menger's theory of money as a general exemplar of his research program, and he produced a particular argument about how the common law developed. But aspects of Hayek's argument with regard to the law also map Mises' regression theorem – although, to my knowledge, Hayek never made this connection. In Hayek's work on the law there is a contrast between *law* and *legislation*. Law emerges out of the evolution of the judge-made common law, whereas legislation is imposed from outside the problem-solving situation of judges resolving disputes. Legislation has the power to thoroughly corrupt the social learning process embedded in customary rules. As Hayek put it: "The basic tools of civilization – language, morals, law and money – are all the result of spontaneous growth and not of design, and of the last two organized power has got hold and thoroughly corrupted them" (Hayek, 1979, p. 163).

Customary rules emerge from within a particular history and reflect the practices of a people as they attempt to resolve disputes. As one contemporary law and economics scholar has written: "Customary law is recognized not because it is backed by the power of some strong individual or institution, but because each individual recognizes the benefits of behaving in accordance with other individuals' expectations, *given* that others also behave as he expects. Alternatively, if a minority coercively imposes law from above, then that law will require much more force to maintain social order than is required when law develops from the bottom through mutual recognition and acceptance" (Benson 1990, p. 12). It is the reciprocal nature of the benefits of customary law that bind individuals to the system. The common law taps into the social learning embedded in custom as judges attempt to formally articulate what was previously held tacitly among social participants in a particular setting – it is in this sense that they *discover* the law.

Market transactions exist across cultures and in all conceivable situations, but the rules which permit the transformation of market transactions into commercial progress must be ones which "stick" (see Boettke 1994a and 1994b). It is not due to an intellectual argument against "Western imperialism" that we must recognize that development is not an issue of simply either writing down the constitutional rules of a Western-style democracy or copying the economic institutions of capitalism, but rather an *epistemological argument* about rules. It is true that economic performance is a function of rules, but rules are a function of "culture." Economic, political, and legal reforms are not just abstract impositions, but rather a process of growing economic, political, and legal institutions within the native soil. Thus, we can conjecture a second – and just as fundamental – statement:

Rules are only RULES if customary practice dictates.

There simply is no way to establish binding rules except through the translation of customary practice into rules of social interaction.[11] As Hayek emphasized in many places, we did not design rules through our reason, but rather we developed reason because we followed rules. This is not conservatism, because no social rule is exempt from our critical scrutiny, but it is a position which insists that the critique must of necessity always privilege some rule context while holding others up for examination – it is impossible to step outside of all context and employ *reason*. The *critical rationalist*, as opposed to the *rational constructivist*, realizes that social experimentation takes place against a backdrop of the customary beliefs and traditions of society. Experimentation cannot be of the root and branch sort, but instead is limited to bold acts on the margin which, if successful, often loop back and mutate previously held beliefs, thus leading to social change. Constructed, large-scale, attempts at social change which are not rooted in the *de facto* norms of existence of the current order are destined to disrupt social order and retard – rather than promote – social betterment.[12]

This is not an easy conclusion for a classical liberal political economist, such as Hayek, to reach. The promise of material progress is not just a matter of adopting certain rules of the game, such as private property and freedom of contract. Economics may establish the properties of alternative rules, but culture and the imprint of history determine which rules can *stick* in certain environments.[13] The problem is not one of private property and freedom of contract generating perverse consequences, but the fact that some social conventions and customary practices simply do not legitimate these institutions.[14] If market transactions – which are universal – are constrained to a *sub rosa* existence, then commercial life and development will be limited. To move from that *sub rosa* existence, legal–political institutions must be adopted, but such adoption is only possible if there is a cultural fit.[15]

One cannot step outside of history and design the appropriate development path. We may *know which* institutions are more amenable to wealth creation and material progress, but that doesn't mean that transformation is simply a task of "institution building." Of course, institution building – including questions of political governance – is a key factor in development (probably *the* key variable under our "control"), but some cultures are hostile and the necessary rules will not stick. This conclusion mirrors Hayek's other critical theory tension within the classical liberal project – that of moral rules for the extended order of the Great Society (see Hayek 1976, pp. 133–52). If we are a product of rules that emerged in our evolutionary past, then we may be "hardwired" genetically for the face-to-face society of our tribal past. Modern life, on the other hand, demands that we develop moral rules for the anonymous society of the extended order. Thus, we are in tension with ourselves. Our survival now depends on the maintenance of the extended order, yet our inner selves long for a tribal past. In other words, even when the culture legitimates the institutions of commercial society, a tension exists between the abstract rules of the extended order and our atavistic urge for the intimate order.

Similarly, we may know what it takes economically speaking to create an economic miracle, even though we cannot create one as we desire. The liberal promise – the simultaneous and mutually reinforcing project of individual liberty, economic prosperity, and peaceful coexistence between peoples and nations – can only be fulfilled if a people's customary norms and belief systems are so inclined to legitimate liberalism.[16] Lifting a people from beneath the struggle for survival is rare in history and is by no means a universal promise to all. The *only* path is an indigenous one, independent of whether it is one of progress or stagnation.[17]

In other words, we can assume that policy-makers possess only the best intentions, and that they *know what* it takes to make an economic miracle, but they will still be humbled in the face of social reality, as the *know how* of economic miracles lies beyond their ability to articulate, let alone control. In fact, and in an ironic manner, it is precisely because our *know how* of social cooperation exceeds our *know what* of social cooperation that the social dilemma can be overcome and advanced material production can be accomplished. As Peter Berger has argued, "it is quite clear that the state as such is not the bearer of development. At best, states can institute policies that *leave room* for the real agents of development – enterprising individuals, families, clans, *compadre* groupings, and other traditional units, and more modern associations such as cooperatives or credit unions" (Berger 1985, p. 14).[18]

Some illustrative examples

The focal argument that I have made so far can be restated as follows:

1 People respond rationally to incentives.
2 Incentives are a function of the rules of the game.
3 Rules are only RULES if customary practice dictates.

Combine this argument with the subsidiary arguments that the international aggregate data (even if we put aside the problems of aggregation in general) cannot unambiguously arbitrate between competing hypotheses on the nature and causes of the wealth of nations, and that this sort of data cannot reach the customary foundations of the rule regime, and the upshot of the argument is that if we want to understand why some countries are poor, while others are rich, and perhaps, even more importantly, why some that were poor became rich, while others that were rich became relatively poor, then we have to open ourselves up to alternative forms of empirical argument.[19] We have to find a way to understand the ideas, beliefs, habits that are indigenous to an area, and then see how the political, legal, and economic institutions that are correlated with economic development fit in to the social ecology. It is precisely in intellectually respecting the given social ecology that an answer to how we can square the two seemingly contradictory propositions with which I started the chapter can be reconciled in a non-*ad hoc* manner. Using economic reasoning, I am suggesting, we find out that we know quite a bit about what makes for economic progress, and part of what we know is that there are limits to what we can construct. As the prayer goes: "God grant me the serenity to accept the things I cannot change, the courage to change the things I can, and the wisdom to know the difference." Perhaps the secular version of that relates to our ability in political economy to learn the difference between the application of reason to social affairs, and the hubris of rationalism, between cultivating the social environment for enterprise, and attempting to control it to achieve optimality.

A rather "thin" reading of some cases (both negative and positive) can illustrate the point. In J. Stephen Lansing's (1991) study of the Balinese water temples, the argument is made that the embodied wisdom in tradition exceeded the scientific *know how* of Western experts on the production of rice. The water temples scattered across Bali were places of worship of various gods; they also managed the irrigation schedule. In the 1960s and early 1970s the International Rice Research Institute sought to eradicate the backward native practices of rice production throughout Asia – this was known as the "Green Revolution." Native methods of rice production would be replaced with a variety of rice that required the use of fertilizers and pesticides. In Bali, the government introduced an agricultural policy in conformity with the "Green Revolution," which promoted continuous cropping of the new rice. Rice farmers were encouraged to plant rice without taking account of traditional irrigation schedules. The immediate effect, as could be expected, was a boost in rice production, but the policy soon resulted in a shortage of water and a severe outbreak of rice pests and diseases. The traditional method of rice production proved more efficient in managing resources than the scientific knowledge of high-yielding rice production. In other words, customary practice was rooted in an understanding of the world which the enacted change failed to respect, and the result was an unintended undesirable outcome of good intentions in public policy.[20]

Robert Blewett (1995) offers a similar story with regard to the pastoral policy of the Maasai of Kenya. The Maasai had followed a practice of communal ownership, although with tacit norms of restrictive access. What Blewett argues is that the Maasai practice evolved as a method to reduce the transaction costs associated with the collective action necessary for cooperation – including pastoral coordination and environmental risk-management. Unfortunately, during the colonial and even post-colonial period where explicit contracts substituted for the tacit norms (and were in conflict with these tacit norms rather than codifying them) the complex institutional structure of the Maasai was disrupted and, as a result, the long-term viability of the common land was destroyed. British ideology failed to respect the social ecology of the Maasai and, as such, ran into direct conflict with the indigenous economic reality. As a result, Blewett argues, the Maasai social structure was undermined and British rent-seeking behavior became the norm during the colonial period. Again we have an example of where the contextual knowledge embedded in tradition outdistanced the acontextual and articulated knowledge that sought to replace traditional ways of living, with the result being undesirable from the perspective of the people.[21]

But modernization and social change should not only be looked upon in the negative. As Peter Berger (1976, p. 193) states, "modernity does not appear on the traditionalists' horizon *only* as a threat. It *also* appears as a great promise – of a longer and better life, of a plentitude of material goods (the 'cargo'), but also of individual liberation and fulfillment." Social change and the discarding of myths are not always to be associated with failure. When social change begins with a respect for the customary practice and mutates, or when the customary practice already is conducive to economic experimentation (and the reward structure which induces such behavior), then modernity's unintended positive side is revealed.

In Stephen Innes' (1995) study of the economic culture of Puritan New England, for example, it is argued that the social ecology of Puritanism led to the success of the Massachusetts Bay Colony in the seventeenth century. A mutated cultural mix of British culture with Puritan ideology combined to free the economy of restraints and place moral sanction on private property and the work ethic. The fierce devotion to God in this case led to a social commitment to engage the world and prosper. This underlying customary belief system was reinforced by explicit public policy within the Puritan Commonwealth to promote economic growth and development. The Massachusetts Bay success story was not a result of "finding a treasure" in terms of rich natural resources, but rather requires explaining precisely because the success was from transforming a resource-poor environment into a thriving international economy.

In the past decade, New Zealand represents another example of such a transformation. As Gwartney *et al.* (1996), p. 179, point out: "In 1985, New Zealand was plagued by an expansionary and unstable monetary policy, restrictions on foreign currency holdings, high marginal tax rates, a large transfer sector, exchange rate controls, and capital market restrictions. Much has changed in the last decade." According to the index of economic freedom developed by Gwartney *et al.*, New Zealand now ranks as the third most free economy in the world, and after years of sluggish economic growth, real GNP increased at an annual rate of 5.2% in 1993 and 6% in 1994. David Harper (1994) delves deeper into the causes of this transformation than the superficial public policies adopted. Of course, the public policy aspect is vital (if you double the money supply you will double the price level), but what caused the shift in policy and what forces legitimate that shift are crucial questions to answer. In Harper (Ibid., pp. 44–75), an attempt is made to access the "intractable determinants" of growth that are embedded in a national culture, and he offers a comparative rating of New Zealand in terms of the acceptability of entrepreneurship. Harper contends, following Carson's work on entrepreneurship, that these cultural components are not intractable after all. Actually, Harper's analysis of the entrepreneurial content of New Zealand's culture is not wholly positive when compared to the US and Japan. But, as he reminds the reader, a nation's culture is not static, but dynamic. His argument is that the changes that have occurred in New Zealand are mutating the culture in a direction further toward the entrepreneurial end of the spectrum.[22] Harper further argues that a social ecology conducive to the entrepreneurial element must be embedded in an institutional framework.

Barry Weingast (1995) in an ambitious paper has conjectured that the appropriate institutional framework for development is what he terms "market-preserving federalism." In this work, Weingast examines the take-off periods of the Dutch Republic, England after the Glorious Revolution, and the United States in the nineteenth century. He then applies this argument to examine the contrast between Chinese and Russian reform efforts. The basic proposition in his paper is that the basic paradox of government – that a government strong enough to establish limits to its powers is usually strong enough to break those bonds on its behavior – has to be solved by the institutional framework of governance if economic agents are going to engage in the investment and entrepreneurial acts that lead to growth and development. The basic problem is one of political commitment – constitutional constraints serve to tie the ruler's hands.

The Dutch Republic example is an excellent one to highlight the issues raised in this chapter.[23] Again, the Dutch success was not due to "finding a treasure" of natural resources, but rather a result of cultural attitudes toward experimentation and ideas becoming codified in an institutional framework which led to an expansion of trade and innovation in the financial industry. One of the most common themes in histories of the Dutch Republic is the role of religious tolerance, which fueled the growth of the population – the influx of new and varied people with different ideas and beliefs toward commerce, etc. – and thus the expansion of economic activity. The institutional framework and social norms (which gave rise to the institutions) were conducive to enterprise. As Reuven Brenner (1994, p. 58) writes: "Whereas elsewhere people could, at best, buy or lease farms and other small properties, the Dutch, even of small and moderate means, could – and did – put their savings into shares in ships and mills, into fishing and trading voyages, and into the much-trusted loans to the city of Amsterdam, the province of Holland, or the United Provinces. The Dutch had the incentive to plough back profits and savings in commercial enterprises, an incentive people in other countries lacked." One interpretation of the difference between the Dutch Republic and other countries puts the causal weight on the decentralized nature of governance, as Weingast's work suggests. "In two or three generations," Simon Schama (1988, p. 223) states, "the Republic had risen from a ramshackle and beleaguered confederacy of towns and provinces into a global empire of apparently unlimited prosperity and power ... It was, indeed, a phenomena. For the Dutch state drew power from federalism when absolutist centralization was the norm."

A significant literature has emerged in the past few decades which explains the European miracle as an outgrowth of this polycentricism.[24] The social infrastructure of polycentricism establishes limits to political opportunism, while also encouraging political (and decentralized units of social pressure, be they formal or informal) to discipline the opportunistic behavior of others. The social ecology is one of secure commitments against confiscation, and thus one of trust in social dealings. If this is combined with cultural attitudes which tolerate dissent from old habits, then the entrepreneurial spur required for development will follow. The difficult task is to "maintain a society poised between tradition and change. This is the condition necessary for creativity, for the emergence of novelty, for prosperity" (Brenner 1994, p. 62). When these conditions are met, then the type of investment in more roundabout processes of production [and the emergence of financial market institutions which lower the cost of this activity (including institutions of financial intermediation and insurance)] that are associated with economic growth and development can be expected to follow.[25] However, if the underlying cultural beliefs are at odds with the institutional framework of decentralization and precommitment, then the institutions will lack legitimacy and fail to "stick."

Conclusion

Culture as a concept should not be held up in contrast to economic principles. The importance of culture as a core concept in social analysis can only be understood through the aid of economic logic. Economic logic establishes certain necessary, although not sufficient, propositions for social theory. Culture establishes limits to the *acceptance* of policy implications of economic logic in an above-ground and transparent setting. When culture and economic logic coincide, commercial experimentation flourishes and material progress lifts the masses of people from subsistence. Absent this coincidence, and the struggle for survival continues, as economic behavior is diverted either into a *sub rosa* existence or manifests itself in counterproductive "rent-seeking" games. Unfortunately, there is no escape from the struggle except through the cultivation of the indigenous institutions of a society in a direction more amenable to the rules of private property, freedom of contract, and monetary responsibility.

Acknowledgments

Earlier versions of this chapter were presented at the Southern Economic Association Meetings, in New Orleans, Lousiana (November 1995); the Department of Economics, Boston University, Massachusetts (February 1996); the Department of Economics, Wake Forest University, North Carolina (February 1996); the Institute for Humane Studies, Fairfax, VA (July 1996); George Mason University, Virginia (October 1996); and the Department of Economics, Baruch College, New York State (February 1997). Comments from participants at these seminars are gratefully acknowledged. Financial assistance from the J. M. Kaplan Fund and the Austrian Economics Program at New York University is gratefully acknowledged. Responsibility for remaining errors is my own.

References

Barnett, R. (1992) "The Function of Several Property and Freedom of Contract," *Social Philosophy and Policy* 9(1).

Bates, R. (1990) "Macropolitical Economy in the Field of Development," in J. Alt and K. Shepsle (eds.) *Perspectives on Positive Political Economy*, New York: Cambridge University Press.

Benson, B. (1990) *The Enterprise of Law*, San Francisco: Pacific Research Institute for Public Policy.

Berger, P. L. (1976) (first published 1974) *Pyramids of Sacrifice: Political Ethics and Social Change*, New York: Anchor Books.

Berger, P. L. (1985) "Speaking to the Third World," in P. L. Berger and M. Novak, *Speaking to the Third World: Essays on Democracy and Development*. Washington, DC: American Enterprise Institute for Public Policy Research.

Berger, P. L. (1986) *The Capitalist Revolution*, New York: Basic Books.

Blewett, R. A. (1995) "Property Rights as a Cause of the Tragedy of the Commons: Institutional Change and the Pastoral Maasai of Kenya," *Eastern Economic Journal* 21(4) (Fall).

Boettke, P. J. (1989a) "Evolution and Economics: Austrians as Institutionalists," *Research in the History of Economic Thought and Methodology*, 6.

Boettke, P. J. (1989b) "Austrian Political Economy: A Reply," *Research in the History of Economic Thought and Methodology*, 6.

Boettke, P. J. (1990a) *The Political Economy of Soviet Socialism: The Formative Years, 1918 – 1928*, Boston: Kluwer Academic Publishers.

Boettke, P. J. (1990b) "Institutions and Individuals," *Critical Review* 4(1–2): 10–26.

Boettke, P. J. (1993) *Why Perestroika Failed: The Politics and Economics of Socialist Transformation*, New York: Routledge.

Boettke, P. J. (1994a) "The Political Infrastructure of Economics Development," *Human Systems Management* 13(1).

Boettke, P. J.(1994b) "The Reform Traps in Economics and Politics in the Former Communist Economies," *Journal des Economistes et des Etudes Humaines*, 5(2–3).

Boettke, P. J. (ed.) (1994c) *The Collapse of Development Planning*, New York: New York University Press.

Borner, S., Brunetti, A. and Weder, B. (1995) *Political Credibility and Economic Development*, New York: St Martin's Press.

Brenner, R. (1994) *Labyrinths of Prosperity*, Ann Arbor: University of Michigan Press.

Buchanan, J. (1993) "Asymmetrical Reciprocity in Market Exchange," *Social Philosophy and Policy* 10(2) (Summer).

Buchanan, J. (1995) "Economic Science and Cultural Diversity," *Kyklos* 48(2) (Fall).

Ellickson, R. C. (1993) "Property in Land," *Yale Law Journal* 102 (April).

Geertz, C. (1973) *The Interpretations of Cultures*, New York: Basic Books.

Gellner, E. (1994) *Conditions of Liberty: Civil Society and Its Rivals*, New York: Penguin.

Gwartney, J., Lawson, R. and Block, W. (1996) *Economic Freedom of the World: 1975–1995*, Vancouver: Fraser Institute.

Harper, D. A. (1994) *Wellsprings of Enterprise*, Wellington: New Zealand Institute of Economic Research.

Harriss, J., Hunter, J. and Lewis, C. N. (eds.) (1995) *The New Institutional Economics and Third World Development*. London: Routledge.

Hayek, F. A. von (1973) *Law, Legislation and Liberty*, vol. 1, Chicago: University of Chicago Press.

Hayek, F. A. von (1976) *Law, Legislation and Liberty*, vol. 2. Chicago: University of Chicago Press.

Hayek, F. A. von (1979) *Law, Legislation and Liberty*, vol. 3. Chicago: University of Chicago Press.

Hirschman, A. (1986) *Rival Views of Market Society, and Other Essays*, Cambridge, MA: Harvard University Press.

Higgs, R. (1987) *Crisis and Leviathan*, New York: Oxford University Press.

Ikeda, S. (1996) *The Dynamics of the Mixed Economy*, New York: Routledge.

Innes, S. (1995) *Creating the Commonwealth: The Economic Culture of Puritan New England*, New York: Norton.

Israel, J. I. (1995) *The Dutch Republic: Its Rise, Greatness and Fall 1477–1806*, Oxford: Oxford University Press.

Kuttner, R. (1997) *Everything for Sale: The Virtues and Limits of Markets*, New York: Knopf.

Lansing, J. S. (1991) *Priests and Programmers: Technologies of Power in the Engineered Landscape of Bali*, Princeton: Princeton University Press.

Lucas, R. (1988) "On the Mechanics of Economic Development," *Journal of Monetary Economics* 22(1).

Lucas, R. (1993) "Making a Miracle," *Econometrica* 61(2).

McGuire, M. and Olson, M. (1996) "The Economics of Autocracy and Majority Rule: The Invisible Hand and the Use of Force," *Journal of Economic Literature* XXXIV (March).

Mankiw, G. (1995) "The Growth of Nations," *Brookings Papers on Economic Activity*, 1.

Mayhew, A. (1987) "Culture: Core Concept Under Attack," *Journal of Economic Issues* 21(2).

Mischel, K. (1996) "Are We Too Thin for Our Own good?" Department of Economics and Finance, CUNY–Baruch College, NY unpublished manuscript.

Mises, L. von (1980) (first published 1912) *The Theory of Money and Credit*, Indianapolis, IN: Liberty Classics.

Mises, L. von (1981) (first published 1922) *Socialism: An Economic and Sociological Analysis*. Indianapolis, IN: Liberty Classics.

Mises, L. von (1949) *Human Action: A Treatise on Economics*, New Haven: Yale University Press.

Nelson, R. and Pack, H. (1995) "The Asian Growth Miracle and Modern Growth Theory," unpublished manuscript.

North, D. (1990) *Institutions, Institutional Change and Economic Performance*, New York: Cambridge University Press.

North, D. and Weingast, B. (1989) "Constitutions and Commitments: The Evolution of Institutions Governing Public Choice in Seventeenth Century England," *Journal of Economic History* 49(4).

Olson, M. (1993) "Dictatorship, Democracy, and Development," *American Political Science Review* 87(3).

Platteau, J.-P. (1994a) "Behind the Market Stage Where Real Societies Exist – Part I: The Role of Public and Private Order Institutions," *Journal of Development Studies* 30(3) (April).

Platteau, J.-P. (1994b) "Behind the Market Stage Where Real Societies Exist – Part II: The Role of Moral Norms," *Journal of Development Studies* 30(3) (April).

Rabushka, A. (1987) *The New China*, Boulder, CO: Westview Press.

Raico, R. (1994) "The Theory of Economic Development and the 'European Miracle'," in P. J. Boettke (ed.) *The Collapse of Development Planning*, New York: New York University Press.

Rodrik, D. (1996) "Understanding Economic Policy Reform," *Journal of Economic Literature* XXXIV (March).

Rothbard, M. N. (1993) (first published 1962) *Man, Economy and State*. Auburn, AL: Ludwig von Mises Institute.

Rutherford, M. (1994) *Institutions in Economics*, New York: Cambridge University Press.

Schama, S. (1988) *The Embarrassment of Riches: An Interpretation of Dutch Culture in the Golden Age*, Berkeley, CA: University of California Press.

Streeten, P. P. (1995) *Thinking About Development*, New York: Cambridge University Press.

Voigt, S. (1993) "Values, Norms, Institutions and the Prospects for Economic Growth in Central and Eastern Europe," *Journal des Economistes et des Etudes Humaines*, 4(4) (December).

Weingast, B. (1995) "The Economic Role of Political Institutions," *Journal of Law, Economics and Organization* 11 (April).

Wittman, D. (1995) *The Myth of Democratic Failure*, Chicago: University of Chicago Press.

16 Concluding remarks

Critics of economics and political economy often argue that the discipline artificially constrains our imaginations. Martha Nussbaum (1991), for example, argues that the economic way of thinking impoverishes our sense of life. "If political economy," she argues, "does not include the complexities of the inner moral life of each human being, its strivings and perplexities, its complicated emotions, its perplexity and terror, if it does not distinguish in its descriptions between a human life and a machine, then we should regard with suspicion its claim to govern a nation of human beings; and we should ask ourselves whether, having seen us as little different from inanimate objects, it might not be capable of treating us with a certain lack of tenderness" (Nussbaum 1991, p. 886).

I actually have great sympathy with some of these criticisms. To the extent that economic reasoning reduces the choice problem of individuals to one of simple maximization and the interactions between individuals to a mechanical procedure, then economic reasoning should be viewed with great skepticism. As argued in the essays in this collection, when, for the sake of mathematical tractability, we model the economic system in such a limiting manner, we fail to appreciate the underlying political–legal–social institutions within which economic processes are played out in the real world. This intellectual failure results in poor judgment among economists about fundamental issues in economic and social organization.

Ironically for those who see free-market economists as lacking in compassion, poor judgment among economists was never more evident than when the majority of the economics profession sided with Oskar Lange during the socialist calculation debate. Institutional differences between economic systems were ignored in the proposed models of market socialism, and thus the problems which socialism in practice would have to tackle were not adequately addressed. The consequences of this intellectual shortcoming are hard to measure. We can say, however, that by providing an intellectual justification to a social system of production that impoverished and tyrannized the populations within which it was implemented, *real* compassion for humanity was ill-served by the discipline of economics. Economic analysis, and thus economists' judgment, also tends to go astray when it proceeds unanchored to the real choices of individuals within the economic system under investigation and instead focuses exclusively on the relationship between aggregate variables, as was the case during the heyday of Keynesian demand management.

Martha Nussbaum moves from her criticism of the truncated view of human life that results from economism to a critique of the meaninglessness of aggregate notions of well-being contained in figures such as GNP per capita. These figures fail to capture what is most important to living a meaningful life. She insists that we need to find better ways to measure the quality of life. Instead, she proposes that we move beyond strictly monetary considerations and include the non-monetary factors that are important for human life in our deliberations over human welfare. She suggests we look at life expectancy, infant mortality, health care, education, political participation, and the quality of racial relations (Nussbaum 1991, pp. 904–5).

Nussbaum is joined in this effort to redefine measures of well-being in economics by Amartya Sen (1999). Sen makes persuasive arguments that we must adopt broader goals for development than growth rates in per capita income. In particular, Sen argues that we must concentrate on increasing human capabilities. Wealth is an enabling factor and thus necessary, but it is not sufficient for explaining human progress. Development is a process of expanding the real freedoms of a people. And this requires removing the sources of unfreedom, including poverty, tyranny, and restricted opportunities (both economic and political). Good health, educational opportunity, life expectancy, democratic decision-making, and tolerance of alternative lifestyles are all important components of human well-being that are unfortunately left out of traditional economic measures. Sen argues that we must expand our measures of well-being to include these factors, if we want our work to have relevance to the dialog on the human condition.

I do not disagree with either Nussbaum or Sen on the shortcomings of the preoccupation with per capita GNP calculations. However, there is a general pattern to be found between the adoption of the policies of economic freedom, the wealth of a nation, and the health and well-being of its people. Wealthier is healthier, and we should keep that in mind when talking about these broader issues of well-being. Our compassion is not truncated by the teachings of economics, as Nussbaum suggests, but, instead, that compassion is redirected toward an appreciation of the institutional and preconditions which provide individuals with the material means that enable them to rise up and realize their potential as human beings.

Statistical correlation is *not* causation. I am convinced, however, that we have "good reasons" to argue that a country that is pursuing policies which respect private property rights, freedom of contract and pricing, open international trade, monetary responsibility, and fiscal restraint will experience better economic growth than countries that do not follow this policy path. And furthermore, countries that experience better economic growth tend to provide more of the things Nussbaum and Sen argue are required to live a meaningful life. In short, economic freedom leads to economic growth, and economic growth leads to improvements in human well-being.

We can see this relationship in the data, and, while I believe that we should be skeptical of this sort of crude economic measurement, and cross-country comparisons in particular, the pattern in the data is important to present (see Appendixes 1 and 2).The pattern presented provides us with some additional information that reinforces a general conclusion of the essays contained in this book – there is no third way to transition from an underdeveloped to a developed economy. The socialist option has been proven to be a chimera. The economies in transition will continue to flounder unless they follow the path of limited government and economic freedom. The potential paradox in this move toward constitutional constraint is that it might require a strong government to establish the credible commitment to limit itself. This is not an argument against limited government, but simply the age-old dilemma of limited government, which is to get the ruler to tie his/her own hands. Without solving this dilemma and effectively binding the discretion of the ruler, economic development will continue to be thwarted within these nations. The fear of predation (from either public or private actors) will continue to limit economic activity and shorten the time horizon of investment. If, on the other hand, a credible commitment to limited government can be made and effectively signaled, and policies of economic freedom are adopted, then economic actors will be willing to bet on their ideas; they will be able to engage in rational calculation concerning those bets, find the financial backing to bring those bets to life, and coordinate their plans with the plans of others in the economy to realize the mutual gains from exchange. In such a world, miracles do happen and the people will be empowered to live peaceful and prosperous lives. It is my sincere hope that such a fate is in store for the peoples of Eastern and Central Europe and the former Soviet Union.

References

Nussbaum, M. C. (1991) "The Literary Imagination in Public Life," *New Literary History* 22: 877–910.

Sen, A. (1999) *Development as Freedom*, New York: Alfred Knopf.

Appendix 1

Economic freedom and wealth

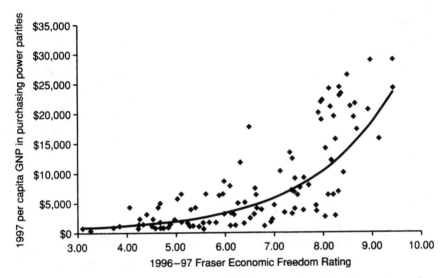

Figure A1.1 1997 GNP measured at PPP in dollars vs. 1996–7 Fraser Economic Freedom
Rating

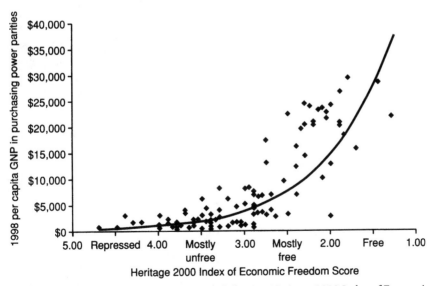

Figure A1.2 1998 GNP measured at PPP in dollars vs. Heritage 2000 Index of Economic
Freedom Score

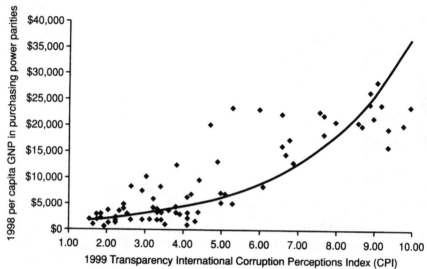

Figure A1.3 1998 GNP measured at PPP in dollars vs. 1999 Transparency International Corruption Perceptions Index (CPI)

Table A1.1 Economic freedom indices and GNP

Country	Fraser rank	Fraser 1996–97 summary rating	Heritage rank	Heritage 2000 score	CPI Rank	1999 Transparency International Corruption Perceptions Index (CPI)	GNP measured at PPP per capita dollars 1997	1998
Hong Kong	1.0	9.4	1.0	1.3	13.0	7.7	24,350	22,000
Singapore	2.0	9.4	2.0	1.5	6.0	9.1	29,230	28,620
New Zealand	3.0	9.1	3.0	1.7	3.0	9.4	15,780	15,840
United States	4.0	9.0	4.0	1.8	N/A	N/A	29,080	29,340
United Kingdom	5.0	8.9	6.0	1.9	11.0	8.6	20,710	20,640
Ireland	6.0	8.7	5.0	1.9	13.0	7.7	17,420	18,340
Australia	8.0	8.6	6.0	1.9	10.0	8.7	19,510	20,130
Canada	7.0	8.6	9.0	2.0	5.0	9.2	21,750	24,050
Netherlands	9.0	8.5	12.0	2.1	7.0	9.0	21,300	21,620
Switzerland	10.0	8.5	6.0	1.9	8.0	8.9	26,580	26,620
Argentina	11.0	8.4	14.0	2.1	56.0	3.0	10,100	10,200
Denmark	12.0	8.4	19.0	2.3	1.0	10.0	23,450	23,830
Belgium	13.0	8.3	14.0	2.1	23.0	5.3	23,090	23,480
El Salvador	16.0	8.3	9.0	2.0	39.0	3.9	2,860	2,850
Japan	14.0	8.3	16.0	2.2	22.0	6.0	24,400	23,180
Panama	15.0	8.3	24.0	2.4	N/A	N/A	6,890	6,940
Chile	20.0	8.2	9.0	2.0	16.0	6.9	12,240	12,890
Finland	18.0	8.2	17.0	2.2	2.0	9.8	19,660	20,270
Spain	17.0	8.3	24.0	2.4	19.0	6.6	15,690	16,060
Thailand	19.0	8.2	31.0	2.7	53.0	3.2	6,490	5,840
Costa Rica	23.0	8.1	39.0	2.9	25.0	5.1	6,510	6,620
Germany	21.0	8.2	17.0	2.2	12.0	8.0	21,170	20,810
Norway	22.0	8.1	20.0	2.3	8.0	8.9	24,260	24,290

Table A1.1 (continued)

Country	Fraser rank	Fraser 1996–97 summary rating	Heritage rank	Heritage 2000 score	CPI Rank	1999 Transparency International Corruption Perceptions Index (CPI)	GNP measured at PPP per capita dollars 1997	1998
Austria	28.0	8.0	12.0	2.1	15.0	7.6	22,010	22,740
Bolivia	25.0	8.1	30.0	2.7	62.0	2.5	2,810	2,820
France	26.0	8.0	27.0	2.5	19.0	6.6	22,210	22,320
Portugal	24.0	8.1	20.0	2.3	18.0	6.7	14,180	14,380
Sweden	27.0	8.0	23.0	2.4	3.0	9.4	19,010	19,480
Italy	29.0	7.9	20.0	2.3	30.0	4.7	20,100	20,200
Peru	31.0	7.9	N/A	N/A	N/A	N/A	4,580	N/A
Philippines	30.0	7.9	39.0	2.9	43.0	3.6	3,670	3,540
Mexico	32.0	7.7	51.0	3.0	46.0	3.4	8,110	8,190
Mauritius	33.0	7.6	N/A	N/A	N/A	N/A	9,230	9,400
Paraguay	34.0	7.6	37.0	2.8	69.0	2.0	3,860	3,650
Malaysia	35.0	7.5	31.0	2.7	25.0	5.1	7,730	6,990
Trinidad and Tobago	36.0	7.5	N/A	N/A	N/A	N/A	6,460	6,720
Greece	41.0	7.4	34.0	2.8	29.0	4.9	12,540	13,010
Guatemala	37.0	7.4	31.0	2.7	53.0	3.2	4,060	4,070
Hungary	39.0	7.4	N/A	N/A	N/A	N/A	6,970	N/A
Jamaica	40.0	7.4	27.0	2.5	40.0	3.8	3,330	3,210
Uruguay	38.0	7.4	29.0	2.6	31.0	4.4	9,110	9,480
South Africa	42.0	7.3	41.0	2.9	27.0	5.0	7,190	6,990
Korea, South	43.0	7.3	24.0	2.4	40.0	3.8	13,430	12,270
Indonesia	44.0	7.2	75.0	3.5	74.0	1.7	3,390	2,790
Czech Republic	45.0	7.1	N/A	N/A	N/A	N/A	10,380	N/A

Dominican Republic	47.0	7.0	41.0	2.9	N/A	N/A	4,690	4,700
Ecuador	46.0	7.0	57.0	3.1	63.0	2.4	4,700	4,630
Honduras	48.0	7.0	67.0	3.4	72.0	1.8	2,260	2,140
Nicaragua	49.0	6.9	80.0	3.6	55.0	3.1	1,820	1,790
Estonia	51.0	6.8	N/A	N/A	N/A	N/A	5,090	N/A
Kenya	50.0	6.8	55.0	3.1	69.0	2.0	1,160	1,130
Latvia	52.0	6.7	N/A	N/A	N/A	N/A	3,970	N/A
Botswana	55.0	6.6	50.0	3.0	21.0	6.1	7,430	8,310
Egypt	56.0	6.6	75.0	3.5	49.0	3.3	3,080	3,130
Lithuania	53.0	6.6	41.0	2.9	40.0	3.8	4,140	4,310
Turkey	54.0	6.6	N/A	N/A	N/A	N/A	6,470	N/A
Israel	58.0	6.5	34.0	2.8	17.0	6.8	17,680	17,310
Sri Lanka	57.0	6.5	N/A	N/A	N/A	N/A	2,460	N/A
Ghana	60.0	6.4	57.0	3.1	49.0	3.3	1,610	1,610
Namibia	59.0	6.4	41.0	2.9	23.0	5.3	5,100	4,950
Slovenia	61.0	6.3	N/A	N/A	N/A	N/A	11,880	N/A
Tunisia	62.0	6.3	51.0	3.0	27.0	5.0	5,050	5,160
China	64.0	6.2	68.0	3.4	46.0	3.4	3,070	3,220
Haiti	63.0	6.2	96.0	4.0	N/A	N/A	1,260	1,250
Jordan	65.0	6.1	41.0	2.9	31.0	4.4	3,350	3,230
Slovak Republic	67.0	6.1	N/A	N/A	N/A	N/A	7,860	N/A
Uganda	66.0	6.1	51.0	3.0	66.0	2.2	1,160	1,170
Morocco	68.0	6.0	34.0	2.8	35.0	4.1	3,210	3,120
Poland	70.0	6.0	37.0	2.8	34.0	4.2	6,510	6,740
Venezuela	69.0	6.0	63.0	3.3	59.0	2.6	8,660	8,190
Brazil	71.0	5.9	75.0	3.5	35.0	4.1	6,350	6,160
India	72.0	5.8	87.0	3.8	57.0	2.9	1,660	1,700
Côte d'Ivoire	73.0	5.7	73.0	3.5	59.0	2.6	1,690	1,730
Colombia	74.0	5.6	41.0	2.9	57.0	2.9	6,570	7,500

Table A1.1 (continued)

Country	Fraser rank	Fraser 1996–97 summary rating	Heritage rank	Heritage 2000 score	CPI Rank	1999 Transparency International Corruption Perceptions Index (CPI)	GNP measured at PPP per capita dollars 1997	1998
Pakistan	75.0	5.6	68.0	3.4	66.0	2.2	1,580	1,560
Tanzania	76.0	5.6	68.0	3.4	71.0	1.9	620	490
Zambia	77.0	5.5	41.0	2.9	44.0	3.5	910	860
Russia	78.0	5.4	84.0	3.7	63.0	2.4	4,280	3,950
Bangladesh	79.0	5.4	86.0	3.8	N/A	N/A	1,090	1,100
Bulgaria	80.0	5.3	N/A	N/A	N/A	N/A	3,870	N/A
Nepal	81.0	5.3	80.0	3.6	N/A	N/A	1,090	1,090
Cameroon	82.0	5.1	68.0	3.4	77.0	1.5	1,770	1,810
Gabon	83.0	5.1	N/A	N/A	N/A	N/A	6,560	6,660
Iran	84.0	5.0	N/A	N/A	N/A	N/A	5,690	N/A
Zimbabwe	85.0	5.0	94.0	3.9	35.0	4.1	2,240	2,150
Benin	86.0	4.9	41.0	2.9	N/A	N/A	1,260	1,250
Niger	87.0	4.8	87.0	3.8	N/A	N/A	830	830
Croatia	90.0	4.7	N/A	N/A	N/A	N/A	4,930	N/A
Mali	88.0	4.7	41.0	2.9	N/A	N/A	720	720
Nigeria	89.0	4.7	63.0	3.3	76.0	1.6	860	820
Senegal	91.0	4.7	55.0	3.1	46.0	3.4	1,690	1,710
Malawi	93.0	4.6	83.0	3.7	35.0	4.1	700	730
Romania	92.0	4.6	63.0	3.3	49.0	3.3	4,270	3,970
Togo	94.0	4.6	87.0	3.8	N/A	N/A	1,460	1,390
Chad	96.0	4.5	N/A	N/A	N/A	N/A	950	N/A
Ukraine	95.0	4.5	N/A	N/A	N/A	N/A	2,170	N/A

Syria	97.0	4.4	96.0	4.0	N/A	N/A	3,000	3,000
Albania	99.0	4.3	N/A	N/A	N/A	N/A	2,170	N/A
Central African Republic	98.0	4.3	N/A	N/A	N/A	N/A	1,310	1,290
Burundi	101.0	4.2	96.0	4.0	N/A	N/A	620	620
Congo	100.0	4.3	94.0	3.9	N/A	N/A	1,290	1,430
Algeria	102.0	4.1	73.0	3.5	N/A	N/A	4,250	4,380
Madagascar	103.0	3.9	61.0	3.2	N/A	N/A	900	900
Rwanda	104.0	3.7	96.0	4.0	N/A	N/A	650	690
Sierra Leone	105.0	3.2	87.0	3.8	N/A	N/A	410	390
Congo, Democratic Republic	106.0	3.1	104.0	4.7	N/A	N/A	760	750
Cambodia	N/A	N/A	51.0	3.0	N/A	N/A	1,290	1,240
Guinea	N/A	N/A	57.0	3.1	N/A	N/A	1,790	1,760
Mongolia	N/A	N/A	60.0	3.2	33.0	4.3	1,490	1,520
Lebanon	N/A	N/A	61.0	3.2	N/A	N/A	6,090	6,150
Papua New Guinea	N/A	N/A	63.0	3.3	N/A	N/A	N/A	2,700
Burkina Faso	N/A	N/A	68.0	3.4	N/A	N/A	1,000	1,020
Ethiopia	N/A	N/A	75.0	3.5	N/A	N/A	500	500
Lesotho	N/A	N/A	79.0	3.6	N/A	N/A	2,490	2,320
Kirghiz Republic	N/A	N/A	80.0	3.6	66.0	2.2	2,180	2,200
Kazakhstan	N/A	N/A	84.0	3.7	65.0	2.3	3,530	3,400
Mauritania	N/A	N/A	87.0	3.8	N/A	N/A	1,650	1,660
Mozambique	N/A	N/A	87.0	3.8	44.0	3.5	690	850
Yemen	N/A	N/A	93.0	3.9	N/A	N/A	N/A	740
Azerbaijan	N/A	N/A	100.0	4.2	74.0	1.7	1,520	1,820
Vietnam	N/A	N/A	101.0	4.3	59.0	2.6	1,590	1,690
Uzbekistan	N/A	N/A	102.0	4.4	72.0	1.8	N/A	2,900
Angola	N/A	N/A	103.0	4.5	N/A	N/A	820	840
Macedonia, FYR	N/A	N/A	N/A	N/A	49.0	3.3	3,180	3,660

Appendix 2

Economic wealth and welfare

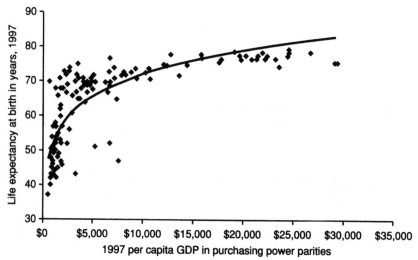

Figure A2.1 Life expectancy at birth in years, 1997 vs. 1997 GNP measured at PPP in dollars

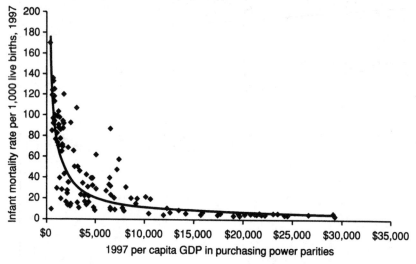

Figure A2.2 Infant mortality rate per 1,000 live births for 1997 vs. 1997 GNP measured at PPP in dollars

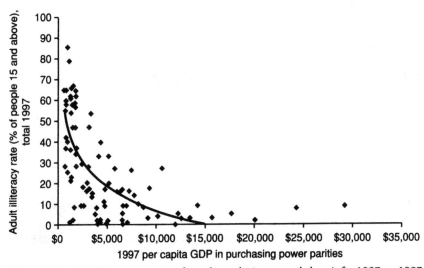

Figure A2.3 Adult illiteracy rate (% of people aged 15 years and above), for 1997 vs. 1997 GNP measured at PPP in dollars

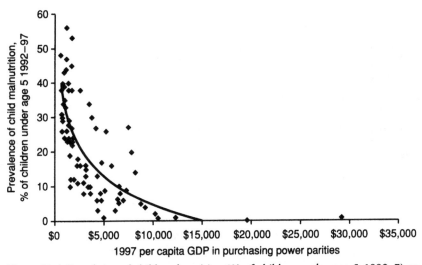

Figure A2.4 Prevalence of child malnutrition (% of children under age 5 1992–7) vs. 1997 GNP measured at PPP in dollars

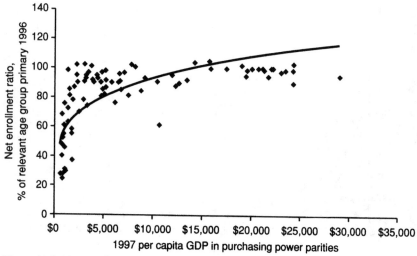

Figure A2.5 Net enrollment ratio,% of relevant age group, primary school, 1996 vs. 1997 GNP measured at PPP in dollars

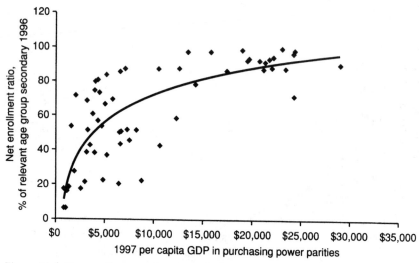

Figure A2.6 Net enrollment ratio, % of relevant age group, secondary school, 1996 vs. 1997 GNP measured at PPP in dollars

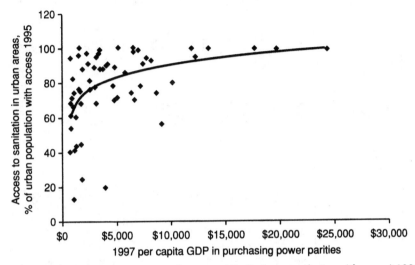

Figure A2.7 Access to sanitation in urban areas (% of urban population with access) 1995 vs. 1997 GNP measured at PPP in dollars

Table A2.1 GNP and measures of human well-being

Countries	GNP measured at PPP per capita dollars in 1997	Life expectancy at birth (years) in 1997	Infant mortality rate per 1,000 live births in 1997	Adult illiteracy rate (% of people aged 15 and above) Total 1997	Prevalence of child malnutrition (% of children under age 5), in 1992–7	Net school enrollment ratio for 1996 (% of relevant age group) Primary	Net school enrollment ratio for 1996 (% of relevant age group) Secondary	Access to sanitation in urban areas (% of urban population with access) in 1995
Albania	2,170	72	26	N/A	N/A	102	N/A	97
Algeria	4,250	70	32	40	13	94	56	N/A
Angola	820	46	125	N/A	35	N/A	N/A	71
Argentina	10,100	73	22	4	2	N/A	N/A	80
Armenia	2,540	74	15	N/A	N/A	N/A	N/A	N/A
Australia	19,510	78	5	N/A	0	95	92	N/A
Austria	22,010	77	5	N/A	N/A	100	88	N/A
Azerbaijan	1,520	71	20	N/A	10	N/A	N/A	N/A
Bangladesh	1,090	58	75	61	56	N/A	N/A	41
Belarus	4,820	68	12	1	N/A	85	N/A	N/A
Belgium	23,090	77	6	N/A	N/A	98	99	N/A
Benin	1,260	53	88	66	29	63	N/A	60
Bolivia	2,810	61	66	16	8	N/A	N/A	77
Botswana	7,430	47	58	26	27	81	45	91
Brazil	6,350	67	34	16	6	90	20	74
Bulgaria	3,870	71	18	2	N/A	92	74	N/A
Burkina Faso	1,000	44	99	79	33	31	N/A	N/A
Burundi	620	42	119	55	38	N/A	N/A	N/A
Cambodia	1,290	54	103	N/A	38	98	N/A	N/A
Cameroon	1,770	57	52	28	N/A	N/A	N/A	N/A
Canada	21,750	79	6	N/A	N/A	95	93	N/A
Central African Republic	1,310	45	98	58	23	N/A	N/A	N/A

Country							
Chad	950	49	100	N/A	39	46	6	74
Chile	12,240	75	11	5	1	88	58	95
China	3,070	70	32	17	16	102	N/A	68
Colombia	6,570	70	24	9	8	85	50	70
Congo, Democratic Republic	760	51	92	N/A	34	54	17	53
Congo	1,290	48	90	23	24	N/A	N/A	N/A
Costa Rica	6,510	77	12	5	5	91	43	100
Côte d'Ivoire	1,690	47	87	57	24	55	N/A	N/A
Croatia	4,930	72	9	2	1	82	66	71
Czech Republic	10,380	74	6	N/A	1	91	87	N/A
Denmark	23,450	75	6	N/A	N/A	99	87	N/A
Dominican Republic	4,690	71	40	17	6	81	22	89
Ecuador	4,700	70	33	9	17	97	N/A	70
Egypt	3,080	43	107	47	15	93	68	95
El Salvador	2,860	66	51	20	11	78	21	89
Eritrea	1,040	50	N/A	N/A	44	30	16	12
Estonia	5,090	51	62	65	N/A	87	83	N/A
Ethiopia	500	70	10	65	48	28	N/A	N/A
Finland	19,660	77	4	N/A	N/A	99	93	100
France	22,210	78	5	N/A	N/A	100	94	N/A
Gabon	6,560	52	87	67	N/A	N/A	N/A	N/A
Gambia	1,440	53	78	N/A	N/A	87	71	N/A
Georgia	1,980	73	17	N/A	N/A	87	87	N/A
Germany	21,170	77	5	N/A	N/A	100	87	N/A
Ghana	1,610	60	66	34	27	N/A	N/A	75
Greece	12,540	78	7	3	N/A	90	87	N/A
Guatemala	4,060	64	43	33	27	N/A	N/A	91
Guinea	1,790	46	120	N/A	24	37	N/A	24
Haiti	1,260	54	71	54	28	N/A	N/A	43
Honduras	2,260	69	36	29	18	90	N/A	91
Hong Kong	24,350	79	5	8	N/A	90	71	N/A

Table A2.1 (continued)

Countries	GNP measured at PPP per capita dollars in 1997	Life expectancy at birth (years) in 1997	Infant mortality rate per 1,000 live births in 1997	Adult illiteracy rate (% of people aged 15 and above) Total 1997	Prevalence of child malnutrition (% of children under age 5), in 1992–7	Net school enrollment ratio for 1996 (% of relevant age group)		Access to sanitation in urban areas (% of urban population with access) in 1995
						Primary	Secondary	
Hungary	6,970	71	10	1	N/A	97	87	N/A
India	1,660	63	71	47	53	N/A	N/A	N/A
Indonesia	3,390	65	47	15	34	97	42	88
Ireland	17,420	76	5	N/A	N/A	100	86	N/A
Israel	17,680	77	7	5	N/A	N/A	N/A	100
Italy	20,100	78	5	2	N/A	100	N/A	N/A
Jamaica	3,330	75	12	14	10	N/A	N/A	99
Japan	24,400	80	4	N/A	N/A	103	98	N/A
Jordan	3,350	71	29	13	10	N/A	N/A	N/A
Kazakhstan	3,530	65	24	N/A	8	N/A	N/A	N/A
Kenya	1,160	52	74	21	23	N/A	N/A	N/A
Korea, South	13,430	72	9	3	N/A	92	97	100
Kirghiz Republic	2,180	67	28	N/A	11	95	N/A	N/A
Lao PDR	1,300	53	98	N/A	40	72	18	N/A
Latvia	3,970	69	15	0	N/A	90	79	90
Lebanon	6,090	70	28	16	3	76	N/A	N/A
Lesotho	2,490	56	93	18	16	70	17	76
Macedonia, FYR	3,180	72	16	N/A	N/A	95	51	N/A
Madagascar	900	57	94	N/A	34	61	N/A	N/A
Malawi	700	43	133	42	30	68	N/A	94
Malaysia	7,730	72	11	14	20	102	N/A	94
Mali	720	50	118	65	40	28	N/A	61

Country								
Mauritania	1,650	53	92	62	23	57	N/A	44
Mauritius	9,230	71	20	17	N/A	N/A	N/A	N/A
Mexico	8,110	72	31	10	14	101	51	93
Morocco	3,210	67	51	54	10	74	N/A	97
Mozambique	690	45	135	60	26	40	6	68
Nepal	1,090	57	83	62	47	N/A	N/A	74
Netherlands	21,300	78	5	N/A	N/A	99	91	N/A
New Zealand	15,780	77	7	N/A	N/A	100	97	N/A
Nicaragua	1,820	68	43	37	12	78	27	88
Niger	830	47	118	86	43	25	6	N/A
Nigeria	860	54	77	40	39	N/A	N/A	82
Norway	24,260	78	4	N/A	N/A	99	96	100
Pakistan	1,580	62	95	59	38	N/A	N/A	75
Panama	6,890	74	21	9	6	N/A	N/A	99
Paraguay	3,860	70	23	8	N/A	91	38	20
Peru	4,580	69	40	11	8	91	53	78
Philippines	3,670	68	35	5	30	101	60	88
Poland	6,510	73	10	N/A	95	85	N/A	
Portugal	14,180	75	6	9	N/A	104	78	N/A
Romania	4270	69	22	2	6	95	73	N/A
Russia	4,280	67	17	1	3	93	N/A	N/A
Rwanda	650	40	124	37	29	N/A	42	N/A
Saudi Arabia	10,540	71	21	27	N/A	61	N/A	68
Senegal	1,690	52	70	65	22	58	N/A	N/A
Sierra Leone	410	37	170	N/A	N/A	N/A	N/A	N/A
Singapore	29,230	76	4	9	N/A	N/A	N/A	N/A
Slovak Republic	7,860	73	9	N/A	N/A	N/A	N/A	N/A
Slovenia	11,880	75	5	N/A	95	N/A	100	N/A
South Africa	7,190	65	48	16	9	N/A	51	78
Spain	15,690	78	5	3	N/A	105	N/A	N/A
Sri Lanka	2,460	73	14	9	38	N/A	N/A	81

Table A2.1 (continued)

Countries	GNP measured at PPP per capita dollars in 1997	Life expectancy at birth (years) in 1997	Infant mortality rate per 1,000 live births in 1997	Adult illiteracy rate (% of people aged 15 and above) Total 1997	Prevalence of child malnutrition (% of children under age 5), in 1992–7	Net school enrollment ratio for 1996 (% of relevant age group) Primary	Net school enrollment ratio for 1996 (% of relevant age group) Secondary	Access to sanitation in urban areas (% of urban population with access) in 1995
Sudan	1,370	55	71	47	N/A	N/A	N/A	N/A
Sweden	19,010	79	4	N/A	N/A	102	98	N/A
Switzerland	26,580	79	5	N/A	N/A	N/A	N/A	N/A
Tajikistan	1,100	68	30	1	N/A	N/A	N/A	N/A
Tanzania	620	48	85	28	31	48	N/A	N/A
Thailand	6,490	69	33	5	N/A	N/A	N/A	98
Togo	1,460	49	86	47	19	85	N/A	76
Trinidad and Tobago	6,460	73	12	2	N/A	N/A	N/A	N/A
Tunisia	5,050	70	30	33	9	98	N/A	100
Turkey	6,470	69	40	17	10	96	50	N/A
Turkmenistan	1,410	66	40	N/A	N/A	N/A	N/A	N/A
Uganda	1,160	42	99	36	26	N/A	N/A	60
Ukraine	2,170	67	14	N/A	N/A	N/A	N/A	N/A
United Kingdom	20,710	77	6	N/A	N/A	100	92	N/A
United States	29,080	76	7	N/A	N/A	95	90	N/A
Uruguay	9,110	74	16	3	1	93	N/A	56
Venezuela	8,660	73	21	8	4	84	22	74
Vietnam	1,590	68	29	8	5	N/A	N/A	N/A
Yemen	720	54	96	58	45	52	N/A	40
Zambia	910	43	113	25	29	75	17	66
Zimbabwe	2,240	52	69	9	16	N/A	N/A	N/A

Notes

1 Introduction

1 See Zaslavskaya (1984). This report was originally presented in April 1983 in a closed session organized by the economics department of the Communist Party Central Committee, the USSR Academy of Sciences, and Gosplan.

2 See Boettke (1990 and 1993) for discussions of the origin and collapse of Soviet socialism. Boettke (2000) provides a documentary history of the theoretical debate over socialism in the twentieth century.

3 There are serious problems with taking these data at face value. First, there is the problem of the overestimation of Soviet statistics, so that the base figures are problematic in the comparison. Second, there are problems of miscalculation associated with the Soviet situation. In a shortage economy, for example, the calculation of real wages will be confusing. The standard technique of dividing nominal wages by the price level (W/P_0) will not provide even a reasonable guess of real wages because P_0 is an administered price set below market clearing levels. In shortage situations, the official price is not an effective price, as many actors cannot obtain the goods at that price. Thus, while if we look only at the explicit situation then letting prices rise to clear markets will appear to reduce real wages – $W/P_0 > W/P_1$. In reality, however, what has occurred is that the freeing of prices rather than reducing real wages has lowered the real price of obtaining goods by eliminating the queue and the shortage situation. A similar miscalculation occurs with regard to production in general. Under the Soviet system of planning, many enterprises were what we now term "negative value added" firms – which means that the value of inputs used by firms was actually greater than the value of the output produced by the firms. If this is your base point for comparisons, then a recorded decline in production should actually be viewed as a positive step toward reorienting your economic system toward a more rational system of production. Finally, the third problem with official statistics is that they underestimate economic activity because of non-recorded activities such as black market and barter.

4 The essays in this book are not intended as a conspiratorial type of criticism of the foreign aid policy as followed in Russia, such as that offered in Wedel (1998). However much sympathy I might have with a general critique of foreign aid in general (see Boettke 1994), I do not believe that there was a conscious effort by individuals to impose policies that they knew would not work in order to garner riches for themselves. Instead, I choose to write of intellectual shortcomings in the analysis of the problem, rather than moral weakness and political opportunism. I simply do not believe that whatever foreign aid program that was followed would have worked.

5 See Peter Murrell (1995).

6 See, for example, Shleifer and Treisman (2000), Shleifer and Vishny (1998), Boycko *et al.* (1995), and Åslund (1991, 1995).

7 It is important in discussions about the determinants of economic development to

distinguish between those factors that we must treat as given and those that we can legitimately treat as subject to choice. In the basic thought-experiment, an economy basically consists of people (attitudes and beliefs), resources (natural endowment), and institutions (rules of the game). Human nature is pretty much given to us. We might wish that people were more kind and gentle in their interactions with others, but the human disposition is not really something that we can control. Similarly, we might wish that there was an abundance of natural resources, but wishing for more oil or sunshine does not provide us with either more oil or more sunshine. The one factor that is to some extent under our control is the set of institutions within which individuals decide how to utilize resources and interact with others. Changes in the institutions (government structure, laws, and public policies) will change the way that individuals decide how to use resources and interact with other individuals. Under certain institutional settings they will seek to better their lot in life by finding ways to interact in positive-sum games (win–win), while within other settings they will pursue zero-sum games (win–lose), and in some settings they may even be led to pursue negative-sum games (lose–lose). The most important contribution that economics and political economy can make, in my opinion, to improving the human condition is articulating which set of institutions possesses the tendency to promote positive-sum games, as opposed to either zero-sum or negative-sum games.

8 See Buchanan (1998) for a discussion of the importance of this asymmetry for transition political economy.

2 Why are there no Austrian socialists? Ideology, science, and the Austrian school

1 Myrdal, in the preface to the English translation of his book, adopts a position quite similar to Joseph Schumpeter's (1954, pp. 41–5) discussion of *vision* and *analysis* when he argued that it is naïve empiricism to assert that, once all the metaphysical elements of political economy are eliminated, a robust positive theory will remain. Values provide what Schumpeter would later term the pre-analytic vision, from which developments in analysis flow. "Questions," Myrdal points out, "must be asked before answers can be given. The questions are an expression of our interest in the world, they are at bottom valuations" (Myrdal 1929, p. vii). As I have argued before, even if the role of vision in science is not denied, there still is the question of the assessment of the analytical argument of an author. In Boettke (1992), for example, the argument is made that the real divide between Hayek and Keynes on the one hand, and Hayek and the market socialist on the other, was not visionary, but analytical – specifically the analytics employed by the respective theorists with regard to understanding a capital-using economy.

2 The jury is still out, however, on the persuasiveness of E. W. Streissler's thesis that Menger's policy preference can be inferred from these lecture notes. The lecture notes are now available in published form (see Streissler and Streissler 1994). Hans Sennholz (1985) provides an interpretation of Menger's monetary writings which stresses Menger's skepticism toward government intervention in general, and in terms of monetary policy in particular, which provides additional support to Streissler's thesis.

3 For an attempted reconstruction of the analytical arguments in *The Road to Serfdom* and suggestions on why Hayek's argument was misunderstood by his contemporaries and ill-appreciated to this day, see Boettke (1995).

4 On the connection between Austrian economics and classical liberal political philosophy, see Raico (1994).

5 Actually, *before* Weber, Menger (1883, pp. 235–7) had already sketched a criticism of the "so-called ethical orientation" of research in political economy.

6 The desire to address the common complaint that Austrian economics yields only a methodological critique of the work of other economists, and that the school is incapable

of yielding substantive propositions on its own, leads me to introduce a recent book of mine with a list of the six theoretical and empirical propositions concerning comparative political economy that would be explored in the book. By doing so, I hoped to state clearly and boldly the substantive claims of my study on perestroika and the transition from socialism, in order to invite critical dialogue. Certainly the Austrian perspective on methodology is highly critical of mainstream economics, and even alternative schools of thought, but the strength of the school can best be gleaned in the application of its theoretical principles to the understanding of real-world problems (see Boettke 1993, pp. 1–11).

7   Rothbard, as a strong adherent of natural rights, believes that an objective theory of ethics is available. Mises' ethical relativism, and his adherence to utilitarianism, represent a serious problem to the Rothbardian libertarian. For one, if the majority of people within an economy – knowing the full consequences of the policy as pointed out by Mises – choose interventionist policies (for a host of reasons that persuade them to trade off economic prosperity for some other "good"), Mises must remain silent.

8   In Rothbard's system of thought, the limits of praxeology are recognized and the moral philosopher takes over, but, in Hoppe's system, praxeology is extended to include moral philosophy. While Rothbard and Hoppe both develop a libertarian ethic of self-ownership, they ground their respective theories differently. Rothbard grounds his theory in natural rights theory, while Hoppe attempts to ground his theory in the logic of action (as applied to the preconditions for argumentation).

9   The Austrian critique of positivism, however, is also part of the modernist agenda. Mises was a rationalist, and Hayek, while eschewing Scientism, nevertheless embraced the Enlightenment project of at least the Scottish variant. Hayek's project, following David Hume, was to use the facility of reason to whittle down the claims of reason. Both Mises and Hayek were groping for a "scientific subjectivism" that would avoid the formalist and empiricist prejudice on the one hand, and the abyss of relativism on the other.

10   However, G. A. Selgin (1988) provides a contemporary defense of the traditional Austrian position against recent developments in philosophy.

11   Thus, Kirzner's (1994) description of the mainstream of Austrian thought as holding dearly to the doctrine of *wertfreiheit* is accurate as a self-description, but not quite correct with regard to the epistemological status of their work. The epistemological case (as opposed to the pragmatic case) for *wertfreiheit* has been undermined by developments in philosophical thought.

12   My use of the terms Methodology and methodology is meant to highlight the point that while I deny the importance of a Methodology of demarcation I still hold out an important role for methodology. Moreover, I would argue that we must as scientists commit to *a* methodology to do our work. Pluralism is a result or scientific interaction, not a position of any one scientist in that process.

13   My argument holds for classical liberals and libertarians as well. We ignore some questions and minimize other aspects of social reality due to our vision, just as others may misunderstand points that we consider elementary analytical propositions because they do not share our vision. The complex interaction between vision and analysis (although not using those terms) is explained by Buchanan in reflecting on the reception of his ideas: "As my ideas approach mainstream, at least in some aspects, I find myself being challenged to defend foundational normative sources that I had long considered to be widely shared. The fact that my own acknowledged normative starting points do not seem widely accepted as I should have expected may possibly account for the apparent oversight of propositions that seemed so obvious to me. In other words, my normative mindset may be more important that I have ever realized" (Buchanan 1992, p. 155).

14   See Kenneth Boulding (1971) "After Samuelson, Who Needs Adam Smith?" *History of Political Economy* 3 (Fall): 225–37.

15   See Peter J. Boettke (1992) "Analysis and Vision in Economic Discourse," *Journal of the History of Economic Thought* 14 (Spring): 84–95.

16 Polanyi (1962) *Personal Knowledge*, Chicago: University of Chicago Press.
17 Kuhn (1958) *The Structure of Scientific Revolutions*, Chicago: University of Chicago Press.
18 Toulmin (1958) *The Uses of Argument*, Cambridge: Cambridge University Press, and *Human Understanding* (1972), Princeton: Princeton University Press.
19 See D. N. McCloskey (1985) *The Rhetoric of Economics*, Madison: University of Wisconsin Press, p. 37.
20 See Peter J. Boettke (1995) "Why Are There No Austrian Socialists?" *Journal of the History of Economic Thought* 17 (Spring): 35–56.
21 See Ricardo Crespo (1998) "Is Economics a Moral Science?" *Journal of Markets and Morality* 1(2) (October): 201–11.
22 Kirzner (1994) "Value Freedom," in *Elgar Companion to Austrian Economics*, ed. P. J. Boettke, Aldershot, UK: Edward Elgar Publishing, pp. 313–19.
23 I owe this formulation of the problem to David Schmidtz
24 Of course, the introduction of terms like *voluntary* and *coercion* introduce moral distinctions into the language of economic analysis. I do not want to object to this aspect of Crespo's argument, or to the theory-laden aspect of all social thought. However, I believe that by taking a pragmatic turn in our defense of value-neutrality we follow certain argumentative procedures that advance our ability to understand the limits and potential of social organization. If we deny that the economic way of thinking can make this step, then we must waive the knowledge that economics can provide in our attempt to advance the moral science of political economy.
25 I owe this terminology to Father James Sadowsky.
26 Buchanan (1987) "The Constitution of Economic Policy," *American Economic Review* 77 (June): 748–50.

3   Economic calculation: the Austrian contribution to political economy

1 Joe Salerno is the scholar whose work most forcefully pushes for the dehomogenization of Mises and Hayek, and specifically on the issue of "calculation" versus "knowledge" (see Salerno 1990, 1993, 1994, 1996). Rothbard (1991) also deserves to be singled out as advancing the Salerno thesis. One of the important points raised by Salerno and Rothbard is to focus on Mises' contributions to the socialist calculation debate in *Human Action*, where it must be admitted that in the standard history Mises' contributions are limited to his writings in the 1920s, and Hayek's work in the 1930s and 1940s moves to the center of the analysis. On the other hand, see the challenges to the Salerno thesis that have come from Yeager (1994, 1996) and Kirzner (1996). On the importance of the shared research program of Mises and Hayek for contemporary Austrian Economics, see Kirzner (1987).

2 Frank Knight, in the capital theory debates with Hayek and Mises, thought that he was responding to a shared analytical tradition. Kenneth Boulding, in discussing his moderate Keynesianism, would insist that Mises and Hayek raised important and disturbing questions to the Keynesian enterprise. Mises did not shy away from attacking the former students when he thought that they were in error, for example, Machlup, Habeler, and Morgenstern. Mises did criticize Hayek's *The Constitution of Liberty* as flawed because the last third (where Hayek makes concessions to the welfare state) of the book undermined the solid first two-thirds (which presented the principles of classical liberalism) (see Mises 1960, pp. 218–19). Hayek sees his own 1937 paper as a decisive break with Mises on economic methodology, but, as Hayek has said, he was always puzzled that Mises found the article to be a solid contribution to economic science (see Hayek 1994, p. 72). In other words, Mises did not see the article as contradicting his own position. Hayek's 1937 paper can be read as establishing that the pure logic of choice is a necessary although not sufficient component of an explanation of the equilibrating market process. To move from individual equilibrating action to systematic market-level equilibration requires

the introduction of subsidiary *empirical* assumptions. The reasons that Mises did not object to this rendering of the market process by Hayek would demand speculations beyond the scope of this chapter, but it would be a fruitful topic to pursue. But, for our present purposes, what should be noted is that at a crucial stage in Mises' discussion of the problem of economic calculation under socialism Mises cites Hayek precisely on the point that socialism would have to forgo the "division of intellectual labor which under capitalism provides a practicable method for economic calculation" (1949, p. 709, fn. 6). Mises cites *Individualism and Economic Order* (pp. 119–28), which are Hayek's three papers on the socialist calculation debate. In other words, on this issue, Mises saw his position as presented in *Socialism* and Hayek's in these essays as making essentially the same critical point against socialist proposals. As a scholar, Mises was not charitable in his practice of citation and he did not shy away from criticizing his students, so we are not on "thin ice" in inferring basic agreement from a footnote citation, as we might be in some other instances.

3   Thus, the intellectual *context* of their respective arguments was different. I am willing to admit with post-modernist writers that knowledge is always *contextual*. Where I differ with post-modernism is that I insist on the distinction between ontological and epistemological statements, which is sometimes blurred in certain traditions of post-modernist writings. Just because one admits from an epistemological stance that all knowledge is *contextual*, it does not follow that an ontological reality (independent of that context) does not exist. I can insist that an objective reality exists, yet admit that our human ability to present representations of that reality is limited. It is this philosophical "middle ground" position which accepts the critique of scientism, yet holds out hope for reason and evidence to improve our understanding of the world that, I would contend, has been an underlying theme within Austrian circles since its founding by Menger. For the purposes of this chapter these broader philosophical issues are not directly relevant. What I am concerned with is identifying the *different context* of Mises' and Hayek's argument. Mises wrote primarily to answer a nineteenth- and earlier twentieth-century political economy of socialism, Hayek wrote primarily to answer a twentieth-century technical economics argument that socialism could achieve efficiency in the same way as formal models of the market suggested that capitalism did. Of course, Mises and Hayek had arguments to offer concerning each others respective *context*, and it is here that the point of comparison must be made. In other words, what matters in assessing the respective contributions of Mises and Hayek on the issue of socialism is to put each argument in its respective *context*.

4   Economic calculation, as Mises put it, "is a method available only to people acting in the economic system of the division of labor in a social order based upon private ownership of the means of production. It can only serve the considerations of individuals or groups of individuals operating in the institutional setting of this social order ... Economic calculation in terms of money prices is the calculation of entrepreneurs producing for the consumers of a market society. It is of no avail for other tasks" (Mises, 1949, p. 216).

5   As Mises pointed out, "mere information" conveyed by technology is not enough to solve the economic problem.

> Here computation in kind as applied by technology is of no avail. Technology operates with countable and measurable quantities of external things and effects; it knows casual relations between them, but is foreign to their relevance to human wants and desires. Its field is that of objective use-value only. It judges all problems from the disinterested point of view of a neutral observer of physical, chemical, and biological events. For the notion of subjective use-value, for the specifically human angle, and for the dilemmas of acting man there is no room in the teachings of technology. It ignores the economic problem: to employ the available means in such a way that no want more urgently felt should remain unsatisfied because the means suitable for its attainment were employed – wasted – for the attainment of

a want less urgently felt. For solutions of such problems technology and its methods of counting and measuring are unfit. Technology tells us how a given end could be attained by various means which can be used together in various combinations, or how various available means could be employed for certain purposes. But it is at a loss to tell man which procedures he should choose out of the infinite variety of imaginable and possible modes of production.

(Mises 1949, p. 207)

6   It must be noted that Salerno has made a significant contribution to the development of a modern Austrian theory of the market process, despite my contrasting position with him on the dehomogenization of Mises and Hayek. That contribution is to refocus attention again on the issue of entrepreneurial *appraisement* and the forward-looking role of monetary calculation. But in Salerno's presentation, the forward-looking role is, ironically, overemphasized. In Mises' theory, monetary calculation is an indispensable aid to the human mind precisely because it is essential for both prospective and retrospective calculations. The price system, as an entire system, provides *ex ante* information which economic actors employ in deciding the future course of action; *ex post* information which informs economic actors of the appropriateness or inappropriateness of their past course of action; and the very discrepancy (i.e. *disequilibrium*) between the *ex ante* and *ex post* motivate economic actions (e.g. entrepreneurs) to *discover* better ways to arrange scarce means to satisfy ends. On the threefold advantage of the private property market price system see Mises (1922, p. 99).

7   See David Ramsey Steele (1992) for an extensive survey of the various attempts by socialist writers to answer Mises' challenge.

8   The importance of this emphasis on private property should not be underestimated. Without private property the very exchange process which generates the informational inputs into the decision process would not be produced. All the data that are given in many of the models that we will discuss shortly would not exist. In other words, it is not that in the absence of private property in the means of production it is more difficult to access economic knowledge; rather, the knowledge is not available to anyone (centralized, decentralized, or computer planners) because it will not come into existence. Thus, the Austrian argument moves beyond the complexity argument evident in Pareto, and is assumed to be the argument by Lange and others in later generations of mechanism design models of economic administration.

9   I should make it clear that I am not denying the universal validity of marginalist principles. There is no doubt that profit-maximization will be achieved when production is at that level where marginal revenue equals marginal costs; that all least-cost technologies will be employed when production is at that level which minimizes average cost; and that the efficiency in exchange, production and product mix will be achieved when a firm's price is equal to marginal costs (which implies that the full opportunity costs of production are taken into account). However, the way in which the propositions of neoclassical economics are interpreted is important. In a market process perspective, the filter of competition leads economic agents to adopt these rules of maximization to the limit, and thus the institutional environment of decision is crucial for this process. Economic actors cannot even begin to guess what the maximization rules (in terms of the system, as opposed to the individual) would be in the absence of this process. This, of course, is what I claim is Mises' real genius. Solving the problem by hypothesis is no solution, because this problem cannot be solved by assumption.

10 Mises made an identical point in *Socialism*. As he put it: "To understand the problem of economic calculation it was necessary to recognize the true character of the exchange relations expressed in the prices of the market. The existence of this important problem could be revealed only by the methods of the modern subjective theory of value" (Mises, 1922, p. 186). Ricardian classical political economy reduced economic development to

the physical–technical possibilities. The human element in decision-making is obscured in the Ricardian analysis. In the Austrian-marginalist rendition of economics, the human decision-maker moves to the forefront of analysis. It is the subjective assessment of trade-offs by individuals that must be communicated to others in the exchange ratios of the market, if the economic decisions of entrepreneurs are to dovetail with the desires of consumers.

11 Here Hayek makes a fundamental point, which should be stressed, as it anticipates his more mature development of the theory of spontaneous order: "… it is not necessary for the working of this system, that anybody should understand it. But people are not likely to let it work if they do not understand it … It needs special training of the economist to see that the spontaneous forces which limit the ambitions of the engineer themselves provide a way of solving a problem which otherwise would have to be solved deliberately" (Hayek, 1935a, p. 8).

12 Brutzkus's book *Economic Planning in Soviet Russia* was extremely important to Hayek in that it was an empirical illustration of Mises' thesis. When Hayek published his edited volume, *Collectivist Economic Planning*, Brutzkus's book was published as a companion volume. Unfortunately, the subsequent debate in economics was diverted into statics, and the historical examination of Soviet planning was diverted into a comparison of growth rates with Western economies. Both the theoretical and empirical direction distorted our understanding of Soviet economic reality and the implications of that reality for the issue of socialist planning. I have tried to repair the theory/history split with Boettke (1990) *The Political Economy of Soviet Socialism: The Formative Years, 1918–1928*. The Mises–Hayek thesis is applied to the Gorbachev reform era in Boettke (1993) *Why Perestroika Failed: The Politics and Economics of Socialist Transformation*.

13 Hayek did not see his own contribution on this issue as original. Originality belonged to Mises, and Hayek was ready to give credit to Mises. "The essential point where Professor Mises went far beyond anything done by his predecessors was the detailed demonstration that an economic use of the available resources was only possible if this pricing (i.e. prices expressed in money) was applied not only to the final product but also to all the intermediate products and factors of production, and that no other process was conceivable which would take in the same way account of all the relevant facts as did the pricing process of the competitive market" (Hayek 1935a, p. 33).

14 Although it should be pointed out that Weber does cite Mises on this issue. Weber claimed, however, that he came to his critique of economic calculation under socialism *before* he had read Mises' 1920 article.

15 The professional responses to one's mentor's work can be a legitimate motivating factor in scholarship. When Lavoie's revisionist interpretation of the socialist calculation debate was published there were two basic lines of criticism. First, some scholars claimed that Lavoie's work did not account for the success of Soviet planning. Second, other scholars claimed that Lavoie's work did not account for the model of workers' self-management. In part the dissertations written by myself and Prychitko were produced to counter these criticisms (see Boettke 1990; Prychitko 1991).

16 Hayek (1940) states that two chapters within the socialist calculation debate should be seen as closing with Mises as the clear victor. The first chapter was the idea that socialism could dispense with monetary calculation, and the second chapter was that the mathematical solution could replace the market mechanism. In both cases, the solutions proposed failed to meet Mises' challenge, according to Hayek. Mises also anticipated most of the possible responses that socialists would come up with, and offered criticisms before the fact (see Mises 1922, pp. 173–94).

17 Compare this with Hoff (1949, p. 207).

18 Despite the obvious clarifications to the literature that emerge within Salerno's writings on the role of entrepreneurial appraisement, the reading of Hayek that is presented is quite neoclassical and, as such, reinforces the mainstream interpretation that Hayek

was concerned with the informational efficiency of *equilibrium* prices, as opposed to the adaptive efficiency of *disequilibrium* prices.

19   Hayek thought that the problem was a preoccupation with equilibrium that had misled a generation of leading economists. The economists to whom he addressed his argument included, besides Lange, Dickinson, Durbin, Schumpeter, and Lerner (Hayek's student).

20   It is important to keep in mind that Mises is not here assuming *omniscience*. Throughout his examination of socialism, and government policy in general, he does insist on the assumption of *benevolence*. In this manner, the critique cannot be said to involve value judgments. On the other hand, Mises intended to dispel the notion of the *omniscience* of the state. In fact, if *omniscience* is granted – along side of *benevolence* – then Mises admitted that "one cannot help concluding that the infallible state was in a position to succeed in the conduct of production activities better than erring individuals" (Mises 1949, p. 692). Against this model of socialism – one assuming *benevolence* and *omniscience* – the economist critic can only insist on the poor judgment of the advocate in postulating a model which assumes away all the problems which, in the real world, the proposal would have to confront. But the economist critic cannot show the logical flaw, as Mises put it, the inference that the state should run all production was "logically inescapable as soon as people began to ascribe to the *state* not only moral but also intellectual perfection" (Ibid., p. 692).

21   This, of course, is the contribution that Israel Kirzner has made to theoretical economics. While mainstream models of price adjustment cannot explain the *path* to equilibrium with a theory of *disequilibrium* adjustments, Kirzner's theory of the entrepreneurial market process provides precisely the *disequilibrium foundations of equilibrium economics* that are required to complete our understanding of market theory and the price system. The theoretical conundrum that one can only get in equilibrium if one begins in equilibrium is a major intellectual puzzle. Kirzner's theory of entrepreneurial alertness offers a theory of adjustment which is endogenous to the model, and as such does not require an *ad hoc* assumption in order for a solution to the puzzle to be found. The absence of the entrepreneur in modern models of market competition was precisely due to the inability to deal with disequilibrium in theories of general competitive equilibrium.

22   This, of course, is the very important point stressed by Yeager (1994) against the dehomogenization project of Salerno. In order to calculate, actors require knowledge of the inputs into the decision process. Absent the market process and this knowledge does not exist, so they cannot calculate. Knowledge and calculation go hand in hand. Attempting to calculate in the absence of knowledge is impossible, and calculation, assuming that *all* knowledge is available, is a trivial matter. If knowledge is assumed to exist on, say, a shelf, and then the question is a matter of pulling it down off the shelf in an optimal manner, then the planning problem simply becomes a search problem, and Mises' challenge has no force. If, on the other hand, no knowledge is said to be required, then the arithmetic without any input variables provides no solution. But, it is precisely because the knowledge required for solution is only available within a certain institutional configuration that projects which propose to change that institutional configuration run into an insoluble problem. Prices without property are an illusion. Calculation without prices is impossible. On the issue of knowledge and calculation, also see Kirzner (1996, p. 150), where he states: "To be unable to calculate the worthwhileness of a prospective action taken in a market society, is, after all, to not know the importance to others of the goods and services one commits to that action, and the importance to others of the goods one will obtain from that action."

23   This is a point that I have stressed in my applied work on the political economy of socialism (see Boettke 1990, 1993).

24   For an examination of some of the theoretical and empirical questions that emerge in the post-Communist world that Austrian economists must address, see Boettke and Prychitko (1996).

4 Hayek's *The Road to Serfdom* revisited: government failure in the argument against socialism

1 For example, I am not contesting Higgs' claim that Hayek does not cite the contemporary public choice literature. Hayek, indeed, does not cite this literature, neither does he cite contemporary work in Austrian economics. His failure to cite either line of literature, however, should not be taken as evidence of his lack of treatment of the issues developed in either of these literatures. Hayek is no less of an Austrian economist because he fails to cite the work of Israel Kirzner and Murray Rothbard, let alone Mario Rizzo, Gerald O'Driscoll, Roger Garrison, Lawrence White, and Don Lavoie, and an interpreter of his work would be "misreading" Hayek to suggest otherwise. Similarly, the fact that Hayek does not cite the work of Buchanan, Tullock, or other public choice scholars, should not be read as a disregard for the analytical issues raised in the public choice literature.

Moreover, I am not contesting Higgs' contention, expressed in private correspondence dated 16 June 1994, that Hayek's public policy positions leave much to be desired from a libertarian position. This is a point recently emphasized by libertarian theorists, such as Hans-Hermann Hoppe (1994) and Walter Block (1994). These thinkers are undoubtedly correct, Hayek is not a modern libertarian. I am not suggesting that people read Hayek for libertarian policy prescriptions, but for a series of analytical arguments which will improve our understanding of the organizational principles of political processes. The fact that, in my own view, if one consistently pursues these analytical arguments they will generate libertarian policy positions far beyond the imagination of Hayek is beside the point of the present chapter.

2 This opinion misses out on the strength of Hayek's research program and its unity throughout his career. Very little of Hayek's work, in fact, is devoted to a critique of central planning, although this critique forms the core of his analysis of various alternative proposals for government action to direct the economic process (including the demand and supply of public goods, the issuance of currency, the contract between legislation and common law, etc.). One of the most disappointing features of the published obituaries on Hayek was their lack of appreciation of the economic theory underlying Hayek's political liberalism (i.e. the private-property, limited-government program of classical liberalism). But Hayek's liberalism was shaped by his Austrian understanding of the nature of economic processes. Thus, the subtle critique of central planning is much more an issue of general economic theory than public policy. This theoretical critique permeates all of Hayek's work, from capital theory to legal philosophy. In this regard, see Kirzner (1991) and Boettke (1992a).

3 For example, in neither Dennis Muller's (1989), Joe Stevens' (1992), nor David Johnson's (1991) basic textbooks on public choice economics does Hayek warrant even one mention in the index or bibliography. Within the constitutional political-economy group of scholars, however, Hayek's work appears to be more fundamental to the core of theory development, as is evidenced by a quote from Hayek which adorns the masthead of the journal, *Constitutional Political Economy*. Moreover, it is quite clear that Buchanan and Vanberg represent the two modern scholars within the public choice tradition who have devoted the most energy to incorporating (and/or revising) Hayek's work on law and politics to forge a revitalized political economy and social philosophy. Special mention, however, should also be made of Gordon Tullock's – in my opinion sorely undervalued – examination of bureaucratic planning, where the Hayekian argument concerning the "knowledge problem" forms the core of his crucial third section (Tullock 1987, pp. 120–220).

4 On Schumpeter's assessment of the economic and organizational logic of socialism, see Schumpeter (1942, pp. 172–99; 1954, p. 989). If socialism was to confront any problems in operation, Schumpeter asserted, then it would be at the level of practical administrative difficulties, and *not* in the realm of pure economic logic as Mises and Hayek contended.

5 In Boettke (1993, pp. 46–56), the Mises–Hayek critique of socialism is examined in

each of its constituent parts – property incentives, informational complexity, the contextual nature of knowledge, and political organization.

6 As I will argue, it is this assumption which led to many of the misunderstandings concerning Hayek's work, because many – even those sympathetic with liberalism – did not understand the import of Mises' demonstration.

7 See Raico (1993) and Hoppe (1993, pp. 93–110) for an examination of interest-group theory in classical liberalism in general and Austrian economics in particular.

8 See, for example, Hayek (1944, p. 77) where he argues that: "Those most immediately interested in a particular issue are not necessarily the best judges of the interest of society as a whole. To take only the most characteristic case: when capital and labor in an industry agree on some policy of restriction and thus exploit the consumers, there is usually no difficulty about the division of spoils in proportion to former earning or on some similar principle. The loss which is divided between thousands or millions is usually either simply disregarded or quite inadequately considered." Fairness in planning, Hayek goes on to argue, would require that the gains and losses of policies be equally considered by the planning authority, but, given the complex chain of events and the indirect nature of the effect of policies, there is no compelling reason why the costs "divided between thousands or millions" would be adequately incorporated into the decision-making process. The discretionary nature of planning, however, forces the authorities to make more and more judgments of precisely these kinds. Abandoning the rule of law for the discretion of planning, Hayek argues, amounts to an unintended return to the rule of status rather than contract.

9 See, for example, Przeworski and Limongi (1993) for this type of argument. There are several problems that immediately come to mind. First, this was not the liberal argument put forth by either Hayek (1944) or Friedman (1962). Second, the analysis assumes that economic development is synonymous with growth rates (i.e. the difficulties of aggregate economics are not adequately addressed). Finally, the *de facto* political structure of the society in question is left unexplored in these studies. For example, in contemporary China, much of the "success" of the economic reforms can be attributed to the *de facto* political decentralization that occurred in the mid- to late 1980s (Weingast 1993, pp. 33–40).

10 It is not impossible to attempt to centrally plan a complex industrial economy, it is only impossible to do so "successfully." Success here means achieving the stated socialist ends of increased prosperity, efficient use of resources, elimination of the business cycle, elimination of monopoly power, and an equitable distribution of wealth.

11 As we will see later, this is where Hayek parted company with Keynes. It is somewhat ironic that Oscar Wilde – and not Keynes – saw the impossibility of mixing socialist economic planning with bourgeois values. Wilde argued in his essay "The Soul of Man Under Socialism" that perhaps socialism would yield a better economic performance than the market economy, but it would destroy artistic freedom. Hayek's argument would simply compound the Wilde-type case against socialism by pointing out that the socialist system could not outperform the market society on the economic front either.

12 For an application of this Hayekian-type argument to the debate over the rise of Stalinism within the Soviet context, see Boettke (1990, pp. 34–8). For an application of the argument in the context of decentralized socialism, such as case of the former Yugoslavia, see Prychitko (1991).

13 Hayek discusses federalism in *The Road to Serfdom* in the chapter, "The Prospects of International Order" (Hayek 1944, pp. 219–38). Also see Hayek (1948, pp. 255–72, and 1960, pp. 176–92).

14 On the issue of *vision* and *analysis* in economic reasoning see Schumpeter (1954, pp. 41–5).

15 For example, consider Frank Knight's (1936; 1938, pp. 867–8) dismissal of the crucial Misesian argument concerning the impossibility of economic calculation under socialism. Knight believed that the problems with socialism were political and not economic.

However, see Knight (1940), where he argued that the fundamental economic problem of socialism arises due to the dynamic nature of economic life which demands continuous adjustment and adaptation on the part of economic decision-makers in response to ever-changing conditions – which, of course, was a key component of Mises' original argument (Mises 1922, pp. 105, 120–1).

16 For a *contra*-Whiz history of thought with regard to the tool-kit of economic analysis, and namely the model of perfect competition, see Machovec (1995).

17 Milton Friedman has pointed out to me, in private correspondence concerning this chapter, dated 9 August 1994, that when Knight was asked later for permission to reprint these lectures, he replied "I wish I could unprint them."

18 Hayek understood this development quite well and directed a criticism against what could be termed the "democratic fetishism" of the time, or as he put it:

> The fashionable concentration on democracy as the main value threatened is not without danger. It is largely responsible for the misleading and unfounded belief that, so long as the ultimate source of power is the will of the majority, the power cannot be arbitary [*sic*.] ... There is no justification for the belief that, so long as power is conferred by democratic procedure, it cannot be arbitrary; the contrast suggested by this statement is altogether false: it is not the source but the limitation of power which prevents it from being arbitrary. Democratic control *may* prevent power from becoming arbitrary, but it does not do so by its mere existence. If democracy resolves on a task which necessarily involves the use of power which cannot be guided by fixed rules, it must become arbitrary power"
>
> (Hayek 1944, p. 71, emphasis in original)

19 See, for example, Frank Knight's review (1946), in which he suggests that "comparatively little is explicitly said which Hayek, or any opponent of 'planning,' in its current meaning of 'planned economy' (a more appealing synonym for state socialism), would need to disagree." As Knight goes on to argue, the dominant impression that one gets after reading the book is "one of glaring contradiction between the tone and evident implications of virtually the whole argument and the definite commitments to any position on social policy." Also see the lengthy review of Wootton's book by John Jewkes (1946).

20 Also see Merriam's radio debate with Hayek over *The Road to Serfdom*, as transcribed in Hayek (1994, pp. 108–23). The general tone of negative reviews in leading scholarly journals was not limited to Hayek. In reviewing Mises' *Bureaucracy*, Harvard professor Pendleton Herring wrote, "If this volume were written as a campaign document, it would merit attention at the technical level as a contrivance for obfuscating debate in accordance with the adage: 'If you can't convince them, confuse them.' It is offered, however, as a serious piece of analysis." What was it about Mises' book that most annoyed Herring? Apparently, Mises' insistence that "the main issues of present day politics are purely economic and cannot be understood without a grasp of economic theory." We do not need, Herring informs the reader, "a course in economic theory as preached by the 'Austrian School' " (Herring 1945).

21 Suffice it to say that the "last few pre-war years" in the Soviet Union constituted the political purges of the 1930s, as well as the consequences of collectivization and industrialization on the masses. All three Stalinist policies combined to form a policy of genocide as horrific as those instituted by the Nazis, as has now been established in the historical literature by such ideologically diverse scholars as Robert Conquest and Roy Medvedev.

22 For a response to Heilbroner's argument that Mises and Hayek possessed a more prescient vision, although not necessarily a correct economic analysis, see Boettke (1992b).

23 The tenet in question would be stable preferences. Austrian economists agree with mainstream theorists that economists do not have much of value to say about the origin

or source of preferences. However, that is not the same as strictly holding the assumption of stable preferences through time. In the Mises–Rothbard analysis of "demonstrated preference," individual preference mappings could indeed be ever-changing.

24 Frank Knight understood the central importance of capital theory to the analytical structure of Austrian economics, and that is why, as a critic, he devoted so much of his review of Mises' *Nationalökonomie* to the issue, when in fact Mises' tome did not devote much space to an explicit treatment of capital theory. Appearances can be deceiving, however, because actually Mises' book is – as Knight was suggesting – almost exclusively about capital theory (Knight 1941).

25 Instead, the equilibrium of any policy set is explored as, for example, when Gary Becker (1991, pp. 369–74) explains the social security system as an equilibrium response to the "market failure" in the human capital market, or when George Stigler (1992) suggests that subsidies to the sugar industry are an efficient outcome by virtue of the fact that nobody has been able to provide a lower cost alternative. Also see, Becker (1985), where the theoretical argument for the "efficiency" of the competitive process among pressure groups in a democratic system (i.e. a system with a large degree of access to the political system) is laid out. The Virginia School, on the other hand, seeks to expose the economic inefficiencies associated with many public policies. The real question which must be raised is whether they can consistently explore these problems while retaining their commitment to neoclassical price theory. In private correspondence dated 13 September 1994, Gary Becker has objected to my interpretation of Chicago political economy. I cannot address his concerns in the present chapter, but I do think the notions of equilibrium and efficiency, whether in market or political environments, are more troublesome than is usually admitted in the Chicago-style studies in political economy. Many of the philosophical, methodological, and economic theory issues associated with the Chicago notion of efficiency are addressed by scholars from various schools of thought, in the symposium "Can Economists Handle Change?" in the research annual *Advances in Austrian Economics* (Boettke and Rizzo 1994, 3–196).

26 A tentative attempt at producing a modern hybrid Austrian–public choice theory of the political process can be found in Richard Wagner (1989, pp. 207–12). For an application of this type of theorizing as applied to the political–economic situation in the former Soviet Union, and in particular the Gorbachev era, see Boettke (1993).

5 Coase, Communism, and the 'Black Box' of Soviet-type economies

1 Coase also cites the following reasons: his lack of training in Latin prevented him from studying history (which was his first choice) and his lack of aptitude for mathematical reasoning prevented him from studying chemistry (his second choice) and thus his study of commerce was the default option. But this choice was a happy one because his socialist leanings led to an interest in economic and social problems. For an intellectual biography of Coase, see Medema (1994).

2 Coase's influence on the economics of organization is documented in Steven Medema (1995). This development is often associated with the work of Oliver Williamson (1975, 1985), but it would also have to include the literature on the property rights theory of the firm as developed by Armen Alchian (1977) and Harold Demsetz (1988, 1989a, 1989b); the work in evolutionary economics associated with Richard Nelson and Sidney Winter (1983); and the work of Richard Langlois (1986). William Lazonick's (1991) work on business organization should also be mentioned. A rigorous textbook formulation of the modern economics of organization is provided in Milgrom and Roberts (1992).

3 This last point – monetary calculation – was first put forth as an interpretation of Coase's article by Murray Rothbard. Rothbard interpreted Coase's work on the firm in light of Mises' proposition about monetary calculation. See Rothbard (1962, pp. 544–50). Also, see the recent work by Peter Klein (1996) on this issue.

4 "The Soviet economy," wrote Alain Besançon in describing the contract between the "thin" description approach of economists and the "thick" description approach of areas studies scholars, "is the subject of a considerable volume of scholarly work which occupies numerous study centres in Europe and the United States and which provided material for a vast literature and various academic journals. But those born in the Soviet Union or for those who approach Soviet society through history, literature, travel or through listening to what the émigrés have to say, find that they cannot recognize what the economists describe. There seems to be an unbridgeable gap between this system, conceived through measurements and figures, and the other system, without measurements and figures, which they have come to know through intuition and their own actual experience. It is an astonishing feature of the world of Soviet affairs that a certain kind of economic approach to Soviet reality, no matter how well-informed, honest and sophisticated, is met with such absolute skepticism and total disbelief by those who have a different approach that they do not even want to offer any criticism – it being impossible to know where to begin" (Besançon 1980, p. 143).

5 While it is important to stress that, *de jure* pronouncements notwithstanding, the system operated on the basis of *de facto* property rights claims, it is vital for understanding the systemic inefficiencies that we recognize how the lack of *de jure* status to these claims attenuates these claims and thus produces incentives for behavior that, while individually rational, fails to generate an economically efficient social order. By "efficient" here I do not mean the typical Pareto-Efficient state of affairs, but rather the adaptive efficiency associated with theories of the market process and tendencies for plan coordination among economic actors. Boycko *et al.* (1995, p. 36) make the point about the existence of, but limits to, the property rights arrangements: "The structure of ownership under Soviet socialism was thus both different from the textbook model and highly inefficient. The politicians had almost all the control rights, and no cash flow rights. The managers had some of the control rights, but no cash flow rights either. The objectives of the politicians who possessed the control rights were very far removed from the public interest. The virtually complete political control without countervailing cash flow rights to moderate political temptations did not constitute an efficient ownership structure."

6 The original formulation of this type of policy proposal was made by Edgar Feige (1990) of the University of Wisconsin at Madison. However, many of the auction models for privatization that were proposed – including the notion behind "people's capitalism" and voucher privatization – draw upon this rough sketch for inspiration.

7 I have developed this argument concerning the reform trap in more detail in Boettke (1994).

8 See, for example, Coase (1988a, pp. 1–31), especially p. 3, where he states that "The preoccupation of economists with the logic of choice, while it may ultimately rejuvenate the study of law, political science, and sociology, has nonetheless had, in my view, serious adverse effects on economics itself." In mainstream economics, Coase continues, "Exchange takes place without any specification of its institutional setting." It is exchange *within* an institutional setting that motivates the Coasean program.

9 The basic problem with the Pigouvian solution was that for the government official to set the correct tax/subsidy scheme to correct the harmful effect of markets, a level of information was assumed to be available that, if it were available, would make the Pigouvian solution irrelevant because market participants would have already produced the solution. In other words, the Pigouvian remedy was either redundant or irrelevant due to impracticality as a solution. This is also a point made by Buchanan in his basic work on opportunity costs in economic theory.

10 This style of reasoning was prominent in several thinkers at the time Coase wrote his "The Theory of the Firm" paper – including Knight, who in his influential work, *Risk, Uncertainty and Profit*, first develops a model of the world in which there is no risk or uncertainty and thus no profit. The first model is developed with the express purpose of isolating those conditions which in fact bring rise to the phenomena of profit. Hayek, in

the 1930s, maintains a similar use of the assumption of full employment equilibrium to explain the business cycle. In Hayek's critique of Keynes, one of the main arguments (beside a critique of aggregation) was that one cannot explain the phenomena of unemployment unless one begins with the assumption of full employment, and then explains the conditions which give rise to unemployment – in the case of the business cycle "the cluster of errors" which characterize the downturn. In both Knight and Hayek, the purpose of the frictionless model is not description, but to aid the task of isolating the real frictions which affect the economic system. Just as the friction between the sole of my feet and the floor enables me to walk, so the frictions in the economic system enable the system to achieve the degree of order that we witness. When we assume away the frictions, we are able to see how the enabling institutions often logically disappear. Coase's work is in this tradition – we can refer to it as *a political economy of everyday life*.

11 See Paul Rubin (1996) for a discussion of the evolution of the legal infrastructure required for post-Communist transformation.

12 The transaction costs associated with "buying out" current benefactors of the existing system may be too high, and thus, if included in the political economy cost–benefit analysis, would suggest that the costs to reform may outweigh the benefits (see Tollison and Wagner, 1991). This problem, referred to as "the transitional gains trap," as termed by Tullock, forces the analyst to shift the focus of attention away from past inefficiencies to questions concerning the future of rules which will prevent future economic deformities.

6 The Soviet experiment with pure Communism

1 Michael Polanyi (1953) "The Foolishness of History: November, 1917–November 1957, *Encounter* IX(5) (April): p. 33.

2 Paul Craig Roberts (1971) *Alienation and the Soviet Economy*, Albuquerque: University of New Mexico Press.

3 Laszlo Szamuely (1974) *First Models of the Socialist Economic Systems*, Budapest: Akademiai Kiado.

4 This is not a point of mere antiquarian interest, but plagues commentators today when they try to understand the meaning or assess the possibility of perestroika. In this essay, however, I will limit my discussion to the three-year period when Lenin, Trotsky, Bukharin, *et al.*, attempted to implement their socialist project, leaving aside current Soviet policy. For a discussion of how a proper historical understanding is fundamental to understanding the current reform movement, see Paul Craig Roberts (1988) "The Soviet Economy: A Hopeless Cause?" *Reason* July: 57, where he argues that: "The Soviet story is one of the interaction of speculative excess or utopian aspirations with refractory reality. But scholars cannot see this as long as they believe that Soviet central planning originated not in an effort to eliminate the market but in a decision to squeeze agriculture in order to rapidly industrialize." Unless commentators understand the "grand tale" of the Soviet experience with Communism, they will be paralyzed in their attempt to understand the meaning of the Gorbachev phenomenon.

5 Polanyi, p. 36.

6 For example, Thomas Remmington (1984) *Building Socialism in Bolshevik Russia: Ideology and Industrial Organization, 1917–1921*, Pittsburgh: University of Pittsburgh Press, and Silvana Malle (1985) *The Economic Organization of War Communism, 1918–1921*, New York: Cambridge University Press, 1985.

7 William Chamberlin (1935/1987) *The Russian Revolution, 1917–1921*, two volumes, Princeton: Princeton University Press, vol. 2, p. 105.

8 H. G. Wells (1921) *Russia in the Shadows*, New York: George H. Doran, p. 137.

9 This economic collapse was also depicted in such literature as Boris Pasternak's *Doctor Zhivago* and Ayn Rand's *We the Living*. As Alain Besançon has pointed out, those scholars who approach Soviet society through the study of literature, travel or émigré reports

"find that they cannot recognize what the economists describe" (Besançon (1980) "Anatomy of a Spectre," *Survey* 25(4) (Autumn): 143.

10 Moshe Lewin (1985) *The Making of the Soviet System*, New York: Pantheon Books, 211.

11 Stephen Cohen (1971/1980) *Bukharin and the Bolshevik Revolution*, New York: Oxford University Press, p. 123.

12 See Alec Nove (1969/1984) *An Economic History of the U.S.S.R.* New York: Penguin Books, pp. 46–187, and G. Warren Nutter (1962) *The Growth of Industrial Production in the Soviet Union*, Princeton: Princeton University Press, pp. 3–10.

13 Tom Bottomore (1986/1987) "Is Rivalry Rational?" *Critical Review* 1(1) (Winter): p. 45.

14 Maurice Dobb (1948) *Soviet Economic Development Since 1917*, New York: International Publishers, p. 122.

15 Ibid.

16 Ibid., p. 101.

17 Ibid.

18 Ibid., p. 100.

19 Although it is not my purpose here to outline a Marxian theory of alienation and exploitation, it is necessary to realize that the decision-making cadre of the Soviet government were revolutionary Marxists who sought to rid Russian society of the evils of capitalism. The Marxian theory of alienation is intimately connected to commodity production, exchange and, in particular, the monetary economy. Alienation to Marx was an objective condition coexistent with commodity production, i.e. the separation of production from use. It is *not* a psychological or subjective condition felt by frustrated man. The transcendence of alienation means to Marx the transcendence of market relations. Viewing Marx as an organizational theorist enables the student of Marx to see a tremendous unity in Marx's life-work that is denied by those who wish to split Marx into a young Marx and a mature Marx. The young Marx, just like the mature Marx, was concerned with transcending the organizational form of alienation, i.e. the commodity production of capitalist social relations, as Marx argued himself in the *Economic and Philosophical Manuscripts of 1844* (Moscow: Progress Press, 1977, pp. 78–9): "Just as we have derived the concept of private property from the concept of estranged, alienated labor by analysis, so we can develop every category of political economy with the help of these two factors; and we shall find again in each category, e.g. trade, competition, capital, money, only a particular and developed expression of these first elements." See also Marx's discussion, in the *Manuscripts*, of money as the "alienated ability of mankind" (pp. 127–32). On Marx's theory of alienation and central planning, see Roberts; Roberts and Matthew Stephenson, *Marx's Theory of Exchange, Alienation and Crisis* (New York: Praeger, 1973/1983); David Reese (1980) *Alienation, Exchange and economic Calculation*, unpublished PhD thesis, Virginia Polytechnic Institute, Blacksburg, VA (revised manuscript, 1985); and Don Lavoie, *Rivalry and Central Planning* (New York: Cambridge University Press, pp. 28–47).

20 Dobb, pp. 102–3.

21 For an excellent discussion of these events see Paul Avrich (1974) *Kronstadt 1921*, New York: W. W. Norton.

22 Dobb, p. 123. However, see Richard Sakwa (1987) "The Commune State in Moscow in 1918," *Slavic Review* Fall–Winter: 431. Sakwa argues that:

> In the chaotic conditions of late 1917, however, the development of direct democracy and decentralization in both political and economic spheres, was not so much a policy implemented by the Bolshevik party as one that emerged largely regardless of its wishes and out of circumstances. The institutions of the dictatorship of the proletariat were only consolidated by June 1918. The practical implementation of commune ideas before then has given rise to a highly idealized if barely credible vision of a golden age of Bolshevism that came to end in spring 1918.

23 Dobb, p. 120.
24 E. H. Carr (1952/1980) *The Bolshevik Revolution,* three volumes, New York: Norton, vol. II, p. 270.
25 Ironically, many other commentators point out the same connection between War Communism and war socialism as evidencing the theoretical nature of War Communism as an experiment with Marxian central planning. See Szamuely; see also Vladimir Treml (1969) "Interaction of Economic Thought and Economic Policy in the Soviet Union," *History of Political Economy* 1(1) (Spring): 187–216. For a discussion of the German ideas of planning that had a direct influence upon the Bolsheviks, see Judith Merkle (1980) *Management and Ideology,* Berkeley: University of California Press, pp. 172–207; Walter Rathenau (1921) *In Days to Come,* New York: Alfred A. Knopf, pp. 63–128; Nicholas Balabkins (1978) "*Der Zukunftsstaat:* Carl Ballod's vision of a leisure-oriented socialism," *History of Political Economy* 10(2) (Summer): 213–32. Also see Mises' (1919/1983) discussion of war socialism in *Nation, State and Economy,* translated by L. B. Yeager, New York: New York University Press, pp. 141–7.
26 Carr, p. 271.
27 Ibid., p. 273.
28 Ibid.
29 Ibid., p. 207.
30 Ibid., p. 162.
31 Ibid., p. 175.
32 Ibid., p. 157.
33 Ibid., p. 151.
34 Ibid., p. 157.
35 Ibid., p. 172.
36 Carr, p. 172. Carr may have a point here, in that policies tend to take on a life of their own after they are instituted, especially when survival of the party is at stake. As Robert Higgs has demonstrated within the American context, institutions that are initiated to conduct policy within a crisis situation tend to outlive the crisis and become counterproductive to economic prosperity. See Higgs (1987) *Crisis and Leviathan,* New York: Oxford University Press. Despite these unintended results, the original plans and purposes of the actors who initiated the policies should not be discounted too heavily. And, as will be discussed later, the Bolsheviks themselves saw a connection between models of war planning and positive socialist construction.
37 Carr, p. 198.
38 Ibid., p. 197. But see Carr's discussion of the beginnings of planning on 36 ff., which implies that both ideology and emergency played a role. Carr is particularly confusing in this part of his discussion. He argues that planning was not possible until 1920, because of the civil war. The institutions of planning, i.e. the Supreme Economic Council, the State bank, nationalization of industry, etc., were established in 1918 and 1919, but they took on an *ad hoc* character because of civil war. Real, centralized planning, therefore, could not be instituted until 1920. Thus, here he admits that central planning was instituted in 1920, not 1928. The economic collapse of 1921 thus occurs during the regime of economic planning and not civil war.
39 Carr, pp. 205–6.
40 Ibid., p. 205.
41 Ibid., p. 216.
42 Ibid., p. 228.
43 Ibid., p. 271.
44 Ibid., p. 246.
45 Ibid., p. 260–1.
46 Ibid., p. 275.
47 See Szamuely, pp. 84–91, for a discussion of the debate among Bolshevik decision-makers over the introduction of NEP and the defense of War Communism by Larin, Kristman, *et al.*

48 Carr, p. 275.

49 Ibid., p. 276. Here again Carr does not maintain a consistent position. The confusion over War Communism was even represented within official Soviet publications. Consider the following statement from an article in *Bol'shaya Sovetskaya Entrsiklopediya* vol. XII (1928):

> It would be a great error not to see, behind the obvious economic utopianism of the attempt of war communism to *realize an immediate marketless–centralized reorganization of our economy*, the fact that fundamentally the economic policy of the period of war communism was imposed by the embittered struggle for victory ... The historical sense of war communism consisted in the need to take possession of the economic base by relying on military and political force. But it would be *incorrect* to see in war communism only measures of mobilization imposed by war conditions. In working to adapt the whole economy to the needs of the civil war, in building a consistent system of war communism, the working class was at the same time laying the foundation for further socialist reconstruction.

> (quoted in Carr, p.275, n.l., emphasis added)

While Carr can argue that Marxian language was an *ex post* justification for policies that were unavoidable, it seems just as possible that war emergency language is an *ex post* excuse for a dream that proved unrealizable.

50 Stephen Cohen (1972) "In Praise of War Communism" in *Revolution and Politics in Russia*, A. and J. Rabinowitch (eds.) Bloomington: Indiana University Press, p. 193.

51 Nikolai Bukharin (1924/1967) *The Path to Socialism in Russia*, New York: Omicron Books, p. 178, quoted in Szamuely, pp. 108–57.

52 Bukharin (1922) "R.S.F.S.R." *Pravda*, December 3: p. 3, quoted in Cohen (1972), *Bukharin*, p. 146.

53 Bukharin (1924) *O likvidatorstve nashikh duei*, quoted in Alec Nove (1924/1979) "Bukharin and His Ideas," *Political Economy and Soviet Socialism*, London: George Allen and Unwin, p. 86. See also Cohen "Rethinking Bolshevism," *Bukharin*, pp. 123–59.

54 It seems that Jurgen Habermas, arguably the leading leftist academic in the world today, recognizes this point when he argues that even radical democratic socialism might be impossible:

> All modern economies are so complex that a complete shift to participatory decision-making processes, that is to say, a democratic restructuring at every level, would inevitably do damage to some of the sensitive requirements of contemporary organizations. If we wish to maintain such organizations at their present level of complexity, then it is probably that the idea of socialism can no longer (and need no longer) be realized by means of the emancipation from alienated labor. It may be that initiatives to democratize global economic priorities and to create humane working conditions can only come from outside in future, by which I mean that a thoroughgoing internal reorganization of the economy in accordance with the principles of self-administration is neither possible nor necessary.

> (Habermas 1986)

"Ideologies and Society in the Post-War World" in P. Dews *Habermas: Autonomy & Solidarity* [interviews with Jurgen Habermas], London: Verso, p. 45. But Habermas, while admitting these problems, holds fast to his criticism of the market – blind to the possibility that the radical solution of the social ills that concern him lies in the radical decentralism of a truly market-based society.

55 My concern is not so much with what Marx meant by socialism, although this is obviously

a point of importance, but rather what leading European and Russian Marxist thinkers thought Marx's project entailed. In particular, with regard to the Russian experience, what did Lenin, Trotsky, Bukharin, *et al.*, think a Marxian world should look like?

56   Alexander Gerschenkron (1969) "History of Economic Doctrines and Economic History," *American Economic Review* LIX(2) (May): p. 16. Also see Joseph Berliner (1964) "Marxism and the Soviet Economy," *Problems of Communism* XII(5) (September–October): 1–10, who argues that Marxism has had little impact on Soviet socialism, and that economists writing about Soviet economic policy and institutions should not find it necessary to consider Marxian theory.

57   See Nove, p. 47.

58   This misunderstanding of Marx's project is because many believe that Marx's analysis is limited to a critique of capitalism and suggests nothing for the implementation of socialism. But, as Don Lavoie has argued in depth, Marx's negative view of capitalism implies a positive view of socialism. See Lavoie (1985, pp. 28–47); Don Lavoie, *National Economic Planning: What is Left?* Cambridge: Ballinger, pp. 11–24, 211–45.

59   Karl Marx (1906) *Capital: A Critique of Political Economy*, New York: Modern Library, p. 92.

60   Marx, *Economic and Philosophical Manuscripts*, p. 97.

61   See Karl Marx and Friedrich Engels (1969) "Manifesto of the Communist Party," *Selected Works*, three volumes, Moscow: Progress Publishers, vol. I, pp. 98–137; vol. I, "The Class Struggles in France," pp. 186–299; vol. I, "The Eighteenth Brumaire of Louis Bonapart," pp. 394–487; vol. II, "The Civil War in France," pp. 178–244.

62   Radoslav Selucky (1979) *Marxism, Socialism, Freedom*, New York: St Martin's Press, has argued that Marx's project of the rationalization of the economy may be inconsistent with the rationalization of politics that Marx envisioned. The concept of a centrally planned unity in economic life is mutually exclusive from the ideal of full democratic participation within political life. The line of reasoning is consistent with basic Marxian materialist philosophy, which argued that the material base (economic life) determines the superstructure (the realm of ideas). Selucky argues that: "No Marxist may legitimately construct a social system whose political superstructure would differ structurally from its economic base. If one accepts Marx's concept of base and superstructure, a centralized, hierarchically organized economic subsystem cannot coexist with a pluralistic, horizontally organized self-governed political subsystem" (Selucky 1979, p. 78).

63   Lavoie, *National Economic Planning*, pp. 18–19.

64   Alexander Rustow (1950–7/1980) *Freedom and Domination: A Historical Critique of Civilization*, Princeton: Princeton University Press, p. 571.

65   Ludwig von Mises sparked the debate in 1920 with his challenging article, "Economic Calculation in the Socialist Commonwealth," which was later translated and reprinted in the 1935/1975 volume: *Collectivist Economic Planning*, F. A. von Hayek (ed.), New York: Augustus M. Kelley. Mises (1922/1981) refined his argument in *Socialism: An Economic and Sociological Analysis*, Indianapolis: Liberty Press. Mises' conclusion that rational economic calculation was (is) impossible under socialism was endorsed by Max Weber (1922/1978) *Economy and Society*, two volumes, G. Roth and C. Wittich (eds.), Berkeley: University of California Press, vol. I, pp. 63–211, especially pp. 100–13. This triggered responses from German socialist writers such as Karl Polanyi and Eduard Heimann; see Mises, *Socialism*, pp. 473–8. Also see William Keizer (1987) "Two Forgotten Articles by Ludwig von Mises on the Rationality of Socialist Economic Calculation," *Review of Austrian Economics*, 1: 109–22, for a more extensive discussion of the Central European debate of the 1920s.

Mises' contention was later challenged in the English-language journals during the 1930s and 1940s. The counterargument was made by Oskar Lange (1939/1970) *On the Economic Theory of Socialism*, Benjamin Lippincott (ed.) New York: Augustus M. Kelley; and Abba P. Lerner (1944) *The Economics of Control*, New York: Macmillan, among others. Mises' student and associate, F. A. von Hayek, was an active participant in the debate with the market socialist writers; see Hayek's 1948/1980 essays in *Collective Economic Planning* and *Individualism and Economic Order*, Chicago: University of Chicago Press.

The debate has been a subject of growing interest among economists, and useful summaries can be found in Hoff (1949/1981) *Economic Calculation in the Socialist Society,* Indianapolis: Liberty Press; Murray N. Rothbard, "Ludwig von Mises and Economic Calculation Under Socialism," in L. Moss (ed.) *The Economics of Ludwig von Mises,* Kansas City: Sheed and Ward, pp. 67–77; Karen Vaughn (1980) "Economic Calculation Under Socialism: The Austrian Contribution," *Economic Inquiry* 18 (October): 535–54; Peter Murrel (1983) "Did the Theory of Market Socialism Answer the Challenge of Ludwig von Mises?" *History of Political Economy* 15(1) (Spring): 92–105. The most extensive treatment of the debate, however, is provided by Lavoie's *Rivalry and Central Planning.*

66 Hayek, "Foreword" in Boris Brutzkus (1935/1981) *Economic Planning in Soviet Russia,* Westport: Hyperion Press, p. ix.

67 K. Leites (1922) *Recent Economic Developments in Russia,* New York: Oxford University Press.

68 Arthur Shadwell (1927) *The Breakdown of Socialism,* Boston: Little, Brown & Co.

69 Leo Pasvolsky (1921) *The Economics of Communism: With Special Reference to Russia's Experiment,* New York: Macmillan.

70 Boris Brutzkus, *Economic Planning in Soviet Russia,* for which the original essay was written in 1920.

71 Polanyi, "The Foolishness of History," p. 35.

72 Ibid.

73 This policy of introducing ideological justifications only to discount them is perhaps the greatest fault I find with both the Remmington and Malle books.

74 As will be suggested later, the move to NEP, and not taking power prematurely, constituted Lenin's real deviation from Marx.

75 Roberts, *Alienation and the Soviet Economy,* p. 37.

76 Ibid., p. 39.

77 "Chernovoi proekt tezisov obrashchenia k internatsional'noi sotsialisticheskoi komissii i ko vsem sotsialisticheskim partiiam," *Polnoe sobranie sochineii* 30: 278–9, quoted in Alfred Evans (1987) "Rereading Lenin's *State and Revolution,*" *Slavic Review* 46(1) (Spring): 18–79.

78 Lenin (1977) "Resolution on the Current Situation," *Collected Works,* 45 vols., Moscow: Progress Publishers, vol. 24, p. 310.

79 This ripeness issue, which many commentators get stuck on, is actually a weak reed upon which to rest one's interpretation of the events. One would be hard-pressed to argue that Marx, who throughout his lifetime kept close watch for any and all possible chances for revolution, would have behaved differently from Lenin, given the same situation. Marx, we should remember, did not hesitate to propose a proletarian revolution in France in 1848. Moreover, from a Marxist perspective, an analysis that finds an easy way out from the ripeness issue is not sufficiently critical. Regardless of Marx's own revolutionary activity, or whether or not he would have agreed with Lenin's use of his doctrines to come to power, concentration on the ripeness issue leads to a fundamental misunderstanding of the Soviet experience, and of socialism in general. As Lavoie points out:

> The reasons for Lenin's failure to achieve either democratic political goals or a prosperous economy are seldom traced to intrinsic elements of socialist aspirations. Russia, it is pointed out, began without democratic political traditions and with a backward economy. These special difficulties and not flaws within socialism itself, it is widely believed, brought Lenin's dream to its rude awakening. This interpretation of Soviet history in effect lets socialism off the hook for whatever political crimes or economic irrationalities the USSR is shown guilty of.

(Lavoie 1986–7, pp. 1–2)

80 "Speech in Favour of the Resolution on the Current Situation, April 29 (May 12), 1917," *Collected Works,* vol. 24, p. 308.

81 Ibid., p. 311.
82 *Collected Works*, vol. 25, pp. 327–69.
83 Ibid., pp. 333 ff.
84 Ibid., pp. 360–61.
85 Ibid., pp. 61–2.
86 *Imperialism*, in Lenin's *Collected Works*, vol. 22, pp. 185–304, was written from January to June 1916 and was published in Petrograd in late April 1917. *The State and Revolution*, in *Collected Works*, vol. 25, 384–497, was written in August and September 1917.
87 Lenin, *Collected Works*, vol. 25, p. 448.
88 Ibid., pp. 302–3.
89 Lenin, *Collected Works*, vol. 25, p. 448.
90 Ibid., pp. 431–2.
91 Ibid., p. 478.
92 Ibid., p. 497.
93 Trotsky (1932/1987) *The History of the Russian Revolution*, three volumes, New York: Pathfinder Books, vol. 3, pp. 323–4. Also see John Reed (1919/1985) *Ten Days That Shook the World*, New York: Penguin Books, pp. 117 ff.
94 Shadwell, p. 23.
95 See Szamuely, *First Models*, 10ff., and Chamberlin, *The Russian Revolution* vol. 2, 96 ff., for a discussion of these policies. Also notice that prominence is not given to grain requisitioning in this outline of the socialist program of the Bolsheviks from 1918 to 1921. While undoubtedly grain requisitioning was a major policy, it was not the major element in the program of socialist transformation. Concentration upon the food procurement policy of requisitioning, while ignoring the various other competents of the Bolsheviks' economic and social policy (such as banking policy) leads one to emphasize the emergency requirement of gathering food for the Red Army. Cf. Lars Lih (1986) "Bolshevik *Razverstka* and War Communism," *Slavic Review* 45(4) (Winter): 673–88.
96 Victor Serge, *Memoirs of a Revolutionary 1901–1941* (1963) New York: Oxford University Press, p. 115. Also see Vasil Selyunim (1988) "The Origins" [English title], *Novy Mir* May: 162–89.
97 See Remington, 78ff., for an extended discussion of the labor mobilization initiatives of the Bolsheviks. In particular, see his discussion of Trotsky's military organization of labor and Trotsky's desire for the full implementation of the principle of one-man management.
98 See Malle, p. 322, for a general discussion of the theory and practice of food procurement in Bolshevik Russia.
99 As Trotsky would later (1922) describe their efforts toward socialist construction during War Communism:

> How did we start? We began ... in economic policy by breaking with the bourgeois past firmly and without compromise. Earlier there was a market – we liquidate it, free trade – liquidate it, competition – we abolish it, commercial calculation – we abolish it. What to have instead? The central, solemn, sacred, Supreme Economic Council for National Economy that allocates everything, organizes everything, cares for everything: where should machines go to, where raw materials, where the finished product – this all will be decided and allocated from a single center, through its authorized organs. This plan of ours has failed.
> (See Szamuely, p. 94, where he discusses Trotsky's speech at the Eleventh Party Congress in March 1922)

100 Lenin, *Collected Works*
101 Malle, pp. 32–3.
102 Lenin, *Collected Works*, vol. 27, 268–69.
103 Quoted in Shadwell, p. 24.

104 Quoted in Leon Smolinsky (1967) "Planning without Theory, 1917–1967," *Survey* 64 (July): 113.

105 Quoted in Lancelot Lawton (1932) *An Economic History of Soviet Russia*, two volumes, New York: Macmillan, vol. I, p. 108.

106 Quoted in Szamuely, p. 34.

107 Nikolai Bukharin and Eugene Preobrazhensky (1919/1966) *The ABC of Communism* Ann Arbor: University of Michigan Press. The appendix of this book contains the adopted Party program, pp. 373 ff. Bukharin wrote all of Part One, the theoretical exposition on the decay of capitalism. He also wrote the introduction to Part Two, which concerns itself with the dictatorship of the proletariat and the building of Communism. In addition, Bukharin wrote the chapters on the organization of industry, the protection of labor and public hygiene. Preobrazhensky wrote the remaining chapters.

108 Bukharin and Preobrazhensky, p. 70, emphasis added. It is the accomplishment of this program of rationalization that Milyutin announced with pride in June 1920. "All enterprises and all industrial branches," he stated, "are considered like a single enterprise. Instead of competition, instead of struggle, Soviet Power with determination implements the principle of unity of the national economy in the economic field." See *Narodnor khoziaistvo Sovetskoi Rossii* (1920, p. 8, quoted in Malle, pp. 320–7). It is this very project of achieving *ex ante* coordination that Mises directly challenged; while Bukharin stated that the planner would know in advance how, to what and for whom to allocate resources, Mises merely asked the planners how, in the absence of monetary calculation, they would know which projects were economically feasible and which ones were not. It is this disregard on the part of the Bolsheviks for economic calculation that finally led to the collapse and retreat to NEP.

109 Bukharin and Preobrazhensky, p. 74. Bukharin does, however, admit that this program is not fully realizable at the moment. Two or three generations would have to grow up under the new conditions before the project was fully realizable; then "the bureaucracy, the permanent officialdom, will disappear" and the state would wither away. Bukharin, at least here, did not seem to understand the threat of the growing bureaucracy associated with the Communist scheme. For a discussion of the bureaucratization of social life under Soviet rule, see Bruno Rizzi (1930/1985) *The Bureaucratization of the World*, New York: Free Press; Milovan Djilas (1957) *The New Class*, New York: Praeger; and George Konrad and Ivan Szelenyi (1979) *The Intellectuals on the Road to Class Power*, New York: Harcourt Brace Jovanovich.

110 Bukharin and Preobrazhensky, pp. 72, 77. See also Bukharin (1920/1979) "The Economics of the Transition Period," in *The Politics and Economics of the Transition Period*, ed. K. J. Tarbuck (ed.) Boston: Routledge & Kegan Paul, p. 155, where Bukharin argues that "Money represents the material social ligament, the knot which ties up the whole highly developed commodity system of production. It is clear that during the transition period, in the process of abolishing the commodity system as such, a process of 'self-negation' of money takes place. It is manifested in the first place in the so-called devaluation of money and in the second place, in the fact that the distribution of paper money is divorced from the distribution of products, and vice versa. Money ceases to be the universal equivalent and becomes a conventional – and moreover extremely imperfect – symbol of the circulation of products."

111 Bukharin, "The Economics of the Transition Period," p. 155.

112 "Program of the Communist Party of Russia (adopted at the Eighth Party Congress Held March 18 to 23, 1919)," in Bukharin and Preobrazhensky, p. 390.

113 Bukharin and Preobrazhensky, p. 396. Also see Lenin, "Draft Programme of the R.C.P. (B.)," *Collected Works*, vol. 29, pp. 98–140. Lenin proposed that "the R.C.P. will strive as speedily as possible to introduce the most radical measures to pave the way for the abolition of money, first and foremost to replace it by savings-bank books, cheques, short-term notes entitling the holders to receive goods from the public stores and so

forth ... " (pp. 115–16). Lenin argued for the eventual elimination of hand-to-hand currency and its replacement by a system of cashless accounting, i.e. sophisticated barter.

114 "Appendix: Documents of the Revolution" in Chamberlin, *The Russian Revolution*, vol. 2, p. 490.

115 "Decree of the Supreme Economic Council on the Nationalization of Small Industrial Enterprises, of November 29, 1920," in Ibid., p. 494.

116 Lenin, *Collected Works*, vol. 32, pp. 329–65.

117 Ibid., vol. 27, 340.

118 Ibid., 339.

119 "The New Economic Policy and the Tasks of the Political Education Departments" (October 17, 1921) in *Collected Works*, vol. 33, p. 62.

120 Ibid., vol. 35, p. 475.

121 F. A. von Hayek, "The Use of Knowledge in Society" in *Individualism and Economic Order*, p. 78.

122 Lavoie, *National Economic Planning*, p. 214.

123 I have argued this position in my 1990 book, *The Political Economy of Soviet Socialism: The Formative Years, 1918–1928*, Boston: Kluwer, 1990, pp. 63–111. Also see my 1990 article, "The Political Economy of Utopia," *Journal des Economistes et des Etudes Humaines* 1(2): 91–138. For classic presentations of this interpretation of Soviet history, see Boris Brutzkus (1935/1981) *Economic Planning in Soviet Russia*, Westport, CT: Hyperion Press; Paul Craig Roberts (1971/1990) *Alienation and the Soviet Economy*, New York: Holmes and Meier; and Laszlo Szamuely (1974) *First Models of the Socialist Economic System*, Budapest: Akademiai Kiado.

124 Leon Trotsky (1923/1960) "Theses on Industry" (March), in R. V. Daniels (ed.) *A Documentary History of Communism*, vol. 1, New York: Vintage, p. 235. Also see Trotsky, *The New Course* (1924/1975), in *The Challenge of the Left Opposition (1923–1925)*, New York: Pathfinder, p. 120, where he argued that the development of "state industry [was] the keystone of the dictatorship of the proletariat and the basis of socialism." The principal concern of Gosplan "must be development of state (socialist) industry."

125 Trotsky, "Theses on Industry," pp. 236–7.

126 Trotsky, quoted in Richard Day (1973) *Leon Trotsky and the Politics of Economic Isolation*, New York: Cambridge University Press, p. 82.

127 See Alec Nove (1981) "New Light on Trotskii's Economic Views," *Slavic Review* 40(1) (Spring): 84–97.

128 Nikolai Bukharin, quoted in Nove (1979) "Some Observations on Bukharin and His Ideas," in Nove, *Political Economy and Soviet Socialism*, New York: Allen and Unwin, p. 86.

129 Nikolai Bukharin (1919/1970) *The Economic Theory of the Leisure Class*, New York: Augustus M. Kelley. In the preface to the book Bukharin wrote that his "selection of an opponent for our criticism probably does not require discussion, for it is well known that the most powerful opponent of Marxism is the Austrian School" (p. 9).

130 Nikolai Bukharin (1925/1982) "Concerning the New Economic Policy and Our Tasks," in Bukharin, *Selected Economic Writings on the Transition to Socialism*, New York: M. E. Sharpe, p. 188.

131 Ibid., p. 189.

132 Ibid.

133 For a recent discussion of Bukharin's views of the market see John Salter (1990) "L. I. Bukharin and the market question," *History of Political Economy* 22(1) (Spring): 65–79.

134 See my *The Political Economy of Soviet Socialism*, pp. 11–61.

135 Nove has recently argued this point in his 1983 book, *The Economics of Feasible Socialism*, London: Allen and Unwin.

136 Don Lavoie (1985) *Rivalry and Central Planning*, New York: Cambridge University Press, pp. 29–30.

7   The political economy of utopia: Communism in Soviet Russia, 1918–21

1   See Pasvolsky (1921), Leites (1922), Shadwell (1927), and Brutzkus (1935/1982) for some of the first interpretations of this period by political economists and historians.

2   See Dobb (1948) and Carr (1980).

3   See Roberts (1971) and Remington (1984). Also see Boettke (1988 and 1990). Silvana Malle seems sometimes to take this point of view (e.g. in Malle, 1985), but, as pointed out by a referee for this journal, she had also in many occasions taken the opposite point of view.

4   See McCloskey (1985) for a discussion of the crisis within modernist methodology.

5   Gadamer (1960/1985, pp. 264–6).

6   For Leon Trotsky's views on the proletariat revolution and the importance of the European revolution for Russian success, see Trotsky (1983, pp. 337–52). Also see Trotsky (1947) and Trotsky (1932/1987, vol. 3, pp. 351 ff.). As Trotsky stated, "the Bolsheviks categorically rejected as a caricature the idea imputed to them by the Mensheviks of creating a 'peasant socialism' in a backward country. The dictatorship of the proletariat in Russia was for the Bolsheviks a bridge to a revolution in the west. The problem of a socialist transformation of society was proclaimed to be in its very essence international" (p. 380). I would also like to point out that in the preface to the second Russian edition of the *Communist Manifesto*, Marx and Engels wrote: "If the Russian Revolution becomes the signal for a proletarian revolution in the West, so that both complement each other, the present Russian common ownership of land may serve as the starting-point for a Communist development." See Marx and Engels (1969, pp. 100–1).

7   See Heller and Nekrich (1986, pp. 50–110). Heller and Nekrich argue (p. 93) that Lenin believed that the spark of the Russian revolution would ignite the fire of world revolution. In his view, conflict with Poland, a potential "Red bridge" to the West, was inevitable. None of the Bolsheviks doubted the necessity of "forcing the Polish bridge"; the only question was when and how to do it. Trotsky, who had said, "The road to London and Paris goes through Calcutta," declared at the end of 1919: "When we have finished off Denikin, we will throw all the strength of our reserves against the Polish front." By such a continued assault, Lenin became convinced that he could bring Communist independence to the world.

This perspective can also help us understand the debate between Lenin and the left wing (Bukharin *et al.*) within the Bolshevik party over the Brest–Litovsk peace agreement (signed 3 March 1918). At the time, Lenin agreed to peace with Germany (which cost the Soviets Poland, the Ukraine, and the Baltic region, and required the cessation of all revolutionary propaganda abroad), in order to regroup the country's resources and hold out until the world revolution began (which he argued might be within a few days or weeks). The peace was a necessary strategic retreat for Lenin, a retreat that would, in a short time, be reversed. Bukharin, on the other hand, argued that the conditions of peace would reduce the international significance of the Russian revolution to nothing and that, therefore, the peace treaty should be annulled and the proper preparations should be made to create a combat-ready Red Army that would help bring the revolution to the West. Both Lenin and Bukharin believed that the international workers' revolution was essential to the success of the Russian revolution. See Lenin and Bukharin on the peace agreement in Daniels (1960b, pp. 135–43). Also see Daniels (1960a, pp. 70–80).

8   Daniels (1960a, p. 53), emphasis added.

9   From Bukharin's report on the war and the international situation, excerpted in Daniels (1960b, pp. 95–6, emphasis added).

10   See Daniels (1960b, p. 97).

11   Roberts (1971, p. 26).

12   See Cohen (1972, p. 193).

13   Polanyi (1951/1980, p. 132, fn. 1).

14 Bettelheim (1976, p. 144).
15 Zaleski (1962/1971, p. 17).
16 This is where the standard account usually begins discussion of the nationalization of industry, thus discounting the earlier nationalization efforts of the Bolsheviks. (Discounting their efforts has the effect of making the emergency interpretation more cogent.)
17 See Zaleski (1962/1971, pp. 16–20) and Dobb (1948, p. 106). The armistice with Poland was signed in October 1920 and the decree nationalizing small-scale industry was published in November 1920, *after* the civil war.
18 While the standard account views this substitution as a product of war, I contend that it is the consistent application of Marxian ideology, and this is where the difference in interpretation lies.
19 Dobb (1948, p. 107).
20 See Remington (1984, pp. 78 ff.) for a discussion of the militarization of labor during this time period.
21 Zaleski (1962/1971, p. 18, fn. 27). While Dobb and Carr see this emission of paper money as a result of war emergency, Preobrazhensky argued that the breakdown of the capitalist system could be accomplished through inflationary destruction of the currency. See Preobrazhensky, 1920. The importance of monetary policy for understanding the ideological interpretation of War Communism will be brought out later in this chapter.
22 See Zaleski (1962/1971, pp. 24 ff.) and Malle (1985, pp. 202 ff).
23 Malle (1985, p. 202).
24 Prychitko (1989) makes a compelling case for an "essential tension" in Marx between his organizational theory of economic centralization and his praxis philosophy of radical decentralization and participatory self-management. Prychitko has also argued elsewhere that there is an organizational logic in Marx's praxis philosophy and the attempt to abolish commodity production that leads to centralization in economic life. See Prychitko (1988).
    For the purpose of this chapter, I am dealing mainly with this logic of the Marxian attempt to abolish the system of commodity production. I leave to others the question of decentralized revisionism of Marx's project.
25 See Marx (1867/1906, p. 92). Also look at Marx's various criticisms of "the chaotic" process of market coordination. Within his negative view of the capitalist process of exchange and production, there lies a positive view of how the socialist mode of production would work; otherwise, by what point of reference would he be criticizing the anarchy of capitalism?
26 Marx (1977, p. 97).
27 See Marx and Engels (1969, vol. 1, pp. 98–137, pp. 186–299, pp. 394–487; vol. 2, pp. 178–244).
28 Marx (1978, p. 161, emphasis added).
29 Marx and Engels (1969, p. 126).
30 Marx (1867/1906, vol. 1, pp. 836–7).
31 Some of the classic treatments of this question can be found in Carew Hunt (1969), Wilson (1940), and Berdyaev (1937/1972). Also see Kolakowski (1978/1985, pp. 304–527), Rustow (1950–7/1980, pp. 537–58, and 564–84), Johnson (1983, pp. 49–103, and 261–308), and Besançon (1981).
32 Lovell (1984, p. 197).
33 Held (1980, p. 35).
34 Jay (1984, p. 537).
35 One of Habermas's attempts to articulate this program can be found in Habermas (1984). An excellent discussion of Habermas's project can be found in McCarthy (1985).
36 Stojanovic (1987, p. 453). Also see Stojanovic (1988).
37 Selucky (1979).
38 See Selucky (1979, p. 78).

39 Alexander Rustow provides an insightful discussion of the evolution of the Marxian
heritage among the political élite within the first decade of Soviet rule, although I believe
that he does not address clearly enough the subtle point of how Stalinism can be seen as
an unintended consequence of Marx's project. See Rustow (1950–7/1980, pp. 571–2),
where he argues that:

> There can be no doubt that Lenin acted as a Marxist during his seizure of power
> and viewed his mission as one of carrying out the Marxist program under his regime.
> What followed was a dictatorship of the proletariat without foreseeable end, in
> which the totalitarian components of Marxism dominated. The ideal of a classless
> society was maintained as the ultimate aim, although it gradually faded into the
> background. Despite the deviations to which Lenin increasingly saw himself forced
> by circumstances, he himself remained a convinced Marxist until his death. Not so
> with Stalin, who, unlike Lenin, was not an intellectual. As a seeker after power,
> pure and simple, he let surrounding realities and opportunities rather than programs
> and ideologies determine his actions. The eschatological promises of Marxism lay
> beyond his intellectual horizon. Hence the idealistic aura, which in Lenin's time
> still surrounded the Communist Party and its policy, disappeared completely under
> Stalin, at least for the members of the ruling stratum. Stalin experienced no inner
> struggles in abandoning the doctrine of abolition of the division of labor as well as
> the hallowed Marxist dogma of the 'withering away of the state.' The new Russia
> placed the orthodox Marxist doctrine in the position of a state religion, or rather of
> a state theology, in place of the Greek Orthodox doctrine of the Russian church.
> Orthodoxy has been strictly enforced with the help of heresy trials,
> excommunications and executions.

40 Lavoie (1985a, pp. 18–19).

41 Lavoie (1985a, p. 19). Also see Lavoie (1985b, p. 29), where he argues that, "Marx's
scientific socialism was not merely an excuse for avoiding any examination of socialist
society. It was a recommendation of a particular method for the conduct of such an
examination – that is, that socialism be described through a systematic critique of
capitalism."

42 The gambling metaphor is important to keep in mind. It is not that the despotism was
an unseen consequence of rationalization, just as it is not an unseen consequence of
poker that one may lose a hand or money. Rather, the despotism in the gamble story
was the possible outcome that the Bolsheviks, and specifically Lenin, were trying to
avoid, just as the poker player tries to avoid losing. This has the result, I contend, of
obscuring the economic problem that the Marxian social relations of production would
have to confront in any socioeconomic situation, no matter how favorable.

43 The classic presentation of this thesis is found in Wittfogel (1957/1964, pp. 369 ff.).
Wittfogel argues that Russia's development since 1917 deserves the most careful scrutiny.
For reasons of historical development, Wittfogel supports the February revolution, but
opposes the October one. As he states (1964, p. 9):

> The marginally Oriental civilization of Tsarist Russia was greatly influenced by the
> West, though Russia did not become a Western colony or semi-colony. Russia's
> Westernization radically changed the country's political and economic climate,
> and in the spring of 1917 its antitotalitarian forces had a genuine opportunity to
> accomplish the anti-Asiatic social revolution which Marx, in 1853, had envisaged
> for India. But in the fall of 1917 these antitotalitarian forces were defeated by the
> Bolshevik champions of a new totalitarian order. They were defeated because they
> failed to utilize the democratic potential in a historical situation that was temporarily
> open. From the standpoint of individual freedom and social justice, 1917 is probably
> the most fateful year in modern history.

Wittfogel argues, therefore, that those intellectuals who profess adherence to Marxism and its promise of radical democracy "will fulfill their historical responsibility only if they face the despotic heritage of the Oriental world not less but more clearly than did Marx" (Ibid.).

Glen Holman combines Wittfogel's analysis of oriental despotism with the interpretation of Soviet economic history found in Boris Brutzkus and Paul Craig Roberts, in his interesting and informative study, "War Communism," on the *Besieger Besieged: A Study of Lenin's Social and Political Objectives from 1918 to 1921*. Although his interpretations of the intent of the policies from 1918 to 1921 are similar, Holman's understanding of the economic problems that War Communism faced differs considerably from the analysis here. To Wittfogel or Holman, the economic irrationality of War Communism is a result of underdeveloped historical conditions, which leads to the restoration of the Asiatic mode of production and Oriental despotism with Stalin. The claim here is stronger, the economic irrationality experienced during War Communism is of any attempt to completely supercede market modes of production. This is a crucial distinction to keep in mind, especially with regard to understanding Bukharin's extreme swing from the left to the right of the Bolshevik party. Bukharin admits that from the "point of view of economic rationality" the attempt to implement comprehensive central planning during War Communism was "sheer madness," but that holds only for the historical stage that the Bolsheviks found themselves in the 1920s. NEP, to Bukharin, was to last for quite some time, until the forces of production were developed enough to implement full Communist methods of production.

44 Daniels (1960a, p. 9, emphasis added).
45 As Lavoie (1986/1987, pp. 1–2) points out:

> The reasons for Lenin's failure to achieve either democratic political goals or a prosperous economy are seldom traced to intrinsic elements of his socialist aspirations. Russia, it is pointed out, began without democratic political traditions and with a backward economy. These special difficulties and not flaws within socialism itself, it is widely believed, brought Lenin's dream to its rude awakening. This interpretation of Soviet history in effect lets socialism off the hook for whatever political crimes or economic irrationalities the USSR is shown guilty of.

But, as Lavoie argues later, this should not be the case. Rather we should see that: "In the failure of War Communism and the retreat to NEP the impossibility of planning as articulated theoretically in the Mises–Hayek critique was directly demonstrated in practice" (p. 10).

46 Besides the point of whether Marx would or would not have agreed with Lenin's use of his doctrine to come to power, this focus in scholarly literature is symptomatic of two shortcomings. First, it represents an *uncritical* acceptance of Marx's interpretation of historical development. Second, because of the latent historicism of the first shortcoming, it represents a bias on the part of historians and social theorists to view historical events only as the intentional outcome or design of the major actors, and to disregard unintended consequences in human interaction. For a criticism of this approach to social theory see Hayek (1952/1979, especially pp. 111–52). Also see Mises (1957/1985, p. 195), where he argues that:

> History is made by men. The conscious intentional actions of individuals, great and small, determine the course of events insofar as it is the result of the interaction of all men. But the historical process is not designed by individuals. It is the composite outcome of the intentional actions of all individuals. No man can plan history. All he can plan and try to put into effect is his own actions, which, jointly with the actions of other men, constitute the historical process. The Pilgrim Fathers did not plan to found the United States.

And neither Marx nor Lenin planned to found the Soviet society of Joseph Stalin. Nevertheless that should not absolve them from responsibility or deny the important role that they (or their ideas) played in the establishment of the system.

47 In fact, it is the belief that Russia had already begun its capitalist development that led George Plekhanov to move from a populist (who believed that the peasant commune could serve as the foundation of anarcho-socialism) to a Marxist by 1883. See Harding (1983, pp. 41 ff.). Also see Baron (1962, pp. 42–54), and his more elaborate treatment in Baron (1963).

48 See Trotsky (1932/1987, vol. 1, pp. 332 ff.).

49 See Rabinowitch (1978, pp. 310 ff.) for an excellent discussion of the events from the July uprisings to the October revolution. In particular, see Rabinowitch's reflections upon the reasons for the Bolshevik success in 1917.

50 Lenin (1977, vol. 24, pp. 96–106).

51 "The Tasks of the Proletariat in the Present Situation," Lenin (1977, vol. 24, pp. 21–6).

52 It is interesting to note that the name Bolshevik was an accident of history; during the 1903 conference Plekhanov sided with Lenin on the organization of the party and, thus, created the Bolshevik (majority in Russian) wing of the social democratic party. In reality, the Bolsheviks constituted a minority of social democrats until their assumption of power in 1917.

53 Among other things, Lenin called for the immediate amalgamation of all banks into a single national bank, and decreed that control over the bank be immediately turned over to the Soviets of Workers' Deputies. Again, the stress was on moving toward the abolition of commodity production and, with that, social relations built upon money, i.e. the alienating ability of humankind. As Marx argued in *Capital*, p. 99, fn. 1, attempts to abolish money while retaining commodity production were like trying to *"retain Catholicism without the Pope."*

54 Lenin (1977, vol. 24, p. 33, emphasis added) "Notes for an Article or Speech in Defense of the April Theses".

55 Lenin (1977, vol. 24, pp. 38–41) "Dual Power". Also see Trotsky (1932/1987, vol. 1, pp. 206–15).

56 I am mainly documenting Lenin's convictions on the ripeness issue, but it should be emphasized that Marx during his lifetime was constantly watching for revolutionary chances – even France and Germany of the 1840s. Commenting on the rigid interpretation of historical preconditions that many "revisionist" Marxists held, Trotsky argued that: "Apparently Marx in 1848 was a Utopian youth compared with many of the present-day infallible automata of Marxism!" (quoted in Day 1973, p. 8). Moreover, from a Marxist perspective, this ripeness question represents a meek argument (allowing any failure of Marxism to be in principle excusable), and should be rejected as undialectical and not sufficiently materialist in its analysis. It represents a cop-out for something that claims to be a critical social theory. Marxian theory is built (supposedly) upon the connection between theory and praxis, and any analysis that is neither grounded in historical praxis nor sufficiently self-critical is to be rejected. The historical precondition response does not answer the questions raised by a critical Marxist concerning the problems of the Soviet experience. See the discussion above of both the Frankfurt School, and especially the Praxis group philosophers, for a more fruitful approach to the problem at hand.

57 Lenin (1977, vol. 24, p. 53, written in April 1917).

58 Lenin did not intend to abolish war planning but to transform it into a model of socialist organization. As he wrote in December 1916:

> The war has reaffirmed clearly enough and in a very practical way ... that modern capitalist society, particularly in the advanced countries, has fully matured for the transition to socialism. If, for instance, Germany can direct the economic life of sixty-six million people from a single, central institution ... then the same can be

done, in the interest of nine-tenths of the population, by the non-propertied masses if their struggle is directed by the class-conscious workers ... All propaganda for socialism must be refashioned from abstract and general to concrete and directly practical; expropriate the banks and, relying on the masses, carry out in their interests the very same thing the W.U.M.B.A. [i.e. the Weapons and Ammunition Supply Department] is carrying out in Germany.

(quoted in Evans 1987, p. 18, fn. 79).

59 Lenin (1977, vol. 24, pp. 309–12).
60 This reference is supplied in the explanatory reference notes of Lenin (1977, vol. 24, p. 603, fn. 106, emphasis added).
61 Also, see Lenin (1977, vol. 24, pp. 424–30) "Inevitable Catastrophe and Extravagant Promises".
62 "The 'April days,' " Trotsky argued, "were the first candid warning addressed by the October to the February revolution. The bourgeois Provisional Government was replaced after this by a Coalition whose fruitlessness was revealed on every day of its existence. In the June demonstrations summoned by the Executive Committee on its own initiative, although perhaps not quite voluntarily, the February revolution tried to measure strength with the October and suffered a cruel defeat" (Trotsky, 1932/1987, vol. 1, p. 458).
63 Lenin's program of control, which he argued could be established by a workers' state by decree "in the first weeks of its existence," consisted of (1) nationalization of all banks and the creation of a central bank; (2) nationalization of syndicates; (3) abolition of commercial secrecy; (4) compulsory syndication; and (5) compulsory organization of population. The creation of a central bank, in particular, was essential to Lenin, because the principal nerve center of modern economic life was the bank, and one cannot regulate economic life without taking over banks – control over the bank allowed the unification of accountancy. See Lenin (1977, vol. 25, pp. 333 ff.).
64 Also see Lenin, "Who is Responsible?" (1977, vol. 25, pp. 151–2), where he argues that: "In times of revolution, procrastination is often equivalent to a complete betrayal of the revolution. Responsibility for the delay in the transfer of power to the workers, soldiers and peasants, for the delay in carrying through revolutionary measures to enlighten the ignorant peasants, rests wholly on the Socialist-Revolutionaries and Mensheviks. They have betrayed the revolution ... "
65 *Imperialism* (Lenin 1977, vol. 22, pp. 185–304) was written from January to June 1916 and was published in Petrograd in late April 1917. *The State and Revolution* (1977, vol. 25, pp. 384–497) was written in August and September 1917.
66 This standard Marxist analysis of the operation of capitalism is based upon faulty reasoning, as discussed in Lavoie (1985b) and Boettke (1990, Chapter 2). Also, see Rothbard (1970, vol. 2, pp. 547 ff. and pp. 581–6). The problem of economic calculation puts a limit on the potential size of any firm within an economic system – the evolution of the economy into one big firm is not technically possible from an economic point of view.
67 In contrast, see the discussion of the economic and political reasons why the most meaningful definition of monopoly is a state grant or privilege given to a business enterprise to be the sole producer of a commodity or service, in Rothbard (1970, pp. 560–660), Armentano (1978, pp. 94–110), and Demsetz, (1982, pp. 47–57). For a historical discussion of "political capitalism" and the strategic use of the state by business managers to either guarantee or protect their profits, see Kolko (1964) and Weinstein (1968).
68 Although Lenin is a harsh critic, he gets most of his theoretical insights on the operation of finance capital from the Austro-Marxist, Hilferding (1910/1985).
69 Lenin concludes that "again and again the final word in the development of banking is monopoly" and he points to America where "two very big banks, those of the multi-millionaires Rockefeller and Morgan, control" most of the capital (1977, vol. 22, pp.

219–20). It is true that the Morgan banks dominated the financial system in the US, but this is a result of the system of political capitalism. The New York (Morgan) banks were losing their market share to the St Louis and Chicago banks prior to 1913. They tried to keep their market share through a cartel arrangement, which would have allowed them to overissue notes, but the cartel could not be maintained. So they sought to establish a government-enforced cartel and the Federal Reserve System (established in 1913) supplied just that for the "House of Morgan" see Rothbard (1984, pp. 89–136).

70 For the same theoretical reason that the realization of socialism is impossible and the assessment of increasing concentration of capital under capitalism is flawed, Lenin's assessment of the desirability of central banking is also questionable. Central banking is not capable of bringing the economic life process under control – in fact, central banks operate in the dark. "They are not well-equipped to know whether an adjustment in the supply of money is needed or not because they lack the necessary economic knowledge" (see Selgin 1988, pp. 89–107).

71 Lenin's argument here is that colonization supplies low-cost labor and natural resources which allows the capitalist to receive increased profits. This argument of the economic logic of imperialism should be kept in mind, especially later when we discuss the internal imperialism advocated by Preobrazhensky, and later Stalin, during the industrialization debate.

72 As Marx argued in the *Critique of the Gotha Programme*, p. 17:

> What we have to deal with here is a Communist society, not as it has developed on its own foundations, but, on the contrary, just as it emerges from capitalist society; which is thus in every respect, economically, morally and intellectually, still stamped with the birth marks of the old society from whose womb it emerges.

The "first phase of Communist society," Marx later added (p. 19) "will have certain inevitable defects" as it has "just emerged after prolonged birth pangs from capitalistic society."

73 Polan (1984, p. 57).

74 Daniels (1960a, pp. 51–2).

75 Barfield (1971, p. 50), emphasis added. Barfield argued that Lenin researched the book from January to February 1917, the notebooks which constitute "Marxism on the State." Barfield's argument suggests that the utopianism evidenced in *The State and Revolution* permeates all of Lenin's political writings – although I would agree that I think Barfield places his finger upon the wrong utopianism – a sort of anarcho-libertarian belief in the masses. Instead, Lenin's utopianism is better represented by the ease with which he thought Marx's project of rationalization could be accomplished.

76 Evans (1987, p. 3).

77 Evans (1987, p. 3).

78 Lenin here is discussing the idea that full democratic participation is impossible under capitalism because the state will be used to exploit the many to the benefit of the few, i.e. the capitalists. Under socialism, however, classes will disappear and, with their demise, formal institutions of democracy will also disappear. Polan has suggested that this theory of the state eliminates all possible checks against abuse and results in the lodging of power in the hands of a few – exactly what happened under Bolshevik rule. See Polan (1984, pp. 129–30), emphasis added, where he argues:

> The central absence in Lenin's politics is that of a theory of political institutions. All political functions are collapsed into one institution, the Soviet, and even that institution itself will know no division of labor within itself according to different functions. It allows for no distances, no spaces, no appeals, no checks, no balances, no processes, no delays, no interrogations and, above all, no distribution of power. All are ruthlessly and deliberately excluded, as precisely the articulations of the

disease of corruption and mystification. The new state form will be transparent, monotogical and unilinear. It is, in sum, a gigantic gamble; the gamble is that it will be possible to set about constructing this state in 'the best of all possible worlds.' The odds against the gamble are astronomic. *It does not simply demand the absence of the peculiarly unhelpful conditions of post-1917 Russia – although those conditions themselves have for a long time conspired to suggest the essential innocence of the model. It* also demands a situation devoid of all political conflicts, of all economic problems, of all social contradictions, of all inadequate, selfish or simply human emotions and motivations, of all singularity, of all singularity, of all negativity. *It demands, in short, for Lenin's political structures to work, that there be an absence of politics.*

The crime of Lenin's text, Polan argues, is not that it did not work: the crime is that it did work. Lenin's theory eliminated any of the possible checks that would have made the Gulag less likely.

79   Lenin seems completely naïve in his understanding of the complexity of economic organization. As A. J. Polan (1984, pp. 61–2, emphasis added) states:

> Lenin seems to suggest that the economic problem that can be resolved by the adoption of the model of the 'postal service' is simply one of efficiency: where the multi-faceted confusions of the competitive mechanism have been removed, there is no 'economic' problem of organization. However, the problem remains that the capitalist mechanism, in the form of the market, accomplished the task of allocation and distribution of rewards and resources, while this task remains to be performed in the absence of the market. Confident assertions of the possibility of extending the 'postal' model to embrace the whole economy ignore the fact that the absence of a market forces the state *to inherit a task of immense complexity.*

This is essentially the point of departure for Polanyi's criticism of central administration of economic life, see "The Span of Central Direction," in Polanyi (1951/1980, pp. 111 ff.). On the nature of complexity in social relations also see Hayek (1967/1980, pp. 22–42), and Hayek (1973, vol. 1, pp. 35–54, and vol. 2, pp. 107–32).

80   The Bolsheviks and their allies among the Left Socialist-Revolutionaries overthrew the Kerensky government on 25 October [7 November] 1917. The Council of People's Commissars was established with Lenin as chairman and Trotsky as the Commissar of Foreign Affairs. The Revolutionary Military Committee of Petrograd Soviet of Workers' and Soldiers' Deputies declared that the provisional government had been overthrown and that "the cause for which the people have fought – the immediate proposal of democratic peace, the abolition of landed proprietorship, workers' control over production and the creation of a Soviet government – is assured" (Daniels, 1960b, p. 117). Also see Lenin "The Bolsheviks Must Assume Power," "Marxism and Insurrection," "The Tasks of the Revolution," and "Can the Bolsheviks Retain State Power?," all in Lenin (1977, vol. 26, pp. 19 ff.) and Trotsky (1932/1987, vol. 3, pp. 124 ff.).

81   As Trotsky wrote (1932/1987, vol. 3, p. 172, emphasis added): "If it is true that an insurrection cannot be evoked at will, and that nevertheless in order to win it must be organized in advance, then the revolutionary leaders are presented with the task of correct diagnosis. They must feel out the growing insurrection in good season and supplement it with a conspiracy. The interference of the midwife in labor pains – however this image may have been used – remains the clearest illustration of this conscious intrusion into an elemental process."

82   Trotsky provides an eloquent discussion of Lenin's first appearance before the Congress after taking power (1932/1987, vol. 3, p. 325).

Lenin, whom the Congress has not yet seen, is given the floor for a report on peace. His appearance in the tribune evokes a tumultuous greeting. The delegates gaze with all their eyes at this mysterious being whom they had been taught to hate and whom they have learned, without seeing him, to love. "Now Lenin, gripping the edges of the reading-stand, let little winking eyes travel over the crowd as he stood there waiting, apparently oblivious to the long-rolling ovation, which lasted several minutes. When it finished, he said simply, 'we shall now proceed to construct the socialist order.'" Also see Reed (1919/1985, pp. 117 ff).

83 Leites (1922, p. 65).

84 Shadwell (1927, p. 23).

85 See Szamuely (1974, p. 10 ff.). Also see Chamberlin (1987, vol. 2, pp. 96 ff.).

86 Notice that prominence is not given to grain requisitioning in this outline of the socialist program of the Bolsheviks from 1918 to 1921. While, undoubtedly, grain requisitioning was a major policy, it *was not* the major element in the program of socialist transformation. Concentration upon the food procurement policy of requisitioning, while ignoring the various other components of the Bolsheviks economic and social policy, leads to an overemphasis on the emergency situation aspect of gathering food for the Red Army. See Lih (1986, pp. 673–88). Also see Malle (1985, pp. 322–465) for a discussion of the ideology of food procurement and the expediency of *prodrazverstka*.

87 See Holman (1973, pp. 7–10), for a discussion of the evolution of the terminology from Communism (Bukharin and Kristman) to militant Communism (Alfred Meyer) to military Communism (Trotsky) to War Communism (Dobb, Carr, etc.). Also consider the following statement by Victor Serge (1963, p. 115): "The social system in these years was later called War Communism. At the time it was called simply 'Communism,' and any one who, like myself, went so far as to consider it purely temporary was looked upon with disdain." Also see Selyunin (1988, pp. 162–89).

88 Pasvolsky (1921, p. 21).

89 Pasvolsky (1921, p. 26).

90 Lenin's concept of the role of financial institutions within economic coordination is strikingly similar to the role predicted by some economists under a completely unregulated banking system. Lenin thought that under socialism monetary circulation would cease and that the People's Bank would keep account of transactions, i.e. the medium of exchange would be separated from the unit of account. In fact, eventually media of exchange would disappear altogether and all that would remain would be accounting. On the other hand, legal restrictions theorists argue that under a completely deregulated financial system, money as we know it would also disappear and banks would merely keep account of transactions made with, say, mutual funds or some other interest-bearing media (sophisticated barrier). The banks would serve as a central clearing-house in economic coordination. Of course, there is a world of difference in the organizational form of all the banks merged into one central bank as under Lenin's scheme, and the decentralized banking system advocated by the legal restrictions theorists. But both schemes underestimate the importance of monetary calculation in the coordination of economic activities and do so for ironically similar reasons, i.e. the apparent simplicity of human control over economic activities. Lenin did so because he thought that the task of achieving *ex ante* coordination was easy, legal restrictions theorists do the same because of the misplaced concreteness of general competitive equilibrium; they mistake the model for the real world. Since, in the model, money is not necessary for coordination (because the agents possess perfect information and face zero transaction costs), without any real-world legal restrictions the demand for cash balances would disappear. Lenin's mistake results because he ignored the knowledge problem. Legal restrictions theory fails because it assumes that the knowledge problem is solved already (by hypothesis). For a history of legal restrictions theory, see Cowen and Krozner (1987, pp. 567–90). For a presentation of the theory see Wallace (1983, pp. 1–17). Also see the criticisms of legal restrictions theory in White (1984, pp. 699–712), White (1987, pp. 448–56), and Selgin (1987, pp. 18–24).

91 Lenin (1977, vol. 27, p. 259) invokes the Taylor system as an example of the technological innovations of capitalism that the Soviet system must experiment with and adopt. The Taylor system was expected to increase the productivity of labor, which was deemed a

necessary condition for socialist construction. The Taylor system fitted neatly into the social engineering bias of the Bolsheviks and other socialist thinkers at that time. Trotsky, for example, argued that the Minister of Trade and Industry should be a technician, an engineer, who would work under the overall control of the Council of People's Commissars. See Trotsky's memo to Comrade Sijapnikov in Trotsky (1964, p. 3). Also see the discussion in Remington (1984, pp. 113–45). This is also connected to Lenin's reliance upon the model of German War Planning as a means to achieve socialist planning: see Merkle (1980, pp. 172 ff.). The principle of one-man management (OMM) represents, both in military organization and technological management within industry, the latest stage of scientific development.

92   Malle (1985, pp. 32–3).
93   Lenin argues here that the Soviet dictatorship of the proletariat provides the political basis for social transformation, while the German war planning machine provides the economic basis. The task of the Soviets, therefore, was to study the German system and "spare no effort in copying it and not shrink from adopting dictatorial methods to hasten the copying of it" (1977, vol. 27, p. 340). Despite accounts that argue that Lenin *et al.* did not have a model of socialist organization because Marxism was confined to a critique of capitalism, it seems there was little doubt in Lenin's mind what was required to build socialism. Compare this assessment with Kauffman (1953, pp. 243–72), and Smolinsky (1967, pp. 108–28), who argue that neither Lenin nor the other Bolsheviks had any theoretical framework from which to develop an approach to economic planning.
94   Trotsky, as quoted in Shadwell (1927, p. 24).
95   Trotsky, Socbinenia, Moscow (1927, vol. XV, p. 215), as quoted in Smolinsky (1967, p. 113).
96   Smolinsky (1967, p. 112). Neither was the nationalization of the banks and the inflationary monetary policy that was being followed intended to be "simply used to finance government expenditures, just as in so many other countries" as Malle seems to suggest (Malle, 1985, p. 175).
97   See Marx (1977, pp. 127 ff.) and Marx (1973, pp. 115 ff.). Also see Vorhies (1982). Smirnov, for example, representing the left Communists, argued in June 1918 that: "the financial and monetary crisis may not be solved by the restoration of finance and monetary circulation, which leads back to a bourgeois system, *but by the liquidation of the monetary-financial system, leading toward the socialist organization of production.*" See the 1918 *Kommunist*, 4 (June): 5, as quoted in Malle (1985, p. 163, emphasis added). Smirnov (along with Osinskii and Savel'ev) was asked by Lenin to organize the Supreme Economic Council only days after the October revolution. See Remington (1984, p. 60).
98   His reports were published in several articles and pamphlets during this time. See Bukharin (1979, p. 212, fn. 5). These articles were collected and later (1928) published in the Soviet Union as *Gosudarstvennyi kapitalizm voennogo vremeni v Germanii* (1914–18). Larin, who was a Menshevik, died in 1932 before "the Terror" destroyed the rest of his colleagues of the War Communism period. He was buried in the Kremlin Wall with honors. See Remington (1984, p. 30). Larin's daughter, Anna Mikhailovna Larina, became Bukharin's wife and has led the struggle for Bukharin's rehabilitation within the Party in the post-Stalin era. See the 1988 article, "Taking a Closer Look at Bukharin: An Interview with Anna Mikhailovna, the Widow of Bukharin," *The Current Digest of the Soviet Press*, XIL(5) (2 March) and Remnick (1988, pp. E1 and E4).
99   Larin, as quoted in Lawton (1932, p. 108).
100 Larin as quoted in Malle (1985, p. 165).
101 Malle explains the policy of all-out nationalization of industry pursued in November 1920, after the armistice with Poland in October 1920, as an attempt to extend this cashless payment system. As she states: "One of the reasons for the overall nationalization of industry in November 1920 was the attempt to extend the system of non-monetary accounts to the sphere of small-scale and kustar industry, which had been working under war Communism on the system of cash payments. A decree of Sovnarkom in July 1920

did, in fact, extend the rules of non-monetary payments to contracts negotiated with private institutions." (1985, p. 172).

102 See the 1920 article, "Bezdenzhnye raschety i ikh rol v finansovom khozyaistve," *Narodnoe Khozyaistvo*, 1–2, pp. 8–9, emphasis added, as quoted in Szmauely (1974, p. 34). Also see Malle (1985, p. 174), where she quotes Krestinskii, who was one of the Commissars of Finance, as arguing that the Bolshevik financial policies during War Communism were a result of their conviction that "the period had begun in which monetary tokens would become unnecessary and it would be possible to get rid of them without any damage to the economy. From such perspective originated our easy attitude towards monetary issue and our lack of concern to increase the value of the rouble."

103 See Bukharin and Preobrazhensky (1919/1966). The appendix of this book contains the adopted Party program (see pp. 373 ff.).

104 Bukharin and Preobrazhensky (1919/1966, p. 70). It is this program of rationalization that Milyutin announced with pride in June 1920. "All enterprises and all industrial branches," he stated, "are considered like a single enterprise. Instead of competition, instead of struggle, Soviet Power with determination implements the principle of unity of the national economy in the economic field." See Milyutin (1920, p. 8) *Narodnoe khoziaistvo Sovetskoi Rossii*, as quoted in Malle (1985, p. 320) in 1927. It is also this very project of achieving *ex ante* coordination that Mises directly challenged, while Bukharin stated that the planner would know in advance how, what and for whom to allocate resources, Mises merely asked the planners how, in the absence of monetary calculation, they would know which projects are economically feasible and which ones were not. As we will see, it is this disregard on the part of the Bolsheviks for economic calculation that finally led to the collapse and the retreat to NEP.

105 Bukharin and Preobrazhensky (1919/1966, p. 74). Bukharin does, however, admit that this program is not fully realizable at the moment. Two or three generations would have to grow up under the new conditions before the project was fully realizable and "the bureaucracy, the permanent officialdom, will disappear" and the state would wither away. Bukharin, at least here, did not seem to understand the threat of the growing bureaucracy associated with the Communist scheme. For a discussion of the bureaucratization of social life under Soviet rule, see Rizzi (1935/1985), Djilas (1957), and Konrad and Szelenyi (1979).

106 Bukharin and Preobrazhensky (1919/1966, p. 72). Also see Bukharin (1979), where he argues that

> Money represents the material social ligament, the knot which ties up the whole highly developed commodity system of production. It is clear that during the transition period, in the process of abolishing the commodity system as such, a process of *self-negation* of money takes place. It is manifested in the first place in the so-called devaluation of money and in the second place, in the fact that the distribution of paper money is divorced from the distribution of products, and vice versa. Money ceases to be the universal equivalent and becomes a conventional – and moreover extremely imperfect – symbol of the circulation of products.
>
> (Bukharin 1979, p. 155)

107 Bukharin and Preobrazhensky (1919/1966, p. 77).

108 Bukharin (1979, p. 155).

109 Program of the Communist Party of Russia (adopted at the Eighth Party Congress Held 18–23 March 1919), in Bukharin and Preobrazhensky (1919/1966, p. 390).

110 Bukharin and Preobrazhensky (1919/1966, p. 397). Also see Lenin (1977, vol. 29, pp. 115–16). Lenin proposed that "the R.C.P. will strive as speedily as possible to introduce the most radical measures to pave the way for the abolition of money, first and foremost to replace it by savings-bank books, cheques, short-term notes entitling the holders to receive goods from the public stores and so forth ... " Lenin argued for the eventual

elimination of hand to hand currency and its replacement by a system of cashless accounting, i.e. sophisticated barrier.

111 Appendix: Documents of the Revolution, in Chamberlin (1987, vol. 2, p. 490).

112 Chamberlin (1987, vol. 2, p. 494).

113 Bukharin would try to "apologize" for the economic destruction – not by reference to civil war or foreign intervention – but by reference to the dialectics of the transition period. This goes for his theory of expanded negative reproduction as well as his justification of non-economic coercion. The contradiction inherent in the transition period – "where the proletariat has already left the confines of capitalist compulsion, but has not yet become a worker in communist society" – demands it. See Bukharin (1979).

114 Chamberlin (1987, vol. 2, p. 105).

115 Wells (1921, p. 137).

116 Lewin (1985, p. 211),

117 Cohen (1971/1980, p. 123).

118 For example, Boris Pasternak's *Doctor Zhivago* or Ayn Rand's *We the Living* give explicit details of the destruction of economic and social life under Soviet rule during this period. Also see the memoirs of Emma Goldman (1923 and 1924) and Arthur Ransome (1919).

119 Besançon (1981, p. 278).

120 Lawton (1932, vol. 1, p. 107).

121 As early as 1912, Mises had argued the essential organizational connection between private property in the means of production and monetary calculation. See Mises (1980, p. 41), where he states: "The phenomena of money presupposes an economic order in which production is based on division of labor and in which private property consists not only of goods of the first order (consumption goods) but also in goods of the higher order (production goods)."

122 Lawton (1932, vol. 1, p. 108).

123 Lawton (1932, vol. 1, p. 111).

124 Mises (1920/1975, p. 125).

125 "Etapy revoliutssi," *Izvestiya*, 12 March 1921, as quoted in Daniels (1960a, p. 144).

126 Avrich (1970, p. 163).

127 Ibid. Avrich seems to think this naïve, but, given the evidence presented above concerning the economic program of the Bolsheviks, and the economic coordination problems that program ran into, the Kronstadter's assessment might not be that naïve after all. Avrich also seems to suggest that the Kronstadt rebellion was a result of the "failure" of the Bolsheviks to implement Marxian socialist programs, but this is because he interprets the socialist project to be one of a radical democratic decentralization of economic and political life. The Marxian ideal of both the rationalization of economic and political life is, thus, misunderstood. Nevertheless, Avrich provides perhaps the best history of the rebellion. Also see Daniels (1960a, pp. 137–53).

128 *Pravda o Kronshtadte* (The Truth about Kronstadt) (1921, pp. 164–5) as quoted in Avrich (1970, pp. 163–4).

129 Shapiro (1990/1971, p. 211).

130 Pasvolsky (1921, p. ix).

131 Lavoie (1985a, p. 214, emphasis added).

132 "The Roots of Stalinism: Four Essays," *Nauka i Zhizen*, (November 1988–February 1989), reprinted in *The Current Digest of the Soviet Press* XLI(10–13) (April 1989).

133 Tsipko (reprinted in 1989, pp. 3 and 5).

8 Soviet venality: a rent-seeking model of the Communist state

1 See Anderson and Tollison (1993) for a discussion.

2 This was a very complex issue for the transition to socialism after the Bolsheviks assumed power. The problem of bureaucracy was assumed to be irrelevant because, with the revolution, a new age had been ushered in, and, within a generation, the socialist culture

would produce socialist man, a being wholly different from his pre-socialist predecessor. Since, in this new society, a permanent division of labor would be absent, those running the bureau of planning today would be working somewhere else tomorrow, and thus bureaucratic interests would not present a problem. See Boettke (1990, pp. 63–111, 150–1, and the references therein to the relevant works of Marx and Lenin on the question of the division of labor and the problem of bureaucracy).

3   Many writers have noted this problem, but have otherwise maintained the conventional view of socialism as ideologically driven (for example, see Pejovich 1990).

4   This rent sharing (other than open sale) may have been motivated by the Soviet rulers' desire to increase their internal security – the autocrat preferring to sacrifice some potential returns from the sale of monopolies in exchange for greater control over choosing the individuals occupying strategic positions in the economy.

5   Various estimates of the size of this economy ranged from 10 to 40% of Soviet GNP. This was in addition to the legal private economy, which probably contributed between 10 and 20% of Soviet GNP. A RAND Corporation report prepared for the Department of Defense estimated that 11.5% of total household income in USSR came from private sources. See Ofer and Vinakur (1980), and O'Hearn (1980). In some regions and for some products, the second economy was simply the predominant provider.

6   It was estimated by Gosnab in 1990, for example, that 80% of the volume of output in the machine-building industry was manufactured by monopolists and that 77% of the enterprises in machine-building were monopoly producers of particular commodities (see Kroll 1991, pp. 144–5).

7   In one incident, the director and chief engineer of a construction trust supplied state farms with building materials and obtained bribes of between 20,000 and 40,000 roubles from each farm that the trust had dealings with, in order to expedite deliveries. Similarly, an official in the Novolipetsk Metallurgical Combine took large bribes for many years (which included cases of champagne) for releasing supplies (see Simis 1977, p. 149).

8   In the early 1970s, for example, the President of the Supreme Soviet of the Soviet Republic of Azerbaijan sold pardons to convicted felons, and charged 100,000 roubles in cases involving the promise of long imprisonment. During the same period, the Azerbaijan Communist Party allegedly sold appointments to various government posts for large sums: 30,000 roubles for District Public Prosecutor, 50,000 for Chief of the District Militia, 80,000 for manager of a Sovkhoz collective farm, and 20,000 for appointment as First Secretary of the Party District Committee (see Voslensky 1984, p. 191).

9   According to Grossman (1977a: 32–3), the "price" of admission varied with the quality of the institution, and also across republics. The scale of bribes necessary to secure admission to the universities in Moscow and Leningrad (now St Petersburg) varied between 1,000 and 3,000 roubles, but admission to the medical institute in Georgia cost 15,000, and in Azerbaijan, 30,000 roubles.

10 Harris (1986, pp. 24–30) lists numerous examples of "socialist graft" in the People's Republic of China at the time when it represented a variant form of the Soviet-style economy.

11 The examples listed here involve monetary bribes, but bribes in the form of transfers of goods and services (and favors) were probably more important and more widespread, because they were inherently more difficult to trace (see Grossman 1977b, p. 841).

12 See the discussion in Hough (1969, chapters 1–2) and Voslensky (1984, chapter 3).

13 An official description (from 1968) of the activity of industrial instructors employed by the Communist Party lists official responsibilities: "Preparing of reports for the bureau and the plenum, sending trucks to harvest, organizing city celebrations and improving city amenities, procuring supplies for enterprises ... and hundreds of other problems have to be dealt with without delay" (see Andrle 1976, p. 102).

14 For an examination of the opulent lifestyle enjoyed by Soviet élite compared with the average citizens, see Zemtsov (1985).

15 See, for example, Zaleski (1980) and Rutland (1985).

9 Credibility, commitment and Soviet economic reform

1　See Boettke (1993) for an examination of perestroika. This chapter draws freely from that earlier treatment.

2　I will not directly address the problems associated with socialist reform attempts, such as Lenin's War Communism or Stalin's collectivization, in this chapter, but instead concentrate on the difficulties of liberalization within a socialist regime. On the difficulties associated with socialist reforms, see Boettke (1993, pp. 46–56 and the literature cited therein).

3　See Klein (1990), Klein and O'Flaherty (1993), and Roderik (1989) for components of the theoretical argument that follows.

4　Roderik (1989) argues that policy overshooting can reduce informational confusion. The more severe the credibility gap, however, the more drastic the policy overshooting must be in order to send the appropriate signal.

5　For an examination of the policies of War Communism, see Boettke (1990, pp. 63–111).

6　Alan Ball (1987, p. 23). Also see N. Gubsky (1927) for a contemporary account of the Civil Code.

7　The Soviet constitution barred from voting or holding office:

1　people using hired labor to make profits;
2　people living on "unearned income," which included income from private enterprises and property; and
3　private traders and middlemen.

　　The *lishentsy* could not have careers in the military, or join cooperatives or trade unions, or publish newspapers or organize gatherings. In addition, they had to pay higher fees for utilities, rent, medical care, schools, and all public services.

8　As Robert Conquest explains: "When the market mechanism had failed to give satisfaction, requisition made up the shortfall, and the government then went back to the market. *But from the peasant point of view, the market was no longer a reasonably secure outlet, but one that might be superceded at any moment by requisition.* And in the further deterioration of market relations thus produced, the government remembered the success it had with forced requisition, and did not reflect that it was the requisition of grain produced with the incentive of the market, and that in the new circumstances this was certain to shrink in quantity" (Conquest 1986, p. 93).

9　See the discussion of Khrushchev's speech in Nove (1992, pp. 336 ff.).

10　As Nove points out, however, Khrushchev's agricultural policies crowded out the only remaining sphere of autonomy left to the peasants after collectivization – the private plot. As such, Khrushchev's agricultural policies were counterproductive. See Nove (1992, pp. 372–7).

11　See the discussion in Hewett (1988, pp. 223–7), Nove (1992, pp. 351–4), and Gregory and Stuart (1990, p. 143).

12　Coordination problems included duplication of supply arrangements, components manufacturing and that all decisions (minor as well as major) required approval from Moscow.

13　See Hewett (1988, p. 226, table 5-1) for an examination of the growth rates during this period.

14　Liberman's original article was published in *Pravda*, 9 September 1962. See Hewett (1988, pp. 227–45). Also, see Pejovich (1969) for a critical examination of the divergence between "announcement" of a reform, the content of a reform proposal, and the implementation of a reform proposal. In the language of this chapter, it is precisely the discrepancy between the announcement and the content and implementation which generates the credibility gap that must be closed before economic reform can be expected to generate positive results.

15 For a discussion of the Soviet bureaucracy and the difficulties that this system presented for reform, see Gregory (1990). Also, see Rutland (1993) for the involvement of local party organs in the economic management bureaucracy.

16 See Linz (1987 p. 156) for the report of these interviews.

17 As John Litwack explains, "A Soviet manager ... is often averse to expending resources for improving the performance of his or her firm. But this is not because of a well-defined progressive tax scheme that requires sharing future benefits with the government. The problem is that the tax scheme tomorrow is at the discretion of superiors in the hierarchy. They will determine conditions only after observing the performance of the firm today. In the absence of long-run commitment, these superiors naturally attempt to extract surpluses from those subordinate organizations that reveal themselves to be more productive. In addition, poorly performing enterprises are typically 'bailed out.' ... The expectation of discretionary extraction and bailouts creates an incentive problem at lower levels" (Litwack 1991a, p. 257).

18 As Belkindas (1989) points out, opportunities for unearned income originate because of the shortage economy. Illegal housing transactions, medical care, admission to an institution of higher education, and so forth are just some examples of how illicit transactions can "correct" for the failings of the official economy.

19 See Belkindas (1989, pp. 37–97) for an overview of the development of private cooperatives in the Soviet Union. In addition, see Jones and Moskoff (1991).

20 See Jones and Moskoff (1989). With regard to the hostility toward the emerging cooperatives, they state that "cooperative activity has ... engendered a great deal of hostility from two groups; the consuming public, which it is supposed to serve, and the bureaucracy, which it threatens" (Ibid. 1989, p. 32). Also see the discussion of the economic environment within which cooperatives had to operate and the array of official responses in terms of restrictions, interference and taxation that stifled the development of cooperatives, in Jones and Moskoff (1991, pp. 34–77). In addition, see Goldman (1991, p. 113). "The half-hearted toleration of cooperative and private trade," Goldman states, "was guaranteed to sabotage the whole effort."

21 The evolution of working capital markets, for example, depends on the ability of the state to be bound by commitments that it will not confiscate assets. "The shackling of arbitrary behavior of rules and the development of impersonal rules" that successfully bind the state are key components of institutional transformation. See North (1990, p. 129) and Litwack (1991b).

22 See the 1993 *Radio Free Europe/Radio Liberty (RFE/RL) Research Bulletin* 3 February: 2–3.

23 For an examination of the inter-enterprise debt, see Ickes and Ryterman (1992).

24 Thus, it was ironic when Western critics of "shock therapy" blamed the poor results on "monetarism." The monetarist policy prescription is predicated on control of money supply – the Central Bank of Russia (under parliament's direction) pursued a loose monetary policy to bail out the failing state enterprises. The struggle between the government policy-makers and the Central Bank guaranteed that a uniform monetary policy would not emerge. On 21 September 1993 – along with disbanding the parliament – Yeltsin transferred control of the Central Bank to his government.

25 See, for example, Shelton (1989). Shelton, building on the work of Soviet émigré economist Igor Birman, challenges Soviet budget records, pointing out, for example, that there was a gap between claimed revenues and identified sources of revenue in the budget figures in 1987 of around 146.4 billion roubles. This gap, she says, was persistent from 1970 onwards, and ranges from a 20% gap in 1970 to a 36% gap in 1987. Shelton concludes that the internal budget mess in the Soviet Union was severe even before Gorbachev.

26 The debate over bread price decontrol is illustrative of the problem with the Russian reform package. Complete decontrol of bread prices was first scheduled for 1 October

1993, but postponed until 15 October 1993. On 12 October, Chernomyrdin announced that the government was reconsidering the decision to decontrol bread prices. Bread allowances subsidize consumption to low-income citizens at an estimated 1,400 roubles per month. See *RFE/RL,* 13 October 1993.

27 The 1993 budget approved by parliament, for example, included a 22.4 trillion rouble deficit that amounted to about 25% of gross national product (see *RFE/RL,* 26 August 1993). As pointed out in an *Izvestiya* article, each liberalization of the Russian economy has been accompanied by promised subsidization, so the fiscal strains on the Russian budget continue to grow (see *RFE/RL,* 30 August 1993). Moreover, because Russia lacks a well-developed securities market, deficit financing translates immediately into pressure to monetize; that is, the government cannot borrow and therefore must finance its affairs either through taxation or inflation.

28 Interview with Professor Gennadi Zoteev, Vice-Director of the Economic Research Institute, Ministry, of Economics of the Russian Federation, in his Moscow office on 25 January 1993.

29 See Boettke (1993, pp. 138–44) for a discussion of some of the opposition, both from conservative and liberal reformist factions, to Yeltsin's policy design.

30 See *RFE/RL,* 3 August 1993, where it is reported that *Izvestiya* announced that an insurance fund had been established by the State Investment Corporation and the European Agency for Export Guarantees to protect foreign investment from political uncertainty in Russia. The fund's founding capital consisted of gold and precious metals to the value of about $100 million and would be deposited in a Western European country.

31 See Burke (1993). Also note that thirty of the eighty-nine republics and regions of the Russian Federation are withholding taxes from Moscow. Some, for example Chechenya–Ingushetia, are simply refusing to pay any taxes to the center. Others, such as Bashkir and Tatar, have declared "fiscal sovereignty" – a unilateral decision on their part as to how much tax revenue will be sent to Moscow.

32 See *The Economist,* 22 January 1994, pp. 52–3.

33 It is important to stress that one cannot legitimately conclude that shock therapy failed in Russia because it was never tried. Thus, it is particularly ridiculous when Chernomyrdin argues that the Russian government has already tried to guide the process of transition with monetary controls and failed and that now it is time to shift to non-monetary means of control (i.e. wage and price controls) to guide the transition. What shock therapy amounted to was a reform announcement followed by partial steps toward implementation and then reversal of the policy. Yeltsin has simply repeated the general pattern of the Soviet reformer, as I have tried to document.

34 The evolution of liberal institutions of governance is in no sense guaranteed. Instead, effective liberal revolutions result from a peculiar mix of indigenous institutions and cultural practices, combined with careful design of liberal rules that can tap into these indigenous traditions and cultivate a sustainable liberal order.

35 See the discussion of the evolution of institutions of public choice in seventeenth-century England, in North and Weingast (1989).

10 Perestroika and public choice: the economics of autocratic succession in a rent-seeking society

1 See Lavoie (1986–7), Roberts (1971), Rutland (1985), and Zaleski (1980) for a detailed examination of the reality of "central planning."

2 For a discussion of the inner workings of rent distribution within the Soviet system, see d'Encausse (1980), Simis (1982), Voslensky (1984), and Willis (1985).

3 Selyunin (1988, pp. 15–16), argues that Soviet "planners" should also pay close attention to world market prices for resources, which they should then proceed to copy. This is a

point repeatedly stressed by Ludwig von Mises, in his analysis of real existing socialism. See, for example, Mises (1981, p. 535).

4 See Voslensky (1984) for a discussion of the *nomenklatura* system. Also see Winiecki (1990).

5 See the "Novosibirsk Report" by Tatyana Zaslavskaya (1984). Also see Goldman (1983 and 1987).

6 For a history of perestroika, see Abalkin (1987), Aganbegyan (1988 and 1989), and Aslund (1989). For a representative sample of the "zigs and zags" of Soviet reform, see the conflicting proposals for "restructuring" offered in Abalkin (1989), Ryzhkov (1989 and 1990), Shatalin *et al.* (1990), and the Supreme Soviet's "Guidelines for Stabilizing the Economy" (1990), which attempted to merge the Ryzhkov and Shatalin plans.

7 See Gorlin (1986), Desai (1989), Schroeder (1987 and 1989), and Thom (1989) for a discussion of the problems with perestroika. Also see Boettke (1991).

8 The complete text of the Law on the State Enterprises was published in *Pravda* (1 July 1987); translated in *The Current Digest of the Soviet Press* 39: 30–1 (1987) (hereafter cited as *CDSP*).

9 As a report in the *Moscow News* stated: "It is as though the directors were being forced to swim with their hands and feet tied." *Moscow News* (10 April 1988), as quoted in Thom (1989, p. 40).

10 See, for example, the 1990 *CDSP* 42(24): 13–15.

11 See *The Economist* (20 October 1990, p. 11) for a discussion of these problems.

12 The Ryzhkov government's proposal for 1991, for example, was to change those figures to 60% centrally fixed prices and 40% unrestricted pricing. The breakdown for the consumer market in 1991 for light industry goods was to be 60% fixed prices, 30% regulated prices, and only 5–10% unrestricted pricing. For cultural, consumer and household goods, those figures were to be 40%, 35%, and 25% (see Ryzhkov 1990).

13 Hewett (1988, p. 310), describes Gorbachev's "reforms" as a form of patronage reallocation.

14 Smith claims that "the record of Mikhail Gorbachev in making personnel changes early in his tenure in office has eclipsed that of any previous leader of the USSR," and adds that by January 1987, only nineteen (of fifty-odd) ministers remained at their posts who had been in place at the time of Gorbachev's succession (Smith 1987, p. 347).

15 In October 1990, before the onset of recent, even more "conservative" (i.e. traditional Communist) policies, the Gorbachev plan for economic reform called for the continuation of the central planning system, central control over basic raw materials, the retention of central direction of prices, and made no commitment to the privatization of land. See *The Economist* (20 October 1990, p. 61).

16 See Hazan (1990, p. 221) for an example of such an interpretation.

17 A newspaper article by Keller (1991) describes the case of the Uralmash Machine Tool Works as a kind of microcosm of the interlocking monopolies, and near-total reliance on centralized decision-making, which continues to characterize the industrial structure of the supposedly "reformed" Soviet Union.

18 Hewett interprets the Gorbachev reforms as oriented toward

> the future industrial structure as one in which a few thousand large, vertically integrated, national-level enterprises would handle national-level markets, while local and regional markets, as well as some of the needs of these ... would be handled by enterprises founded and operating under republican and national authorities.
>
> (Hewett 1988, p. 331, fn. 45)

that is, a form of socialism, albeit partially decentralized.

19 The current "anti-corruption campaign" has been portrayed as an example of the economic liberalization under perestroika. In fact, instead of increasing effective competition, the clamp-down on bribery and graft has probably made markets *less* competitive in practice.

Enterprises which for decades utilized bribery and other black-market transactions to overcome the chronic shortages and delays associated with central planning now find that their ability to do "end runs" around the planners is greatly restricted. A number of comparative systems scholars have noted that *bribery* has long played a vital role in keeping the "centrally planned economy" minimally functional. The Gorbachev "anti-corruption campaign" may have seriously impeded the operation of this "safety valve."

20   See Voslensky's discussion of the origin of the ruling class in the Soviet Union (Voslensky 1984, pp. 14–67). As he points out,

> In 1930, 69 per cent of the regional and district secretaries and secretaries of the central committees of the Union's constituent republics had joined the party before the revolution. In 159, 80.5% had joined the party only after 1924, i.e. after Lenin's death. Of the 1,939 secretaries, 91% were under forty; in other words, they were adolescents at the time of the revolution. The figures for the secretaries of regions and towns are similar. In 1939, 93.5% had joined the party only after 1924, and 92 per cent were under forty.
>
> (Voslensky 1984, p. 61)

Stalin's purge of the "Old Bolsheviks" served, among other things, to create a layer of very young and loyal *apparatchiks*.

21   Soon after Gorbachev became Chairman, *Pravda* printed several letters which called for an across-the-board Party purge. In 1985, if such a suggestion appeared in *Pravda*, by definition it had the Chairman's approval. Gorbachev publicly dismissed this suggestion, but stated that the Party was carrying out a non-violent and more selective "cleansing" (*ochishcheniye*), mostly by means of retirements. See Colton (1986, p. 89).

22   The text of the law on the press and other media was published in *Pravda* (20 June 1990); *CDSP* 42(25) (1990). Gorbachev (July 1990) had announced that television should function independently of all political and public organizations. At the same time, however, the Gorbachev announcement reaffirmed Moscow's control over television by stating that "all legal acts of republican and local authorities aimed to change the legal and property status of television are invalid." Altogether, this is an excellent example of a "reform" that superficially appears to herald a dramatic shift, but really gives away little or nothing. *See Radio Free Europe/Radio Liberty Daily Report* 133 (16 July 1990, p. 8). Hereafter cited as *RFE/RL*.

23   There are numerous cases like that of Sergei Kuznetsov, a journalist for *Glasnost* magazine, who annoyed Gorbachev and was first deposited in a psychiatric institution, then sentenced to three years hard labor after being accused of "slandering the Soviet state." See Ledeen (1990, p. 15). Also relevant is that in spring 1990, the Soviet government passed a law protecting the President's honor from "slander in the press." See *CDSP* 42(21) (1990). Valeriya Novodvorskaya, one of the leaders of the "Democratic Union," was arrested and sentenced to 15 days' imprisonment for "defaming the CPSU, the Congress of People's Deputies and the dignity of the President of the USSR." See *RFE/RL* 148 (6 August 1990, p. 9).

24   For example, *Izvestiya* published an exposé of the lavish lifestyle and extensive property of Alexsey Boyko, chief of the Turkmenian KGB, which facilitated Boyko's subsequent dismissal. This episode is typical of the campaign in the press against the KGB, usually followed shortly by reports of the dismissal of the accused officials. In February 1988 alone, the dismissals of the KGB chiefs in five republics (Ukraine, Kazakhstan, Lithuania, Tadzhikistan, and Kirgizia) were announced, and many of their assistants were fired as well (see Hazan 1990, p. 153).

25   The marginal tax rates range from 15% for incomes up to 3,000 roubles a year, to 65% on incomes above 6,000 roubles. The *patenty* fees are set by region, and are also high. For example, in the Russian Republic, the *patent* for a private taxi costs 560 roubles, which implies that the taxi-driver must – during his hours off from his "day" job, when

he/she works for the state – earn the equivalent of at least three months' wages before he/she can clear any net revenue from taxi-driving (Hewett 1988, pp. 340–1). The perverse consequences of this are described in the Moscow diary of Taubman and Taubman (1989, pp. 46–7).

26 Western estimates of the extent of the Soviet "second economy," pre-Gorbachev, ranged from 15% to 30% of GNP (Lacquer 1989, p. 203, fn. 10); granting *de jure* legality to a business which has long had *de facto* legality might not have much net effect on the aggregate level of such activity. Also see Feldbrugge (1989) for a discussion of the underground economy in the Soviet Union.

27 For example, the combined tax burden on private traders and manufacturers in 1924/ 25 was equal to 53% of the private traders' reported profits, and 42% of the private manufacturers' (Ball 1987, p. 54). These figures do not include the various license fees imposed by the central government and by local authorities, which were substantial (Ibid., p. 29).

28 See Gorbachev (1989) for an outline of the official tax policy in relation to the cooperatives.

11 The reform trap in economics and politics in the former Communist economies

1 See, for example, the article by Alexander Dallin (Dallin, 1992, pp. 279–302). A neo-conservative autopsy on Sovietology is performed in *The National Interest*, 1993.

2 My own attempt to assess Hayek's work for a popular audience can be found in "Friedrich A. Hayek (1899–1992)," Boettke (1992a, pp. 300–3).

3 This was the basic argument presented by Robert Heilbroner (Heilbroner 1990, pp. 1097–114). For an examination of the analytical issues that Hayek raised during the debates with Keynes and the market socialist, see Boettke (1992b, pp. 84–95).

4 My own attempt to address these issues can be found in Boettke (1993). At a theoretical level this work is influenced by Mises, Hayek, Buchanan, and Tullock and seeks to develop a hybrid political economy framework out of these (and other) scholars' respective bodies of work. The main thrust of this approach is to comparatively analyze the epistemic function of alternative political, legal and economic institutions and practices.

5 For a discussion of the issues involved in the privatization debate and the different approaches, see Gligorov (1992, pp. 45–58). Gligorov, however, while correctly challenging the technocratic approach to privatization favored by Western advisors, wrongly rejects the spontaneous privatization process, for reasons that I will allude to later.

6 This position owes much to G. Warren Nutter's critique of attempts to construct a social system of production which would generate the incentives and signals of a market economy without the institution of private property. See Nutter (1983, pp. 94–102).

7 See McKinnon (1991). McKinnon uncovered the important phenomenon of negative value added firms within the state sector. McKinnon's conclusion, however, about the necessity of adopting a cautious trade policy does not necessarily follow from his analysis of the distinction between state enterprises that make losses and those firms which are value subtractors. Without the introduction of market discipline, it is difficult to determine how prevalent negative value added firms are in the system. We now have good reasons to believe that the phenomenon is of much greater magnitude than even McKinnon first imagined. Many East German firms, which were viewed as the flagships of socialist industrial development, once exposed to Western markets were revealed to be not only inefficient producers, but negative value added firms. Market competition not only provides incentives, but generates information which is simply not available in its absence. Moreover, unless the link between microeconomic inefficiency and macroeconomic policy is severed, liberalization will not result. The "negative" results on

the current economic system from severing that link are symptoms of reforms working, not of reforms failing.

8   See Michnik (1990, p. 24).
9   Smith (1776/1937, p. 423).
10 See Knight (1921/1971).
11 See Coase (1988).
12 See Knight (1935).
13 This should not be construed as a conservative intellectual or political statement. The assessment that we have lost a certain intellectual wisdom that can be found in earlier writers does not imply that all we need to do is return to their writings, or even that their writings were entirely correct. All that is implied is that the Whig theory of history of ideas is not correct.
14 See Lange (1939/1970). Also see Lavoie (1985).
15 See Arrow (1951). The claim that Arrow's results should not be surprising to students of politics was, of course, the astute observation of Buchanan and Tullock regarding Arrow's proof of the voting paradox.
16 See, for example, Schumpeter (1942, p. 254).
17 See the discussion of Arrow's theorem in Stevens (1993, pp. 143–6).
18 The classic criticism of Arrow's market failure theory is in Demsetz (1969/1989, pp. 3–24).
19 This is particularly ironic, given that his work in political failure theory pre-dates his work in market failure theory.
20 The "important point," Hayek wrote, "is that all coercive action of government must be unambiguously determined by a permanent legal framework which enables the individual to plan with a degree of confidence and which reduces human uncertainty as much as possible. See Hayek (1960, p. 222). Also see Rizzo (1980, pp. 291–318).
21 See Lange (1970, pp. 61–2).
22 Adam Przeworski, for example, mentions the calculation debate and even seems to agree with central components of the argument, but nevertheless argues that:

    1   he is skeptical that forms of property ownership have consequences for firm performance, and
    2   that even if socialism is unfeasible, capitalism is irrational.

    Market socialism may have difficulties, and it does not reflect complete democracy, but it does appear more attractive than capitalism because of the distributional effects. Market socialism would be more egalitarian than capitalism. See Przeworski (1991, pp. 100–35).
23 See, for example, Thornton (1992).
24 Viktor Vanberg has summed up this point nicely by distinguishing between "conditional" and "unconditional" normative claims concerning market competition. The normative claims concerning the superiority of the market, Vanberg argues, can be made only to the extent that the competitive environment conforms to certain specified characteristics. The framework which Vanberg establishes in his discussion is one which (despite subtle differences in emphasis) I share – it combines a positive individualist evolutionary selection process with a normative conditionality for collective choice. See Vanberg (1993). Compare with Boettke (1993) – see pp. 65–9 for a discussion of the difference between unconditional and conditional competition within the Soviet-type context and p. 183, n. 15, for a distinction between rule design and rule selection within political economy.
25 See the discussion of these theoretical issues in Klein (1990, pp. 1–19) and Klein and O'Flaherty (1993, pp. 295–314).
26 Player 1 (the government) does possess a wealth-maximizing incentive to commit to liberalization. However, if the ruling regime's time horizon becomes short sighted, the revenue-maximizing strategy is to confiscate. Commitment technology, in other words,

allows the regime to adopt an encompassing view, as opposed to a narrow self-interest perspective (see Olson 1983). Commitment technologies are often stumbled upon rather than emerging from the brow of any genius. As Hayek has remarked "Individual liberty in modern times can hardly be traced back farther than the England of the seventeenth century. It appeared first, as it probably always does, as a by-product of a struggle for power rather than as the result of deliberate design." (Hayek 1960). Also see Kiser and Barzel (1991, pp. 396–422).

27 See North (1990, p. 129).
28 I am defining democratic politics here as electoral politics and not the other values implied in the democratic vision, such as openness, open-endedness, autonomy and public transparency. For a discussion of the democratic vision and its contemporary relevance, see Lavoie (1992, pp. 435–55). To my mind, however, Lavoie's discussion does not adequately account for how "democracy in the narrow" (i.e. electoral politics) may undermine "democracy in the broad" (i.e. the democratic vision). As a result, Lavoie does not deal with the constraints on "democracy in the narrow" that are required to sustain democracy in the broad.
29 On this distinction, see Hayek (1960, pp. 103–17).
30 See *The Federalist Papers* (1961, p. 322).
31 See Hayek (1978, pp. 157–8). Also see Hayek (1979, p. 3), where he states that:

> The tragic illusion was that the adoption of democratic procedures made it possible to dispense with all other limitations on governmental power. It also promoted the belief that the "control of government" by democratically elected legislation would adequately replace traditional limitations, while in fact the necessity of forming organized majorities for supporting a program of particular actions in favor of special groups introduced a new source of arbitrariness and partiality and produced results inconsistent with the moral principles of the majority.

32 See Oi (1992, pp. 99–126). Also see the discussion of developments in China in *The Economist* (1993, pp. 41–2). The problem with contemporary discussions which see China as a paradox (for example, Kristof 1993, pp. A1, A10) is, as Herbert Spencer pointed out long ago, that they tend to confuse ends and means. Rights are the claims and limitations which are deemed necessary to pursue the objects of life. Social arrangements which maintain these rights, Spencer stated, are what we mean by the term "government." A basic analytical problem, and the corresponding confused state of political discourse, arises when these instruments for maintaining rights come to be viewed as rights themselves (see Spencer 1897, pp. 174–80).
33 See Hayek (1944/1976) and Friedman (1962/1982).
34 Hayek (1944/1976, pp. 91–2).
35 I have argued that much of the early experience with attempts at reforming the Soviet system reflects the fact that Lenin understood this basic liberal point, and sought to avoid falling into the liberalization dynamic during the New Economic Policy of the 1920s by banning all political opposition (see Boettke 1990, pp. 34–8).
36 See Ackerman (1992).
37 Pipes (1990, p. 838).
38 See Arendt (1958).
39 A contemporary defense of the twin liberal project of open markets and open politics can be found in Lavoie (1992, pp. 435–55) and Lavoie (1993, pp. 103–20).
40 See Havel *et al.* (1985).
41 The Russian rule, I was informed during my stay in Moscow in January 1993, was "what I watch is mine." The predominance of *de facto* property claims, and the implications for reform, will be discussed later.
42 It is also not an easy transformation, for the reasons discussed by Buchanan (1993, pp. 51–64). The historical story of the development of Russian culture is radically different

from the one told concerning the development of European civilization, let alone the United States. Moreover, the collective experience with the market under the Soviet system was one of monopolistically dictated terms of exchange. Citizens could either wait on long lines to buy lousy products or they could go to the black market and pay higher prices to buy mostly the same products (with some Western products unavailable elsewhere). There simply were not many alternative sources of supply other than the state sector for most products (most products offered in the black market in fact were stolen from the state sector). In a shortage economy, the transformation of non-monetary costs to consumers (such as waiting in line) into monetary benefits for sellers (such as bribes) does not necessarily yield either efficient or just outcomes. It would be like limiting the market experience of a people to the search and occupation of rent-controlled apartments.

43   In Boettke (1993, pp. 108–12), I distinguish between three liberal traditions:

1   the Locke–Nozick natural rights tradition;
2   the Hobbes–Buchanan social contractarian tradition; and
3   the Hume–Hayek evolutionary morality tradition.

My argument is that the Hume–Hayek evolutionary morality tradition avoids the pitfalls of the first two approaches, while maintaining its strengths. The Hume–Hayek approach also highlights the necessity of the growth of indigenous institutions and customary practices for economic and political progress.

44   See Tocqueville (1856/1955, p. 167).

45   In their discussion of Chinese and Taiwanese development, Thomas Metzger and Ramon Myers introduce the useful terminology of the uninhibited center, the inhibited center and the subordinate center. See Metzger and Myers (1991, pp. xiii–xiv). The transformation that I am alluding to in the text (the move from customary rules to established rules) is the one from the inhibited center to the subordinate center. Most discussion concerning Eastern and Central Europe and the former Soviet Union focuses on the move from the uninhibited center (the Communist power structure) to the subordinate center (constitutional democracy) and side-steps completely the inhibited center (the *sub rosa* political and intellectual culture and the *de facto* power centers outside the Soviet system of governance) – a move which I believe, for the reasons to be discussed in the text, to be epistemologically impossible, however desirable we would find it in the abstract.

46   See Hayek (1973). Also see Leoni (1972) and Benson (1990, especially chapters 2–7). The issues are also addressed in Aranson (1992, pp. 289–319). Aranson's article is significant in that it disputes the neoclassical reading of the efficiency of the common law. This neoclassical reading, however, must be distinguished from the one that Hayek offers. Just as Hayek's defense of the private property order is not predicated on the efficiency claims of Pareto optimality and the model of general competitive equilibrium, the superiority of the common law found in Hayek's writings does not rely on its Pareto efficiency properties. Efficiency in Hayek's writings – if we can use that word – deals with adaptive efficiency and not static efficiency.

47   See, for example, Naishul (1991a). Also see Naishul (1991b, 1992, pp. 489–96, and 1993, pp. 29–44).

48   Hernando de Soto raises a similar point with regard to reform in Peru. De Soto focuses his discussion on the fundamental role in economic development of the formal recognition of the already accepted informal claims to property rights. He ends his discussion with a nice story which is worth repeating: "When I was growing up in Peru, I was told that the farm I visited belonged to farming communities and not to the individual farmers. Yet as I walked from field to field, a different dog would bark. The dogs were ignorant of the prevailing law; all they knew was which land their masters controlled. In the next

150 years those nations whose laws recognize what the dogs already know will be the ones who enjoy the benefits, of a modern market economy." See de Soto (1993, p. 12).

49 See Naishul (1991b, p. 5), translated by Clifford Gaddy, as quoted in Leitzel (1993).

50 See the article in *The Economist* (1992, p. 46).

51 See Vite and Travin (1991, p. 9). Also, see Tollison and Wagner (1991, pp. 57–70). Tollison and Wagner demonstrate that under plausible conditions it is often impossible to recapture past losses from distorting government policies.

52 This general theoretical conjecture can be seen as part of the underlying rationale behind many of the conjectural history stories told in Austrian economics. Menger's story of the evolution of money, and Mises' regression theorem, for example, are but two examples. "Business usage alone," Mises argued against state theorists of money, "can transform a commodity into a common medium of exchange. It is not the state, but the common practice of all those who have dealings in the market, that creates money." The implications of this theoretical insight, according to Mises, were profound, because it provided both a confirmation of Menger's theory of the evolution of money, and a refutation of alternative theories which argued that the state could consciously create a monetary system through a general agreement independent of commercial activity. See Mises (1980, p. 93; also see the discussion on pp. 129–93). For a contemporary application of Mises' monetary theory to the monetary reform during the transition, see Selgin (1994) The argument in the text concerning rules can be interpreted as an application of Mises' regression theorem to the area of social norms and the establishment of formal rules.

53 An excellent discussion of the theoretical differences between arguments from complexity and arguments from knowledge can be found in Thomsen (1992).

54 See, for example, Fischer and Gelb (1991, pp. 91–105).

55 Hayek spent considerable time throughout his career explicating the impact of competition on social learning. See, for example, Hayek (1978a, pp. 179–90).

56 See Hayek (1948/1980, pp. 255–72).

57 See, for example, *US News and World Report* (1993, pp. 42–6).

58 See, for example, Buchanan (1975).

59 See, for example, Baechler (1975) and Berman (1983).

60 On the importance of competition between governments for the discovery of alternative social arrangements which enhance well-being, see Vihanto (1992). Also see Boettke (1993, pp. 106–31).

61 See, for example, Weingast (1992). Also see Bish (1988, pp. 351–68).

62 See Higgs (1987) for a discussion of the breakdown of federalism in the US during the twentieth century. Also, see Higgs (1988, pp. 369–86).

63 Federalism, however, is not sufficient. Hayek may have pointed the way to an examination of the most important constraint on government discretion – the denationalization of money. I argue the case for free banking on the grounds of precommitment, in Boettke (1993, pp. 123–5).

12 Promises made and promises broken in the Russian transition

1 Financial assistance from the J. M. Kaplan Fund is gratefully acknowledged. The usual caveat applies.

2 See, for example, George Soros (1997). Also, see Amsden *et al.* (1994) for the argument that the task of restructuring the economies in Eastern Europe is far too complex to leave to the forces of the market economy.

3 For a political–economic history of the Gorbachev years, see Boettke (1993). It is important to stress that market-like mechanisms existed throughout Soviet history – even during the periods of hard-line Communism (e.g. War Communism, 1918–21) – in the form of black-market consumer goods, and "vertical and horizontal" negotiating

and trading within the plan itself. The bribe economy was vast, and the *de facto* organizing principle of economic life cannot be captured in the central planning models represented in standard textbooks. See Anderson and Boettke (1997) for a presentation of a "mercantilist" model of the Soviet economic system.

4   See *The Economist: Survey on Russia* (12 July 1997). "Russia today," the survey states, "is a land of unpaid wages, unpaid taxes, strikes, subsistence, dubious privatization, clapped-out industry, crime, corruption, pollution, poverty. It is a land of excess vodka and early death." Also, see David Remnick (1996) for a general account of contemporary Russia.

5   On the failure of development planning, see Bauer (1979) and Boettke (1994).

6   Mises (1922) demonstrates how the ability to assess the economic merits of alternative uses of scarce resources is directly tied to the establishment and enforcement of private property rights and free pricing. Thus, Mises' argument against socialism stressed private property as a necessary prerequisite for the ability to engage in economic calculation, as well as the motivational problems of collective property, and the political problems of unlimited state power.

7   This graph is implied in Epstein (1995, p. 13) and Buchanan (1975, pp. 107–29). The original graphical presentation is developed in Roberts (1971, pp. 48–69).

8   A cost–benefit argument is employed in the case for the flat-tax by Hall and Rabushka (1995), the time consistency argument is presented by Brennan and Buchanan (1985, pp. 67–96), and the argument for the importance of stable rules in a dynamic world is developed by Rizzo (1980). For our present purposes, it is not important to discriminate between these various arguments for permanence and stability.

9   See Boettke (1995) for an elaboration of this argument, and illustrative examples from various reform periods in Soviet and post-Soviet economic history.

10   Weingast (1995, p. 1). Also see Weimer (1997) for a variety of case studies exploring this paradox and, in particular with regard to Russia, see the papers by Frye and Litwack (on Russian privatization), Kiman, Bell and Smith (on legislative politics and property rights in Russia), and Ericson and Jones (on enforcement of property rights in St Petersburg).

11   See Anderson (1995) for a discussion of what she terms "The Red Mafia."

13   The Russian crisis: perils and prospects for post-Soviet transition

1   Between 1948 and 1951, the US provided $13.3 billion to European countries for post-war reconstruction, about $90 billion in today's dollars.

2   On the origins of the Soviet system, see Boettke (1990). On the nature of the Soviet system in practice, see Boettke (1993, 57–72).

3   See Anderson and Boettke (1997). Also, see Krugman (1998), where he argues that post-Soviet Russia is run by a "looting" band of oligarchs (or what Mancur Olson modeled as roving bandits). Because of the lack of security in the right to the flow of rents, these oligarchs have a very short-term time horizon. Krugman argues that the root of Russia's current crisis lies in the inability to collect taxes from these ruling oligarchs who control Russia's natural resources such as oil, gas diamonds and gold, and the current crop of politicians. And thus, while the problem is not so much that the Russian government is spending too much, the revenue short-fall has generated a fiscal imbalance, which manifests itself in rising pessimism about the Russian government's solvency. I do not deny Krugman's account, but I would stress the continued subsidization of inefficient economic organizations (which exacerbates the budget imbalance), rather than the inability to collect taxes, as the crucial problem.

4   For an economic and political history of the Gorbachev years, see Boettke (1993).

5   Marshall Goldman (1991, pp. 37, 110), makes a similar point first about Khrushchev's and then Gorbachev's reform proposals. The proposed policies were treated as a "big lie" under Khrushchev and the "indecision" and "inconsistency" associated with

Gorbachev resulted in a discrediting of the reform efforts in both instances of attempted, but ultimately failed, social transformation.

6 On the credibility and commitment issue as it relates to Soviet and post-Soviet economic history, see Boettke (1993, pp. 88–105), Boettke (1995), and Boettke (1998).

7 It is important to stress that the "mafia" in Russia is a direct outgrowth of the government system and is intertwined within the power structure. See Anderson (1995).

8 In January 1992 the Rb/US$ exchange rate was 198, but by May 1995 the exchange rate was 5,054. This was during a period when Russia was supposedly following "monetarism." Political leaders, such as Viktor Chernomyrdin, repeatedly made statements that the monetarist program had failed, or that the era of market romanticism must end. After the pro-inflation central banker Viktor Gerashchenko was replaced with Sergei Dubinin in 1994, a "monetarist" program of restrictive monetary policy was followed. But the necessary changes in the state budget and banking system were not made. Gerashchenko is now back in charge of monetary policy. In the aftermath of the currency crisis in Russia, the Institute for the Economy in Transition (Moscow) forecasts that the inflation rate for 1998 under four alternative scenarios will range from a low of 223% to a high of 297% (see the September 1998 economic report at http://koi.www.online.ru/sp/iet/trends/sep98eng/3.html).

9 For all the strides toward privatization, one must keep in mind that the Russian state owns more than 10% of roughly one-third of all privatized corporations and more than 20% of one-quarter of privatized ones. Of the top fifty corporations, the state retains over one-third of interests in them. Moreover, there are still several thousand firms that were never privatized in the coal, precious metals, health, and communications industries. See Blasi *et al.* (1997). Writing from a slightly earlier vantage point, Goldman (1996, p. 271) points out that "the most important indicator that privatization has had only a superficial effect is that thus far there has been relatively little product or managerial restructuring. As of 1995, only about 10% of newly privatized enterprises have had a change in management and that was initiated by a hostile vote of the stockholders."

10 The intimate connection between monetary and fiscal policies and the more general-level rules of the game changes that are required for effective change is recognized by Marshall Goldman (1996, p. 144), when he states that:

> Under the best of circumstances the reform would still have required decades to undo all the damage inherited from the decades of central planning. Nonetheless, Yeltsin and Gaidar and their associates and Western advisors can and should be faulted for concentrating so much on monetary, fiscal and price reforms and not enough on new investment and institution and infrastructure building. Had they done the latter, there would still have been difficulties, but there might also have been a few more success stories.

On the general relationship between private property and economic prosperity, see Bethell (1998).

11 44.4 million as estimated in September 1998. See Hiatt (26 October 1998). Also, see the Associated Press report (18 November 1998).

12 Immigrant studies are, of course, problematic because of the systematic bias that those who chose to immigrate are more risk-taking than their contemporaries at home. Nevertheless, if the people have a problem, then even the risk-takers should do relatively worse than other immigrant populations who do not have the problems of cultural resistance to capitalism and democracy. I have not found evidence in the literature that would suggest that Russians are disproportionately disadvantaged in adjusting to the new environments of capitalism and democracy.

13 On the development of "market-preserving Federalism" in China, see Montinola *et al.* (1995).

14 Robustness, rather than ideal efficiency, can become the welfare standard. How robust

are institutions in the wake of opportunistic behavior, on the one hand, and sheer ignorance, on the other? Comparing states of affairs when people are both omniscient and benevolent does not provide us with much insight into real-world political economy. See Mises (1966, p. 692), where he states that socialism becomes an inescapable inference:

> as soon as people began to ascribe to the *state* not only moral but also intellectual perfection. The liberal philosophers had described their imaginary state as an unselfish entity, exclusively committed to the best possible improvement of its subjects' welfare. They had discovered that in the frame of a market society the citizens' selfishness must bring about the same results that this unselfish state would seek to realize; it was precisely this fact that justified the preservation of the market economy in their eyes. But things became different as soon as people began to ascribe to the *state* not only the best of intentions but also omniscience. Then one could not help concluding that the infallible state was in a better position to succeed in the conduct of production activities than erring individuals. It would avoid all those errors that often frustrate the actions of entrepreneurs and capitalists. There would no longer be mal-investment or squandering of scarce factors of production; wealth would multiply. The 'anarchy' of production appears wasteful when contrasted with the planning of the *omniscient* state. The socialist mode of production then appears to be the only reasonable system, and the market economy seems the incarnation of unreason.

Mises left the assumption of benevolence alone, but challenged the assumption of omniscience. He focused particularly on the fact that even given perfect technological knowledge, economic planners without the assistance of the practices and institutions of the market process would be unable to determine the relevant economic knowledge required to assess the alternative use of scarce factors of production. Public choice scholars, on the other hand, have generally taken the different tack of challenging the assumption of benevolence. A robust political economy should work from a starting point which accepts neither benevolence nor omniscience. I believe that there is a good case in human affairs for striving to build institutions from pessimistic assumptions about motivation and knowledge, and thus guarding against worst-case situations.

14 The political infrastructure of economic development

1   See the chapters by Prybyla (China), Ayittey (Africa), and Kamath (India) in Boettke (1994).

2   See, for example, the chapters by Choi (Korea) and Naka, Brough and Tanaka (Japan) in Boettke (1994).

3   These three "facts" of the social world (rules, institutions, and culture) combine to form the social or institutional infrastructure of any society.

4   P. T. Bauer has argued that the term "Third World" emerged merely to represent those countries receiving foreign aid from the developed world. My classification does not intend to challenge Bauer's etymological accuracy. Rather, I am just pointing out that a new classification scheme emerged to reflect the perceived fact that capitalism was no longer the only path to industrial development.

5   See Weber (1961, p. 252). Also see Rosenberg and Birdzell (1986, pp. 113–433).

6   See the chapter by Raico in Boettke (1994) for a literature survey on the "European Miracle."

7   This is what economists in the tradition of Boehm-Bawerk mean when they discuss "roundaboutness" or a deepening of the capital structure.

8   North and Weingast (1989) argue that the emergence of new institutions in the wake of the "Glorious Revolution" of 1688 enabled the government to credibly commit to

upholding property rights. This ability by the government to successfully commit to non-confiscation of wealth creation led to a tremendous growth in investment activity.

9   On the theoretical implication of this observation, see the provocative paper by Israel Kirzner on the limits of the market (1994).

10   Hayek spent considerable time throughout his career explicating the impact of competition on social learning. See, for example, Hayek (1978).

11   Federalism entails a system of governance that possesses the following characteristics:

1   hierarchy of government;
2   delineated scope of authority;
3   guarantee of autonomy; and
4   the locus of economic regulation is decentralized.

The system of governance is, therefore, organized in such a manner that:

1   authority is not at the highest governmental level, and
2   lower levels of government cannot eliminate competition with trade restrictions, etc.

The benefits of federalism for economic development are considerable. It provides a unified market region, at the same time that the prohibition on trade restrictions amongst local governments encourages competition and economic experimentation – both of which lead to innovation and technological development. Federalism also represents a contractual technology which minimizes the ability of the federal government to confiscate the wealth created at the lower levels of government.

12   In other words, federalism represents one model of how to capture the benefits of polycentricism at the same time as minimizing the potential disruptions and costs associated with fighting factions.

13   The terminology of uninhibited, inhibited, and subordinate states is borrowed from Metzger and Myers' analysis of developments in Mainland China and Taiwan. Although I freely borrow their terminology, they are absolved regarding any misapplication of their ideas that I may commit.

14   I would dispute the argument that Russian culture is inherently authoritarian and anti-capitalistic. Obviously I cannot debunk this general impression persuasively here, but let me suggest some alternative evidence. For one, there have been anti-authoritarian movements indigenous to Russia throughout its history, including some of its great writers and poets, as well as a *samizdat* literary culture and dissident political culture. In other words, even at the height of totalitarian rule there was an underground culture which provided something akin (admittedly in a very constrained manner) to civil society. Moreover, there is nothing inherent in the Russian personality that prevents Russians from achieving capitalist success. Large underground markets existed throughout the history of the Soviet regime. In addition, émigré studies (even allowing for the bias contained in the sample population employed in such studies) do not show Russian émigrés to be significantly less capable of adapting to capitalist economies. In fact, Russians tend to be a rather successful group.

15   For a discussion of how the divergence between announcement and implementation affects the credibility of the reformer, and thus the economic environment, see Boettke (1993, pp. 88–105).

16   See Boettke (1993, pp. 138–44) for a discussion of some of the opposition, both from conservative and liberal reformist factions, to Yeltsin's policy design.

17   At the Second International Conference on Banking Operations held in Moscow on 19 October 1993, Western bankers argued that Russia was the highest political risk for investors in the world after Iraq. Political and economic instability was cited, along with

crime, corruption, bureaucracy and incompetence, as the factor undermining the investment climate in Russia.

18   The evolution of liberal institutions of governance is in no sense guaranteed. Instead, effective liberal revolutions result from a peculiar mix of indigenous institutions and cultural practices, combined with careful design of liberal rules that can tap into these indigenous traditions and cultivate a sustainable liberal order.

19   See the discussion of the evolution of institutions of public choice in seventeenth-century England, in North and Weingast (1989).

15 Why culture matters: economics, politics and the imprint of history

1   On property rights in land and economic performance, see Ellickson (1993) and Randy Barnett (1992) for an examination of the "knowledge" function of several property. On the importance of a "rule of law" and constraints on the arbitrary behavior of government for economic performance, see North and Weingast (1989) and Weingast (1995). Also, see Borner *et al.* (1995) for an empirical analysis in support of the hypothesis that political credibility is the key factor in economic development.

2   See Brenner (1994) for an argument critical of mainstream approaches to the question of growth and development – one that argues that we do know what economic policies are responsible for growth and development and that modern economics simply serves to obfuscate the basic insights that can be found in economic science.

3   One of the theoretical difficulties is that the persistent application of economic theory (at least understood by mainstream economists) may in fact push one to the conclusion that inefficiency is only an illusion. Consider the following problem: statement 1 – there are efficient and inefficient policies in the world, and some inefficient policies have a rather long life (statement about the world); statement 2 – we know that some policies are efficient and others inefficient on the basis of economic reasoning (statement about the application of economics); statement 3 – the same economic reasoning that informs us that there are efficient and inefficient policies also insists that inefficient policies cannot persist (statement about theory). How does one square statements 1–3 in a coherent manner from an economic point of view? Donald Wittman's work (1995) suggests that mainstream economic logic does insist that the inefficiency of political institutions is indeed an illusion, supposedly inefficient policies are viewed as such simply because the analyst has not accurately measured the appropriate costs associated with alternative arrangements. The survivorship principles in politics, in other words, are just as relevant a signal of efficiency as in the market. At least that is what scholars such as Stigler, and now Wittman, were compelled to conclude on the basis of economic reasoning.

4   This distinction goes back to the philosopher Gilbert Ryle and was appropriated by Hayek to aid in his examination of the tacit domain of knowledge in social processes of coordination. See, for example, Hayek (1973, p. 72).

5   For a recent examination of these issues, see Buchanan (1995). The argument in this chapter for the importance of culture and the imprint of history is consistent although slightly different from the one that Buchanan's makes. Also, see Buchanan (1993).

6   In his recent critique of modern economics and the political–cultural implications which mainstream economics has had for US society, Robert Kuttner (1997, p. 34) makes the following telling observation about the economistic penchant for "thin" description:

> Apprentice economists, and fellow travelers in other disciplines, were spared the time-consuming process of reading history or studying the details of complex institutions. They had only to devise the models, collect the statistics and crunch the numbers ... You didn't really need to know anything, and you could know everything about everything. Some of the most prestigious economists today are

astonishingly expert in everything from trade to labor markets to income distribution to financial markets to macroeconomic policy – and by the age thirty-five. It suggests either remarkably protean intellects – or dubious shortcuts.

In an otherwise quite confused work, Kuttner touches the right chord with regard to the rather dubious shortcuts to which "thin" description taken alone can lead.

7   For a subtle reading of the institutionalist argument, see Rutherford (1994). The usual dichotomies between institutional economics and neoclassical economics are more complex than is often assumed.

8   Thus, the three pillars of contemporary economics analysis – endowment, technology, preference – must make room for an explicit treatment of the fourth (historically implicit) pillar – institutions within which economic behavior is embedded. See the articles by North, Bates, and Toye in Harris *et al.* (1995, pp. 17–68) for an examination of the implication of this new institutional economics insight for the field of development studies. Also, see Platteau (1994a and 1994b). In Platteau (1994b) the argument is made that the generalized norms that underlie economic progress can neither be created by fiat nor expected to evolve spontaneously.

9   Mises states that:

> Monetary calculation is the guiding star of action under the social system of the division of labor. It is the compass of the man embarking upon production. He calculates in order to distinguish the remunerative lines of production from the unprofitable ones, those of which the sovereign consumers are likely to approve from those of which they are likely to disapprove. Every single step of entrepreneurial activities is subject to scrutiny by monetary calculation. The premeditation of planned action becomes commercial precalculation of expected costs and expected proceeds. The retrospective establishment of the outcome of past action becomes accounting of profit and loss. The system of economic calculation in monetary terms is conditioned by certain social institutions. It can operate only in an institutional setting of the division of labor and private ownership of the means of production in which goods and services of all orders are bought and sold against a generally used medium of exchange, i.e. money.
>
> (Mises 1949, p. 229)

In developing this argument, Mises pioneered an alternative way to understand the institutions of *civil society*, which differed radically from the understanding that emerged from Durkheim (and has come to dominate much of the sociological thinking on social cooperation). On the concept of *civil society*, see Gellner (1994).

10   See Mises (1949, chapter 15, and part Six).

11   In writing this section I was continually reminded of a scene from Woody Allen's movie, *Bananas*, from the 1970s. The revolutionary dictator finally takes charge and in his first decree he announces that from now on everyone will wear their underwear on the outside of their pants. Confused, each of the revolutionary supporters looks at one another. Such decrees do not "stick" in my sense of the term, simply because they are so alien to the context within which they are made. Similarly, decrees to adopt this or that plan for development which lie outside of the context of the people are alien and fail to "stick."

12   This is a position not limited to Hayek and his followers, but also is recognized by an advocate of strong government action to promote development, such as Paul Streeten. As he has put it:

> [T]he 'absorptive capacity' of developing countries is limited not only for capital, but also for technical assistance. To teach skills effectively, much more is needed than teaching. Human attitudes and social institutions in a complex social system

may have to be changed if the teaching is to have an impact. Teeth-gritting humility, patience, curiosity and independent thinking are called for in learning how superior foreign technology works and how it can be improved. Without these conditions the technical assistance 'does not take'. The cut flowers wither and die because they have no roots.

(Streeten 1995, pp. 11–12)

Streeten, however, remains persuaded that while it may be true that the state is too big to accomplish small tasks, the state is too small to accomplish the big tasks required by economic development. It is precisely because Streeten reduces all knowledge to *know that,* even though he seems to recognize the *know how* latent in indigenous traditions, that enables him to remain persuaded of the large role of the state in economic development.

13 As Hayek has put it: "The process of articulation will thus sometimes in effect, though not in intention, produce new rules. But the articulated rules will thereby not wholly replace the unarticulated ones, but will operate, and be intelligible, only within a framework of yet unarticulated rules" (Hayek 1973, p. 78).

14 This is why ideology and belief-systems and how they underlie the common practices of a people must be examined alongside the self-interest explanations that follow from a rational choice framework – in order to *understand* development processes. Institutions are not only constraints against which actors maximize, but they also shape the perceptions of actors as to what it is that is to be maximized.

15 Richard Nelson and Howard Pack (1995) divide researchers attempting to explain economic growth and development into two camps: accumulationists and the assimilationists. Accumulationists place argumentative weight on the level of investment and the marshaling of resources, whereas assimilationists place the argumentative weight on learning and entrepreneurship and specifically on the use of new technology. The emphasis in this chapter is on the complex institutional structure which underlies both the accumulationists' and assimilationists' stories of the growth and development of nations. This, of course, is a point that has been repeatedly made by Douglass North (see, for example, North 1990).

16 To borrow the language from China specialists Ramon Myers and Thomas Metzger, we must distinguish between the uninhibited center, the inhibited center, and the subordinate center. Development requires the establishment of a subordinate center (i.e. transparent and credible rules which constrain even the actions of the center), but the key question that must be answered is whether a subordinate center can be established without passing through the inhibited center of customary practice. The contention of this chapter is that the attempt to go from an uninhibited center to a subordinate center is an epistemological impossibility.

17 This is one of the reasons why liberalized foreign trade is so vital to development – not just because of the importation of a price structure, competition, technology, etc., but because the flow of goods and services is a major factor in cultural mutation which generates social progress and transforms the existing culture – not necessarily into a replica of the "invading" cultural values, but a new mutation.

18 Berger adds that there is an urgent moral aspect of this argument that must be stressed. A moral responsibility must fall on those who impose public policy on developing societies, especially since the imposition of unproductive and inefficient economic arrangements are often introduced in conditions of hunger, disease, and degrading poverty. The necessary moral dimension to development policy has been a long-time theme of Berger's writings, see Berger (1976, especially pp. 149–209).

19 The most obvious "recent" example of a country that was considered rich that became poor is probably Argentina. On the other hand, a country that might be considered in bad economic shape that has had a recent reversal would be New Zealand.

20 On the general phenomena of unintended consequences in public policy, see Ikeda (1996). The argument that I am presenting in the text is different from Ikeda's more traditional Austrian theory of interventionism, but I would contend that the arguments are complementary.

21 Blewett's analysis, however, represents a different case from the one reported by Lansing, in that, in Lansing's case, the undesirable effects were felt by both sides, whereas, in Blewett's analysis, the undesirable component of the enacted change fell on the indigenous people, and the agents of enacted change were able to exploit the situation to their advantage.

22 The fluidity of culture and the manifold mutations that can occur must be recognized in the analysis of any changing society. For example, the Eastern and Central European national cultures of 1989 are in the process of going through a process of radical transformation. An interesting examination of these issues can be found in Voigt (1993).

23 For a comprehensive treatment of the Dutch Republic, see Israel (1995).

24 See Raico (1994) for an overview of this literature.

25 For a clear presentation of the position with regard to roundaboutness and economic development, see Rothbard (1993, chapters 5–9, and pp. 832–9).

Index

Brezhnev, economic policy under: bureaucratic expansion 165; centralization of price setting 165; incentive scheme for state enterprises 164

Brezhnev, Leonid 154, 164–5, 184

bribery 3–4, 177

Brutzkus, Boris 36, 87, 291, 303, 306

Buchanan, James: culture and history, importance of 334; Hayek failure to cite public choice work of 47, 293; 'here and now' origins of reform 207; incorporation of Hayek's work 293; on LSE approach to economics 39; on market asymmetry, transition and 286; moral philosophy, influence on developments in 15; on pre- and post-constitutional levels of analysis 24–5; 'productive' and 'redistributive' states, distinction between 50–1; on productivity of rules 330; on Russian cultural development, shortage economy and 327; on Russian experience, contrast with Western 227; trivialization of result of non-market allocation by 60–1; on vision, interaction with analysis 287

Bukharin, Nikolai: anti-market references of 82; Austrian School as most powerful opponent 8, 306; bureaucratic threat, lack of awareness of 317; on central planning during War Communism 310; on Communism and the dictatorship of the proletariat 94–5, 96, 97; economic architect of War Communism and the NEP 84; on economic destruction 318; Marxian project, faithful interpreter of 113; money, self-negation of 317; peace considered detrimental to revolution 307; private economic initiatives under NEP, call for 160–1; socialism, intention for 107; state capitalism and the NEP 96, 97; War Communism as 'normal' economic policy 98–101; *see also* Bolsheviks; Lenin, V.I.

bureaucratic: expansion 165; threat 305, 317; transformation 182, 184

calculation, monetary: basis for market economy 256; Bolshevik disregard for 305; central importance of 30, 32–5; conditioned by social institutions 225; decision-making, the market process and 31, 32; foundation of main contributions of Austrian School 30; Hayek's

development of the argument 34–7; impossibility of, without private property 31, 32, 36; Lenin's concept of replacement by accounting and control 94; practical meaning of 31; pure socialism and the impossibility of rationality in 4; Stalinism and 135

capital theory 295–6

capitalism, imperialist stage of 121–2

capitalist production, abolition of 88

Carr, E.H.: discounting Marxian aspirations to eliminate money 101; influential commentator 78; on institutional development 299–300; interpretive influence of 87; Lenin's political double-speak and 97; skepticism, growing, towards position of on War Communism 106; War Communism, confusion on 300–1; War Communism, emergency interpretation of 79; War Communism, view on economic effects of 81–4

Central Bank of Russia 170, 321

Central Committee of the Communist Party 285

central planning: apparatus and restriction rents 145–7; Bukharin on, during War Communism 310; challenge to, in recent years 177; comprehensive and non-comprehensive 98, 135; concealment of rent-flows and 147; essential nature of 128–9; failure to appreciate economic and political problems in 55; inconsistency with democracy 55–6, 302; 'knowledge' problem for 8, 29; monitoring and control functions of 150–1; origins of 298, 300; perestroika and new leadership for 181–2; process entrusted to statistical bureaus 95; public interest and the planners 144; public-interest assumptions of 318–19; reality of 322; relative importance of need and 51; Soviet system of 140–1; War Communism and 300–1; workers' control and 93, 128

Chamberlin, William 78, 133, 298, 305, 317, 318

Charles University, Prague 152

Chernobyl 1

Chernomyrdin, Victor 170, 322, 331

Chicago School of public choice analysis 60

China 200–1, 228, 252

choice: collective 196–7; freedom under perestroika 186–7; strategies and rules 24–5